Vaishnava Temple Music in Vrindaban:

The Rādhāvallabha Songbook

Vaishnava Temple Music in Vrindaban: The Rādhāvallabha Songbook

Compiled, Recorded, and Edited
by
Guy L. Beck

With original Braj Bhasha text,
Roman transliteration, and English translations
by
Rupert Snell, Charles S. J. White,
H. S. Mathur, Heidi R. M. Pauwels, R. S.
MacGregor, Chandrakala Pandey, and Guy L. Beck

Blazing Sapphire Press
715 E. McPherson
Kirksville, Missouri 63501
2011

ISBN 978-0-9817902-4-4 (0-9817902-4-0)

Library of Congress Control Number: 2011939601

Published by:
Blazing Sapphire Press
715 E. McPherson
Kirksville, Missouri 63501

Available at:
Nitai's Bookstore
715 E. McPherson
Kirksville, Missouri, 63501
Phone: (660) 665-0273
http://www.nitaisbookstore.com
http://www.blazingsapphirepress.com
Email: neal@blazingsapphirepress.com

स्फुरद्वदनपङ्कजः कनककुटदेहद्युतिः
प्रशस्तसुखसम्पदां निधिरपूर्वमानप्रदः।
सकृष्णवृषभानुजाचरणमाधुरीचञ्चुरः
सदा मधुरवाक्पटुर्जयति साधुवैयासकिः॥

He whose lotus face is glowing,
Whose skin shines like a sunlit peak,
Rarest honors he's bestowing,
Treasure-house of the joys most seek,
He who relishes ambrosia
At Vṛsabhānu's daughter's feet
Along with her much loved Kṛṣṇa,
He whose words are expertly sweet,
May sage Vyāsa's holy son
Be known as the glorious one.[1]

---

[1] Kṛṣṇadāsa, second son of Śrī Hita Harivaṃśa, *Karṇānanda* (1578 CE), verse 1. Translation by Neal and Elizabeth Delmonico.

Cover picture: Śrī Rādhāvallabhajī

Picture by Guy L. Beck

Samples of a few of the songs described in this book can be downloaded and listened to at our website: www.radhavallabha-songbook.com. In addition, a collection of samples filling two CDs is available for free to buyers of the book in a variety of formats. The complete set of all the songs (filling 18 CDs in all) may be purchased separately at www.radhavallabha-songbook.com. Please visit the website to find other extras connected with the book and to place your order.

Vaishnava Temple Music in Vrindaban:

The Rādhāvallabha Songbook

Contents

**Chapter Two: The Rādhāvallabha Songbook Volume
   II   145**

Foreword

The strong relationship between music and religion is well known to millions of the world's citizens—people who belong to a host of contrasting religious traditions. Some of these religions go so far as to take a stand against the power of the tie between religion and music, aiming to rescue the holy word from the vanities, distractions, and deformities that might pollute it if allowed a musical manifestation. When a religion embarks on a sonoclastic campaign of this sort, however, that effort only serves to underscore the strength of the connection that is sought to be dismantled. One of the ongoing embarrassments of the field of Religious Studies is that we represent this bond so feebly in the classroom. All too few Religion departments have a course called "Religion and Music" or some variant of that title. Yet every department should, and Guy Beck, taking a single religious tradition as his example, shows us why.

What you have in hand isn't a book, really, but a library—a library of sound. The musical samples that accompany the text represent one of India's great musical traditions, and they do so with a fidelity that no written document could possibly match; a complete set of eighteen CDs is available by subscription. In the pages and disks that comprise *Vaishnava Temple Music in Vrindaban*, Beck, whose musical sensitivities have been honed in long years of performing the vocal repertoire of north India, underscores the powerful bond between word and sound that is an article of faith in the worship of Krishna. Those connected to Vrindaban affirm that *bhakti*, participation in a life with God, can hardly exist without *bhajan*, devotional song. These two words, in fact, are formed from a single Sanskrit root. Beck presents here the mutual resonance between *bhakti* and *bhajan* as it is performed by a particular religious community within the complex that makes up Vrindaban's whole—a community that traces its history to the time when Vrindaban's distinctive religious culture took shape in the early years of the sixteenth century. Adherents of the Rādhāvallabha Sampradāya believe they stand at the epicenter of the relationship between *bhakti* and *bhajan*, since they eschew from ritual performance any aspect of human experience that cannot take its place in the charmed circle that forms around the love exchanged between Krishna and Rādhā. Rādhāvallabhis therefore insist that they are the bearers of a musical style—*samāj gāyan*—as distinctive as the charmed circle itself.

In the early years of the eighteenth century the great king Jai Singh II, ruler of Amer and Jaipur and a key figure in the administration of the Mughal empire, urged that the Rādhāvallabha community join forces with a pan-sectarian effort designed to align the Vaishnava theological traditions of north India with what he took to be the overarching history of Vaishnava religion in India as a whole. They, like Vrindaban's other *sampradāyas*, were expected to claim a prior lineage that would connect them to one of the theological traditions established in south India well before the sixteenth century, or to show that their doctrines were based on Vedic fundamentals as transmitted in the *Brahma-sūtras*, the Upaniṣads, and the *Bhagavad-gītā*. Other *sampradāyas* connected to Vrindaban and the Braj region acceded to this demand—some, indeed, may have inspired it—but the most important Rādhāvallabhī spokesman at the time, Rūplāl Gosvāmī, refused to go along. He seems to have believed that the special magic of Vrindaban, Krishna's paradigmatic place, ought not to be diluted by canons pertaining to any external agency—even Vedic, Vaishnava ones—just as Krishna himself should not be subordinated to any other deity, even Vishnu himself. Here was a supremely confident, inwardly concentrated theological and musical tradition that felt it did not have to compromise with the demands of state.

It was a dramatic moment, and had dramatic consequences. For a time, we are told, Rūplāl and the central leadership of the Rādhāvallabha Sampradāya had to withdraw from the Vrindavan it so cherished. But they retained the truest Vrindaban, Krishna's own Vrindaban, in their liturgy. In the text that follows and in the recorded music that accompanies it, Guy Beck does a superb job of conveying this deeply devoted Rādhāvallabhī spirit to those of us who stand outside the charmed circle that its songs are intended to evoke. He offers us an invitation to enter.

John Stratton Hawley
Barnard College, Columbia University

Acknowledgments

This book is dedicated primarily to the musicians of the Rādhāvallabha Sampradāya for their unswerving devotion and diligence in maintaining the living tradition of Samāj-Gāyan. Ignoring the distractions of worldliness and fame, the devotees of Rādhāvallabha are to be admired for their steadfastness. I would like to thank first of all Pandit Rajendra Prasad Sharma and his group of Samāj musicians in Vrindaban, including Śrī Kunj Bihari Das. Heartfelt thanks are offered to the trustees of the Śrī Rādhāvallabha Temple, the Choti Sarkar temple complex, and the Śrī Satsanga Bhūmi ("Hita Ashram," directed by Śrī Hitdas Maharaj Ji), for allowing me to tape record extensively throughout the 1992-1993 season, as well as previously in 1976, 1978, 1979, 1980. These institutions have provided the bulk of the recorded material as well as the inspiration to bring this project to completion. Financial support for the extensive research conducted in 1992-1993 was provided by the Council for the International Exchange of Scholars (C.I.E.S.) in the form of a Fulbright Research Grant, and by the American Institute of Indian Studies (A.I.I.S.) in the form of a Senior Research Fellowship.

The work of collecting recordings and translations, beside being a labor of love for me, required countless hours of listening, sorting out song selections, scouring the Hindi literature for the precise texts, consulting with authorities in Braj Bhasha language and literature, and working alongside recording engineers in order to pull all of this material together. My thanks and admiration are accorded to the translators who dedicated themselves to this project, especially to Śrī Hari Shankar Mathur who did the majority of the translating work; Prof. Chandrakala Pandey for her help in translating poems in Calcutta, and Rupert Snell, Charles S. J. White, Heidi R. M. Pauwels, and Robert MacGregor for their previously published translations. I will thank both Jason Smith and William Kelley of the LSU School of Music Recording Studio for their roles in the CD production: Jason Smith for his patient work on the transfer from cassette to CD, and William Kelley for his fine mastering work leading to the final eighteen CDs. Financially, the final product would not have been possible without the continuing support of the LSU Foundation (Urmila and Gopal Singhal Fund) in the recording and publishing phases. Special thanks go to Prof. John Whittaker of the Department of Philosophy and Religious Studies for overseeing the Singhal Fund and assisting in various ways.

I would like to thank the members of the staff of the Sri Vrindaban Shodh Samsthan (Vrindaban Research Institute), Vrindaban, (U.P.) for their hospitality and helpful assistance with their facilities, archives and personal guidance in the study of Braj musical traditions. Especially, I remember the kind aid of Dr. Naresh Bansal in Braj Vaishnavism, Śrī Vrindaban Bihari Goswami in Braj Bhasha language and literature, Śrī Gopal Ghosh in local Braj religious traditions, and Śrī Punit Goswami for his pleasant companionship during visits to Agra.

Thanks to Dr. Neal Delmonico and the Blazing Sapphire Press for accepting this project in its complete form, along with the eighteen CDs; a daunting challenge for any publisher. Thanks as well to Dr. Elizabeth Delmonico for her work in editing the volume.

This project is the result of the contributions of many individuals. My ardent desire is that it be acceptable to the members of the Rādhāvallabha Sampradāya. However, if there are any errors in content or interpretation, I take full responsibility and, if such is the case, I apologize and pray for forgiveness at the lotus feet of Śrī Hita Harivaṃśa and Śrī Śrī Rādhāvallabhajī.

Jaya Śrī Hita Harivaṃśa!
Śrī Śrī Radhavallabha kī Jaya!
Guy L. Beck
New Orleans, January, 2009

Introduction
by Guy L. Beck

Vrindaban is the principal center of Krishna worship in India, and a truly magical place. While the historic and geographic site of Vrindaban is located within the region of Braj, just south of New Delhi in northern India, its place in the Hindu imagination is boundless and timeless, as it radiates an aura of mystery and serves as "window" into a transcendent sphere of reality. From its location nestled among the hamlets along the Yamunā River, it is especially enchanting in the late evening hours during the autumn season of Karttik. If one carefully listens to the devotional music emanating from the various temples in this small town, what was a noisy and bustling pilgrimage site during daylight hours is now transformed into a serene sanctuary that belongs only to its permanent residents. One night in 1988, as the temple bells rang to signify the final Darshan (viewing) in the main Rādhāvallabha Temple, the musicians began their closing song, a lullaby for laying the deity of Rādhāvallabha (Krishna) to rest for the night. After the curtain closed at 10 p.m., and the Samāj-Gāyan music session ended with the final clap of the hand cymbals, the lead singer (at that time, Śrī Damodar Das "Mukhīya") suddenly stood up and walked over to me, seated in the audience. Without a word, he dropped a large *laḍḍu* (sweetball), taken from the temple *prasādam* (holy food) given by the temple priests, into my open right palm. While I was savoring this delicious confection, the drummer wrapped his instrument (*pakhavāj*) in a large white cotton cloth, and the *esrāj* (bowed lute) player, Śrī Ramnath Prasad, put away his instrument in a colorful quilted case. Śrī Prasad, the only person who could speak English among the musicians, attempted to explain to me the meaning of the beautiful songs and ballads that I had just enjoyed for the past three hours. After a few passionate comments about Vaishnava aesthetics and the writings of Jayadeva and Śrī Hita Harivaṃśa, he spoke the following soliloquy in a calm tone of voice:

> After we sing these songs, the entire sound vibrates in our minds night and day, bringing a deep and unspeakable joy. The *līlās* or pastimes of Lord Krishna were composed in the form of these ballads right by the side of the Yamunā River. The nature and activities of Lord Krishna and Rādhā have been described by our poets in such a way that it will take years to explain them. Even then, it is not possible to give the full explanation. That is why we go on singing these songs. Our only activity is to observe the love affairs of Rādhā and Krishna by singing these songs. Then the divine beauty manifests in different colors, aspects, and forms. I have been singing these songs here for over forty years.[2]

For me, after only a few nights of listening to the enraptured sounds of the Rādhāvallabha temple music, I was permanently transfixed and felt that I was to become a lifelong *chelā* (devotee).

As is perhaps evident from this passage, and is certainly so upon close observation of the worshipping community, musical activity in the Rādhāvallabha Sampradāya (RVS) is a vital and central occupation of its members. It would be a mistake

---

[2]Interview conducted with Sri Ramnath Prasad at the Rādhāvallabha Temple in Vrindaban, U.P. on July 20, 1988. The content was transcribed and edited from an audiotape.

to assume that their musical worship is a kind of extra feature, a decoration or "window-dressing." On the contrary, the entire devotional life of the community of followers and initiated members has revolved around the twice-daily musical sessions of Samāj-Gāyan ("group singing") held in the temples, based primarily in Vrindaban, for centuries. This particular form of devotional singing is the central core of their religious practice, and the focus of this book.

Scope of this Book

Within the context of the Vaishnava worship of Krishna in northern India, this book presents and examines a special collection of Rādhāvallabha *bhakti* poetry in Braj Bhasha (a dialect of Hindi), referred to as the "Rādhāvallabha Songbook." This devotional poetry is utilized musically as part of the seasonal liturgical worship of the image of Krishna known as Rādhāvallabha, "Dearest of Rādhā." The Vaishnava sect known as the Rādhāvallabha Sampradāya is one of the foremost *bhakti* devotional movements, founded in the sixteenth century CE in the region of Braj. Yet it is strangely unknown outside of its immediate environment.

Based on extensive research at the headquarters of the Rādhāvallabha Sampradāya in present-day Vrindaban within the Braj region of Uttar Pradesh, and in consultation with relevant literature, this book seeks to expand the resources for the study of Hindu liturgy and music by presenting material that is new to Westerners despite having been a vital part of Vaishnava worship in India for nearly five hundred years. In textual and audio forms, it makes available 108 songs, many for the first time in English translation.

Over the course of several visits, including over an entire liturgical year, the author collected and recorded many of the most important songs from this tradition. All of these songs date from roughly 1530-1850 CE, and their lyrics, in Braj Bhasha, appear in the three-volume published anthology known as the *Śrī Rādhāvallabhajī kā Varṣotsava.* This anthololgy will be signified by the letters RV, or as simply the Rādhāvallabha Songbook. Beside the poems of the founder Śrī Hita Harivaṃśa (c. 1502-1552 CE), this expansive anthology contains many poems from both prominent and lesser-known members of the *sampradāya* (tradition), such as Harirāma Vyāsa, Damodara Dāsa, Dhruva Dāsa, Nāgarī Dāsa, Cācā Vṛndāvana Dāsa, and Rūpa Lāla, as well as from non-sectaries like Sūra Dāsa, Nanda Dāsa, and Svāmī Haridāsa. These poems are each placed in the text according to the liturgical season. Most of them display a free metrical structure comparable with some Western hymnody. They are performed in the musical style known as Samāj-Gāyan ("group singing"), which is a unique vocal music tradition of Braj. It is related to classical Dhrupad and largely based on Hindustani *rāgas* (scale formulas reflective of distinct emotional moods or *rasas*) and *tālas* (rhythmic cycles). Set within fixed daily or seasonal formats, these poems are sung on specific days by trained singers along with musical accompaniment of harmonium, *tanpura* (lute), *pakhavāj* (barrel drum), and cymbals. The liturgical calendar of the sect, based on the solar/lunar system, is composed of a series of festivals and observances extending from Spring (Basant) to Holi, Pāvas Ritu (Rainy season), Rāsa Dance, and Kārtik. As part of this prominent living tradition in northern India, all of these songs, and many others not included, are embedded into the seasonal liturgical worship of the image of Krishna by the Rādhāvallabha Sampradāya.

Following this introduction, this book presents, over the course of three chapters and an appendix, the Braj Bhasha texts of many of the original songs (in the appendix), their Roman transliteration, and their English translation. There are also brief notes explaining the genre, context and structure of each of the songs, including mention of the *rāga* (melodic scale), *tāla*, (rhythmic cycle), and other specifics of the performance rendition. The songs have been presented in the same sequence according to the seasonal chronology represented by the three volumes of the original anthology.

Volume I (Chapter One): songs of spring (Vasant, Holi) and the appearance day of Śrī Hita Harivaṃśa.

Volume II (Chapter Two): songs of summer (Rainy Season) and early autumn, and the appearance days of Śrī Krishna and Śrī Rādhā.

Volume III (Chapter Three): songs of mid-autumn (Rāsa Līlā) and late autumn, as well as evening worship songs.

English translations of some of these songs have been previously published in the works of Charles S. J. White (1977), Rupert Snell (1991), Heidi R. M. Pauwels (1996, 2002), and R. S. McGregor (1973). In addition to incorporating these, as appropriate, translations of many other poems by H. S. Mathur and Dr. Chandrakala Pandey, done in collaboration with the present author, are included.

Two compact disks are available free for those who buy this book, each filled with samples of representative songs.[3] A full set of eighteen compact disks, containing many complete songs and portions of other of the 108 songs is also available separately.[4]

Rādhāvallabha Scholarship

Previous scholarship on the Rādhāvallabha Sampradāya, praiseworthy for its detail, has focused almost exclusively on the literary output of the founder Śrī Hita Harivaṃśa and his

[3]The sample compact disks as well as several free songs for download and listening are available at www.radhavallabha-songbook.com.

[4]Available from www.radhavallabha-songbook.com.

immediate follower Śrī Harirāma Vyāsa, with comparative analyses of vocabulary, grammar, meter, and syntax as evidenced in a variety of manuscripts. These works, like many scholarly studies of *bhakti* poetry, have often overlooked the important ritual and liturgical contexts of the poems, especially their musical performance within living communities.

The Rādhāvallabha tradition had been all but ignored in Western scholarship until the work of Charles S. J. White and Rupert Snell. Orientalist writings had mentioned it in passing or in footnotes. In his 1977 translation of the poems of the *Caurāśi-Pad* (*CP*, "Eighty-four Songs") of Śrī Hita Harivaṃśa, the first lengthy study of the Rādhāvallabha tradition, Charles S. J. White provided an introductory section on the religious beliefs and ritual traditions of the Rādhāvallabha Sampradāya, drawing mostly upon the earlier Hindi scholarship of Vijayendra Snatak (1957, 1968), the first Indian scholar to give serious attention to the Rādhāvallabha tradition. Charles S. J. White had also translated Śrī Hita Harivaṃśa's *Sphuṭa-Vāṇī* (SV, "Clear Speech") as well as two letters to his disciple Śrī Viṭṭhaladāsa, called *Śrī Mukha Pātrī* ("Chief Vessel," 1996). His translations of the Harivaṃśa poems into English attempted to carry over the poetic effects of the Braj Bhasha lyrics into English verse. Some of his translations of the *Sphuṭa-Vāṇī* have been included in this collection.

Because of the unabashedly erotic nature of much of the Rādhāvallabhite poetry, however, Indian natives of this tradition have been reluctant to have these poems translated and discussed by foreigners, with the attendant risk of misinterpretation of spiritual meanings as mere sexual imagery associated with ordinary human relationships. Their concern has validity. In several poems in which erotic situations between Rādhā and Krishna are distinctly portrayed, some editions of the *CP* have employed the terms "sexual" and "sexual desire" in their English renderings, to the possible detriment of the intended sublime and spiritual meaning of the poetry. The translations of Rupert Snell (1991) have been selected for inclusion in this collection, as they are most sensitive to the issues in question, and are able to convey the amorous nature of the divine encounters without the need to reduce them to gross sensuality. Snell has also been able to successfully nuance the many varieties of romantic expression of the Braj Bhasha language into attractive English renderings in both prose and poetry. Because of the unique, I would say "spiritually aesthetic," nature of Braj Bhasha Vaishnava poetry, it is very unlikely that its naive beauty can be transferred by endeavoring for similar effects in English. In addition, it is our contention that a proper appreciation and understanding of the depth of musical expression of these poems precludes any tendency to view them as comparable to ribald European expressions. As becomes evident through sustained study and analysis of the context of Braj devotional poetry, the poems were themselves written as songs, and composed for the purpose of offering them in liturgical worship for the pleasure of the deities, Rādhā and Krishna. Thus the poem/songs are believed to have been divinely inspired. This inspiration affects and includes the rhythms and repetitions which pull the listener into the experience of devotional joy in all its playfulness and energy. A tiny sample in English is appended to show something of how the Braj Bhasha lyrics might sound if composed in English. The remaining translations in this project have been rendered in simple prose without the extra endeavor of placing them in poetic format. The intention is for the reader to be exposed directly to the Braj Bhasha sounds as composed, by virtue of the CD recordings, as they are sung and performed in their original context.

Heidi R. M. Pauwels, in *In Praise of Holy Men: Hagiographic Poems by and about Hariram Vyas* (2002) thoroughly analyzed the poetical output surrounding the Rādhāvallabha poet Śrī Harirāma Vyāsa. Her earlier work, *Kṛṣṇa's Round Dance Reconsidered: Harirāma Vyāsa's Hindi Rās-pañcādhyāyī* (1996), had provided the complete Braja Bhasha text with English translation, and notes, of Śrī Harirāma Vyāsa's lengthy poem on the Rāsa-līlā theme, "Rāsa-pañcādhyāyī" ("The Five Chapters on the Circle Dance"). Other issues discussed by Pauwels are the debates surrounding Harirāma Vyāsa's actual religious affiliation.

The first scholarly work that attempted to analyze specific Rādhāvallabha songs in musical performance is an article by Rupert Snell (1983). Though not strictly examining musical elements, he discussed the metrical structure of about eight poems of the *CP* of Hita Harivaṃśa, and how these structures were manifest in performance in terms of their rhythms. Regarding the context of his recording, he stated, "The recording ... was made by me in the Radhavallabhi temple of Choti Sarkar, Vrindaban, in the summer of 1977. The *gāyana samāja* [group of singers] consists of the *mukhīya*, who plays harmonium, a small chorus, one of whose members plays the *jhāñjh*, and a tabla player. The ensemble sits on the *jagamohana*, the raised section of the temple floor immediately in front of the shrine."[5] More details about the musicians will be given later.

While Rupert Snell does not mention the names of the performers on his recording, the precise location and the specific performing artists studied by him are essentially the same as the source informants for this book. Over the course of 1975-1980, I regularly visited the Rādhāvallabha Temple and Choti Sarkar, which also houses an image of Rādhāvallabha. It has been independently confirmed that Snell's informant-singer was Śrī Rajendra Prasad Sharma, the same individual whom I recorded and studied with later in 1992-1993. Śrī Sharma ("Masterjī") would sing daily at Choti Sarkar in the early evenings about 5:00-6:30 PM. In 1975, 1976, and 1979, I had also recorded Śrī Damodar Das Mukhiya, who sang at the main Rādhāvallabha Temple for over fifty years until re-

[5]Rupert Snell (1983), 361.

tirement in 1996. Three of his recordings are included in the present anthology, as well as two by Śrī Krishna Bhatt, another important singer of Rādhāvallabha poetry in Vrindaban. By the time of my 1988 summer visit, Śrī Sharma and his accompanying musicians were also performing nightly, just after their session at Choti Sarkar, at Śrī Satsanga Bhumi in Hitashram, the residential temple of Śrī Hita Dasji Maharaj, an important living *guru* of the Rādhāvallabha Sampradāya. This location was slightly outside the main streets of the town of Vrindaban. The second sessions there began at 7:30 P.M. and lasted until about 9:00 P.M. Unless otherwise specified, all of the songs on the eighteen CDs in our collection were sung by Śrī Rajendra Prasad Sharma and his musicians, either at Choti Sarkar or at Śrī Satsanga Bhumi.

Regarding scholarship of Braj musical traditions including Rādhāvallabha, mention must be made here of the recent work of Selina Thielemann. In *Musical Traditions of Vaisnava Temples in Vraja: A Comparative Study of Samaja and the Dhrupad Tradition of North Indian Classical Music* (2001), based on her Ph.D. dissertation at Benares Hindu University, Thielemann presents and analyzes many examples of Braj songs in both Indian and Western notation. In the first volume of this large two-volume work, she examines selections from the five major musical traditions of Braj, beginning with the Caitanya Sampradāya, followed by Rādhāvallabha Sampradāya, Nimbārka Sampradāya, Haridāsī Sampradāya, and Vallabha Sampradāya (Puṣṭimārga). While containing many insights valuable to musicologists, there are no recordings to accompany her discussions.

Her section on the Rādhāvallabha temple music (pp. 143-215) includes analyses of six songs in performance: three from the *Caurāśi-Pad* (23, 27, 28), one from the *Sphuṭa-Vāṇī* (16) of Śrī Hita Harivaṃśa, one of Śrī Rāmarāya Prabhu, and one from the most prolific of RV poets, Cācā Vṛndāvana Dāsa. The first selection is not included in our collection. The remaining five songs are listed in our collection as numbers 1, 2, 62, 7, and 20. Thielemann's intention is to compare different renderings of the same composition to show that various interpretations exist. She thus points out differences between the versions sung by the aged Śrī Damodar Das Mukhiya, recorded in 1994 just two years before his retirement from leadership, and those led by Śrī Jayesh Khandelwal, a musically untrained lay singer-follower who performs occasional Samāj-Gāyan. As she recognizes, the recordings she transcribes are flawed. Regarding Śrī Damodar Das Mukhiya, "the voice of the aged mukhiya is no more able to utter the pitches distinctly—the pitches sung by him do not correspond to the notes he plays simultaneously on the harmonium." (167) Regarding Jayesh Khandelwal's group, "the singers are not always in tune. It should be kept in mind that here, one has to deal with lay musicians and devotees rather than professional singers as in the temple." (173)

The three lengthy examples of the singing of Śrī Damodar Das Mukhiya that are included in our CD collection were recorded when he was in his prime (1970s), when his vocal production was excellent beyond description. It is significant that nowhere in Thielemann's writings is there mention of Śrī Rajendra Sharma, our singer/informant, who is the most competent representative of the Rādhāvallabha tradition by virtue of his training in classical music and his close following of the texts and oral traditions. And the Śrī Satsanga Bhumi, where Śrī Sharma leads Rādhāvallabha Samāj-Gāyan every evening, is the quintessential location for experiencing the fruits of this tradition.

Thielemann's other books (1998, 2000, 2002) contain chapters that represent reprinted articles, lectures and seminar papers with considerable overlap. A more useful volume is *The Music of South Asia* (1999), representing her wide-ranging interests in many aspects of religious music in South Asia, including Śrī Lanka and Nepal.

Another few words of caution regarding definitions are in order at this point. The term Samāj-Gāyan is often misleadingly translated as "congregational singing" in some of the above works (i.e. Selina Thielemann 1998, 59, 199, 292; 2001, Vol. I, 31; 2001, Vol. II, 916; 2002, 55, 58). While the word *samāja* may signify society, community, congregation, etc., in ordinary Indian usage, in the context of music it refers to a specific genre of religious music that is a form of high art. Samāj-Gāyan is no more "congregational" than Gregorian Chant, Lutheran Chorales, or Vedic chant. Also, in Thielemann (2001), the term *samājagāyana* is inappropriately used in a kind of generic sense to refer to all five traditions of temple music in Braj. The term must only refer to the particular group singing style that was founded and developed by the Rādhāvallabha, Haridāsī, and Nimbārka sampradāyas. For example, in the Puṣṭimārga tradition, the Vallabha Sampradāya, there is no Samāj-Gāyan, and so the term cannot be used as a description of their temple music. Samāj-Gāyan is occasionally performed within the Caitanya Sampradāya, but since the Caitanya Sampradāya is essentially a Bengali tradition, its primary form of music is Bengali *kīrtana* and *nāmasaṅkīrtana*, the chanting of divine names in congregation. It is only in the Braj "branches" of the Caitanya tradition that Samāj-Gāyan is practiced. Thus, employing the term Samāj-Gāyan for all of the music of the Caitanya tradition is also misleading. As Samāj-Gāyan is not found in Bengal where the *sampradāya* was founded, it represents a native Braj tradition that has been adopted by the Caitanya Sampradāya.

Research and Study

After several shorter visits to the region, I obtained grants which enabled me to remain in Braj for a full year, studying the Rādhāvallabha musical worship over the many seasons of the annual calendar. Due to the rather stringent religious piety of the informants, most of the songs are only performed on specific days of the calendar. Thus, if one arrives in the spring or summer seasons, only those particular songs would be heard. It should be added here that these songs have a unique charm and are jealously guarded by followers of the sect. As suggested above, it takes a considerable period of time before one can obtain the good graces of the singers and persuade them to reveal these songs and perform them, much less allow them to be recorded.

Out of the eight songs of Śrī Hita Harivaṃśa that Rupert Snell discussed in his 1983 article, six are included in this book as well as on the accompanying CDs. In his article, Snell pioneered a particular venue of scholarship, the metrical and rhythmic analysis of the Rādhāvallabha songs. Snell's later monumental work (1991), the full translation and analysis of Śrī Hita Harivaṃśa's *Caurāśi-Pad* (CP), is especially appreciated, as he has permitted some of these translations to be incorporated into the present work. The present author only wishes to enlarge and enhance what Snell had originally accomplished, and to build upon his information and methodology. Careful linguistic scrutiny and analysis of each song in the entire RV anthology, however, would fill volumes, and so that is not the object of this book. Rather, this work places over a hundred of the important songs in their ritual and musical context with introductory comments. It is hoped that other scholars and interested parties will continue to mine this extraordinary field of material and examine it in various levels of depth and precision.

A unique aspect of the present book is that the Rādhāvallabha songs included here in their transliterated textual form are supplemented by their authoritative audio rendition taken from field recordings of Rādhāvallabha musicians, and compiled into a series of eighteen CDs. The CDs contain my complete archive of one hundred and eight (108) Rādhāvallabha songs that were collected and recorded over several visits in 1975, 1976, 1977, 1978, 1988, and during the year-long research trip in 1992-1993 that was funded by a Fulbright Research Grant and the American Institute of Indian Studies (A.I.I.S.). Thus the reader will have both the audio and textual version of each song presented. The number one hundred and eight, while normally considered very auspicious within Hindu religious circles, was arrived at by chance. There is no implicit relation between this number and the total number of songs in this archive.

A close study of all of these hymns in context reveals a vast multi-leveled "auditory environment" in the total mixture of songs descriptive of Krishna *līlā*, in *rāga* scales and in emotional moods associated with various times of the day and seasons of the year. This book suggests that hymns in Rādhāvallabha worship can only be fully comprehended when they are viewed as a contributive part of an interlocking network of liturgical meaning, created from the unique combination of a number of independent variables such as *rāga*, time of day, season, mood, theology, and song lyrics.

The complex relationships revealed by this type of presentation point toward broader comparative issues such as the relation between metrical song and theistic worship in other religious traditions. Furthermore, these studies are enhanced and complemented through conversation with the fields of liturgy and music in Western religions. Referring to Western liturgical traditions, Mary McGann in *Exploring Music as Worship and Theology* (2002) observed that in ritual, song texts are inseparable from other aspects of the social, cultural, and religious communication that takes place musically. Furthermore, concepts in liturgical studies such as "auditory environment" or "tonal landscape" as discussed by Edward Foley in *Ritual Music: Studies in Liturgical Musicology* (1995), and vernacular "corporate song" as explained by Robin A. Leaver in *Liturgy and Music* (1998), are enriched by the Hindu data and are also shown to be useful in fostering general insight about function of music in theistic religious life, where "hearing is believing." The present book is a partial response to the critical need for studies in traditions that effectively combine religion and music. It seeks to provide a salient example of how music is inextricably intertwined with religious thought and ritual in northern India, with special attention to the Rādhāvallabha tradition in Vrindaban.

Background: Music and the Study of Religion

Religion and music are clearly acknowledged by experts as distinct universal features of human culture and society. A commonly repeated tenet of musicologists and ethnomusicologists is that music is a universal aspect of culture and civilization. Yet the special bond that frequently exists between music and religion in religious belief and thought, and their integral relationship in religious practice, are important dimensions that have been largely overlooked by scholars of both religious studies and musicology.

The pressing need for more studies in the field of religion and music has been outlined in the Introduction to my recently edited volume, *Sacred Sound: Experiencing Music in World Religions* (2006). A concluding statement from this book may be cited here:

> Encountering and incorporating sacred sound enhances the ability to understand religion at its deepest levels. Music and chant are most often located at the core of religious life in any culture, tied in with ritual and liturgical action. Just as it is unthinkable to approach or understand a religious liturgy without the oral dimension, it is just as impossible to effectively penetrate a religious tradition without the

musical dimension.[6]

Just as it would be deficient to study Christianity without looking at Protestant hymns and Gregorian chant as part of the religious services, or to approach Islam without recognizing the significance of the oral recitation of the Qur'an, in the same way it is partial at best to study *bhakti* poetry and Hindu *bhakti* traditions in India without a basic knowledge and appreciation of Indian music. With overpowering evidence from all corners of the world, the field of phenomenology of religion, then, must include music and chant as essential elements in the study of religion.

While there may be a wide variation in the definitions of and approaches to religion, scholars of the discipline generally strive to collect data in order to validate, or invalidate, the presence of "religion" in its many forms. One prominent form of interpretation of this data, for example, is to perceive a religion, including the cultic and social dimensions, as a kind of artistic creation expressing the existential human response to the presence of the "wholly other," which is frequently labeled the sacred or the divine, but also that which is of ultimate value and importance. As a "work of art," a religion elicits interpretation through the methods of the humanities rather than through the purely logical explanations (*erklarung*) often employed in the social and natural sciences. Referred to in this way as the phenomenology of religion or the history of religions, many thinkers in religious studies stress that all "religious worlds" contain authentic voices that when assembled express, in various ways, the universal human condition. In this view, any foreign or unfamiliar religion may be understood or apprehended by outsiders through a kind of "empathetic understanding" (*verstehen*) that draws upon our common human experience of finitude and the need to grasp life

[6]Guy L. Beck (2006), 8-9.

in it greatest possible totality.[7] Phenomenology of religion as a method in religious studies also purports to give primacy to the experiences of the believers themselves.

There is evidence that early historians of religious studies as a budding academic discipline did seriously consider religion and music as important overlapping categories. For example, Rudolf Otto in his classic work, *The Idea of the Holy* (German 1917, English 1923) declared that the feelings associated with music are very similar to feelings of the holy itself, the numinous, which is something "wholly other": "Music, in short, arouses in us an experience and vibrations of mood that are quite specific in kind. The resultant complex mood is, as it were, a fabric, in which the general human feelings and emotional states constitute the warp, and the non-rational music-feelings the woof. The real content of music is not drawn from the ordinary human emotions at all, and is in no way merely a second language, alongside the usual one, by which these emotions find expression. Musical feeling is rather (like numinous feeling) something 'wholly other.'"[8] Consequently, the human response to music is composed of similar feelings and experiences as toward the numinous, such as *mysterium tremendum* (mystery and awe) and *fascinans* (attraction).

The phenomenologist of religion Gerardus van der Leeuw, in his now famous work *Religion in Essence and Manifestation* (1938), enlarged upon Otto's insights by affirming that "musical expression of the holy occupies an extensive domain in worship. There is hardly any worship without music." His other major work, *Sacred and Profane Beauty: The Holy in Art* (1963), reaffirms that "Almost all worship uses music—religion can no more do without singing that it can without the word. . . . Music represents the great struggle of reaching the wholly other, which it can never express."[9]

---

[7] Guy L. Beck (2006), 3.

[8] Rudolf Otto (1923), 49.

[9] Gerardus van der Leeuw (1938), 453, (1963), 225, 227.

Unfortunately, however, additional studies that further pursue this connection between religion and music along the lines of Otto and van der Leeuw, are relatively scarce. As such, the detailed study of sacred or religious music seems to have played a relatively minor role in the overall development of the disciplines of phenomenology of religion, comparative religion, or the history of religions. But this in no way should obscure the significance of music in the study of religion. In fact, the emerging sub-disciplines of ritual studies and liturgical studies have partially taken up the slack and have contributed further inspiration for the present book and its methods of approach.

The object of ritual studies and liturgical studies is the liturgy itself, apprehended as a pivotal dimension of a living community. Liturgy is the structured series of rites combining word, action, music, and physical space. Accordingly, it becomes a useful category for approaching religious practices associated with musical worship in Hinduism. Yet scholarly studies in Indian music have mostly focused on private and non-liturgical contexts, such as domestic devotion, rites of passage (wedding songs), popular entertainment (film songs), and secular courts (*darbari dhrupad, khayal, thumri, ghazal*), leaving a paucity of work on the large corpus of religious songs or hymns that are regularly and publicly performed within the context of liturgical rites in Hindu temples. Since a number of well established Vaishnava traditions of Krishna worship in the Braj region have integrated devotional hymns or *kīrtanas* into daily and seasonal rituals known as *pūjā* or *sevā*, there is an unexplored surplus of data for studies of music in Hindu liturgy.

The Spirit of Krishna in Braj: Beginnings

The in-depth study of Krishna traditions in the Braj area of northern India, including Vrindaban, was pioneered in the English language only recently with the book of A. W. Entwistle, *Braj: Centre of Krishna Pilgrimage* (1987). Though some previous studies had been done during the British colonial period, they were sketchy, with serious field work in the region being delayed until the 1980's. Charlotte Vaudeville, John S. Hawley, David Haberman, and A. Whitney Sanford have also made signal contributions in this vein with religio-geographic studies of some of the forests, hills, villages, and rivers of Braj.

In his thoroughly researched book, Entwistle confides that his scholarly approach was neutral and unfettered by the kind of devotional fervor that is so visibly characteristic of the area. He stated, "Though I have attempted to suppress value judgments and be less opinionated than my colonial predecessors, my perspective remains that of an outsider who, being charmed by the aesthetics and vivacity of Braj culture, has remained stubbornly impervious to the theology and mysticism. I am intrigued by the sentimental and emotional appeal of Krishna devotion, but have failed to let it sweep me off my feet."[10]

In my own case, the opposite disclaimer is advanced. I was "swept off my feet" by the same object of study, from the very first time that I was exposed to the music of Braj and Vrindaban. In 1974, while working as a Sanskrit editor for a well-known Indian Studies publisher in New York, the Bhaktivedanta Book Trust, one of my associates who had just returned from India presented me with a short audio tape of a recording that he had made in the Rādhāvallabha Temple. Knowing I was "into music," he thought I might find it interesting. Somehow I could not stop listening to it! The unusual melodies in Indian *rāgas*, along with the unique call-

[10]Alan W. Entwistle (1987), xvii.

and-response style of choral singing, with its repetitions, exclamations, and variations in overall tempo, were things that I had never heard before. The exotic *tāla* rhythmic patterns were also overwhelming. But there was something more—a powerful and intangible element of devotion that penetrated directly to the heart. While I was somewhat familiar with the sounds of the *sitar* and *sarod* which were popular then, this vocal music was on a totally different level, possibly an antecedent to the compositions performed on these instruments. To say that I was merely "blown away" by the emotional effect of this listening experience is an understatement. I became, in fact, "smitten" by the whole mystique of the Krishna myth as expressed in Indian vocal music. The singing on that tape lingered in my mind for a year until I was able to visit the Rādhāvallabha Temple myself in 1975 to make further recordings. This was followed by more lengthy visits in 1976-1980, 1988, and 1992-1993. I am certainly not alone in being enchanted by the culture and music of Braj. Still, in allowing my emotional responses to the musical and religious phenomena of Vrindaban to delay the prompt analysis and publication of my research, I stand in contrast to Entwhistle and those like him.

In addition, my lengthy period studying Indian classical music meant postponing timely and precise scholarly research expected in the humanities and social sciences. That is, rather than scouring libraries for different manuscripts of the poems I had heard, I was repeatedly drawn to taking more and more music lessons in order to collect many compositions in different *rāgas*, as the best means of understanding the performance traditions. In fact, one of the primary motivating factors that led me to enroll in formal Hindustani classical music lessons in Calcutta (1976-1980) was to attempt to comprehend the elusive Rādhāvallabha melodies and rhythms, which were sophisticated and, as I came to appreciate, quite connected to the current classical tradition. More biographical details of my classical training in Indian music are found in my article, "The Magic of Hindu Music," in *Hinduism Today* (Oct/Nov/Dec, 2007: 20-31). In short, I came to realize that the "spirit of Braj," or that intangible element of Krishna devotion, was not limited to a geographic area or spiritual lineage, but permeated the entire field of Hindustani classical music. This spirit or element was thus equally present in the classical compositions (also in Braj Bhasha language) that I received from renowned musical exponents in different parts of India, whether from my Hindu teachers Śrī Sailen Banerjee, Pandit Vijay Kichlu, Pandit Arun Bhaduri, and Śrī Ashish Goswami, or from the Muslim Dagar Brothers and Ustad Latafat Hussain Khan. Furthermore, all of this training reinforced my conviction that the Rādhāvallabha songs were compelling and that they urgently needed appreciation and dissemination. Hopefully, by now, there is sufficient preparation and emotional "distance" between subject and object for credible and articulate scholarly work to take place, resulting in this book and CD collection.

The term "Braj" does not refer to an area with clearly defined boundaries and "has never been used as the official name of a political territory or administrative division."[11] The term comes from the Sanskrit *vraja*, meaning a place where cattle roam, where Krishna tended his cows many centuries ago. Nonetheless, Braj is often defined as the religious and cultural sphere occupying about eighty-four square miles in western Uttar Pradesh and eastern Rajasthan where there is the predominance of the spoken language of Braj Bhasha; it includes the entire districts of Mathura and Bharatpur, as well as adjacent parts of other districts, like the towns of Aligarh, Hathras, Agra, and Alwar.[12] The single most important town within the Braj area in terms of the intensity of Krishna devotion and worship, is Vrindaban, the place where the adolescent Krishna

[11] Alan W. Entwistle (1987), 1.
[12] Alan W. Entwistle (1987), 1.

is believed to have exhibited his childish pranks, heroic feats, and amorous pastimes roughly five thousand years ago.

The people of Braj, or "Brajbasis," as they are usually called, in Entwistle's words:

> have taken the image of the romantic and pastoral Krishna to their hearts and have made him the central character in their folklore. They are proud to be associated with the land in which Krishna spent his youth and delight in telling visitors stories about the deeds he performed in their neighborhood. In keeping with their pastoral background, they are lovers of all dairy products and, if they indulge in a feast, prefer to gorge themselves on butter, ghee, and sweets made from milk, rather than any other kind of delicacy. They are also proud of their dialect, usually referred to as "Braj Bhasha." It is universally admired for its sweetness and is popularly assumed to be the language that Krishna spoke while he lived and played among the rustic people of Braj. Because it was thought to be the dialect most appropriate for describing Krishna's pastoral adventures, it became the most widely used form of literary Hindi from the sixteenth to the nineteenth century. Throughout this period Braj was a centre of inspiration for anyone concerned with the adventures of Krishna and Rādhā.[13]

The geographic Braj remains an important locus today for the study of Krishna, but the "spiritual" Braj which has taken on a life of its own within human consciousness: "Even though there is hardly a trace of his mythological environment, the presence of Krishna remains alive in the hearts and minds of the people."[14]

---

[13] Alan W. Entwistle (1987), 8.

[14] Alan W. Entwistle (1987), 2.

Krishna worship in India generally centers around the human-like form of Krishna who, either as supreme being or as an incarnation of Vishnu, is believed to have manifested in both space (the Braj region of northern India) and time (ca. 3000 BCE). The image forms of Krishna are venerated according to special events in his earthly life, like birth, childhood miracles, adolescent dalliances with cowherd girls, partnerships with his favorite milkmaid Rādhā, marriages with various queens, slaying of adversaries, ruling of dynasties, and speaking of holy teachings (*Bhagavad-Gītā*). Devotees of Krishna normally strive to invoke and recall his real presence. They do so by referring to one or more of these events in ritual worship and by hearing and singing his names and activities, often through the medium of vernacular songs or hymns variously known as *vishnupad, dhrupad, samāj-gāyan, bhajan,* and *kīrtan.* Unique among Vaishnava traditions, the Rādhāvallabha Sampradāya focuses attention almost solely on the romantic/erotic relationship between Rādhā and Krishna. The liturgical tradition of the Rādhāvallabha Sampradāya (community), which venerates Rādhā and Krishna but gives prominence to Rādhā, is one of the oldest and strongest of the various devotional *sampradāyas* established in Braj between 1200 and 1600 CE (the others include the Nimbārka, Vallabha, Haridāsī, and Gauḍīya *sampradāyas*).

Historically, Krishna fits into the broad category of the Hindu tradition known as "Vaishnava," acknowledged to encompass the majority of Hindu believers. Beside Krishna, it includes the veneration of Viṣṇu, Nārāyaṇa, Lakṣmī, Rādhā, Rāma, Sītā, and the remaining *avatāras* (incarnations) with their female consorts, saints, and sectarian leaders and followers. The various "Krishna" traditions within Vaishnavism differ regarding theology and the methods of worship, though nearly all involve music in some form. In a recent work, *Alternative Krishnas: Regional and Vernacular Variations on a Hindu Deity* (2005), I discussed these traditions and separated them into two general camps, one normative, and the other alternative. The normative Krishna tradition is based primarily on a canon of early Sanskrit texts (Purāṇas, epics), while so-called "alternative Krishna" traditions may or may not include these along with regional or vernacular sources.[15]

While the Sanskrit Purāṇas and epic texts describing the life and pastimes of Krishna have proliferated throughout the more elite or literary sectors of Indian society, the production of vernacular versions and descriptions of his *līlās* in the form of devotional songs are gradually being recognized as equally significant for the study of Hinduism. Braj Bhasha scholar Heidi R. M. Pauwels has explained,

> One of the favorite vehicles of the [*bhakti*] movement is the genre of devotional songs in the vernacular of the Braj area, the region closely associated with Krishna. Studying these apparently simple Braj Bhasha devotional songs reveals the complicated processes underlying them. Roughly speaking, the songs are the result of a merging of the brahmanic Puranic tradition (itself complex), Sanskrit poetics usually associated with the courtly tradition, and popular devotional and even secular folk traditions. In other words, these songs are excellent materials for the study of Hinduism.[16]

As this book seeks to focus on an important living vernacular tradition, it gives closer attention to the listening experience of hymns in ritual context, rather than to texts and commentaries.

---

[15]See Guy L. Beck (2005), 65-90, for a discussion of the "Alternative Krishnology" of the Rādhāvallabha Sampradāya.

[16]Heidi R. M. Pauwels (1996), 1.

Rādhāvallabha Sampradāya

One of the most unique of the various “alternative Krishna” subdivisions is the Rādhāvallabha Sampradāya (RVS). This medieval *sampradāya* flourished in northern India from the early 16th Century CE, and remains a potent force of Vaishnava devotion today in Braj, especially at its home town of Vrindaban. The sacred image of Krishna is central to this sect, but within the theology of RVS, Krishna is approached, not as the consummate Godhead, but as the penultimate step toward the supreme Deity which is not Krishna alone but primarily Rādhā, his spouse and only female companion.

The name ”Rādhā-vallabha” refers to Krishna as ”the dearest of Rādhā,” yet Krishna is subservient to Rādhā, who stands supreme in the theological hierarchy. The poetry of this tradition deals almost exclusively with the intimate and erotic relationship between Rādhā and Krishna. This ”alternative” Krishnology, while not totally without precedent in Vaishnava literature, is firmly located within the literature and tradition of the RVS, beginning with the works of the founder.

The Rādhāvallabha Sampradāya was founded in about 1535 CE by Śrī Hita Harivaṃśa (1502-1552 CE) in Vrindaban (cf. Vṛndāvana), near Mathurā, where according to pious tradition, Krishna was born miraculously in roughly 3000 BCE. Śrī Hita Harivaṃśa assisted in the medieval revival of the town of Vrindaban as a major pilgrimage center for Hindus. Along with Caitanya and the Six Goswamis of the Gauḍīya tradition, Śrī Vallabha and the Aṣṭachāp poets, Śrī Bhaṭṭa and Śrī Harivyāsadeva from the Nimbārka Sampradāya, and Svāmī Haridāsa of the Haridāsī Sampradāya, he is recognized by historians as a pioneer in developing Vrindaban. Śrī Hita Harivaṃśa established four important shrines there, each closely related to one of Krishna's pastimes. Sevā Kuñja is the alleged location of the original Rāsa-līlā, or circle dance, in which Krishna multiplied himself in order to dance with each of the townswomen simultaneously. Rāsa Maṇḍala is the site where the Rāsa-līlā plays are staged; Vaṃśīvaṭa is the tree where Krishna played his flute and inaugurated the Rāsa-līlā; and Mānasarovara is the pond where the cow-tending girls, the Gopīs, rested after Rāsa-līlā dance.

Śrī Hita Harivaṃśa's extraordinary life has been briefly summarized by Braj scholar Rupert Snell (1991), from the account of Uttamadāsa, an 18th century disciple of the Rādhāvallabha tradition. Hita Harivaṃśa's family was from the town of Deoband in Uttar Pradesh. His father, Vyāsa Miśra, was a wealthy Brahmin astrologer who served at the royal court but was at first unable to conceive a child. However, Vyāsa rejoiced at his brother's dream of a son who would soon be born to Vyāsa's wife as a joint incarnation of Hari (Krishna) and *vaṃśa* (Krishna's flute). Since the Miśra family was often in transit, Harivaṃśa took birth in the small village of Bada near Mathura, Krishna's own birthplace. From an early age the child was obsessed with the name and form of the Goddess Rādhā, often receiving communication from her in dreams. Rādhā had told him to make known a special *mantra* of her name to the world, and to rescue a Krishna image from a well in his father's garden. Harivaṃśa took these commands seriously by establishing this deity in a temple in his hometown. After marrying and raising three children, Harivaṃśa was further ordered by Rādhā to leave his family behind and proceed to Vrindaban, but only after going to another village and accepting two daughters in marriage from a Brahmin as well as another image of Krishna to be installed there. This image was known as "Rādhāvallabha," and was installed in a new temple in Vrindaban in the year 1535 C.E.

According to the record, "He [Harivaṃśa] established the service of the deity with seven food offerings (*bhoga*) through the eight periods of the day (*yāma*), according to the season."[17] Their unique tradition of Samāj-Gāyan singing began with the inauguration of this temple, drawing first upon the early Braj Bhasha hymns of Hita Harivaṃśa. Samāj-Gāyan, the focus of our study, is a collective style of vernacular hymn-singing resembling the Hindustani classical forms of Dhrupad and Dhamār. This is performed twice daily, in the morning and in the evening. The daily schedule is described more in detail further below.

The Rādhāvallabha scriptural canon is almost entirely in the vernacular dialect of Hindi known as Braj Bhasha. This special language is believed to be the speech of the intimate associates of Rādhā and Krishna in both the earthly Vrindaban and in the corresponding eternal spiritual abode. Braj Bhasha is also said to provide access to a more profound level of spiritual experience than that represented by the Sanskrit "canon," which is thought to be inferior since it is spoken only in the heavens by the various gods and goddesses, and neglects Rādhā as the highest truth. Though a few works in Sanskrit by members of the RVS survive, these texts develop a theology of Rādhā and Krishna rather than build upon standard themes of Vedānta, Mīmāṃsa, Yoga, Nyāya, or Vaiśeṣika philosophies. Moreover, RVS theology does not align itself with classical positions of nondualism or dualism. In the Sanskrit work of Śrī Hita Harivaṃśa known as the *Śrī-Rādhā-sudhā-nidhi-stotra*, "The Treasury of Rādhā's Nectar," the supreme divinity of Rādhā is presented as irrefutable. There are over sixteen commentaries on it written by disciples of the Rādhāvallabha lineage. Beside this, there is a short work in Braj Bhasha, *Sphuṭa-Vāṇī* (SV), and a prayer in Sanskrit to the Goddess Yamunā.

Śrī Hita Harivaṃśa's principal work in Braj Bhasha is the *Caurāśi-Pad* (CP), which has eighty-four verses covering themes of *nikuñja-vihāra* (the intimate love pastimes of Rādhā and Krishna taking place in eternal time), the Rāsa dance, Rādhā's

[17] Rupert Snell (1991), 19-20.

māna or pride, and descriptions of the Spring and Autumn scenery of Vrindaban. His devotional focus is primarily on the *yugala-mūrti*, the combined form of Rādhā and Krishna in loving embrace. Other aspects of Vaishnavism, such as *avatāra* mythology and worship, *vyūha* expansions, theology, personal privations and rituals like fasting on Ekādaśī, etc., are rejected as distractions. In fact, most of what passes as Sanātana Dharma Hinduism, including caste duties, *saṃskāras*, Vedic rituals, etc., are viewed as irrelevant to the central *līlā* of Rādhā and Krishna and are even held with some disdain. Avoidance of all of these conventional components of religious life further underscores the singular importance of music as the primary means of group participation and expression of the faith.

Besides the work of Śrī Hita Harivaṃśa, there is an immense body of poetic literature of the Rādhāvallabha Sampradāya which is unfortunately both unedited and unpublished. Most of the existing writings and manuscripts attributed to members of the various disciplic lineages, with dates, have been tabulated in a book by Śrī Kisori Saran Ali, *Śrī Hita Rādhāvallabhiya Sāhitya Ratnāvalī.* In the fall of 1992, in the Vrindaban home of his grandson/disciple Śrī Jayesh Khandelwal, Śrī Kisori Saran Ali showed me two gigantic closets filled with hand-written manuscripts and transcriptions that had accumulated for generations, pointing out that the poetic riches of this tradition have been largely untapped.

The subsequent development of the Rādhāvallabha Sampradāya incorporated two parallel streams, one dependent on the other. The principal stream is the hereditary line derived from Śrī Hita Harivaṃśa, through his sons and descendents. Those individual householder leaders in the hereditary line are called Goswamis (Gosvāmīs), and the stream is called the Bindu Parivāra ("family from the seed"). The other line is a chain of ascetics linked through initiation (*dīkṣā*). This is called the Nāda Parivāra ("family from the sound"). The ascetic line is not independent and derives its authority from the Goswamis. The Bindu Parivāra (hereditary line) maintains control over the following religious sites: the main Rādhāvallabha temple, Sevā Kuñja and Raṅgīlāla Mandira in Vrindaban. Some of the names in this line are Vanacandra, Kṛṣṇacandra, Hita Rūpalāla, and Vṛndāvanadāsa Gosvāmī. The Nāda Parivāra (ascetic line) maintains the sites at Bād Grām, Māna Sarovara, and the Rāsa Maṇḍala in Vrindaban, and includes the names of Nara Vāhana, Dāmodara Svāmī, Rāmakṛṣṇadāsa, Ativallabha, Sahacārī Sukha, Uttamadāsa, Premadāsa, Vrajajīvana, and Priyādāsa.[18]

The Rādhāvallabha tradition maintains a "Krishnology" that is complex, and believed to represent the highest and truest culmination of centuries of Vaishnavism and Krishna worship. In order to understand and appreciate this consummation of devotion, it is helpful to study the development of Vaishnavism from the initial stages of Vedic religion that gives reference to the deity of Vishnu to the ultimate supremacy of Rādhā over Krishna.

Indian Music and Hindu Devotion

The role of music in Hindu devotion requires some elucidation beginning with a brief description of the development of Dhrupad and Samāj-Gāyan as theoretically derived from Gandharva music, the ancient music contemporary with Vedic ritual and the Sāma Veda. This will assist in providing a deeper understanding of the importance of music and rhythm in Vaishnava worship.

Rather than a secular art or folk expression, music in Hindu traditions is believed to be originally created by the gods for their own amusement, and later bestowed upon humans both

[18]For a complete listing of the members of each line along with their literary contributions, see Vijayendra Snatak (1957, 1968), 573-581.

for enjoyment and as a means of release from mortality. As such, music is seen to be innately possessed of sacred qualities, whereby the individual notes (*svara*) and beats (*mātrā*) reflect natural and cosmic forces. The bestowal of music is said in Hindu mythology to have happened in response to a plea or petition in a time of critical need. Brahmā, after meditating for thousands of years, finally decided to give music to the entire human race when sages begged him to bring relief to the sorrow and hardships of the world. The use of music in various Indian religious contexts is thus more readily understood and expected, since virtually all music, like language, reflects the divine realm.

The Sāma Veda *sāmans* were hymns that were comprised of 3-7 *svaras* or notes. Each note has a specific finger position (*mudrā*): *kruṣṭa* (*Pa*), *prathama* (*Ma*), *dvitīya* (*Ga*), *tritīya* (*Ri*), *caturtha* (*Sa*), *mandra* (*Dha*), *atisvārya* (*Ni*), *anudātta* (*Pa*). The *riks* or verses of the original Rig Veda were chanted in one, two, and three notes that were linked to three accents known as *anudātta*, *udātta*, and *svarita*. There was no percussive element apart from the rhythm of the singing, yet the hand gestures indicated falling and rising moments at appropriate times. In order to create more effect, both aesthetically and spiritually, *stobhas* or semantically meaningless syllables were inserted between notes to conform to patterns of melody and rhythm.

Ancient Indian music was also understood as a form of yoga that served to bring about a state of blissful immortality for the chanter and listener. Sometimes this was referred to as *nāda-yoga*, in reference to the concept of Nāda-Brahman, the cosmic or sacred sound that is believed to pervade the universe but also resides within the human consciousness. Musicians are often cited as having experiences of this Nāda-Brahman while in their performance or private practice. Sanskrit texts have identified this experience and amplified it with the notion of *rasa*, which is equated with that bliss or *ānanda* which is felt when the divine nature of the Self is realized. Music came to be practiced not merely as an aesthetic or mental exercise but as a means toward realization of the knowledge of the *ātman*. The aim of music is to restore equanimity to the mind and induce a state of bliss to the inner self. *ānanda* being an attribute of Brahman or the Hindu God Vishnu or Krishna, it is the most pure, elevating and intense joy that also brings with it an intuition of reality. More details on the Sanskrit philosophy of Nāda-Brahman as well as the Vedic notion of *adṛṣṭa* are found in the author's study, *Sonic Theology: Hinduism and Sacred Sound* (1993).

Indian music, if properly performed according to the canons of musical theory, is said to provide salvation (heaven) and relief from *bhava-sāgara*, the ocean of material suffering. The tradition of Gandharva Saṅgīta, ancient classical music, according to the texts of *Dattila* and *Nāṭya Śāstra*, was based on the Vedic system of sacrifice, in which the correct performance of rites guaranteed entrance into heaven. This was realized through the same principle of *adṛṣṭa*, or unseen merit that accumulated within the soul of the practitioner over a lifetime on earth. Though the rite would finish, the result derived from its execution remained invisible to the performer only to be reclaimed after death. This corresponded to the principle of *apūrva* in Mīmāṃsā philosophy and linguistics.

Solveig McIntosh, in her new study of ancient music, *Hidden Faces of Ancient Indian Song*, states that,

> In general, all formalized music was known as Gandharva and was even considered a secondary Veda. More specifically, it meant music that was intended for *adṛṣṭa phala*, for obtaining the unseen result, for religious merit or praising the gods. This was a highly grammatical music and in the *Nāṭya Śāstra* [of Bharata] was used in a specific sense. The main components of Gandharva were *svara*, *tāla*, and *pada* (tone, time,

> and word or syllable) with specific rules for obtaining unseen spiritual results. Vocal music, *vīṇā* and the flute formed the triad of Gandharva music with the main emphasis on vocal music and with *vīṇā* and flute lending a special harmony.[19]

Gandharva music has been described in detail in the Sanskrit treatise *Dattilam,* written by Dattila (ca. 300 BCE). Based essentially on the Vedic theory of sacrifice, the performers "earned" their way to salvation through the correct performance of traditional music. Mukund Lath, a contemporary interpreter of the *Dattilam,* argues in *A Study of Dattilam* that,

> Gandharva was not only immutable like the Vedic *mantras,* its performance was not unlike the performance of a Vedic sacrifice. It was a special kind of sacrifice in honor of the gods. It was a *yāga* that was free of the immense expenses involved in Vedic sacrifices and was especially pleasing to Lord Śiva. Like Vedic sacrifices, Gandharva was governed by strict commands regarding do's and don't's. Every movement in it had to strictly follow the injunctions or *vidhis* laid down for it. These injunctions were preserved in the manuals on Gandharva (such as the *Dattilam*) ... A properly performed Vedic sacrifice was said to result in *adṛṣṭa* (or *apūrva,* a concept synonymous with *adṛṣṭa*). The same belief existed regarding Gandharva.[20]

Ancient Gandharva music was primarily vocal and employed as its main percussion instrument the *jhānjh,* hand cymbals, which were employed to demarcate the *svaras* or musical notes and the *mātrās* or rhythmic units of *tāla* as they unfolded. Similar types of hand cymbals are used all over India

---

[19]Solveig McIntosh (2005), 79.
[20]Mukund Lath (1978), 82, 84.

today primarily in religious music and are especially found in the Vaishnava temple music traditions. As observed by Lath, "A distinct feature of Gandharva *tāla* was the peculiar nature of the instrument used. *Tāla* measures were demarcated chiefly by sounding bronze cymbals. To this day in India, the *jhānjh* and *mañjīra* (large and small bronze cymbals) are specifically connected with music in a religious or devotional setting."[21] The great musical scholar Śārṅgadeva of the thirteenth century C.E. included a small section on bells and cymbals and their proper usage in his *Saṅgīta-Ratnākara* ("Ocean of Song," 6.1170f). As such, similar notions of earning merit toward liberation in Vedic sacrifices and ancient Gandharva music hold for much of the temple music from the medieval periods to the present.

The later Vaishnava temple songs, while grouped according to *rāga* and *tāla*, incorporate the basic principle of *adṛṣṭa* which functions independently of the particular *rāga* or *tāla* that may be employed. And as the syllables of the Braj Bhasha text are vocally rendered in the strict manner of rhythmic units or *mātrās*, the *śakti* or power of the letters unfold within the mind of the performer or listener, accumulating merit through the building up of *apūrva*. In addition, the references to the Gandharva musical instruments in later *bhakti* poetry, especially drums, cymbals, and other percussion instruments, are insightful with regard to the soteriological dimension of Vaishnava temple music, such as found in the Rādhāvallabha tradition, in the terms discussed above.

The two most characteristic types of Vaishnava temple singing in Vraja are Samāj-Gāyan, the congregational singing of devotional poetry at fixed times, and Nitya Kīrtan, also known as Haveli Sangit, the soloistic rendition of verses to accompany the temple worship service on a continuous basis from morning until evening. Whereas Samāj-Gāyan is the special

[21] Mukund Lath (1978), 110.

genre of Vraja, in particular the Rādhāvallabha, Nimbārka and Haridāsī Sampradāyas, Nitya Kīrtan is still observed today in the temples of the Vallabha Sampradāya (Puṣṭimārga), which have dispersed throughout Western India. The Hindustani classical form known as Dhrupad forms an integral part of both Samāj-Gāyan and Nitya Kīrtan.

Dhrupad

Dhrupad is the most important classical vocal musical form in North India. It is named as such because its song-texts have a "fixed" (*dhru, dhruva*) relation between the syllable, note (*svara*), and rhythmic unit or beat (*mātrā*). The term Dhrupad is thus nominally related to the ancient theatre songs known as *dhruva*, which were rendered in the vernacular Prakrit dialects of the day. In fact, Dhrupad is the oldest surviving genre of classical singing in India. Its name, derivative of *dhruvapada* — an older variety of devotional music — means simply "refrain", and today means both a form of poetry and a style of music in which the poetry is sung. A Dhrupad composition comprises four parts, usually represented by four lines of a complete poem, that are termed *sthāyī, antarā, saṃcārī*, and *ābhoga*. In theory, these four parts each have a separate melody within the confines of a specific *rāga* that serve to unfold the characteristics of the *rāga*. Modern practice has tended to reduce these to the first two, as in the genre of Khyāl, its direct successor in form and popularity.

The direct connection between Vaishnava temple music and Dhrupad singing is explained by Selina Thielemann with reference to the *Bhāgavata Purāṇa* scriptural text: "While classical musicians often refer to Śārṅgadeva's *Saṅgīta Ratnākara*, and more specifically to the description of *prabandha* contained in it, as the theoretical fundament of classical Dhrupad, the scriptural confirmation of the superiority of the temple Dhrupad over other genres of Vaishnava devotional music is sought not in a musicological treatise, but rather in the text that forms the theological basis of Vaishnavism, namely the *Bhāgavata Purāṇa.*"[22] The verse that specifically refers to devotional music is from Chapter Thirty-three of the Tenth Book (10.33.10), which offers an elaborate description of the Rāsa-līlā, Krishna's famous round dance which he performed with the *gopīs* (cowherd women) of Vraja on the side of the Yamunā River during the full-moon in autumn. The passage describes a musical exchange between the *gopīs* and Krishna.

kācit samaṃ mukundena svarajātīr amiśritāḥ
unninye pūjitā tena prīyatā sādhu sādhviti
tad eva dhruvam unninye tasyai mānaṃ ca bahvadāt

In Graham Schweig's translation: "One of them, together with Mukunda, sang out in pure embellished tones, freely improvising on a melody. Pleased by her performance, he honored her, saying, "Well done! Well done!" Another one sang out that melody in a stylized rhythmic pattern, and he offered her much praise." The footnote states, "in a particular measure of music known as *dhruvam.*"[23]

In Selina Thielemann's translation: "A certain (*gopī*) sang together with Krishna (in a way that) the notes of the scale did not harmonize. She was honored by him, as she had pleased him, (with the words) "Splendid! excellent!". (When) she proceeded to sing to the measured beat (*dhruva*), he paid much respect to her."[24]

In the second half of the stanza, the appearance of the term *dhruva* is very significant. It indeed refers to a type of song in the ancient music style of Gāndharva Saṅgīta. *Dhruva* was a fixed metrical song that was rendered in the vernacular or

[22]Selina Thielemann (2002), 27.
[23]Graham Schweig (2006), 68.
[24]Selina Thielemann (1999), 357.

Prakrit dialect of the time, and survives by name in the Vaishnava tradition of Dhruvapad or Dhrupad, a close relative of the Samāj-Gāyan tradition. In her studies of Vaishnava temple music, Thielemann has commented on this passage:

> The usage of the term *dhruva*, which is nowadays interpreted as *dhruva pada* (i.e. *dhrupada*) and quoted as evidence for the superior position of *dhrupada* among the song types of devotional music. In the present context, the term *dhruva* refers clearly to a melody set to a fixed metric pattern, i.e., to a composition as distinct from a freely improvised melody, but if we keep in mind that *dhruva pada* is most likely to have been the original and principal type of composition in Vaishnava devotional singing, the interpretation of *dhruva* as *dhruva pada* gains indeed authority.[25]

In a later work, Thielemann cites a Vaishnava authority in connection with the interpretation of this passage:

> Interpretations by contemporary *Bhāgavata* scholars equate "*dhruva*" with "*dhruva pada*" i.e. "*dhrupada.*" Thus, Shri Purushottam Goswami ji Maharaj of Vrindaban explained in a commentary on the present verse [sermon on April 26, 1995] that the *gopī* referred to in the text was honored by the lord as she proceeded to sing *dhrupada*, and he continued by saying that *dhrupada* derives its special spiritual significance from the power inherent in the twelve *mātrās* of its metric cycle, i.e. Cautāla.[26]

He also attributed this same spiritual power to the fourteen *mātrās* of Dhamār Tāla. This statement about the power of

[25]Selina Thielemann (1999), 357.
[26]Selina Thielemann (2002), 28.

the *mātrās* serves to validate the connections between Indian musical rhythm and Vedic chanting briefly outlined above.

Like all other Indian classical music, Dhrupad is modal or monophonic music, having a single melodic line and no harmony in the Western sense. The modes are known as *rāgas*, and each *rāga* is a scale but has its own complicated framework of melodic rules. Apart from other genres of folk and popular music, Dhrupad is in slower tempo, mostly in Cautāl (twelve beats) and Dhamār (fourteen beats). It has less melodic development, and a limited set of ornaments. Based on available evidence, Dhrupad seems to have originated as a form of devotional singing in Hindu temples. It is thus believed to have a very long history that is traceable back to the Vedic period, since there is mention of *dhruva* as a kind of vernacular song in ancient texts like the *Dattilam*. Gandharva music was the musical counterpart to the ancient Vedic hymns of the Sāma Veda called *sāmans*.

Dhrupad became popular in both the Hindu and Muslim courts during the medieval times. Abul Fazl, who was the courtier and chronicler at the court of the Emperor Akbar, wrote a work called the *Ain-e-Akbari* in which he defined *dhrupad* as "Four rhyming lines, each of indefinite prosodial length of words or syllables." The four lines, in serial order, are *sthāyī*, *antarā*, *saṃcārī* and *ābhoga*. The subject matter was mostly religious, but also included praise of royal figures, musical symbolism, and romantic themes.

Gradually by the eighteenth century Dhrupad singing began to decline and was replaced by a more fluid improvisatory genre called Khyāl. It allowed for more display of virtuosity and was configured as less religious and more of a courtly entertainment. At this time, new instruments were being developed such as the *sitar* and the *sarod*, that mirrored the rendering of Khyāl with regard to fast tempos and rapid passages in succession.

The classical Dhrupad of today is performed by a solo singer, or a small number of singers in unison, to the beat of a double-headed barrel drum, the *pakhavāj*. The songs are mostly in praise of Hindu deities, but, as in Abul Fazl's time, Islamic or simply regalist lyrics have been composed and added to the repertoire. In concert performance, the text of the *sthāyī* is usually preceded by an introductory improvised section called the *ālāp*, without instrumental accompaniment. Sung without words, it uses instead sets of syllables in a repetitive fixed pattern, such as, *ā re ne na, te re ne na, ri re re ne na, te ne toom ne.* This practice is often called *nom-tom*. These syllables are actually derived from sacred syllables of Vishnu *mantras* like *Om Hari Ananta Narayana*. It has became the trend in modern concerts of Dhrupad that the *ālāp* will comprise the greater part of the performance, lasting up to an hour, beginning in slow tempo with a gradual, controlled development of the *rāga*.

Samāj-Gāyan

As a form of devotional singing that is related to the classical Dhrupad styles, Samāj-Gāyan is based on similar notions of the formal structure and development of the *rāga* and *tāla*. It also employs the *pakhavāj* drum (sometimes the *tabla*) and may utilize a *tanpura* drone. However, principal differences exist between Dhrupad and Samāj-Gāyan. Hand cymbals must always be used in Samāj-Gāyan, while they are virtually absent in classical Dhrupad concerts. There is no *ālāp* in Samāj-Gāyan, and Samāj-Gāyan is never a solo singing event. The harmonium is used in Samāj-Gāyan but rarely in Dhrupad; however, this does not reflect on the structure and age of either tradition. One of the main differences is that Samāj-Gāyan is never for entertainment purposes, whereas Dhrupad had developed as courtly entertainment by the 16th century. Selina Thielemann notes the complexity of Samāj-Gāyan in contrast to the simple four-fold structure of classical Dhrupad:

"The most complex structure is found in Samāj-Gāyan, where the verses may comprise any number of lines from four onwards; very often the texts are extremely extended, and they have to be rendered in full during the performance owing to the sanctity of their devotional content. The sequence of *sthāyī* and *antarā* is repeated for each couplet; *saṃcārī* and *ābhoga* (i.e. the final couplet) are melodically identical with *sthāyī* and *antarā* respectively."[27] Yet many of these differences are circumstantial and do not obscure the fundamental similarities in origin and structure.

The Rādhāvallabha Sampradāya gives a central place to the singing of Samāj-Gāyan within its temple enclosures and sacred shrines. English scholar and researcher Rupert Snell confirms that, "Special importance is attached to the singing of appropriate texts in Samaj, and a large body of sectarian literature, mostly in Braj Bhasha, exists for this purpose."

Members of the Rādhāvallabha Sampradāya utilize music and singing in Braj Bhasha as a vehicle with which to gain direct access to ecstasy and pure religious experiences. American scholar Charles S. J. White, commenting on the musical dimension of this group, says: "Where the tradition of the sect provides for the composition of hymns or *bhajans* for group singing, such music becomes, through participation and understanding, a vehicle for the devotee to move beyond the external forms of the cult to an inner experience of ecstasy based on the intensity of his faith."[28]

While several groups in Vrindaban practice Samāj-Gāyan and hold music and singing as central to their cult worship, the RVS prides itself as the originator of Samāj-Gāyan. As a unique form of devotional singing that has ties with the classical tradition, it is most likely native to the Braj area. The RVS claims that it has maintained this musical tradition continually on a daily basis since its origination in the 16th cen-

[27] Selina Thielemann (2002), 31-32.
[28] Charles S. J. White (1977), 31.

tury. The central temple of Śrī Rādhāvallabhaji established by Śrī Hita Harivaṃśa indeed houses the longest continuing tradition of Samāj-Gāyan in Braj, with performances daily and frequently twice-daily. In addition, several other branch temples have maintained a daily regimen of Samāj-Gāyan as well, including Jaipur and Calcutta. Modern scholarship has reaffirmed this view with reference to a painting of Harivaṃśa, Haridāsa and Harirāma Vyāsa sitting together in Samāj-Gāyan. Thielemann says:

> The musicians of the Rādhāvallabha Sampradāya claim that their practice of congregational singing reaches back to the 16th century when it was initiated by the founder of the *sampradāya*, the poet Hita Harivaṃśa. This opinion is supported by a miniature painting dating from 1538 C.E., that shows Hita Harivaṃśa and his followers performing Samāj-Gāyan to the accompaniment of cymbals, barrel-drum and *tanpura*. Beginning with Hita Harivaṃśa, the Rādhāvallabha tradition has developed a rich poetic heritage, and music has always played a predominant role in this community. The Rādhāvallabhite Samāj is perhaps the oldest tradition of Samāj-Gāyan to have been maintained on a continuous basis to the present. The principal religious center of the *sampradāya*, the temple of Rādhāvallabha in Vrindaban, arranges Samāj performances twice daily[29]

Śrī Rajendra Prasad Sharma, the principal singer of this tradition and the one most prominently featured on the accompanying CDs, stated emphatically in an interview that Samāj-Gāyan began within the RVS: "The origin of Samāj-Gāyan is only in Vrindaban and particularly in the Rādhāvallabha temple. And if held elsewhere outside Vrindaban, it is only in the

[29]Selina Thielemann (1999), 305.

Rādhāvallabha Sampradāya. There is no worship of Rādhāvallabha without Samāj."[30] This claim to seniority, however, has been contested by members of the Nimbārka Sampradāya who state that Śrī Bhaṭṭa, an early Braj Bhasha poet in their tradition, sang Samāj-Gāyan. But while some of the literature of the Nimbārka Sampradāya even claims that the legendary Nārada Ṛṣi of antiquity learned Dhrupad from the gods, there is no reference to Samāj-Gāyan, which is distinct from classical Dhrupad. Classical Dhrupad and Samāj-Gāyan are only sung in non-Sanskritic dialects such as Braj Bhasha, and not in Sanskrit which was the basic language of the gods, of Nārada Ṛṣi, and the Puranic authors. While Sanskrit is called Devanāgarī ("City of the Gods") and is believed to be spoken by the gods, *bhakti* authors of North India claim that Krishna and his associates, who are on a higher plane of power and intimacy, speak and sing in Braj Bhasha, a dialect related to Apabhraṃśa Prākrita and medieval Hindi. Moreover, Braj Bhasha is less formal with regard to grammar and pronunciation, has more allowance for vowel sounds, and is thus sweeter to the ear and more suitable for singing.

Śrī Kisori Saran Ali of the Rādhāvallabha Sampradāya disputes all other claims to seniority by saying that Samāj-Gāyan is a relatively recent practice in other *sampradāyas*: "Samāj-Gāyan has been recently adopted by the followers of Svāmī Haridāsa, while the Nimbārka Sampradāya and others are now also using Samāj-Gāyan in their communities. The Rādhāvallabha Sampradāya is most certainly the originator of this music, as it is attested in older manuscripts of this tradition and lacking in others."[31] Indeed, with specific references to Samāj-Gāyan in early literature of the Rādhāvallabhites, their credentials appear stronger than the others who lack such ref-

[30] Interview with Śrī Rajendra Prasad Sharma in Vrindaban, March 23, 1993. Transcribed from an audio tape and translated from Hindi to English by Śrī Harishankar Mathur, former Director of the Śrī Rangaji Temple in Vrindaban.

[31] Interview with Śrī Kisori Saran Ali in Vrindaban, July 22, 1992. Transcribed from an audio tape and translated from Hindi to English by Śrī Harishankar Mathur.

erences and most probably adopted the style of singing from the Rādhāvallabha Sampradāya. The Haridāsī Sampradāya inaugurated their Samāj-Gāyan as late as the 18th century.

During my own research from 1992-93 on the music of the Rādhāvallabha Sampradāya, I found the most effective "singing" informant to be Śrī Rajendra Prasad Sharma, who sang every evening at two different places in Vrindaban: the Choti Sarkar Temple in Autkhamba from about 6 to 7 P.M., and then at the Hitashram at Śrī Satsanga Bhumi from about 7:30 to 9 P.M. While there were only a few people at the former, including on some days only the *tabla* player and one *jhela* who also played *jhānjh*, at the latter *āśrama* one could readily absorb Samāj-Gāyan at its very best. There, the singer was accompanied by an expert player on the *pakhavāj*, several *jhānjh* cymbals, and a fervent and dynamic chorus of *jhelās* consisting of local disciples but also many wandering, bearded "holy men" who seemed to revel in the assurance that this was where the real "Braj vibrations" were to be heard. Except for occasional bouts of load-shedding (electric power cuts), the sessions were amplified through a microphone which added greatly to the intensity of the music. "Masterjī," as I called him respectfully, allowed me to record his music on a daily basis and was very eager about discussing the tradition, though he was rather limited in English expression. Sometimes I would walk with him from Choti Sarkar to Hitashram, and he stressed that I would now hear *bahut badiya samāj* ("the very best samāj"). I was also invited to some of his private sittings at the home/shrine of the now-deceased guru Śrī Lalitcaran Goswami. There I was able to record, with almost no background noise, rare songs such as "Lāla kī rūpa mādhurī" ("The Boy's Form is Sweet") and "Mohana madana tribhaṅgī" ("Enchanting, Intoxicating Threefold Bending Form"), which are only sung once a year.

Masterjī Śrī Rajendra Prasad Sharma was at that time the best-trained and most authoritative of the singers in this tradition, having a good background knowledge of Sastriya Sangit (classical Hindu music) and many years experience learning the Rādhāvallabha Samāj tradition. I stress his musical qualities because I heard (more than once) some other Samāj-Gāyan singers in Vrindaban, whom I will not mention, who were much less-trained and often out-of-tune. Although not a Goswami, a hereditary descendent of Śrī Hita Harivaṃśa, Masterjī has been pronounced Mukhiya, "chief songster" of this sect by its leaders, having thoroughly studied the style and repertoire of his predecessor singer of the *sampradāya*, Śrī Damodara Dvivedi Das Mukhiya. The latter Mukhiyajī has led the Samāj for over thirty years in the main temple of Śrī Rādhāvallabhajī and is recognized as a person whose singing is *alaukika*, or completely transcendental. Damodara's son, Rakesh, has now been trained by both his father and Masterjī, and is accepting the responsibility of carrying on the tradition of Samāj-Gāyan in the main Rādhāvallabha temple.

Śrī Rajendra Prasad Sharma sang every evening at the Hitashram in Vrindaban, headed by Śrī Hitadas Maharaj. In an interview, Śrī Rajendra Sharma related his background in music and in the tradition of the Rādhāvallabha Sampradāya:

> Music has been my hobby since childhood. I started learning by myself, as my father was not a singer. My original music *guru* was in Kamban, one of the areas of Braj. Then I joined in service as a teacher in Rajasthan. My first post was in Bhulpur, then Rajakhara. Then I learned music from Kallu Khan who was a *sāraṅgī* player. When I came to Vrindaban, I developed contacts with Bābā Jīvan dās, a retired professor of music from the University of Rajasthan who was then living as a recluse-devotee in Vrindaban. But I started learning Samāj-Gāyan on my own when I came to Vrindaban. Within two years, I picked up the style of singing, which I learned from Śrī Lalitacaran Goswami, my spiritual *guru*. I heard

> many singers and used to call many singers to my house for occasions like the birthday of my son, etc.
>
> By and by, I gained a full command of Samāj Gāyaki. I learned primarily by hearing in the company of other musicians. The system of Samāj music is that the *guru* sits face-to-face with the student. The *guru* will sing and the student will hear, and this is the tradition of Samāj-Gāyan. Notation started quite late, but the earlier tradition was that of *guru-śiṣya paramparā* (guru-disciple lineage). Playing the *tanpura*, the *guru* would sing and then I would repeat, sitting in front of him. Memory and grasping power are both necessary to pick up this music. Sitting for many years in the Rādhāvallabha temple and also at other places like Bhattaji's and Tatti Sthan of the Haridāsī Sampradāya, I absorbed many features of devotional music. But my main concentration was on the Samāj-Gāyan of the Rādhāvallabha Sampradāya. After listening to me and testing me for two years, Śrī Lalitacaran Goswami finally gave me permission to sing in the Rādhāvallabha temples. Now I have been performing in Vrindaban for over twenty years.[32]

Another person who is extremely well-informed about the literary tradition as well as the music, is Śrī Kisori Saran Ali. More a scholar than a performer, he has written and published several works including a commentary in Hindi on the *Caurāśī-Pad*. He resides in his own ashram very close to the Vrindaban Research Institute in Raman Reti where there are several manuscripts of the works of Śrī Hita Harivaṃśa and other saints of the RVS. In an interview, Śrī Kisori Saran Ali stressed the unique nature of Samāj-Gāyan and its relation to

---

[32]Interview with Śrī Rajendra Prasad Sharma in Vrindaban on March 28, 1993. Transcribed from an audio tape and translated from Hindi to English by Śrī Harishankar Mathur.

various types of folk music and women's songs in Braj:

> Samāj-Gāyan is very old. It is the form of worship of the Rādhāvallabha Sampradāya, both *upāsanā* and *sādhanā*. It is also a special form of music sung to please the chosen deity. This is a devotional music drawn from certain forms of *lok-saṅgīt* and *lok-gīt*, folk music still alive in the Braj culture today (i.e., the local festivals). In *saṃskāra* ceremonies like the birth of a child, hair shaving, and marriage, there were folk songs sung by ladies with *dholak* and *jhāñjh* in particular tunes, not necessarily in *rāga* and *rāginīs*. One lady addresses another using "eri ha, ari heli, ari sajani," etc. This is proof that Samāj-Gāyan is connected with women's songs of Braj. No man will address another man with the words, "eri or saheli." When you sing Samāj-Gāyan you feel a sort of emotion towards God. It is another method of pleasing God. It was started in the latter part of the 16th century.[33]

The musicians of Samāj-Gāyan employ melodic forms and rhythms drawn from the Hindustani classical tradition of Dhrupad that was developing in the surrounding court *darbars* of the sovereign rulers. Though it is much closer to Dhrupad than the later emerging Khyāl form, there are some differences from the classical Dhrupad, as explained by Śrī Kisori Saran Ali who also shared his views regarding the relationship between Samāj-Gāyan and Hindustani classical music:

> Samāj-Gāyan is not necessarily based only on classical *saṅgīt*, for it has independent *dhuns* (tunes). Classical *rāgas* are there, but they are not rendered in a totally classical style, but in a mixture. These may be called mixed *rāgas*, *miśrit rāgas*, not pure *rāgas*. The

[33]Op. cit. Interview with Śrī Kisori Saran Ali.

> emphasis is rather on emotion and the words that convey the emotion. The intention is not to preserve the pure form of the *rāga*, but more on maintaining the words and their clear meaning. The *ācāryas* of Samāj-Gāyan possess their own independent tunes which cannot be fully defined according to classical *rāga* classification. Yet the *rāgas* have not been totally abandoned. The songs are not wedded to the *rāgas*. The main thing is *bhāva*, the emotional meaning of the words."[34]

Vaishnava Dhrupad, unlike its classical counterpart, is always composed in Cautāl. In fact, the *theka* (the basic structure of claps and waves within the twelve *mātrā* cycle) of Cautāl in all traditions of devotional music is identical with that in Hindustani music. However, the term "Dhrupad" is not used in the RVS, nor equated with Cautāl. To be sure, there are compositions in Cautāl in the RVS, as the reader will find in this collection, but they are not referred to as Dhrupad compositions, simply as Samāj-Gāyan. As clarified by Thielemann,

> The equation of *dhrupada* and *cautāla* is ... strongly rejected and regarded as a terminological confusion by the representatives of Rādhāvallabha Samāj-Gāyan. In the opinion of the Rādhāvallabhite musicians [Śrī Kisori Saran Ali of Vrindaban], *dhrupada* is firstly a singing style (*gāyakī*) rather than a *tāla*, and secondly it belongs to the tradition of North Indian classical music which has to be strictly separated from the *samāja* practice of the Vaiṣṇava temples. ... the Rādhāvallabhite musicians themselves do not employ the term "dhrupada" (or any other specific term denoting song types for that matter)

---

[34]ibid.

with reference to Samāj-Gāyan.[35]

The most celebrated author, scholar, spiritual leader, and *ācārya* (guru) within the Rādhāvallabha tradition was Śrī Lalitacaran Goswami. He has outlined the importance of Samāj-Gāyan in his literary works:

> In the Puṣṭi Mārg and Rādhāvallabha temples, *kīrtankāras* (performers of Kirtan) are appointed to sing *padas* in front of the deity of Krishna at specific hours. The *kīrtankāras* of the Rādhāvallabha Sampradāya are known as Samājīs. The number of Samājīs is at least four, one of whom is the *mukhīya* (leader), one the *pakhawājī* (player of the *pakhawājī* drum), and two *jhelās* (responsorial singers). The *mukhīya* first sings one line of a *pada* which is then repeated by the *jhelās*. One of the *jhelās* usually plays *jhāñjh*, and the other plays *tanpura* or something else.[36]

Accordingly,

> the Rādhāvallabhīya Samājīs have their own distinctive style. Their singing style has been created in such a manner that words or *vāṇī* (speech) must be properly pronounced and distinctly audible to listeners. Whenever the rendering of any *rāga* or *rāginī* with *ālāps* and *tānas* (melismatic passages) was found to be obstructing the pronunciation of the words, a new compound *rāga* was created by mixing the *svaras* of other *rāgas* of the same *ṭhāṭ* (group of *rāgas*), so that the words could be expressed more distinctly and appealingly ... There is no scope for elaborate *tānas* in this style, and only very brief *murkis* (ornaments) are tolerated. [In Samāj-Gāyan,] the attempt

[35] Selina Thielemann (2002), 29.

[36] Śrī Lalitacaran Goswami Maharaj, former *ācārya* of Śrī Rādhāvallabha Sampradāya. "The Musical Style of the Rādhāvallabha Samāj-Gāyan." Translated in Guy L. Beck (1996), 136.

> is made to reproduce the description or subject matter of the various poetic compositions with the help of *svara* (musical notes) and *laya* (rhythmic styles). For example, in the Jhulan compositions where the deity is described as being placed on a swing, the motions of *hindola* (swinging) are recreated in the musical rendering. Similarly, in the compositions of Rāsa-līlā the paces of dancing, and in Holi songs the joy of Phag (Spring), have been expressed musically."[37]

More specifics of Samāj-Gāyan style may be described from first-hand observation by the author. The musicians are generally seated along two rows adjacent to the deity or altar platform. In most cases the percussionist faces the deity toward the end of the rows, and the *jhelās* face each other and the *mukhiya* who may be on either side. After an invocatory prayer in Sanskrit honoring Śrī Hita Harivaṃśa and other *ācāryas*, the leader begins the Samāj session with a slow composition in either Dhāmar *tāla* or Cautāl, which speeds up intermittently according to the dynamics of the call-and-response format. Within the time frame (one to three hours), a number of songs are selected by the leader, and the session is usually closed with a few songs in lighter *tālas* (Dadra or Dīp Chandi) that most everyone knows from memory. Beside these, the songs are generally followed in the hymnal by both the musicians and the congregation. Unlike most other genres of Indian music, Samāj-Gāyan displays a much more intimate interaction between the lead singer and the responders. There is also a close adherence to the text, with little or no attention to individual creativity or improvisation as found in courtly classical traditions. The most conspicuous feature of Samāj-Gāyan is the presence of the two or more *jhelās*, responsorial singers who reiterate each line, or half-line, of the main

[37] ibid.

singer, *mukhiya*. The lines of the text are also broken up into short phrases that are each repeated by the responders with a variety of additional exclamations accompanied by special hand gestures. It is said that without the *jhelās* there can be no Samāj-Gāyan, for the essence of the singing tradition is constituted by the interactive "play" of the participants, who temporarily assume the role of the associates of Lord Krishna and the *gopīs*. Part of the response patterns of the *jhelās* in Samāj-Gāyan include long exclamations of the short phrase "eri ha" or "iha," which is a sign of affirmation believed to have been used by the *gopīs* in association with Krishna. The tempo of the performance intermittently speeds up during the repetition of the refrain, and then resumes its normal slow pace once a new verse is commenced. It is obvious that the *jhelās* are experienced musicians who understand the dynamics of this style of singing.

The instruments which are normally used in Samāj-Gāyan are the barrel-shaped drum known as the *pakhavāj* (sometimes replaced by the *tabla*), hand cymbals known as *jhāñjh* or *kartals*, and the harmonium, a small portable reed organ, to accompany the lead singer. Occasionally a drone instrument such as a *tanpura*, or a bowed lute called a *sāraṅgī*, or *esrāj*, is added for melodic effect. Since the text of the song is the main focus of the singing, there is little or no solo playing of instruments or virtuosity for its own sake. The players are there to accompany the singers and enhance and support the overall effect of the lyrics as rendered in song.

More information regarding the instruments and their techniques of playing may be discussed here. The styles of *pakhavāj* drumming in Samāj-Gāyan are close to that of Dhrupad. Although there are no *jhāñjh* cymbals in concert Dhrupad today, they did have an important role in the *tālas* of temple music.

For example, using "X" to denote the strike of the cymbals (one *mātrā*), and "xx" as double strike (which also counts as one *mātrā*), the most common *tālas*, including the number of unstruck *mātrās* (beats), are given below with their corresponding strikes on the hand cymbals:

Cautāl (12 mātrās): X - - - X - - - X - X -

Dhamār (14 mātrās): X X - X X X - , X X - X X X -

Dīp Chandi (14 mātrās): X X - X - X -, X X - X - X -

Rūpak (7 mātrās): X xx xx X xx X xx

Jhaptāl (10 mātrās): X xx X xx xx X xx X xx xx

Tintāl (16 mātrās): X X X - X X X - X X X - X X X -

Kehervā (8 mātrās): X xx X xx xx X X xx

A familiarity by the reader with these cymbal patterns will lead to their recognition in the recorded examples, which are centered on these basic beats.

A brief note is also given here regarding the musical notation utilized in discussing the song-texts. The Indian diatonic scale is generally written as Sa Re Ga Ma Pa Dha Ni sa (ascending), and sa Ni Dha Pa Ma Ga Ri Sa (descending). In this work, they appear as S R G M P D N sa. The upper Sa is written as sa, lowercase. The Western C-scale note equivalents for the Indian diatonic scale letter-notes correlate as follows: Sa = C, Re = D, Ga = E, Ma = F, Pa = G, Dha = A, Ni = B, sa = upper C. When a note is flattened, it is underlined (<u>G</u>, <u>N</u>), and when sharpened, italicized (*M*). This system covers all of the principal notes used in *rāga* music. However, some of the ornaments used by musicians in certain *rāgas* may employ semitones for aesthetic effect.

North Indian vocal music, as it developed further in the secular courts in the form of Khyāl, contained stylistic elements like *tānas*, rapid patterns and phrases of notes sung with a, i, u, or o, etc. that did not have linguistic meaning. This led to egoistic gestures and mannerisms that were believed to be out of sync with the Vaishnava tradition of solemn and reverent worship, and generated the impression that Indian music had human romantic and sexual overtones. The practice of *tānas* was thus particularly deplored by exponents of Samāj-Gāyan. According to Masterji, "there is no scope for *tānas*, as they will spoil the *śabda*, the meaning of the words. There are some *murkis* [short melismatic phrases] but not *tānas*. There is no scope for artistic display in the form of *tānas*, etc. Such deviations affect the devotion, and are a distraction."[38] According to Śrī Lalitacaran Goswami, "the Rādhāvallabhiya Samājīs have their own distinctive style. To ensure and protect the clear pronunciation of *śabda* (words), *ālāps* have been regulated in this style, and only prescribed *ālāps* are sung with *sthāyī* and *antarā*. There is no scope for elaborate *tānas* in this style, and only very brief *murkis* (ornaments) are tolerated."[39]

The unanimous opinion of the informants regarding Samāj-Gāyan was thus that this music was primarily meant for devotion and worship, and not for virtuosic display of musical skills or for pleasing human audiences. Masterji commented that, "Samāj-Gāyan is basically a *bhakti sangīt*, meant for worship and not for *lok rañjan*, human entertainment."[40]

With regard to improvisation and the insertion of exclamatory syllables, Thielemann has concurred with the above:

> Because of the sacred character of the temple songs, the foremost musical requirement for Samāj-Gāyan of the RVS is simplicity of style and plain melodic rendition that allows for the poetic word to be pronounced with absolute clearness. Melodic embellishments or rapid turns of notes are prohibited because they may affect the comprehensibility of the

[38]op. cit. Interview with Śrī Rajendra Prasad Sharma, March 28, 1993.
[39]op. cit. Śrī Goswami Lalitacaranji Maharaj,136-137.
[40]Sharma Interview.

> text. ... In Samāj-Gāyan of the RVS, only the text-based compositions are sung. The non-metricized *ālāpa* introductions are dispensed with, because they are merely musical entities and of no significance for the rendition of the devotional verse. Improvisation, too, is prohibited.[41]

Thielemann does note that *tālas* follow classical traditions:

> The only type of variation which is not only legitimate, but whose execution is compulsory in Samāj-Gāyan, is the insertion of melodic phrases sung on the syllables *eri ha*. The musicians of the RVS claim to be the originators of the practice of inserting extra syllables, which is followed in Samāj singing of all Vaiṣṇava communities of Vraja. Further additional syllables such as *ri mai* may occur at the end of verses or verse-lines: these serve as verse-fillers in order to adjust the poetic line to the cycle of the musical meter. With regard to the *tāla* cycles, on the other hand, there are no discrepancies between the Rādhāvallabhite temple music practice and the classical tradition.[42]

Within the region of Vrindaban, a select group of highly-trained musicians are regularly employed by the Rādhāvallabha temples or trusts. During most of my recording sessions, there were two very skilled musicians who were faithful to Masterji that I will mention; Śrī Kunj Bihari Das, a Bengali who sang back-up and played the cymbals, and Murari Das, a percussionist who doubled on *tabla* and *pakhavāj*. The basic instrumentalists and singers are paid a small stipend to maintain the daily regimen of Samāj-Gāyan throughout the

[41]Selina Thielemann (1999), 305-306.
[42]ibid.

liturgical year. Occasional substitutes would appear, but generally the same musicians appeared regularly, unless they had accepted other engagements elsewhere.

From a religious viewpoint, by intensely participating in Samāj-Gāyan, it is believed that the participants are not merely observing the pastimes of Rādhā and Krishna, but actually participating vicariously. A "theology" of Samāj-Gāyan would explore and possibly explain the manner and degree of spiritual elation obtained by the singers and their ability to experience aspects of the divine pastimes that are unavailable to persons who may simply read the song-texts. To what extent the current singers in this tradition are on this higher level is difficult to assess from the outside, but has been attested by informants. It seems more than likely in that the singers have committed themselves to a lifetime of devotion in this manner and have eschewed all commercialization. It took many weeks for me to gain the confidence of the singers so that recordings could be made. As a devotee-scholar, I believe that the combination of many years of accumulation of merit through performance plus the grace of the sacred image of Krishna (and particularly of Rādhā) enables the Samāj-Gāyan performers to make valid claims of advanced spiritual states.

Rādhāvallabha Songbook: Hymnal and Liturgical Calendar

The living musical tradition of the Rādhāvallabha Sampradāya possesses an impressive repertoire of songs for different occasions that are distributed over their annual calendar. Most of the songs are strictly linked to the *sevā* in the temple, as well as to the specific pastimes of Rādhā and Krishna, so that outside of these occasions or holidays, they are not sung. Thus nearly all of their music is structured around their solar/lunar calendar of festivals, with dates that of course vary from year to year due to lunar calculations. Śrī Lalitacaranji Maharaj, former *ācārya* for the tradition, notes few exceptions:"Most of the devotional lyrics, except for some prayer *padas* of *bhakti-kāvya* and some didactic stanzas, are linked to various festivals and jubilees. Worship of the deity and other routine functions ... are carried out with the help of these *padas*."[43]

Accordingly, there is little or no general *kīrtan* or *bhajan* for any day or time in the Rādhāvallabha tradition, nor is there *nām kīrtan* as found in groups like the Gauḍīya Sampradāya of Śrī Caitanya. Neither does the RVS attempt to spread their teachings through street singing or processions. Their musical worship remains largely in secluded enclaves, relished only by the *rasikas*, the accomplished devotees who understand and appreciate the aesthetic feelings and devotional nuances of the literature and music. Yet the main temple gets overcrowded on special festival days like Holi, when giant syringes of colored water are squirted on pilgrims by priests from the altar, and Annakut, when the entire altar area is covered with sumptuous food offerings to Krishna.

The current liturgical hymnal of the Rādhāvallabha community, was originally published as the four-volume *Śṛṅgāra-rasa-sāgara* (edited by Śrī Tulasi Das Baba, 1956-1962). This was re-edited by Śrī Lalitcaranji Goswami Maharaj and published as the *Śrī Rādhāvallabhji kā Varṣotsav* (RV) (1978-1980) in three volumes of slightly smaller print. A second edition of Volume II was published in 1994 and of Volume III in 1996. Songs of the *Caurāśī-Pad* (eighty-four songs) of Śrī Hita Harivaṃśa, as well as the complete *Śrī Bayalis Līlā* (forty-two *līlās*, twenty-two *rāgas*) of Dhruva Dās are contained in this collection, one of the largest of its kind in Braj Bhasha literature. Portions of the four hundred and eighty-two verse, thirty-two rāga *Vyāsa Vāṇī* of Harirām Vyāsa are also included.

[43]op. cit. Śrī Goswami Lalitacaranji Maharaj,136-137.

Cācā Vṛndāvanadāsa (18th century), the most prolific poet of the Rādhāvallabha Sampradāya with works numbering in the hundreds, is strongly represented.

The songs in these volumes are organized according to the seasons and holidays that are celebrated in the main temple. The liturgical year begins in Volume I with the season of Basant in the Spring, and ends in Volume III with *bayalis līlā* in the Winter months.

Volume I: Basant (Spring), Holi, Rasiya, Dol, Caitra, and Hita Badhāi (Appearance day of Śrī Harivaṃśa).

Volume II: Phul Racana (Flower arrangements), Van Vihār (Forest pastimes), Grīṣma Ritu-Jal Vihār and Naukā (Summer water and boat pastimes), Ratha Yātrā (Chariot), Pāvas Ritu (Rainy Season), Jhūlan (Swing Ceremony), Rakhi, Sevak Badhāi (Appearance Day of Sevakji Maharaj), Krishna Badhāi (Birthday of Krishna, Janmāṣṭamī), Rādhā Badhāi (Birthday of Rādhā, Rādhāṣṭamī), and Sāñjhī.

Volume III: Rāsa Līlā, Dasahara (Diwāli), Caupar (Game pastimes), Annakūṭ (Feast at Govardhan Hill), Vyahulau Utsav (Wedding of Rādhā and Krishna), Patotsava, Khicari Utsav, Mohan Bhog, Phutkar (assorted songs), Sain ke Pad (lullabies), and Śrī Bayalis Līlā (sung during the Winter months).

The *Śrī Rādhāvallabhji kā Varṣotsav* (RV) anthology contains approximately two thousand four hundred songs, so the one hundred and eight songs that the present author has collected and recorded might be considered an insignificant specimen. However, the songs included in this study represent the principal songs that have been repeatedly performed on the specific holidays, the songs that are the best known by the public congregations. Yet several of the songs included here are rarely performed, sometimes only once in an entire year on the respective holiday. Following the first edition of RV, the complete breakdown of songs in the anthology, with pagination, is as follows:

Voume I —

Basant 1-76, 164 songs
Holi 81-253, 156 songs
Holi Rasiya 254-266, 50 songs
Holi Dol 269-277, 22 songs
Gulāb Phul Dol 282-287, 28 songs
Caitra 288-340, 130 songs
Śrī Hitotsav kī Maṅgal Badhāi 341-504, 244 songs

Volume II —

Phul Racana 10-24, 72 songs
Candan 26-35, 9 songs
Van Vihār 35-44, 31 songs
Usir Kuñja 44-53, 32 songs
Grīṣma Ritu 53-56, 1 song
Jal Vihār 56-59, 3 songs
Naukā Jal Vihār 59-74, 49 songs
Genda Khel 74-76, 3 songs
Rath Yātrā 76-78, 1 song
Pāvas Ritu 78-116, 170 songs
Braj Parikram 116-121, 23 songs
Luhar 121-127, 7 songs
Mehandi Singhār 128-133, 18 songs
Jhulan Utsav 135-193, 137 songs
Pavitra Utsav 194-197, 14 songs

Rakhi Utsav 198-200, 13 songs

Śrī Sevaka Janma Maṅgal Badhāi 201-253, 100 songs

Śrī Lāl Jū kī Janma Badhāi 254-346, 137 songs

Śrī Priya Jū kī Janma Badhāi 347-463, 180 songs

Śrī Ladili Jū kī Pālana ke Pad 464-470, 7 songs

Dāna Kelī ke Pad 471-478, 13 songs

Sāñjhī Utsav 479-522, 50 songs

Volume III —

Dasahara ke Pad 1-4,

Rās ke Pad 109-155, 252 songs

Dīp Malika Hatari ke Pad 156-158, 6 songs

Caupar ke Pad 158-162, 15 songs

Annakūṭ 162-164, 1 song

Vyahula Utsav 164-167, 3 songs

Gaucarana ke Pad 168-169, 4 songs

Rādhāvallabha ke Patotsav 170-175, 11 songs

Himaritu Men Phargula ke Pad 176-180, 16 songs

Khicari Utsav 181-189, 32 songs

Maṅgal ārati ke Pad 189-206, 9 songs

Maṅgal Jugala-Vinod Beli 207-213, 21 songs

Phutkar Pad 213-218, 49 songs

Svāminī Singār Aṣṭaka 219-220, 1 song

Sain ke Pad 221-232, 45 songs

Śrī Bayalis Līlā 233-253, 42 songs

Pada Dhruva 253-254, 4 songs

Several of the festivals on the Rādhāvallabha calendar are actually extended over a fixed number of days. Thus the musicians may perform a variety of *padas* over the time period, as there are so many contained in the songbooks appropriate to the occasion. According to Rādhāvallabha singer Śrī Rajendra Prasad Sharma, the Spring season of Basant lasts for ten days, during which time any song from the chapter labeled "Basant" may be sung, normally in the *rāga* Basant which may be sung any time during Basant season. This is followed by the Holi season during which songs from the Holi section may be sung for thirty days until the full moon in March. Many of these songs, sung in a variety of *rāgas* (classical musical modes), but especially in the *rāga* Kafi, are called Dhamār, often in Dhamār *tāla* of fourteen *mātrās* (beats) but not necessarily. After that, miscellaneous *padas* may be sung until the celebrations of Śrī Hita Harivaṃśa's Appearance begin. This period of Badhāi songs lasts for twenty-five days, from Vaishakh Pūrṇimā (April) to the *ekādaśī* of the second fortnight of the next month.

Then the Phul *padas* start, with beautiful flower decorations in the temples (called Phulbanglas) for a month. Following this, the Rainy season (Sāvan, or Pāvas Ritu) begins with many songs in special *rāgas* like Megh Mālar and Gaur Mālar. Then the Jhulan season starts around mid-July, with many unique songs to accompany the deities of Rādhā and Krishna on their swings. When this is finished, there is preparation for the major festivals of late Summer and Fall, like Krishna Janmāṣṭamī (Krishna's birthday), Rādhāṣṭamī (Rādhā's birthday for one month usually in September), and Sāñjhī (special songs along with beautiful sand paintings of Rādhā and Krishna).

During Karttika (October-November), there is the Rāsa Līlā for one and a half months, then Diwāli and Annakūṭa, followed by the wedding of Rādhā and Krishna with very special songs. After the Full Moon of Diwāli, the Winter season begins, and for two and a half months the Śrī Bayalis Līlā by Dhruva Dāsa is sung in special tunes. Then we come full circle back to Basant again.

Placing the Samāj-Gāyan songs in context, several of the major festivals are listed below along with the titles of a few important songs associated with each. These songs figured prominently in the recordings that I made from August 1992 through April 1993. Their location in the current hymnals is designated by "RV." If they also appeared in the *Caurāśī-Pad* (CP) or the *Sphūṭa-Vāṇī* (SV), both works by Śrī Hita Harivaṃśa, those pages are also given.

1. Basant (10 days in early Spring, February-March)

   madhu ritu vrindavana ananda na thora (CP 27, RV 1.1)

2. Holi (30 days until full moon, March-April)

   prathama yathamati pranaun sri vrindavana ati ramya (CP 57, RV 1.81)

   aho ranga ho-ho-ho-hori khelain sakala kumvari barasane ki (RV 1.117)

3. Śrī Hita Harivaṃśa Appearance (25 Days, April-May)

   jai jai sri hari vamsa vyasa kula mandana (RV 1.341)

4. Rainy Season; Sāvan or Pāvas Ritu (2 months, June-July, until mid-July).

   nayo neha nava ranga nayo rasa (CP 54, RV 2.78, analyzed by Snell, 1983, 371-372)

   dou jana bhinjata atake batana (RV 2.78)

   savana prema sampada layo (RV 2.97)

5. Krishna Janmāṣṭami; Śrī Lālajū kī Badhāi (August-September)

   ananda aju nanda ke dvara (SV 11, RV 2.254)

6. Rādhāstami: Śrī Priyā jū kī Badhāi (30 days, Sept-Oct)

   calau vrishabhana gopa ke dvara (SV 16, RV 2.347)

7. Rāsa Līlā (45 days, October-November)

   mohana madana tribhangi (CP 63, RV 3.5).

   lala ki rupa madhuri nainana nirakha neku sakhi (SV 22, and RV 3.5)

   calahi radhike sujana (RV 3.6, analyzed by Snell, 1983, 365)

   mohani madana gopala ki bamsuri (CP 26, and RV 3.10, analyzed by Snell, 1983, 369)

8. Sain ke Pad (late evening all year)

   nagari nikunja aina kisalaya dala racita saina (RV 3.221)

9. Evening *ārati* song

   rajata nikunja mahala thakurani (RV 3.223)

Liturgical Day

The daily temple schedule of the RVS revolves around the waking, bathing, feeding, dressing, and retiring the deity of Rādhāvallabha, a statue of Krishna playing the flute. Rādhā is present but only as a leaf on a seat (*gaddi-sevā*), signifying her presence as totally divine and other-worldly. The temple priests maintain a strict regimen and must ensure that all worship activities are preceded with the utmost cleanliness of all utensils as well as their own person and dress. Today there are seven daily services before the deities in the Rādhāvallabha temple.

Maṅgal 6:00 A.M. The awakening of the deities [images] and the offering of sweets, including butter and a lump of sugar. Stanzas 3 (Rāga Vilaval, Tāla Dhamār) and 13 of the *Caurāśī-Pad* are sung. The *ārati*, or waving of lights in front of an image, is a feature of all hours of worship.

Śṛṅgār 10:00 A.M. The icon is bathed and adorned; various costumes are prescribed according to the day and season. Incense, curds, and sweets are offered. Stanzas 9 (Rāga Asavari, Tāla Tintāl) and 25 (Rāga Khammaj, Tāla Jhaptāl) of the *CP* are sung at this time.

Rāj Bhog 12:00 Noon. The time of the main meal. Food offered to the deities consists of rice, curry, dal, vegetables, curd, and sweets. Games such as *caupada* are played. From this time onward the songs sung at the hourly services are from works other than the *CP*.

Utthāpan 4:00 P.M. The deities are awakened from their afternoon siesta with music and bathing. The deities go for their evening stroll.

Sandhyā 6:00 P.M. Various sweets are offered and there is singing, together with the arati. The Rāsa Līlā sport begins at this time.

Sāyan 8:00 P.M. The evening meal of fried foods, *puri*, *halva*, *rahani*, and other dishes are taken.

Saiya 10:00 P.M. The time of retiring the deity for the evening.[44]

Scholars looking for any of the above-mentioned songs in notated form, whether in manuscript or published edition, will be disappointed in their quest, as the music of the RVS is passed down only by oral transmission. A couple of songs have been transcribed using Indian (Hindustani) notation in a few Hindi works, but the main corpus of songs remains unwritten musically. But despite the absence of musical notation in the songbooks, native congregations follow a familiar and established pattern of melody and rhythm that has become

[44]Charles S. J. White (1977), 32.

near-habitual. Without necessarily being able to lead a Samāj session, most disciples and their families are familiar with a large corpus of songs and can even recite many of the lyrics by heart.

Some of the songs in the hymnals contain, above the song itself, the names of one of the familiar *rāgas* of current Hindustani classical tradition, such as Sarang, Basant, Kafi, Dhanasri, Gauri, and Malar. Some also contain *tāla* indications. Yet these are not prescriptions in a strict sense and thus are not a reliable guide to the live performance tradition, which differs significantly by exhibiting altogether separate, more specialized, or even unknown, forms of these otherwise general categories of Hindustani *rāgas*. And while some of the songs used throughout the liturgical year of this sect can be readily identified with standard forms of classical *rāgas*, there are several key songs which, though based on the *rāga-rāginī* format, have their own individual character and are generally not to be heard outside the tradition. That is, although bearing a certain *rāga*'s name above the text, the song in performance betrays melody-lines that defy classification. For example, in the *Caurāśī-Pad* of Śrī Hita Harivaṃśa, the clues to which *rāgas* the *padas* are to be sung are given above each of the 84 poems. The present performance tradition is mostly faithful to his indications, but many of the melodies are not strictly in *rāgas*. The frequency distribution in the *CP* may reveal something about the more commonly preferred *rāgas* in the tradition: Sarang 16, Gauri 9, Kanharau 9, Vilaval 7, Dev Gandhar 7, Dhanasri 7, Kalyan 6, Vibhas 6, Malar 5, Kedar 4, Todi 4, Asavari 2, and Basant 2.

The above distribution, however, cannot be squared with the *rāgas* that are most frequently listed in the RV anthology, or heard within the total living tradition. For example, two songs of the RVS are sung in very slow style, the first in Rūpak (7 *mātrās*) and the second in Dhamār (14 *mātrās*) on specific days of every liturgical year. The first, *prathama yathamati pranaun sri vrindavana atiramya* (RV 1.81), from the first volume of the hymnal (also found in CP 57) which inaugurates the Holi season in the Spring, is listed as Gauri, yet cannot be reconciled with any possible form of classical Gauri (flatted R and D). It sounds more like a modified Kafi. And the second example, *lala ki rupa madhuri* (RV 3.5), from the third volume of the hymnal and sung only on the evening of Śārad Pūrṇimā in October, is listed as Rāga Kalyan, but the notes that are performed do not conform to any classical Kalyan, but rather a mixed *rāga*. Thus, instead of strict prescriptions, the *rāga* listings above the poems in Rādhāvallabha Samāj-Gāyan appear to be general guidelines or approximations, manuscript conventions, or simply suggestions for the singers added by the scribes of the manuscripts or the editors of the anthologies. The songs, however, should not be seen as deviations or imperfect renderings of earlier standardized scales or *rāgas*, but might rather be seen as archaic forms of the now classicized *rāgas*, or even survivals of extinct *rāgas*. This is based on observations regarding the extent to which the purity and orthodoxy of their singing tradition is maintained against tendencies for deviation and "popularization" found in other traditions.

Selina Thielemann offers additional explanations for the differences between the *rāgas* in RVS and the Hindustani tradition:

> "The requirement of textual clarity is regarded to be the main reason for changes made to the conventional North Indian *rāga* structures in the musical practice of the RVS. *Rāga* melodies that include difficult or uncommon melodic progressions, or scales in which certain notes have to be rendered with specific embellishments, have been simplified or mixed with other *rāgas* in order to create a melodic structure that is easily sung without disturbing the pro-

> nunciation of the words. The new *rāgas* thus created were not re-named, but retained their original denominations, hence the *rāgas* of Rādhāvallabhite Samāj-Gāyan do not necessarily have the same musical features as their nominal counterparts in North Indian classical music."[45]

In light of the above statement, I will further comment that any anticipation in the study and analysis of the Rādhāvallabha Songbook with regard to "purity of *rāga*" is bound to be disappointed. The song repertoire of RVS is totally unique and represents a valuable corpus that must be examined for its own melodic worth. In fact, many of the *rāgas* that are commonly heard in Hindustani classical music today are less than a hundred years old in their final standardized form. Indian musicologists agree that *rāgas* tend to evolve over time and become more refined with regard to their grammar and rules of performance. There is no original, pure form of any current *rāga* that exists in an ancient musical treatise or tradition. While the Rādhāvallabha Songbook is a glimpse into the remote past of devotional music, the RVS has kept and protected its musical tradition from encroachment from outside so that it may be preserved in its pristine form; but that form does not depend on the purity of a *rāga*. The tradition has its own rules and guidelines that are separate from Hindustani musical expectations. For example, most of the songs in Dhāmar Tāla do not fit into any *rāga* scheme, and so it is irrelevant to judge the compositions, good or bad, according to the purity of *rāga* or any other musicological standard other than the simple *bhakti rasa*, the emotional content that is evoked upon careful and attentive listening and understanding. As an ethnomusicologist I could describe the reactions I have seen within the community. As a devotee-scholar, I speak to my own experience.

---

[45]Selina Thielemann (1999), 305-306.

The music of the Rādhāvallabha Sampradāya in the form of Samāj-Gāyan may thus be studied, with some caution, in the context of Hindustani classical music, particularly Dhrupad, yet may also be viewed as an important predecessor of that as well as an influence upon several other important forms of devotional music that were sweeping the northern regions and extending East and West. The tradition of *padāvalī kīrtan* in Bengal can only be properly understood in relation to the temple music traditions of Vrindaban in the 16th century. Many other varieties of devotional music found in parts of North India can be stylistically traced back to the *bhakti* musicians of the Braj area that especially include the Rādhāvallabhites, the Aṣṭacāp poets, and Svāmī Haridāsa. But as there is still a sizeable amount of manuscript materials that remain to be critically edited, translated, and analyzed, the bulk of scholarly determinations in the West have yet to be formulated with regard to the direct and indirect influences of Samāj-Gāyan on the entire network of devotional music in India.

On the accompanying eighteen CDs, most of the one hundred and eight songs are in their complete form. However, some, due to extreme length, are represented only by the first few lines or stanzas. Yet the basic melodic and rhythmic patterns are established that prevail throughout the duration of these songs. On the two-CD sample set available online there is a judicious selection of sample tracks from the eighteen CD set that represent the various seasonal styles, tunes, and rhythms of this fascinating yet largely unknown tradition of *bhakti* music.

Chapter One: The Rādhāvallabha Songbook, Volume I

[CD 1]

Basant—Spring Season

1. Madhu ritu vrindavana (Spring Season in Vṛndāvana), RV 1.1 (CP 27), Śrī Hita Harivaṃśa

This composition by Śrī Hita Harivaṃśa in *rāga* Basant, the most prominent *rāga* in the Spring season of Basant, opens the Rādhāvallabha Songbook as the first entry in Volume 1. The *rāga* Basant is comprised of the notes, S G *M* $\underline{D}$ N s in ascent, and s N $\underline{D}$ P *M* G *M* G $\underline{R}$ S, with the addition of the interval S M in the ascent, depending on the melody. The first line of this poem, *madhu ritu vrindavana ananda na thora* ("Spring season in Vṛndāvana, bliss knows no limits"), is set to a slow Dhamār *tāla* (14 *mātrās*: 5-2, 3-4, or 3-4, 3-4) which is repeated. In the second line, there is a slow beginning but after three words the song moves into a fast Dīp Chandī (also 14 *mātrās*: 3-2-2, 3-2-2). This *tāla* sustains most of the poem until the last two lines convert into a medium Kehervā (8 *mātrās*: 4-4), followed by a repeat of the refrain (first line) with an end on the word *ānanda* (bliss).

madhu ritu vrindavana ananda na thora /
rajata nagari nava kusala kisora //
juthita jugala rupa-manjari rasala /
bithakita ali madhumadhavi gulala //
campaka bakula kula bibidha saroja /
ketuki medina mada mudita manoja //
rocaka rucira bahai trividha samara /
mukalita nuta nadata pika kira //
pavana pulina ghana manjula nikunja /
kisalaya sayana racita sukha punja //
manjira muraja dapha murali mridanga /
bajata upanga vina vara mukhacanga //
mrigamada malayaja kumakuma abira /
bandana agarasata surangita cira //
gavata sundari-hari sarasa dhamara /
pulakita khaga mriga bahata na vari //
jaya sri hita harivamsa hamsa-hamsini samaja /
aise ho karahu mila juga-juga raja //

Translation: Rupert Snell (1991, 206)

Joy is abundant in springtime Vṛindāvana, resplendent with young skillful ladies and adroit youths. It is rich in two jasmines, in beautiful buds and mango trees, and in bees worn out by rose and spring jasmine. The god of love is delighted by groups of *campaka* and *bakula* flowers, the various lotuses, and the rapture of *ketakī* and *medina*. A pleasant and agreeable breeze of threefold nature blows, half-opened fresh blooms are resonant with cuckoo and parrot. A bed of tender leaves is created as a mass of delights in the dense and lovely bower by the pure riverbank. Anklets, tambourine, frame-drum, flute, barrel-drum, *upaṅga*, noble *vīṇā* and mouth-harp resound. Garments are colored by musk, sandal, saffron, red powder, *bandana* and sap of aloe. The beautiful one and Hari sing a sweet springtime song; birds and beasts are thrilled, and the river checks its flow. Hita Harivaṃśa, may the assembly of swan and pen rule together thus from age to age!

2. Radhe, dekha bana ki bata (O Rādhā, Look What's Happening in the Forest!), RV 1.1 (CP 28), Śrī Hita Harivaṃśa

The next composition, by Śrī Hita Harivaṃśa, is also in *rāga* Basant, but set to a slow Rūpak *tāla* (7 mātrās: 3-2-2). The speed picks up in the last lines and refrain, with a quick Dīp Chandī. Many of the songs follow this pattern. The Sam (the first *mātrā* of the *tāla*) is on the word "*dekha*" (look).

radhe dekha bana ki bata
ritu vasanta ananta mukulita kusuma aru phala pata //
venu dhuni nandalala boli suni va kyon ara sata /
karata kataba vilamba bhamini vritha ausara jata //
lala markata-mani chabilau tuma ju kancana gata /
bani sri hita harivamsa jori ubhaya guna gana mata //

Translation: Rupert Snell (1991, 208)

Oh Rādhā, see what goes on in the forest:
an eternal spring, with leaves and fruits
(and yet) blossoms still in the bud.
Nanda's son has sounded the call of his flute—
why do you tarry when you have heard it?
Why do you still delay, lovely lady,
while the chance passes by uselessly?
With Lāla the handsome emerald,
and you who are golden-bodied,
Hita Harivaṃśa's pair is well met,
both being transported by their host of virtues.

3. Kuca gaddava (Breast-Pitchers), RV 1.5, Svāmī Haridāsa

This song by Svāmī Haridāsa opens as if in *rāga* Bhairava (S R̲ G M P D̲ N s, s N D̲ P M G R̲ S), and then resembles Basant. However, it changes patterns in the words "*rakhyau basanta*" (it is Spring) at the end of the first line to create a unique melodious phrase that is uncharacteristic of Basant. By the second line it changes over to a faster Dīp Chandī. This recording is incomplete and stops at the end of the second line with "*lasanta*" (shines). The special quality of the refrain makes this specimen unique in devotional music. Svāmī Haridāsa is a famous sixteenth-century composer and practitioner of the Dhrupad style of music. He also founded a monastic community and lineage known as the Haridāsī Sampradāya which is still active in Vrindaban. The Rādhāvallabha Songbook contains several of his compositions which are sung in Samāj-Gāyan style.

kuca gaddava jovana maura kancuki vasana dhampi lai rakhyau vasanta/
ye guna mandira rupa bagica men baithi hai mukha lasanta//
koti kama lavanya bihari jahi dekhata saba dukha nasanta/
aise rasika sri haridasa ke svami takaun bharana ain mila hasanta//

Translation: Chandrakala Pandey

It is Spring season and Rādhā covers her youthful beauty with a blouse (*kañcukī*). Her breasts resemble small pitchers. Blooming in loveliness, she sits in the garden with a radiant face. Gazing upon her beauty, all worldly sorrows wither. She is more beautiful than thousands of gods of love. Svāmī Haridāsa worships this girl and happily longs to meet her.

4. Viharata vipina phirata (In the Forest, She Wanders and Sports), RV 1.5-6, Nāgarī Dāsī

This song by Nāgarī Dāsī begins on the word "*vipina*" (forest grove) and is closer to the *rāga* Basant than the previous song. It changes to a fast Dīp Chandī and continues until a repetition of the refrain.

viharata vipina phirata ranga dharaki /
harakhi gulala udaya ladili sampati kusumakara ki //
kasumbhi sari saundhe bhiji upara bandana bhuraki /
coli nila lalita ancala cala jhalaka ujagara ura ki //
mridula suhasa tarala driga kundala mukha alakavali ruraki /
sri nagari dasi keli sukha sani rahe maina lalaka nahin muraki //

Translation: H. S. Mathur

Rādhā wanders playfully in the forest, where many colors are flowing. She is happy throwing red powder, the wealth of springtime. Her saffron *sārī* is moist, and sandalwood powder is upon it. Occasionally her beautiful blue blouse reveals the beauty of her full breasts. As she smiles softly with shifting eyes, her face is hidden beneath the flowing braids of her hair. The poet Nāgarī Dāsī says that this playfulness is an outward expression of the inner pleasure of amorous love, and there is no end to her desire for it.

5. Ritu basanta men (In the Spring Season), RV 1.37-38, Śrī Vallabha Rasika

Only the first two lines of this song by Śrī Vallabha Rasika, who may have been a follower of the Caitanya Sampradāya, are included on the CD.

ritu vasanta men lasanta murata dou baithe nikasi nikunja baga /
lalita gunja manjula latana para ali punjana ki suni suni guna-guna puni puni rasa kau cadhata paga //
maure amana cadhi cadhi baure juga juga vahai kuhakata kokila kula rijhata suni kalarava vibhaga /
praphulita gulalala ki kyari, pavana lagata mahakata lahakari piya pyari cakha lagana laga //
ranga ranga ratana satana ke kuje jatanana gula naragisa son gamsi gamsi takhana bica rakhana salaga /
navala lala nava bala paraspara phuli phuli phulana ke jhora rakhe pencana bica alaga //
lalana kara naragisa ki dandi ati itaraya dharata tiya urapara atha manamatha ura hota jaga /
bala gulalala ki bendi kara ucai dhari lala bhala para yon karata ranga dou rasa tadaga //
lalita lalita ranga ranga bhine lakhi lakhi rijhi bhiji tana bajayau hai madhura vasanta raga /
rati rasa jheli sabai saheli nava ranga bhine jhine bage rage sugala jugala suhaga //
ekana kara bica ranga ranga sisi ratana piyale liye sasi si hulasin ali ananda yaga /

dasana arunai vasana arunai dasana vasana arunai nai lakhi pohi lai piya prema dhaga //
ali sankulita lata halihali neti neti kahata si rahata si thaki thaki sikhavata dikhavata ananga raga /
ananda cika dai dai alabeli ke adhara kusuma kau anupama lampata madhupa mita musikana paraga //
saundhe sani bani coli ten chain chain chavi ki chata chabili chutata chaila chalakyau' nuraga /
chalaki chalaki chala-chala ratipati ki chakana chake lakhi chipi chipi chinu chinu vallabha rasika sakhi cakha sabhaga //

Translation: H. S. Mathur

It is springtime and the couple sits gracefully in a grove. Hearing the humming of bees over the vines increases the pleasure of their love. With peacocks perched on mango trees the couple is further intoxicated as cuckoos sing. Hearing each other's lovely sounds, the birds feel very excited. The flower beds of roses are blooming and the sweet fragrance spreads everywhere with the blowing of the breeze. Rādhā looks enchantingly towards the flowers. The decorated and bejeweled flower pots have been carefully adorned with *nargis* flowers, and have been artfully placed in their niches. Krishna, along with his cowherd friends, carefully separates bunches of flowers and places them on the breasts of Rādhā, and thus awakens the god of love. Then Rādhā takes a sprig of roses and places it on Krishna's forehead. In this manner, both Krishna and Rādhā become immersed in a lake of love. Rādhā's girlfriend Lalitā, watching this play, is squirted and drenched in color, and then sings a lovely song in the *rāga* Basant. All the girlfriends are absorbed in amorous delight. As their thin clothing becomes sprayed and drenched in colors, they all sing together in sweet voices songs of loving union. With bottles of colors in their hands as well as the jewel-studded cups, they get extreme pleasure in the sacrifice of love. Their teeth and clothes are all colored deep red, and it appears as if they are bound up in the threads of love. The vines are full of bees, whose buzzing sounds like a long, low, "nooo, nooo, nooo," teaching pleasure through Cupid's song. Bees kiss Rādhā as if through a transparent curtain, drinking the nectar of her smiling lips. Through her blouse, the beauty of her full breasts is visible. Seeing this, Krishna becomes infatuated. Secretly enjoying the beauty of Rādhā, poet Vallabha Rasika tastes amorous delight to the fullest extent.

Holi Festival

6. Prathama yathamati (First, As Seems Fitting), RV 1.81 (CP 57), Śrī Hita Harivaṃśa

This song by Śrī Hita Harivaṃśa begins the section of Holi songs in the Rādhāvallabha Songbook. It is serious in tone, yet contains many delightful surprises and changes despite its seemingly ponderous pace. The song is in three sections: lines 1-14, 15-21, and 22-23. The first maintains a slow Rūpak (7 *mātrās*). Then it changes to a breaking up of the phrasing with alternate passages as in the first section. The last section moves in a medium Kehervā (8 *mātrās*) with a faster repeat of the last two lines and refrain. The entire piece is rendered in the *rāga* Kafi (S R G̲ M P D N̲ s, s N̲ D P M G̲ r S) with slight variation. This particular recording was made of Śrī Damodar Das Mukhiya and the devotees at the main Rādhāvallabha Temple on the opening night of the Holi season in February, 1976.

> prathama yathamati pranaun sri vrindavana atiramya
> sri radhika kripa binu sabake manani agamya
> vara yamuna jala sincana dinahi sarada-basanta
> vividha bhanti sumanasa ke saurabha alikula manta
> aruna nuta pallava para kujata kokila kira
> nirtana karata sikhikula ati ananda adhira
> bahata pavana ruci dayaka sitala-manda-sugandhu
> aruna, nila, sita mukulita jahan tahan pusana-bandhu
> atikamaniya virajata mandira navala nikunja
> sevata sagana pritijuta dina minadhvaja-punja

rasika-rasi jahan khelata syama-syama kisora
ubhai-bahu-pariranjita uthe unide bhora
kanaka kapisa pata sobhita subhaga samvare anga
nila basana kamini ura kancuki kasumbhi suranga
tala rababa muraja dapha bajata madhura mridanga
sarasa ukati-gati sucata vara bansuri mukha canga
dou mili cancara gavata gauri raga alapi
manasa-mriga bala bodhata bhrikuti dhanusa driga campi
dou kara tarinu patakata latakata ita uta jata
ho-ho-hori bolata ati ananda kulakata
rasika lala para melata kamini bandana dhuri
piya picakarinu chirakata taki-taki kumakuma puri
kabahun-kabahun candana taru nirmita tarala hindola
cadhi dou jana jhulata phulata karata kalola
vara hindola jhakorana kamini adhika darata
pulaki-pulaki vepatha anga pritama ura lapatata
hita-cintaka nija-cerinu ura ananda na samata
nirakhi nipata nainana sukha trina torata bali jata
ati udara vivi sundara surata sura sukumara
jai sri hita harivamsa karau dina dou acala bihara

Translation: Rupert Snell (1991, 233-236)

Firstly, I bow as best I can to Śrī Vṛndāvana the most pleasurable, which would be inaccessible to the minds of all but for Śrī Rādhikā's favor. Irrigated by the Yamunā's excellent water, autumn and spring endure there constantly, and swarms of bees are drunk with the fragrance of many kinds of flowers. On ruddy young shoots cuckoo and parrot warble, while troops of peacocks dance, frenzied with delight. There flows a gentle breeze, cool, gentle, and fragrant; reddish, blue and white lotuses are blooming in every place. A most attractive dwelling adorns the fresh bower, and multitudes of love gods ever serve joyfully with their attendants. Where the youthful Śyāmā and Śyāma play in the lovers' round-dance, the two delighted in each other's arms arise sleepily at dawn. [His] blessed dark limbs are decorated in gold and tawny cloth; the blue-clad loving lady has on her breast a bodice of fine saffron hue. Cymbals, *rabab*, *muraja* and frame drum resound with the sweet barrel-drum and in sweet proclamations excellent flute and mouth-harp indicate the rhythm. The two sing a spring-time song together, tuning their voices to the Gaurī *rāga*. The bow of the brow and the arc of the eye forcibly pierce the deer of the mind [with the arrow of a glance]! Clashing cymbals together, the two go swaying this way and that; "Ho Ho Hori" they cry, calling out in their great delight. The loving lady smears Lāla the voluptuary with [yellow] *vandana* powder; taking aim again and again, the lover sprinkles her with syringes filled with saffron. Sometimes a lively swing is set up in a sandal tree; the two of them mount it and swing to and fro, frolicking and blossoming with joy. The loving lady is greatly alarmed by the lunges of that excellent swing, and with a thrill of delight she wraps her quaking limbs around her beloved's chest. Their well-wishing constant attendants feel an overflowing joy; seeing how great is the pleasure of their eyes they make a protective charm and dedicate themselves [to the pair]. Most illustrious are these two beautiful ones, tender heroes of amorous dalliance; Harivaṃśa, may the pair ever perform their unremitting sport!

7. Ranga ho-ho-ho-ho-hori (Colorful Ho-ho-ho-ho-holi), RV 1.83-84, Śrī Rāmarāya Prabhu

This Holi song by Śrī Rāmarāya Prabhu ("Bhagavān Dāsa") is rendered in Vilaval scale (S R G M P D N s, s N D P D N̲ D P M G M R S), beginning with a slow Dhamār in the first two lines. It then changes the tune with a faster beat of Dīp Chandī. There are only four lines included here, and there are no cymbals.

ranga ho-ho-ho-ho hori khelai ladilau vrajaraja kau /
samvare gata kamala dala locana naika prema samaja kau //
prathamahin ritu vasanta vilase hulase hori dandau ropyau /
manon phaga prana jivana dhana anandana saba vraja opyau //
mrigamada malaya kapura agara kesara brajapati bahu jora dhare /
sarasa sugandha samvari sanga dai rangana kancana kalasa bhare //

prema bhari khilavarana ke hita sukha kau sara singara kiyau /
bhaga apara jasomati maiya bara bara jala vari piyau //
phenta bharai lai janani pai ajna lai vraja isa saun /
nandarai taba ratana peca raci bandhyau giradhara sisa son //
tapara mora candrika sobhita griva dulana lahakata hai /
madana jita kau banon manaun rupa dhvaja phaharata hai //
bhai rangili bhira duvaren pritama darasana karanen /
aba bana thani nikase mandira ten koti kama kiye varanen //
taisei sakha sanga ranga bhine harakhi paraspara mana mohai /
barana barana jyoti ke kamala manaun amrita dinamani sanga sohai //
ananda bhari baje bajata nacata madhu mangala ranga kiyau /
hari ki hamsana dasanana ki kirana nainana ki durana mana moha liyau //
abira gulala udai cale khelata jaisen saba kou harashain /
chirakata bharata chaila navarangi kaha kahiyai rasa ghana barashain //
kou dvarana kou cadhi atarina kou khirakina badana suhaye /
gokula candrama dekhana kaun manaun indu vimanana cadhi aye //
sriradhaju drishti parata hi mohana phuli-phuli nainana ghumyau /
sanamukha hvai piya kalapa tarovara mahabhaga phala rasa jhumyau //
pramadaganamani syama rasika siromani son khelana ai /
duhun disi sobha umangi ranga macyau gana venu dhuna dhuni lai //
nainana bainana khela macyau gaunduka navala-sina mara maci /
kamala naina kara lai picakari mriga nainina ki bhaunha naci //
chirakin chaila chabili bhantina manaharani jovana vari /
ranga-ranga chinta bani tiya vasanana phula rahi chavi phula-vari //
puhupa paraga udai dai raci achana-achana niyaren ai /
dauri damininu ghana gherayau piya bata bani saba mana bhai //
kou mukha madata dai garabahiyan kou paunchata achi chavi son /
alakana bhaunhana-mula ranga rahyau sobha kahi na jai kavi saun //
kou raci pana khabavata pulakita sundara adharana parasa kiyen /
kou bhuja gahi ladakai phaga mangata piya nainana caina diyen //
(sri) radhaju nagara syama sundara para prita umaga kesara dhori /
maha manoharata kau raja abhisheka kiyau kahi ho-hori //
sara suti sahita mahamuni mohe yaha sobha sampati heren /
kahi bhagavan hita ramaraya prabhu hamsi citavana basi jiya mere //

Translation: Chandrakala Pandey

Krishna, the King of Braj and loved by all, is celebrating Holi. As the leader of his love group, he is dark-colored with eyes like lotus petals. The Spring season has arrived, and Holi begins with the beginning of Spring. Each resident of Braj has planted a stick as a symbol of Spring. It now seems as if Krishna, as the life of Braj, has planted life in Braj. Krishna has adorned his body with sandalwood, saffron, camphor, musk and *agara*. All the fragrances fill the air and many cowherd girls follow Krishna carrying golden pitchers full of different colors. They have also decorated themselves with many ornaments as they sprinkle drops of happiness in the atmosphere. Mother Yaśodā is very fortunate, and is satisfying herself with this iridescent beauty. Krishna then asks permission to go out with his cowherd friends. Upon receiving permission, Krishna ties a turban on his head and places on it a peacock feather. At this, he looked like the god of love, and the peacock feather resembles a flag of beauty. In the early morning, many people rush to Nanda and Yaśodā's house. When Krishna comes out to see them, everyone is very anxious just to have a look at him. When he comes out of the house, people begin to observe among themselves—that this posture of Krishna is thousands of times more splendid than that of the god of love. Krishna's friends look just as beautiful as Krishna. The poet offers a simile: Krishna's friends are like lotuses of light around Krishna the sun. As his friends sing, dance and play musical instruments, Krishna laughs, and the rays of light from his teeth spread everywhere and enchant everyone's eyes. They then start throwing *abīra* (red) and *gulāla* (pink) powder on one another, and it seems as if there is a tremendous drizzle from the sky. All the cowherd girls observe this beauty—some sit at their doors, some stand, and some look from the windows. It seems as if a new moon has risen in Braj (Gokula) and many moons are peeking at this moon, sitting in their chariots. The cowherd girls then go toward the *kalpataru* (wish-fulfilling tree) and assemble there to celebrate Holi. Krishna plays his flute, but then he takes a syringe (*picakari*) and squirts various colors on the beautiful girls. The girls look like mutlicolored flowers blooming in the garden, and the fragrance of the flowers spreads throughout the air. The cowherd girls embrace Krishna, appearing like lightning flashes surrounding a cloud. Someone places color on Krishna's cheeks, and someone wipes the colors off his cheeks. With so many colors abounding, Krishna's beauty appears like that of a rainbow. Someone then insists that Krishna have some betel leaf (*pan*), and someone else asks for his syringe to celebrate Holi. The couple of Rādhā and Krishna are the embodiment of love. The poet Śrī Rāmarāya Prabhu observes that Krishna as `beautiful beauty' is set for coronation as King of Braj on this holy occasion. The Goddess Sarasvatī and many sages also admire the entire situation, where Krishna creates a central place in everyone's heart.

8. Radha ravani ranga bhari (Rādhā Covered in Colors), RV 1.95-96, Nanda Dāsa

Only two lines of this song by Nanda Dāsa (1530-1584), a member of the Vallabha Sampradāya, are recorded here. It is rendered in Dīp Chandī *tāla*, without cymbals. There are interjections of "*eriha*" after the word "*ke*" in the second line. Nanda Dāsa was an important poet of the Vallabha Sampradāya. Several other poets of this lineage are included in the Rādhāvallabha Songbook, such as Sūra Dāsa, Caturbhuja Dāsa, Cita Svāmī, and Paramānanda Dāsa.

radha ravani ranga bhari / ranga hori khelen //
apane pritama ke sanga / aho hari hori khelen //

ika pahilen hi rangamagi / ranga hori khelen //
puni bhini ranga ranga / aho hari hori khelen //
ranga ranga ki sanga sahacari / ranga hori khelen //
bani rangili ke satha / aho ranga hori khelen //
pahiren vasana ranga ranga ke / ranga hori khelen //
ranga bhare bhajana hatha / aho ranga hori khelen //
ranga ranga ki kara picakai / ranga hori khelen //
sohata eka samana / aho ranga hori khelen //
manon maina siva para sajyo / ranga hori khelen //
hathana tripi kamana / aho ranga hori khelen //

kahu pai kusuma gunthita chari / ranga hori khelen //
kahu pain aye naye naura / aho ranga hori khelen //
kau pai kusuma genduka calain / ranga hori khelen //
kahu pai nutana maura / aho ranga hori khelen //
kahu pai aragaja ranga kau / ranga hori khelen //
kahu pai kesara kau ranga / aho ranga hori khelen //
kou gaura mrigamada liyen / ranga hori khelen //
hota bhamvara jahan panga / aho ranga hori khelen //
tinamen mukatamani ladili / ranga hori khelen //
sohata ati sukumvari / aho ranga hori khelen //
lataka calati janu pavana te / ranga hori khelen //
komala kancana dara / aho ranga hori khelen //
piya kara picaka dekhi ken / ranga hori khelen //
tiya naina chavi son darahin / aho ranga hori khelen //
khanjana se manau udahinge / ranga hori khelen //
dharaki mina hvai jahin / aho ranga hori khelen //
chirakata piya jaba tiyana kau / ranga hori khelen //
yon mana upajai ananda / aho ranga hori khelen //
manahun indu sincata sudha / ranga hori khelen //
apani kumudina ke vrinda / aho ranga hori khelen //
bhiji vasana tana lapatane / ranga hori khelen //
baranata barani na jai / aho ranga hori khelen //
upama daina na dainhi naina / ranga hori khelen //
gahi rakhata ha-ha khai / aho rnaga hori khelen //
ranga rangili radhika / ranga hori khelen //
rangilo giradhara piya / aho ranga hori khelen //
ye ranga bhine nita basau / ranga hori khelen //
nanda dasa ke hiya / aho ranga hori khelen //

Translation: H. S. Mathur

Śrī Rādhā enjoys playing colorful Holi with her beloved Krishna. O Lord Hari is playing Holi! Already covered in colors, after playing Holi with Krishna she again became drenched with colors. Her girlfriends were also covered with colors and, accompanying Rādhā, were dressed in various colorful garments. Krishna held a water-gun filled with different colors. He looked as if the god of love was there in his shadow, holding a bow in his hands with a string of embedded flowers. Some participants were wearing new head decorations and holding balls of flowers. Some had sweet-smelling paste and saffron coloring; some wore musk. The jewel of all was Śrī Rādhā who was walking like a tender golden vine swayed back and forth by the breeze. Seeing the water-gun in Krishna's hands, she tried to stop him with her glances. Her pupils were like flying *khañjanas* when she widened her eyes. When she lowered them, it was as if they were overturned like fish. When her beloved Krishna sprinkled colored water, it created great pleasure in her heart, as if the moon was sprinkling nectar onto lotus flowers. As her garments began to stick to her body, it is difficult to describe her beauty, and impossible to compare it with anything else. Because her eyes were always changing, Rādhā was detained, held back. Krishna was fully covered in color. `Please stay in my heart in these colorful forms, playing Holi in the heart of Nanda Das.'

9. Yaha jogi basata (Where Is This Yogī's Home?), RV 1.108-110, Cācā Vṛndāvana Dāsa

This lengthy composition by Cācā Vṛndāvana Dāsa (1708-1787), a very prolific poet of the Rādhāvallabha Sampradāya, is sung in the *rāga* Bhairava to Keherva *tāla*. Only the first three lines are included, without cymbals. It begins on the word, "basata."

yaha jogi basata kahan hai /
main parakhyau badi bera te yamen jukti joga ki na hai // teka //
kauna guru upadesa te ina ghara chandyau tatalalita nikata bulayakai
yason bujha marama ki bata //

citavana bhari saneha ki hiyen lalaka kachu aura /
ghara-ghara pyasau sau phirai yake cita ki vritti na thaura //
yaha jogi bhayau tarka son nahin jnana kau anga /
joga javahara jyaun dipai jo kiyau hohi guru sanga //
kai jogi jadu ju kari mohyau rajakumara /
sundarata pai rijha kai lai ayau apane lara //
bahu saun viracyau ju aba pura kautuka kiyau heta /
rupa savadi sau lagai yaha phir-phir pheri deta //
jihi dekhau tana ujari tahan urajhavai naina /
yaha auguna hai joga men satya kahata haun baina //

vaha jogi tuma nripasuta ghatati kahi na jaya /
jo sandeha so bujhiye tau abahi laihun bulaya //
lalita koca joga bala jina tyagyau parivara /
bidhi pratikula tahana bhayau yaha jana pari niradhara //
jogi liyau bulaya kain baithyau sanmukha ai /
hiya ke hiya phule sakhi kachu vastu dari si pai //
sangi nada bajai tu kachu raga rangilau gaya /
vasa bhanupura daihingi pyari sundara kuti chabaya //
singi adharana dhari kain rucira alapyau raga /
vidya phuri ju mohini ati ura ujhalyau anuraga //
rijhi kirati nandini vidya akhila nidhana /
jo kachu iccha ravari aba viramau pura brishabhana //
kauna manoratha kari bhaye tuma ju parama avadhuta /
alakha purusha paracyau nahin lai hiye ju ravari kuta //
griva dhora ravala kahi tuma bhashata ju anita /
parada men ki bhamini kyon lakhain joga ki rita //
jogi kau ghara dura hai ko bhashana samarattha /
guru gama saun pahuncyau tahan jahan natha gahyau dridha hattha //
hatha gahana kaun ko kahan sunasana sau desa /
joga dhyana nahinna sunyau hama karau gorau bhesha //
saba vahi ke barana hain saba vahi ke rupa /
sakala pasarau alakha kau suni beti ravala bhupa //
alakha-alakha jakaun kahata baranau take anga /
jaise phula akasa ke kina dekhe kaise ranga //
dina dasa nagari viramate samajhi tumharau neha /
aba caraca aisi kari paga dharain na tumhare geha //
jogi kula janame nahin joga liyau suni jnana /
raja vibhau hamane taji takau tuma ju karata abhimana //
kauna desa aura kauna kula kauna nama, ko grama /
ravala badana prakasiyai hama saba mila karain pranama //
bhali bhai tuma apa mukha kahi apani adi /
yaha sandeha nivariye bali aura bata saba badi //
nirakhata pyari badana disa hiye men dhakapaka hota /
jaise parasata pavana ke jhakurata ju dipaka jota //
desa rangilau kula badau nama dhama sukha mula /
vidita loka saba janiye premina kula anukula //
saba prani nirbhaya basain saba kau palana hoya /
hama sukha lada tahan pale yamen sandeha na koya //
hama jogi bana bana phirata kahu saun na cinhara /
sukhita bhaye guru jnana son saba birasa ganyau samsara //
ye guna braja-mandala sabai tuma thaharayau kauna /
bujhata kirati nandini mukha ravala gahi rahyau mauna //
rahi-rahi kain bolata sakhi hamsata naina ki kora /
jogi kaidyaun kautuki tana simatata jaise cora //

joga chadama sau ginata ye sakhi na manata ana /
kaise tuma dhinga viramiye suni ninda apane kana //
tuma murata ju saneha ki bacana ami ki dhara /
sravana na tripata ju hota hain syama suniye barambara //
citra nerain au tu laksana parakha nirata /
ravala-ravala kaha kahai jaki caraca aurai ghata //
kesa dhape sira basana saun je bhije ju phulela /
jogi nahin bhogi sakhi ye nanda-suvana ke khela //
suna gahavara bana kaun bhaje sukha ju apurava luta /
mana baji hyahin rahyau gai baga hatha son chuta //
khela bibidha nita-nita racain bhijain ura ahalada /
vrindavana hita rupa jasa gayau sri harivamsa prasada //

Translation: H. S. Mathur

Someone (Krishna) is dressed like a *yogī*. Śrī Rādhā talks about him with her friend Lalitā. She says, "He doesn't appear to be a real *yogī*; he may be a fake. Who is this *yogī* and where does he reside? I have been observing him for quite some time and feel he does not have the character of a *yogī*. Who is his guru? Who advised him to leave his home?"

Rādhā then asks Lalitā to call him near and question him. She says that he has a glance of love and desire, is wandering from house to house, and that his mind is not stable. "He appears to be a *yogī* only by his saying so, but he does not have a trace of wisdom. If he had learned something in the company of a guru he would be shining like a jewel. Or else some *yogī* has enticed a prince by his magic, and being attracted by his beauty, the *yogī* brought the prince to him. Having been trained by the *yogī*, the prince now shows some marvelous tricks. He seems to be a connoisseur of beauty; that is why he comes here again and again. Wherever he sees a beautiful lady, he fixes his eyes there. But this would be a great defect for a real *yogī*."

Lalitā said, "He is a *yogī* and you are a princess; so it is difficult to describe this combination. If you have any doubts to clear up, I will call him right now."

Rādhā concludes that his yogic power is weak, although he has abandoned his family. There is no sense in his being a *yogī*, because of the odd circumstances. At this juncture, Lalitā calls the *yogī* and he comes and sits before them both. At this Rādhā becomes enamored in her heart, as if she had received something unsolicited. She tells him to play something on his flute, like a beautiful *rāga*. If she is pleased, he will get a beautiful hut to stay in in Bhanupur. Krishna puts the flute to his lips and plays a very beautiful *rāga*. A great pleasure comes to her as the music blossoms in her heart. Krishna is a repository of knowledge of music and Rādhā is greatly enamored of him. She tells him he can fulfill all his desires in the town of Vṛṣabhānu (Barsana).

She asks, "What was the desire which turned you into a great *yogī*?'

Krishna replies, "You did not recognize a great saint, yet took something into your heart."

Turning his neck, he says that what she has asked is not proper. "Ladies stay behind curtains. How would they know the ways of *yogīs*? The residence of *yogīs* is very remote, and no one is competent to talk about them. The *yogī* goes to the place of his guru, and the guru holds the disciple's hand firmly. In *yoga* and meditation, we never hear of black or white complexion. Everybody is of the complexion of the Lord, and everybody is of the form of the Supreme Lord. Listen, O daughter of the King, the whole world is an extension of the Lord. The Lord is invisible, but his features are like the flowers in the sky; who can describe the colors of the flowers in the sky? I wander to different towns and I appreciate your devotion, but you have talked about things in such a way that I will never come to your house. I was not born in the house of a *yogī*, but I learned about *yoga* through hearing. I have relinquished all the glory of royalty of which you are so proud."

Rādhā then asks, "To which town and country do you belong? What is your family and what is your name? You describe all these things, and we all salute you jointly. It would be so nice if you would describe yourself in your own words. Please remove these doubts and tell us everything else."

When Krishna looks at the face of Rādhā, there is a palpitation in his heart. Just as the flame of the lamp trembles at the touch of air, so his heart trembles. He replies to her questions, saying, "I belong to a well-known family of this lovely country, with a name and home full of pleasure. We are known to the whole country and our family is united in love. All people live in our country without fear, and all get their nourishment there. There is no doubt that I was nurtured in comfort and love. Yet when I wander like a *yogī* from one forest to another, nobody recognizes me. I have been blessed with knowledge by my guru and have relinquished this world. All these qualities of mine are known in the Braj Mandal."

After describing all these qualities to Rādhā, Krishna becomes silent. The girlfriends (*sakhīs*) speak to Rādhā in intervals, smiling through their eyes, saying, "This *yogī* is frolicsome and he is trying to conceal himself like a thief. He is a deceitful *yogī*. Don't consider him anything else. Having heard such words of defamation, how can you stay near him?"

The girlfriends then say to Rādhā, "You are an icon of love, and your words are like flowing nectar. Hearing them, ears are never satisfied, and a desire arises to hear them again and again."

Citrā comes nearby and says that she can identify his marks, "Why do you call him Raval again and again. He is talked about everywhere. He covers his head with a cloth (*dupata*) to deceive everyone. He is not a *yogī* but a *bhogī* (enjoyer of pleasure), and this is merely a trick of Nanda Bābā's son (Krishna)." Hearing all this, and having enjoyed unusual pleasure in his mind, Krishna retreats to the forest. But his heart remained like a horse without its reins. In this way, Krishna plays various types of games and tricks everyday, which gives great pleasure to the heart. The beauty and form of Krishna is sung by Cācā Vṛndavana Dāsa by the mercy of Śrī Hita Hari-vaṃśa.

[CD 2]

10. Vaghamvara odhe (The Lord Wears a Tiger-skin), RV 1.107-108, Mādho Dāsa

This song by Mādho Dāsa begins in slow Dhamār *tāla* (14 *mātrās*) for the first line, then changes the tune and reverts to a faster Dīp Chandī. The interjection of "*eri*" is made in the first line after the word "*ho.*" Only three lines are included here. The general melody is in the *rāga* Kafi.

vaghamvara odhe samvarau ho yamen yogi kau hunara kaun //
gvala bala kou sanga nahin ho anga vibhuta ramai /
kamala-naina sukha daina kumvari kaun aye hai bhesha banai //
sankha sabda suni suni jita tita ten ghira ain braja nari /
vadana viloka kumvari radhe kau baithe hain asana mara //
danda kamandala dharen mana mohana kati bandhe mrigachala /
bhaunha aniyari naina kamala dala mohin lai braja bala /
kauna disa ten aye ho ravala kahan teri manasa jai //
apanu mauna gahi mere svami dakshina disa batai /
hamsi bujhata vrishabhanu-nandini ravala uttara dehu //
karana kauna bhesha tapasi kau vana taji dolata geha //
singi patra vibhuta na batua sira candana ki khaura /
mere mana esi avata hai kanta visari gaura //
cancala capala catura dikhayata ati mukha madhuri musakana /
jogi nahin kou badau hai viyogi bhogi hai bhamvara nidana //
cutaki-vibhuta dai radhe kon cale hain vaghamvara jhara /
mana hari liyau tanaka citavana men gohana lagi hai kumvari //
nagara bagara aru bhavana-bhavana prati nisa dina phirata udasa /
naina cakora bhaye radhe ke hari darasana ki pyasa //
mana hutau ratana jatana hari linau capala naina ki kora /
sri jagannatha jivana dhana madhau prita lagi duhun ora //

Translation: H. S. Mathur

Krishna wears a tiger skin just like a *yogī*. What are the attributes of a real *yogī*? No cowherd friends accompany him, he is alone, and he has rubbed his body with ashes. It seems lotus-eyed Krishna has come in this peculiar dress to enjoy Rādhā. Hearing the sound of the conch, the ladies of Braj gather on all sides. Seeing the face of Rādhā, Krishna sits cross-legged in the lotus posture. Krishna holds a rod (*daṇḍa*) and a gourd waterpot, and has tied a deer skin around his waist.

With his eyebrows sharply pointed, his lotus eyes have enchanted all the ladies of Braj. They ask him, "O Rāval (king), where have you come from? And where do you wish to go? Like a Swami you do not speak, but only point your hand toward the south."

Rādhā, the daughter of Vṛṣabhānu, asks the *rāval* a question, "Why do you adopt the attire of a renunciate and wander in the forest? You don't have a trumpet, leaves, or purse, and you don't have the paste of sandalwood on your forehead. Have you forgotten your fair-skinned beloved? You appear to be smart and alert, smiling beautifully. You don't appear like a real *yogī*, but more like an enjoyer or amorous person. That is my conclusion!"

Then, Krishna gave a small bit of ash to Rādhā by shaking the tiger skin. And with a slight glance he steals Rādhā's heart; she begins desiring him. Afterwards, Rādhā wanders daily from street to street and house to house in deep longing. In her search for Krishna, it is as if her eyes have turned into *cakora* birds longing for the rain. Rādhā's heart is like a jewel, but by his smart glance and cleverness Krishna snatches it from Rādhā. Krishna is the life and wealth of the universe. The poet Mādho Dāsa says there is a mutual bond of love between them.

11. Rupa anupama mohani (Beauty, Matchless and Enchanting), RV 1.110-111, Nāgarī Dāsī

Only three lines are included here of this song by Nāgarī Dāsī. It is played in a slow Dīp Chandī in the *rāga* Miśra Kafi, which includes both G and G̲: G in ascent and G̲ in descent. This song is similar to number 27 below.

rupa anupama mohini / ranga race lala //
mohe kumvara kishora / lada gahelari, ranga race lala //dhru o //
badana sudha rasa sravata ri //ranga o// pivata naina cakora //lada o//

naina kamala mukha kamala ke //ranga o//
carana kamala kara lala //lada o//
tana mana phule kamala ri //ranga o//
mohana mudita marala //lada o//
hasa kusuma jobana lata //ranga o//
ali asakta tamala //lada o//
vacana racana sura sabda kai //ranga o//
mriga mana mohe rasala //lada o//
ye ghana tuma duti damini //ranga o//
mili vilasau prema suhaga // lada o//
alasa kyaun bali kijiye //ranga o//
hilamila khelahu phaga //lada o//
sunata bhayau cita cau ri //ranga o//
sughara siromani jana //lada o//
sahacari sanca surana liyen //ranga o//
karata madhura kala gana //lada o//
sri kunjabihari khelahin //ranga o//
prema bhare rasa ranga //lada o//
buka bandana melahin //ranga o//
kumakuma kusuma suranga //lada o//
madana mudita anga angari //ranga o//
surata sukhada kala keli //lada o//
ura karavara parasain hamsen //ranga o//
jugala navala rasa jhela //lada o//
pivata sudha rasa madhuri //ranga o//
citrita pika kapola //lada o//
anga-anga anuraga ri //ranga o//
kahata madhura mridu bola //lada o//
raga ranga ati ranga rahyau //ranga o//
sri haridasi binoda //lada o//
vicitra viharina dasa ri //ranga o//
vipula badavata moda //lada o//

china-china prati rati sajahin //ranga o//
kunja sadana sukha rasi //lada o//
madhura prema rasa bilasahin //ranga o//
bali-bali nagari dasi // lada gahela ri ranga race lala

Translation: H. S. Mathur

The beauty of Śrī Rādhā is very enticing, and Krishna is immersed in pleasure. Rādhā has bewitched Krishna with her songs. It is as if nectar is flowing from her body and is being sipped through the eyes by a *cakora* bird. He is lotus-eyed, his entire face is like a blooming lotus, and his feet are also lotus-like. In this manner, the lotus is present all around. Krishna thus appears like a happy swan. In the vine of youth, merriment is like flowers, and dark black bees are enamored of them. The notes and words of her songs, sweet like mangoes, entice even the hearts of deer. Krishna is like a cloud and Rādhā is like the lightning—so both of you go on enjoying the pleasures of love. Why are you dilly-dallying? Play Holi with each other. Even hearing about this creates keen amusement in the heart. Rādhā and her Sakhīs are all singing sweet songs while Krishna is playing Holi full of divine love. Having ground the kumkum powder and *kusuma* flowers into fine color, the girlfriends apply the substances to their foreheads. Kāmadeva, the god of love, blossoms throughout their bodies as they engage in the celebration of love. They hold each others' hands, touch their breasts and laugh. Rādhā and Krishna enjoy this frolic as if they are drinking sweet nectar—their cheeks have become colored. Love spreads through all their limbs as they speak in sweet tones, with a profusion of color and merriment. For the saints Haridāsī, Vihārina Dāsa, and Vipula, this causes great pleasure and happiness. Minute by minute, moment by moment, Rādhā and Krishna experience more pleasure, and enhance each other's pleasure. And the grove where they are playing is a place of sweet pleasure and love. The poet Nāgarī Dāsī feels great affection for all this, and is drowned in divine love.

12. E cali lalana bharen ("Let's Go," Say the Ladies), RV 1.111-113, Harirāma Vyāsa

This composition of Harirāma Vyāsa (1511-1613) is played in a slow Tintāl (16 mātrās: 4-4-4-4) without cymbals. Though set in what seems to be Vilaval scale, it has its own unique tune that defies strict *rāga* classification (see number 14, which is similar). Only the first four lines are given here.

e cali lalana bharen mili /
cali ho cali ali begi giridharana bharahin mili //
bharana kaun pahirain suranga dukula /
navasata abharana saji calin saba angina-angana phula // giridharana
sanamukha avata hori gavata sakhana sahita balavira /
ubhai madana dala umade manahun jure hain subhata ranadhira //
mahuvara canga upanga bamsuri bina muraja mridanga /
dholaka dhola jhanjha dapha bajata kahyau na parata sukha ranga //
brajajana bala rasika gupala khelata ranga bhare phaga /
tana tarangana muni gana mohe chai rahyau anuraga //
ratana jatita picakarina bhari-bhari chirakata catura sujana /
kanaka lakuta chailana para tutata mala dharata bharata bhuja peli /
lala gulala anana para taki-taki karata capala kala keli //
ika bhanapura ki amana gujari harakhi anga na mai /
chailana kheda kahun laun ai haladhara pakare dhai //
ain simita sabai brajabala leta apanaun dai /
manaun sasi avani para gheryau udagana pahunce
i // ekai dhai dharata ankau bhari eka marorata kana /
ika sanamukha hvai saji aratau bahu puja sanamana //
jori sakhana mana mohana dhaye dauju ki bhira /
juvatina jutha sanamukhai umade kuken deta abhira //
juvatina naina saina bhedana men mohana line gheri /
madhumangala hamsata dura bhayau thadyau subala bajabata bheri //
mohana pakari jutha men lyain puja racata banai /
dadhi akshata rori kau tikau ganapati gaura manai //
ekai kuca bica leta lala kaun lai rahata ura jhela /
manahun taruna tamalahin lapati kanaka lata bahu beli //
gaura lepa mohana mukha lepyau likhi chabili bhaunha /
ye dhota vrishabhana rai ke subala tumhari saunha //
pakari sridama coba son madyau lai ain bhari batha /
nandarai yaha dhota jayau dayau hai hamare satha //

bhaji manasukha jasumati pai ayau kahata ature bola /
vrishabhana pura ki jora gujari bhaiyana lai gai ola //
cali mahari taba yaha sukha dekhana jora apane vrinda /
sura nara muni jana eka bhaye hain thakita bhaye ravi cana //
dekhata sobha vrajapati rani ananda mana mana hoi /
aja rohini bhaga hamare tahi na pujai koi //
taba rohini lalitaju boli agen avahun bhama /
kara joren hama karata binati calahu hamare dhama //
taba lalita radha pai ai bata sunahu dai kana /
badi mahari apane ghara bolata payau cahata mana //
taba radha sakhiyana pai ai lagata sabana ke pai /
gavata khelata hamsata hamsavata calahu mahari kain jai //
itanaun sonata sabai jura ain cali mahari ju ke dvara /
brajapati rani drishti pari taba bhaji gaye saba gvara //
agen hvai rohini taba ain aragha pamvade deta /
kancana thara utara aratau bari balaiyan leta //
ratana jatita simhasana anyaun diyau kisori raja /
babaju aba karata binati mola liye hama aja //
aganita meva ganaun kahan laun bhushana basana amola /
prema magana nandarani varashata kahata bacana madhu bola //
nautana bhushana khule sabana tana upajata kotika bhai /
prathama utirana diye vyasa kaun vimala vimala jasa gai //

Translation: H. S. Mathur

The girlfriends (*sakhīs*) call out, "Let us go to meet Mountain-lifter (Krishna)." Wearing colorful new clothes and ornaments and decorated with flowers from head to toe, they rush out to meet him. When they see Krishna coming from the opposite direction singing Holi songs, they approach him, playing musical instruments such as *mahuvara*, *cāṅga*, *upāṅga*, along with drums, cymbals, tambourines. It is difficult to describe the pleasure of this scene—amorous Krishna and the ladies of Braj playing colorful Holi (Phāg) together. There is so much love all around that even the sages (*ṛṣi*) are charmed. Water-squirters (large syringes) decorated with gems are used to spray colored water. On the word of Rādhā, the girlfriends strike Krishna and his friends with golden sticks. But clothes tear and garlands break; still they catch each other in their arms. Red powder (*gulāl*) is thrown on their faces. A simple Gujarī could not contain her pleasure, and when she surrounds and catches Krishna, all the cowherd girls of Braj collect there to take their turn beating him. It is as if the moon is caught on earth and all the stars arrive at the scene. While one girl embraces Krishna, another pricks his ears. Then another girl comes forward and venerates Krishna with worship and a welcoming ceremony.

Suddenly, gathering all his friends together including his brother Balarāma, Krishna tries to make a getaway, but all the cowherd boys cry out with joy and confront the younger ladies, who surround Krishna and stare at him with their slanted eyes. Madhumangal loves this scene and stands apart laughing, while Krishna's friend Subal plays a drum. The girls then catch the Enchanter (Krishna) in the middle of their group and offer him worship. Praying to Gaṇeśa and Gaurī, they place a mark (*tilaka*) of rice and *roli* on his forehead. Then a cowherd girl embraces Krishna between her breasts for a very long time. It looks as if a golden vine with many flowers had entwined itself around a young Tamal tree. Then other girls smear Krishna's face with a white paste, and decorate his lovely eyebrows. They say that he is the darling of Vṛṣabhānu. Subal, I assure you, and Śrīdama catch them with sticks while they hold Krishna in their arms. They say that Nanda Bābā has given his son to us for amusement. Then Manasukha goes to Yaśodā and says with distress that the Gujarī of Vṛṣabhānu is holding Krishna in captivity. Krishna with his friends meanwhile enjoy this scene of pleasure. Gods, humans, and sages all gather to see it, and the sun and moon become ecstatic. Seeing this, the Queen of Braj becomes very happy. She says, "it is our good luck today."

Rohiṇī and Lalitā then come to invite Krishna to their homes and offer worship to him. They say, "We pray you come to our house." Then Lalitā comes to Rādhā and says, "Listen carefully. The senior lady calls you to her house and wants you to be honored." Rādhā approaches her girlfriends, touches their feet, and says, "Singing and playing, let us all go to the house of the lady." Hearing this, her girlfriends gather and go to the Lalitā's house. When Yaśodā sees them, all the cowherds disperse. Rohiṇī comes, worships the feet of Krishna, and makes offerings of dry fruit, and such things. She performs a welcoming ceremony with a golden platter. One cowherd girl brings a jeweled couch for Krishna. Nanda Bābā says, "Today I have purchased Krishna back again." Yaśodā is filled with love and speaks affectionately. New ornaments decorate the bodies of all of the girls. Successfully completing this description, the poet Harirāma Vyāsa sings the spotless glories of Krishna.

13. Aho ranga ho-ho-ho-hori (Oh Colorful Ho-ho-ho-holi!), RV 1.117-118, Śrī Acala Dāsa

This is another recording of Śrī Damodar Das Mukhiya made in 1976 at the main Rādhāvallabha Temple. The composition is by the poet Acala Dāsa of the Rādhāvallabha Sampradāya and displays many unique features. With a scale of Vilaval *rāga*, its rhythm is a slow Dhamār with alternate fast repeats in Dīp Chandī and Kehervā at the end. It is complete and has a duration of forty minutes.

aho ranga ho-ho-ho-hori khelain sakala sumvari barasane ki /
tinamen rasika siromani syama ekahi vaisa samane ki //
ranga ho-ho-ho hori o //teka//
nava nidhi saji singara vividha ranga nakha sikha banin ika bane ki /
kirata prana adhara lali jivana saba desa bhayane ki //
gagara lai bharai mai pai kesara mrigamada sane ki /
komala karana kanaka picakari mani naga racita khacane ki //
bajata tala mridanga jhanjha dapha dhola dhamaka sahadane ki /
gavata ghora jila svara tanana kokila kantha samane ki //
ai hain vata sanketa saghana vana subhaga simba sarasane ki /
sravana sunata aye manamohana saina sakha amane ki //
duhun disi khyala macyau ju paraspara cokhacakha ati thane ki /
ita uta ahuta na manata kou kamalana mara macane ki //
badhi hai relapela bithina men sohai ranga barasane ki /
udata abira kapura dhura mili gagana madhya mandarane ki //

campaka lata gahe manamohana kara sarata kunja basane ki /
candravali pakare bala ju dhapi dhai dhanya maradane ki //
liye damame china ladaiti jiti hai ravala rane ki /
bicare sakha bhaje jita tita kaun nara mana maharane ki //
balaju ki ankha anji mukha mandyau kana na kari badyane ki /
ha-ha khai pani pari chute rahi na kachu virada bane ki //
gahi-gahi cibuka uthabata lalita drishti na jurata khisyane ki /
rahe ju kaha nara nici kari anga anga sakuca lajyane ki //
sakala simita ain kanhara dhinga kari-kari bata bakhane ki /
pare ai basa navala badhuna ke hyan nahi calata sayane ki //
janata hau mana men lalaju chalabala kari bhaja jane ki /
parau pani sri radhaju ke aura na kachu basyane ki //
gavata nari gari hori ki ancala gantha jurane ki /
koti-koti sukha bariye ina para ho-ho kahi hansi jane ki //
rasana eka kahan lagi baranau yaha sukha sindhu samane ki /
nagara bagara ghara gali galyare prema hilora chakane ki //
brahma siva muni karata prasansa gopina bhaga badane ki /
acaladasa giridharana bhaye basa prema ke hatha bikane ki //

Translation: H. S. Mathur

Look! The maidens of Barsana are playing colorful Holi. Among them is an amorous Dark One (Krishna) of the same age. The girlfriends have decorated themselves from head to foot with richly colorful dresses. The well-known girls are heartily loved by all the brothers in the area. Their mothers have filled up their pitchers with water, scented with saffron and musk. In their tender hands the girls hold water-guns of gold studded with small gems. *Tablas*, bells, cymbals, and tambourines are being played and drums are making thundering sounds. The merry-makers sing in high tones resembling the calls of cuckoos. The maidens come to the lovely dense forest, where they gather under a banyan tree. They learn of Mind-enchanter's (Krishna's) arrival with many of his friends. On both sides, a dancing contest with skillful movement of limbs ensues. There appears to be no limit to the playful frolics. In the lanes of colorful Barsana, crowds are increasing. The sky is full of dust mixed with *abīra* (red-scented powder) and camphor. Mind-enchanter is holding a *champak* vine from the bower in his hand, while Balarāma is holding the girlfriend Chandrāvalī with his strong hands. Rādhā, the dearest daughter of the village head, snatches drums from the boys' group, who being vanquished by girls of Nandgaon, run helter skelter. Disregarding the seniority of Balarāma, the cowherd girls smear his eyes and powder his face. Begging and falling at their feet, he somehow rescues himself from totally losing face and dignity. Lalitā raises Balarāma's chin, but he cannot face her out of shame. Folding in all his limbs he cowers with lowered head. The cowherd girls gather around Krishna and start to talk. They say to him, "You have been trapped in the company of newly wedded girls where your tricks have no value. In your heart you are planning to escape by your cleverness. But nothing is of any import except that you bow down before Rādhā's feet." The girls sing Holi taunts for the new couple. With peals of laughter, they pray that plentiful happiness should be bestowed on them. One tongue alone cannot describe the extent of this bliss. In every home, lane and street of the town, waves of love rise to the brim. Brahmā, Śiva, and all the sages praise the good luck of the cowherd girls. The poet Acala Dāsa is himself enslaved to Mountain-lifter (Krishna) out of love.

14. E cali janhi jahan (O Let Us Go Wherever), RV 1.121-123, Rāghava Dāsa

This poem by Rāghava Dāsa is demonstrated musically by presenting only the first stanza (6 lines). It is set to a slow Tintāl, at first without cymbals, in a variation of the *rāga* Kafi. In the last two lines of the stanza, it replicates in part the melody of a famous composition of the Rāsa Līlā season, *Mohana madana tribhaṅgī* (Enchanting, Intoxicating, Thrice Bent Form), Song 68, by also switching to Kehervā (8 *mātrās*). It is similar to Song 12 above.

e cali janhi jahan hari khelata gopana sanga /

ananka bahu baje tala muraja mukhacanga //
gavata suni bhavata manda madhura mukha bani /
janu harakhi paraspara manahu madana gati thani //
cali janhi jahan //teka//
cali janhi jahan kridata nanda-nandana jhanjha panava dapha bhari /
bina mridanga upanga canga bahu deta paraspara gari //1//
kara picaka vikaca mukha kati pata bhesha banayau /
janon gudara daina kaun bani basanta braja ayau //
hataka mani naga khacita vividha kara jeri sajain /
runja muraja nisana dhola dholaka dapha bajain //
avajha ati atura bajain braja jana khelata phaga /
tana tarangana vayu bandhyau chaya rahyau anuraga //2
/ dhuni sunata piyarinu kumakuma bhushana kine /
bahu ranga basana tana javaka caranana dine //
kavari karaja samvara nirakhi upama kaun hari /
manon hataka lata rahi khaga pannaga nari //
sravana tara ura hara chabi aru mukta sarasa sudhara /
janon juga giri bica dekhi kain dhasi surasari dhara //3//
raci tilaka bhala para mrigamada rekha samvari /
janu jugala jibha dhari pannaga pivata sudhari //
khanjana mina adhina dekhi driga saranga lajai /
badana canda bhruva capa svatisuta nasa rajai //
upama kaun avaloki kavi ya sama nahina aura /
manaun kira udagana gahain cugata nahin suni baura //4//
ati adhara aruna chavi aru dasanana duti pai /
manon bijjula bijana bidruma bara banai //
kantha kapota lajyata karana angada jagamagiyau /
manaun jalaja mrinala sarada sasi balaka lagiyau //
pahuncana men pahunci saghana sundara syama supasa /
manahun kanja ke kantha lagi bhringa rahe madhu asa //5//
bani cali hain sakala tiya paga nupura sura bhari /
manon vividha kama kalahamsa karata kilakari //
sakha jabadi sugandha kumakuma kesara ghori /
bhajana bhari lai calin sakala tiya gavata hori //
nakha sikha ten abaloki chabi nagara mohe gana /
manon sangita-sala padhi ghatabadha parata na tana //6//
chabi-sindhu lalana tana dekhata locana bhule /
citavata cita corata anga-anga anukule //
barana-barana sira paga sravana kundala manimaya ati /
manahun syama naga sikhara tarani juga ramata tarala gati //
ura vanamala visala chabi vividha sumana bahu vekha /
manhun jalada men pragata ati satamakha saranga rekha //7//
raci tilaka malaya kau piya kara khaura banai /
manu jugala ahina sasi ghana para dai hain dikhai //

ghana tana dekhi lajyata kanja driga kyaun sama pavahin /
mukha sasi syama bhujana dekha ahi vapuhin lajyavahin //
nakha sikha ten avaloki chabi kati pata pita sudesa /
manahun jalada dhurava sakhi damini rahi paravesa //8//
chabi srimohana tana laghu mati barani na jai /
citavata cita corata manamatha rahyau hai ljyai //
tiyana paraspara harakhi harita kara dage nivaje /
uthe gopa kilakara lagi duhun disi ten baje //
ekana kara kumakuma liyau ekana ghori gulala /
calin sakala braja sundari pakarana madana gupala //9//
sainana hi mohana haladhara diyen hai batai /
gahi nila vasana tana dvai vindu diye chitakai //
bahuryau mohana pakari sabai radha pai lain /
tabahi taruni musikyai sakha bhajana lai dhain /
chintata chirakata bharata bahu prema chaki nanda-nanda /
manahun avani para meghakaun ghori rahe bahu canda //10//
nirakhata vithakita nabha jahan tahan amara vimana /
barasata sura sumanana aru bajai nisana //
rahyau paraspara ranga sakala tiya bhavanana ain /
tabahi tinahin brajaraja vividha pata dai hai mithai //
ai tarani-tanaya salila majjana kiyau balabira /
pahari vasana aye bhavana sanga sakala abhira //11//
pariva sri-mohana rajata pita suvasa /
baithe singhasana bali bali raghau dasa //12//

Translation: H. S. Mathur

Let us go to all those places where Krishna is playing Holi with the cowherd boys. There are various types of musical instruments being played there like the drum, etc. Hearing them all singing with lovely expressions is very nice. It appears as if the god of love has entered into a music competition. Let us go! Other instruments are being played like *jhāñjh* (cymbals), *vīṇā, mṛdaṅga, upāṅga, cāṅga,* and the ladies of Braj start abusing each other in song. Krishna is smiling as he holds a water-gun. He is beautifully dressed with a scarf tied around his waist. It appears as if the Spring season of Basant has come to Braj to register its attendance. Various types of jewels, money, and gold ornaments adorn the hands of all the participants, who begin vigorously playing Holi and playing upon the musical instruments. The atmosphere of love spreads everywhere, and the air appears as if it has been fastened to the sound of musical notes.

The neighbor girls have adorned themselves with *kumkum* and ornaments, and listen to the songs. Wearing multi-colored dresses, with the bottoms of their feet painted red, they arrange their hair with their fingers. It is difficult to offer a simile for them—they appear perhaps like creepers of gold, or birds with serpents. They don beautiful ear ornaments and look exceedingly graceful wearing necklaces of pearls on their necks. These necklaces hang down into the crevices of their breasts and appear like the Ganges flowing down through the openings between them. On their foreheads are marks of musk, which appear like snakes quenching their thirsts with nectar through their two tongues. Their eyes are shaped like both birds and fish; even lotus flowers are shy before them. Their faces are like moons and their eyebrows like bows. They are also wearing pearls on their noses. The poet Rāghava Dāsa says they are peerless, for they are incomparable in beauty. Birds or parrots catch hold of the stars but they do not eat them, thinking them to be new mango blossoms. Their lips are red like coral and their shining teeth are like lightning. Their necks are like those of doves. Their arms, decorated with shining ornaments, look like soft lotus stems or like baby moons. And the beautiful thick ornaments on their forearms look like bees trying to suck the honey out flowers. Thus decorated, all the ladies walk with anklets on their legs making lovely sounds like swans. They are scented with *jaba*, *kumkum*, and saffron.

To play Holi, they carry heavy earthen pots full of color. Seeing their beauty, from top to bottom, and hearing their songs, they seem to have learned music from the masters. Looking at their beauty, people forget themselves, and their eyes forget looking as well. Stealthily they look at and admire the uniformity of their bodies. They are wearing turbans of different colors and earrings of beautiful jewels. As if from a dark mountain top, the sun is shining in a dancing pace. Their decorated breasts appear like many beautiful gardens of flowers, creating a rainbow of different colored rays. With profuse amounts of sandalwood on their faces, their eyebrows appear like two snakes on the face of the moon. Seeing their bodies, lotus flowers feel shy, finding no basis for comparison. Their faces are like moons and their arms make even the serpents feel timid. They are indeed lovely from top to bottom.

Krishna then ties a yellow scarf around his waist. He appears like a small cloud surrounded by lightning. The full gracefulness of Krishna cannot be described by a poet of small knowledge like me. Even the god of love is ashamed to look on the grace and beauty of Krishna. The ladies of Braj advance courteously. Seeing each other, they suddenly cry out and musical instruments start sounding from all sides. They all take red powder in their hands and catch hold of Nanda's Cowherd (Krishna), but he defers to Balarāma with his eyes. Catching holding of Balarāma's blue cloth, they spread colors on it. They then catch hold of Krishna and bring him to Rādhā. All her friends smile and bring different utensils. Spreading and showering colors over Krishna with their hands, they are saturated with love. It appears as if a beautiful cloud is surrounded by many moons. In the sky one can see the chariots of the gods, who are tossing flowers and playing kettle-drums. Finally, all the ladies return to their homes fully drenched in color. At that time, Nanda Baba gives them new clothing and sweets. They then go to the river and bathe. Meanwhile, Krishna and all his cowherd friends return home and don new clothes. Krishna, wearing a yellow, fragrant cloth, sits on a beautiful throne.

15. Sri vrindavana rani (Queen of Vṛndāvana), RV 1.123-125, Śrī Sadānanda Jī

This composition by Śrī Sadānanda Jī begins, rather surprisingly, on the words *aṅga aṅga* ("each limb [is a picture]") in the third line. It then follows with the lines of the refrain in the first line. Only the first three lines are given. It is set to the *rāga* Miśra Kafi in a slow Dhamār that accelerates into Dīp Chandī by the second line. There are no cymbals.

sri vrindavana rani radha sundara rupa nidhana /
banitana gana cudamani mandana mohana jivana prana //
anga anga chabi mana bhamvati ho sajani dekhahu naina nihara //teka//

lalita alaka kusumana son gathita sendura racita simanta /
manon ratipati mriga-krida karana kiyo sakhi udita basanta //
sisa phula rasa mula vadana chabi nava-nava sobha hota /
manon nava graham udapati dhinga baithe jagamaga apani jota //
sundara mastaka bendi rajata lakhi sukha pavata lala /
pragatita bhaga suhaga manon mani dipata manohara bhala //
kanana vara tatankana ki duti jhalaka kapola abhanga /
kanaka kamala men manu pratibimbita chabi son prati patanga //
diragha sundara naina su cancala ancala pata na samahin /
manon sravana kari marajada jyaun badi adhika na jahin //
aruna adhara mili makhi suthi locana bica moti bahu bhanti /
duhun tham ki duti parasa triveni bhai kala gunja kanti //
cibuka sudesa dithauna launa chabi son subhaga suhata /
manon alichauna pi makarandahin baithyau dhinga jalajata //
gaura manohara bhuja virajata balaya balita chabi jala /
manaun bhushana bhushita sobhita komala kanaka mrinala //
udita ujagara ura para manjula rurakata mukta hara /
manaun murati-vanta subhagata karata sudesa bihara //
nabhi sarovara trivali lahari pyari parama pravina /
tamen ranga bharyau dolata sakhi santata piya mana mina //
kankana kinkini nupura bajata rajata chabi vistara /
manon kancana beli vilambita madana muni dhuni caru //
tana-sukha sari subhaga virajata ararauta ati ranga /
aisi chabi son gori hori khelata piya ke sanga //
sakhi samaja madhya piya pyari varashata ami ananda /
udagana koti kalolata manaun vica dolata bibi canda //
baje bajata ghana jyon rajata varashata ranga apara /
bhijata tana mana hari juvati jana prema vihara udara //
aruna abira gagana men ghumadyau manu ghana umadyau lala /
ranga bhari camakata cancala tana damini si nava bala //

vadana chabile naina rangile ghumada gulala suranga /
manaun bhora dinesvara ke madhi mina phirata sasi sanga //
bharata paraspara pritama pyari hiya bhari anuraga /
nirakhi-nirakhi sukha harakhi kahata yon badabhagi yaha phaga //
sri vrindavana kalindi tata khela badhyau sukha sara /
jai sri sadananda hita vyasa suvana bala gavata jugala vihara //

Translation: H. S. Mathur

Śrī Rādhā, the Queen of Vṛndāvana, is an epitome of beauty. She is the crown jewel among the young ladies, and the very life of the Enchanter (Krishna). Friend, look closely at how each part of her body is full of glamour. Her lovely braids of hair are entwined with flowers and her forehead is decorated with *sindur* (red powder). It appears as if the god of love has brought forth the spring season just for sport. Her head ornament and lovely face increases her splendor more and more. She looks like the moon sitting in the center of the nine planets. Shining with its own light is a *bindi* (decorative dot) on her lovely forehead, which is beautiful and gives great pleasure to Krishna. The jewel in the part of her hair is a sign of marriage and good fortune. The brightness of her earrings adorns her cheeks like the reflection of the sun appearing between the petals of a golden lotus. Her large and beautiful eyes dart back and forth; they cannot be concealed by her veil. If her eyes were any wider, they would touch her ears. Her pink lips look pearly and her eyes appear like *guñja* seeds. The black dot (used to protect one from the evil eye) on her cheek increases her beauty; it looks like a baby bumble bee, sitting near a lotus after drinking nectar. Her fair arms are decorated with lovely bracelets like the stems of golden lotuses. A garland of pearls hangs over her bulging breasts, giving the impression that her loveliness has taken physical form and is enjoying there.

On her belly there are three ripples, a very good sign, decorating her navel area and looking like waves in a pond. In that navel pond, the heart of her lover wanders like a fish. Her bracelets, waist-bells, and ankle bells are tinkling beautifully, a lovely sound created by Kāmadeva. A colorful skirt along with a *sārī* adorns her body. With such glamour, Rādhā plays Holi with Krishna among a group of her friends. She spreads oceans of pleasure sparkling like stars playing around the moon. All the musical instruments being played together sound like clouds thundering. Boundless color drenches everyone. The ladies and Krishna are being rained upon by a flow of generous love. So much red powder spreads through the sky, it appears like a giant red cloud. And the resplendent bodies of the ladies shine like lightning. Their bodies are beautiful, their eyes are colorful, and the color red has spread everywhere. It appears as if goldfish are wandering along with the moon. Rādhā fills the hearts of everyone with deep affection, and everybody watching this scene says that it is a very auspicious Holi season. In this manner on the banks of Yamunā River in Vṛndāvana, the game of Holi develops and increases more and more. The poet Śrī Sadānanda, son of Vyāsa, sings in deep appreciation of these love-sports.

16. Sri vrindavana sahaja suhavanau (Śrī Vṛndāvana's Simple Beauty), RV 1.125-127, Śrī Vipula Vihārinī Dāsa

Similar to Song 11, this composition by Śrī Vipula Vihāriṇī Dāsa (17th century) of the Haridāsī Sampradāya is set to the *rāga* Miśra Kafi in slow Dhamār. The part included here starts from the second line (beginning with *ari*), breaking into Dīp Chandī and then a Kehervā.

sri vrindavana sahaja suhavanau //nava nagari e//
ari eri navala nava nagari e // nava nagari neha nidhana // bana //
han-han hamvai // bana hamvai //teka// hori khelana ke mate //nava o//
bana baithe kari thana //bana o//
mana manavata prathama hi //nava o//
e dou karata paraspara ana //bana o//

ronta meti mili khelahin //nava o//
hamsi diye hain dulahini pana //bana o//
navala nikunja birajahin //nava o//
ravi tanaya ke tira //bana o//
bhringa vihanga kulahala //nava o//
nava juvatina ki bhira //bana o//
syama ora ki samvari //nava o//
gori ke gore gata //bana o//
umagi calin cita caumpa son //nava o//
apani-apani gahi ghata //bana o//
saba sakhi mana anusarani //nava o//
una saji lini saba saunja //bana o//
lala ratana mani ki kundi //nava o//
kesara ki ojaoja //bana o//
kasturi karpura son //nava o//
sakha kumakuma adi //bana o//
candana malaya-gira ghase //nava o//
ghasi gaura meda javadi //bana o//
baje bajain anabhatin //nava o//
saba mile hain sanca sura tara //bana o//
bina amriti avajhi //nava o//
vara kinnara kathatara //bana o//
gavata caita suhavanaun //nava o//
meri piya pyari kau heta //bana o//
khelata melahi milavahin //nava o//
una badyau hai sabana sanketa //bana o//
lai lavana langen kasin //nava o//
baini kati son lapatai //bana o//
adhe kuca kancuki kasi //nava o//
ati ananda ura na samai //bana o//
ajna lai sanamukha bhain //nava o//
una dini hai jukti banai //bana o//
aragaja picakari calin //nava o//
saba bharata paraspara dhai //bana o//
coba ke cahale mace //nava o//
bhaye ambara aruna abira //bana o//
hara jita nahin samajhahin //nava o//
ati mana magana gambhira //bana o//
phagu khilavata phula son //nava o//
dain sainana hi sanakara //bana o//
naina kamala kajjala bhare //nava o//
maci hai kataksana mara //bana o//
ika jhuki baithin pitha dai //nava o//
ika manina hvai mukha mori //bana o//

eka manavata dina hvai /nava o//
ika paina parata nihori //bana o//
dina dulahina kaun dularavahin //nava o//
dina dulaha kaun dai gari //bana o//
gavata sukha dai rukha liyen //nava o//
mukha cumvata bhari ankavari //bana o//
saundhe men saundhi sabai //nava o//
kauna pichanen kahi //bana o//
sabai prema rasa ranga rangi //nava o//
rahe hain rasika mukha cahi //bana o//
merau kunjavihari kautiki //nava o//
ihi kautika rahe lubhai //bana o//
matta bhaye rasa madhuri //nava o//
rasa pivata sukha dai dhai //bana o//
hori khelata ranga rahyau //nava o//
saba gori lai hain bulai //bana o//
ko gori ko samvari //nava o//
moson kahau syama samajhai //bana o//
syama kahain gori sabai //nava o//
gori ke tana mana syama //bana o//
nirakhi badana tanamaya bhaye //nava o//
yon saphala kiye saba kama //bana o//
batana rahasi bahasa badhi //nava o//
ihi vidhi khelain phaga //bana o//
(apane) rasikana ki rasa riti kau //nava o//
pragata kiyau anuraga //bana o//
sakhi saheli sahacari //nava o//
sri haridasi sukha rasi //bana o//
sri vipula viharini dasi kon //nava o//
rijhi dai svavasi //bana o//
han-han hamvai // bana hamvai //

Translation: H. S. Mathur

Vṛndāvana is simply beautiful. O new maiden! Vṛndāvana is the epitome of love. Yes, it is so. Many people gather together there to celebrate Holi, sitting and determined. At first, they are miffed, and the girlfriends try to console them. But now Rādhā and Krishna promise each other that they will celebrate Holi together, putting aside their differences. Smiling, Rādhā offers a betel leaf to Krishna. Then they sit together in a new grove on the bank of the river Yamunā. Bumblebees and birds make their sounds as a bevy of young ladies gather there. The dark-skinned girls join the side of Krishna, and the fair-skinned girls join the side Rādhā. Jostling, excited, each trying to take a turn, they are acting as they feel in their hearts. Their necks are decorated with jeweled ornaments—rubies and such. There is a profusion of saffron, musk and camphor, as well as jars of red *kumkum* and sandalwood from the Malaya mountains. Their bodies are rubbed with musk, tumeric powder, and reddish *jabba* flowers. Sweet-sounding musical instruments such as the *vīṇā* are played. Kinnaras strum the *kathatara*'s strings. The ladies sing songs of Caiti for the pleasure of Rādhā. While playing, they also signal each other, each using secret signs (*samketa*). Their clothes are tied around their waists in elegant and stunning beauty, yet their bodices cover only half of their breasts because they are all so full of happiness that it can not be contained in their hearts.

They come out in front with permission from Rādhā, finding a clever new method for celebrating Holi—their water-guns full of scented water. After squirting the water, they quickly refill their water-guns. And then they dig a hole in the earth to hold the supply of colored powder.

As they grab and throw fistfulls of colored powder, the sky turns reddish from all the flying powder. No one minds since they are all deeply engrossed in celebrating Holi. They communicate with each other through the movements of their lotus eyes, lined with collyrium. One wink is enough to make one of the girlfriends sit down and turn her back. Then another turns her face away in a huff, and another tries to appease her by touching her feet and flattering her. Some of the girlfriends appease Rādhā, and some scold Krishna. But all of them sing with happy faces. Embracing, they kiss each others' faces. All drenched in scent and color, they are not even able to recognize each other. Everything is colored by love. Then Krishna as a lover of bliss (*rasika*) wants to kiss their faces, too. As he endears himself to the girls in this way, they all become intoxicated in the sweetness of love as if drinking its nectar too quickly. The celebration of of Holi continues.

All the fair girls are called together, but it is difficult to distinguish between the fair and the dark. Who is fair and who is dark? Tell me. Dark One (Śyāma) then says that all of them are fair-skinned, since they all have Krishna in their bodies and minds. When the girls see his face, they become so engrossed that all their hearts' desires are fulfilled. Their talk of love goes on and on. In this manner, they all celebrate Holi in the manner of connoisseurs (*rasika*), expressing and enjoying the nectar of devotion to Krishna. All the maidens and girlfriends of Rādhā are in fact his companions. Śrī Haridāsa is the treasure trove of this form of happiness, says the poet Vipula Vihāriṇī Dāsa, who is so happy he expresses it by patting himself on the back. Yes, yes, most certainly!

[CD 3]

17. Ari cali navala kisori (O Let's Go Young Lady!), RV 1.127-129, Nanda Dāsa

This song by Nanda Dāsa (1530-1584) is in a slow Dhamār in the *rāga* Misra Kafi. Only two lines are included in the recording.

ari cali navala kisori gori bhori, hori khelana janhi //teka//
ari aisi madhu jamini dekhi bhamini, kyaun tohi bhavana suhahi //
ari uhan (saba) braja vara nara narinu ke, jutha jure hain ai /
ari uhan nanda-nandana puni aye, rangile rasika mani rai //
ari ali tinamen tu nahin dekhi, rahi gaye naina nai /
ari taba ita uta taki mohana piya, mo tana takyau aragai //
sakhi mosaun sainana hi men kahyau kahan, main kahayau griva dhurai /
tabatau ri chabile kumvara to pahiyan, sainana dai pathai //
tu aba na kari gaharu nagari tiya, ani banyaun bhalau dai /
yaha suni navala ladili sahacari tana, musiki naina dhurai //
itane hi parama catura sakhi jina tina, bhuja bhari lai uthai /

gahi nava kancuki saundhe bori, biri dai banai //
puni pada pitha patora ponchi ken, agen dhari samuhai /
cali navasata saji svamini kamini, sakhi ke amsa bhuja lai //
manon kanaka dhatu parvata para, tadita lata camakai /
nava guna navala rupa nava jovana, navala neha hulasai //
jhumaka sari pyari pahiren, calata lanka lacakai /
janu yaha rupa joti jagamaga-si, pavana lage jhakuai //
kamala phiravata karavara bala, mala urasi rurai /
puni ika lata chabi son ju chabili ke, besara rahi arujhai //
manu pritama mana mina ki banasi, bhakha mukata latakai /
lalitadika sakhiyana men sundari, sobhita hain ihi bhai //
janu nava kumudina ke mandala men, indu pagana calyau jai /
kabahunka badana durai ugharata, puni hamsi leta durai //
manjula mukara maricina si manu, china-china chavi adhikai /
aru jaise nava mada matta gayandani, malhakata bahu dhurai //
sobhita sravanana sveda sudanti ke, manon pate cucani /
nivi-bandhana phundava ghanta, kinkini ghana ghungharai //
nupura upara cura rura, manu sankala jhanakai /
cancala ancala camvara virajata, nainku calata jaba dhai //
sakhiyana ke kara kusuma chari te, agadha bane cahun ghai /
madana mahavata kau bala nahin, ankusa deta darai //
sakhiyana men hitu visesha visakha, jyaun tana ki parachani /
so nanda-nandana niyaren jani ken, sahaja uthi kachu gai //
sabahina janyaun sri-radhaju ain, bhaye caugune cai /
je hutin navala kisori ki sathina, te daurin samuhai //
tina sanga mohana dhaye aye, jyon ranka mahanidhi pai /
pahilain hi lala juhara kahyau mridu, murali manhi bajai //
itaten kutila katakshana piya tana, citayau muri musikai /
so sukha piya naina hi janai mo mana men na samai //
cancara denna lagin braja vithinu, rangile ranga upajai /
gavata lagin gvalina gari, sundara lalahin lagai //
radhaju gari suni-suni hamsi-hamsi, hari tana lajyani /
lalanu abira bharata gvalina kaun, (apani) prana priyahin bacai //
aura ju prema vivasa rasa kau sukha, kahata kahyau nahin jai /
jehi sukha kahive kaun kotika sarasuti ki sumati hirai //
sesa mahesa suresa na janen, aja ajahun pachitai /
so rasa rama tanaka nahin payau, jadapi palotata pani //
sri vrishabhanu-suta pada ambuja, jinake sada sahai /
ihi rasa magana rahata je tina para, nanda dasa bali jai //

Translation: H. S. Mathur

A girlfriend addresses Śrī Rādhā, "Oh fair-skinned and simple one, let us go where Holi is being celebrated. O Lady, can't you see that it is such a sweet night? On such a night, why do you want to stay in the house? O friend, at that place all the men and women have gathered together. The Son of Nanda (Krishna) has also gone there. He is a colorful and amorous prince. When Krishna did not see you in the crowd, he lowered his eyes. After glancing here and there, Krishna then looked at me intensely and asked me, only through his eyes, where you were. Then I lowered my head. With only the motion of the eyes, he has sent me to you. You should therefore not delay, for it is a good turn for you."

Hearing this, the young lady smiles and lowers her eyes. Meanwhile, her clever girlfriend catches her by the arms and pulls her up. Catching hold of her blouse, which is scented, she places a jewelry box in front of Rādhā. After decorating herself in sixteen ways, Rādhā starts dressing. She looks like a mountain of gold, or a creeper of lightning. She has new qualities, and fresh form and youth, and new love. Wearing a very beautiful *sārī*, and walking with her waist in motion, Rādhā seems like an embodiment of shining light. With the caress of wind she also trembles. As she massages her lotus hands, the garland moves over her chest. Again and again, her nose-ring (*besra*) get caught in one of her braids.

The heart of Krishna is attractive to her, like bait to a fish. Rādhā looks so graceful walking between friends like Lalitā and others. Rādhā walks as if the moon were advancing in a circle of red lotuses. Sometimes when her veil slips, her concealed smile is revealed. She looks even more beautiful when her reflection falls on a looking-glass; minute by minute she looks more graceful. Long arms relaxed at her sides, sensuous and limber, she struts about like a she elephant. And there is even perspiration around her ears, just like an elephant's.

Hanging along her waist-band, tiny bells are ringing. Ankle bells and bracelet bells also ring as if in a chain. On her chest there is a small necklace (*camvar*), shaking. Her girlfriends have small flower sticks which offer protection from all sides. The god of love has no more control over any of this than he would over an elephant.

Her special friend Viśākhā is like a shadow of her body. She starts singing, sensing that he is near. When her girlfriends know that she has come, their energy surges fourfold. When all the girls come forward as a group, Krishna looks like a poor man who has suddenly inherited great wealth. The blissful boy offers his salutations by playing the flute. With a smile, Rādhā observes him out of the corners of her eyes. Describing this scene, this poet cannot contain the pleasure in his heart, a pleasure only Krishna can know. In Braj, the cowherd girls and boys start singing songs in the meter Cañcar, with mock scolding in the lyrics that appeal to Krishna. Hearing the scolding, Rādhā looks towards her blissful one again and again, smilingly, and feels embarrassed. Krishna then throws colored powder (*abīra*) on the other girls and boys, avoiding Rādhā. The full effusion of love and the pleasure it gives cannot be described. Even the goddess Sarasvatī is baffled when describing this joy, which is beyond the awareness of even Śeṣa, Maheśa, and Indra. Even Brahmā regrets not witnessing it. Lakṣmī has not been blessed with this pleasure either, although she massages the feet of Vishnu. The lotus feet of Rādhā give their help to some persons and such persons are always lost in *rasa*. In this the poet Nanda Dāsa rejoices.

18. Sajani lala phaga (Good Woman, the Red Powder of Holi), RV 1.132-133, Cācā Vṛndāvana Dāsa

This song by Cācā Vṛndāvana Dāsa (1708-1787 C.E.) has a rather long and complex melody line, and the *tāla* is an extended Tintāl. The verses run thirty-two *mātrās* each, ending on the word, *sajanī*, the first word of the refrain. The refrain actually begins on the fourth *mātrā* of the Tintāl on the word *lāla*. The scale for the tune is based again on the *rāga* Miśra Kafi, using G and $\underline{G}$, and with N. The characteristic phrase is M P M G, $\underline{G}$ M P D M P. The tempo picks in the second line in the fast repeat, and then returns to the original pattern by the third.

sajani lala phaga phala payau /
ranga bhari-bhari ken gheri kunja madhi gahi-gahi banha nacayau //
piya kiye priya priya karin pritama badhi gayau ranga sabayau /
bhamvari dai baithare mandala lakhi driga bhagya manayau //
lalita ghunghati syama badana para raci kautuka upajayau /
vari-vari pahupanjali sabahina ati hita saun dularayau //
gaura syama angina ju ranga caunpana caina chirakayau /
tana bhinjana mana bhinjana kau sukha anana ujhala ju ayau //
kusuma chari dai hatha bahuri jhumaka kau khela khilayau /
dulaha dulahina prema mahilau chandana raci-raci gayau //
nyauchavara kiye prana parama kautika hori mana bhayau /
yaha ju apurava lada jhumaka bana-bani darasayau //
aurai caha samajhi kai douna kunja sadana padharayau /
vrindavana hita rupa ghumadi rasa kau ambuda barasayau /

Translation: H. S. Mathur

Good Woman! The red powder of Holi bears fruit. The girlfriends pour color on Krishna in the forest grove, and, holding up his arms, make him dance. When Rādhā and Krishna are confronted in love, the pleasure of Phāg increases manifold (14 times!). The girlfriends then make them sit in-between them, increasing their own good fortune by seeing them in this way. The scene becomes an amusing game as some girls place a veil over Krishna's dark body. Many offerings of flowers are given to them to express their endearment. And then enthusiastically the girls sprinkle colors on Rādhā and Krishna. When their bodies and hearts are submerged in this colorful powder, great pleasure is revealed in their faces. Then they hand them the bouquets of flowers and make them play various games. The deep love of the bride and bridegroom is expressed in beautiful songs that they compose. They sacrifice their own life-forces (*prāṇa*) and enjoy the fun of Holi immensely. Rādhā and Krishna express their unique love in this way. And when the girlfriends think that the pair wants more amorous play, they send Rādhā and Krishna to a forest grove for more enjoyment. The poet Cācā Vṛndāvana Dāsa says a dense cloud of *rasa* is starting to spread.

19. Hori ranga rangili ai (The Colorful Season of Holi is Here), RV 1.141, Kiśorīlāla

This brief song by Kiśorīlāla resembles the traditional Kafi songs of Holi that one hears in Hindustani classical concerts and recordings. Played in medium Dīp Chandī, the refrain begins with "*Raṅga*" and ascends the Kafi scale from S to the Sam on P, descending on "*horī*" (Holi). With a delightful gait, the song proceeds to Kehervā with double-time at the end and in the repeat of the refrain.

hori ranga rangili ai /
khelaungi brajamohana sonhana so atihi mana bhai //
sunahu saheli lalita adi rangana ghorau bahu caina cai /
jai sri kishorilala hita saun mila khelaun kari haun apani hi dai //

Translation: H. S. Mathur and Guy L. Beck

The colorful season of Holi is here. Rādhā says that she will celebrate it with the Enchanter of Vraja (Brajamohan, Krishna) as she wishes. She tells Lalitā and her other friends to prepare many colors. Poet Kiśorīlāla says that after joining them, he will take her turn to play Holi with him.

20. Braja kau dina dulaha (On the Festive Day of Vraja, the Darling Boy), RV 1.141, Cācā Vṛndāvana Dāsa

This is a song from the Holi Rasiyā class of songs in the Rādhāvallabha Songbook. This refers to a lighter variety of folk song, preferably in faster rhythms like Keherva̅ and Dīp Chandī. The tune, which is completed by repeating again the first three words of the refrain, is instantly identifiable and very well-known throughout the Braj area. It is not in any specific *rāga* per se, although one could place it in the Desh mode. There are many poems set to this tune in the Rādhāvallabha Songbook. The classical singer Pandit Jasraj has recorded one of them in a similar tune on a CD of Haveli Sangit songs.

braja kau dina dulala ranga bharyau /
ho-ho-hori bolata dolata hatha lakuta shira mukata dharyau //
gadhe ranga rangyau vraja sagarau phaga khela kau amala paryau /
vrindavana hita nita sukha varshata gana tana suna mana ju haryau //

Translation: H. S. Mathur and Guy L. Beck

On the festive day of Holi, the Darling Boy (Dulāla, Krishna) is drenched in color. Wandering here and there with a stick in his hand and a crown on his head, he covers all of Braj with rich colors while celebrating Holi. According to poet Vṛndāvana Dāsa, it is as if happiness rains from heaven, and all the residents' hearts joyfully hear beautiful music.

21. Ranga rangile dou nava nikunja (The Two Covered with Colors in a Fresh Bower), RV 1.146, Kiśorīlāla

This poem by Kiśorīlāla has an unusual melody that is long and complex, stretching over several cycles of Tintāl. Words and short phrases are constantly being broken up and repeated. It is set in a kind of Miśra Kafi, but again one must be cautious in assigning a *rāga* to many of the selections in the Rādhāvallabha Songbook. Give special attention to the triple four-*mātrā* notes on the syllable "*ho*," first on P, then on upper s, and then on upper g coming back down to sa. This type of song will not be heard anywhere outside of this tradition.

ranga rangile dou nava nikunja madhi prema ranga bhare khelata horiyan,
ho ho ho /

syama varana sakhi syama sanga bhain gori ke sanga saheli saba goriyan,
ho ho ho //
phaintana bhare gulala vividha ranga taka-taka melata navala kishoriyan,
ho ho ho /
jai sri kishorilala hita saun gahi anyau mukha mandyau kari-kari bara joriyan, ho ho ho //

Translation: H. S. Mathur

Both Krishna and Rādhā are drenched in colors, and they celebrate Holi in a new bower, full of love for each other. The girlfriends who are with Krishna turn dark and the girlfriends who are with Rādhā become fair in color. The girls store the scented, red color in their scarves tied around their waists. Poet Kiśorīlāla says, "Glory to Śrī Krishna, whom they caught hold of, forcibly smearing his face."

22. Ari cali bega chabili (O Let's Quickly Go Fair Lady), RV 1.156-157, Nanda Dāsa

This poem by Nanda Dāsa presents another complex melody set to several cycles of Tintāl. The melodic structure resembles Song 18 above. The line "*ari cali bega*" is the key phrase in the refrain that is repeated after each verse. There is a fast repeat on the lines beginning with "*nikasyau hai*" and "*umadyau hai*" Only the first three lines are included here.

ari cali bega chabili! hari son khelen jahin //dhru //
nikasyau hai mohana samvarau bali phaga khelana braja manjha /
umadyau hai abira gulala gagana bica manau mai phuli hai sanjha /
bajata tala mridanga muraja dapha kahi na parata kachu bata /
ranga-ranga bhine gvala bala sanga manon mai madana barata //
ai hain itate juri sundari saba kari-kari apanau thata /
khelata nahin kou kanha kumvara son cahata tumhari bata //
binu raja dala kauna kaja bali uthiye chandiye ainda /
unadyau hai nidhi jyaun navala nanda kau rukata ravari mainda //
uthi hain vihamsi vrishabhanu kumvari vara kara picakari leta /
sahi na sakata kou maha subhata laun sunata samara sanketa //
ai hain rupa agadha radha chabi barani nahin jai /

navala kishora amala candahi manon mili hai candrika ai //
khela macyau braja bithina manhiyan barashata premananda /
damakata bhala gulala bhare manau bandana bhurake canda //
aura ranga picakarina chabi son chirakata hari tana tiya /
kutila kataksha prema ranga bhari-bhari bharata piya kaun hiya //
dura muri bharana bacavana chabi son badyau hai ranga apara /
maina muni si bolata dolata paga nupura jhanakara //
siva sanakadika sarada narada bolata jai-jai-jai /
nanda dasa apane thakura ki jiyau balaiyan lai //

Translation: H. S. Mathur

One girlfriend addresses another, saying: "we should go and meet Mohana (Krishna) because he has come out to celebrate Holi in Braj." Bright red-colored powder spreads throughout the sky, as the evening arrives. Many drums like the *mṛdaṅga* are being played, and it is difficult to describe their beautiful sound. The cowherd boys are all drenched in color and it looks as if the marriage party of the god of love has arrived. From the other side, the handsome ladies of Braj arrive in beautiful fashion. They each tell Rādhā that "no one celebrates Holi with Krishna, who waits for you. Therefore, put aside your pride because there is no pleasure in playing without the king. The flow of Krishna's pleasure is obstructed by your levees (mud walls)." Hearing this, Rādhā smiles and takes a water syringe in her hand. Hearing the sound of her attack, nobody is brave enough to withstand it. The excellent beauty of Rādhā here cannot be described. Krishna is like a faultless moon and Rādhā has joined him like moonlight. In the streets of Braj, Holi play thus starts and love begins to rain down everywhere. The forehead of Krishna is covered with red powder, and shines like the moon. All the girls spray water on Krishna with their syringes. They also with their glances fill his heart with the color of love. Sometimes, they turn or conceal themselves and try to escape. In this way, the beauty of Holi increases considerably. The anklets on the girls' feet ring like the sound of a myna bird. Shiva, Sanaka,

Śārada, Nārada, and all say 'Victory to Krishna,' and the poet Nanda Dāsa also praises his Lord.

23. Cali hai kumvari radhe khelata hori (Maiden Rādhā Goes to Play Holi), RV 1. 158-159, Nanda Dāsa

This poem of Nanda Dāsa is performed in slow Dhamār. Only the first two lines of this rendition are included here, which are more or less within the bounds of the Kafi scale. There are no cymbals.

cali hai kumvari radhe khelata hori /
pankaja paraga vara liyen bhari jhori

ranga ranga rali sanga sohen gana alim /
saphala kari hain saba gokula ki galim //
bajen dapha tala mridanga jhanjh suhae /
madana sadana manon mangala badhae //
gavata sarasa sura aisi mithi dhuni /
haraju jaryau manoja jiyau jai suni //
sohain mukha kachu-kachu amvara durae /
adhe-adhe bidhu manon badarana chae //
abira dhundhara madhi rajain ranga bhini /
manon ditha dara mara sara dhampi lini //
utaten aye mohana bhinen ranga-ranga /
carana luthata aven kotika ananga //
rangili galinu bica khela macyau bhari /
uta hari ita vrishabhana ki dulari //
chirakin chabile ana pyari tiya gana /
rangana barasai manon nutana saghana //
chuten picakari ranga bhari sobha bhari /
chabi saun chutata manon maina phulajhari //
tiyana ke anga ranga kana gana sohain /
kancana jarai jari chari chabi kohai //
itaten ranga ki dhara samvare pai meli /
abahin ulahin manon nava prema beli //
abira gulala mili mandita gagana /
manon abahin ravi cahata ugana //
hamsata-hamsata uta candravali gai /
lala son kahata haun tihari disi bhai //
bamsuri chidai lini chalakai kisori /
tari dai-dai hasain saba kahain ho-ho hori //
radhaju adhara dhari bamsuri viraji /

aisi kabahun samvare piya pain a baji //
vamsi daina misa pyari radhika bulae /
hamsata-hamsata lala ikale hi ae //
kamini ke vrinda syama ghera line aisen /
damini nikara manon nava ghana jaisen //
samvare ke anga sanga sohain tiya aisi /
singara kalapa taru chabi lata jaisi //
nanda dasa aura sukha kahan lon bakhanau /
vidhi hun kahyau hai soi janon soi janau //

Translation: H. S. Mathur

The maiden Rādhā goes to celebrate Holi. Her bag is full of lotus pollen. Her girlfriends accompanying her appear to be fully covered with color, and they all adorn the lanes of Gokula. Drums, trumpets, and other musical instruments are played, as if for an happy meeting at the house of Kāmadeva. They sing with very sweet voices, hearing which even the god of love feels jealous. Their faces are slightly veiled like half-clouded moons. Their powdered faces are moist with color, and partly covered by their *sārīs* for fear of bad influences (like the evil eye). The Enchanter (Mohana, Krishna) arrives there from the other side also covered with color. For his grace, numerous Kāmadevas fall to their knees abashed. In the colorful streets various forms of merriment ensue in a grand manner. Krishna and Rādhā face each other. Adoring ladies are scattered all around. Wet colors are raining down as if from new clouds. Lovely water guns squirt colored waters, as if they are fireworks. Drops of colored water beautify the bodies of the girls in their *sārīs* which are embedded with golden beads. Many girls direct their sprays of color towards Krishna, which sprays appear like new vines of love sprouting. The sky was full of *abīra* and *gulāla* (types of colored powder), making it seem as if the sun were just about to rise. Candra Sakhī goes to Krishna and laughingly says that she has joined his side. Surreptitiously she snatches Krishna's flute. All the other *sakhīs* laugh and clap. The flute looks so nice on Rādhā's lips. Even

Krishna has not played it so well. Rādhā then calls Krishna pretending to return his flute. He comes near, alone and smiling. The girls surround him like bolts of lightning surrounding a new cloud. They appear very enticing together with Krishna, like lovely vines surrounding a celestial wishing tree. The poet Nanda Dāsa says: "How can I describe this pleasure? Even the sages say that one can only enjoy this pleasure by experiencing it."

24. Ranga aja vamsivata (Colorful Today is Vaṃśīvaṭa), RV 1.161-163, Sahacārī Sukha Jī

Similar to Song 24, this song of poet Sahacārī Sukhajī (1635-1697) is also in slow Dhamār in the Kafi scale. There is a fast repeat on the line beginning with "*viharata*" that includes an extension on the phrase "*eri ha.*" Only one line is included here, and there are no cymbals.

ranga aja vamsivata phaguna vividha vihara /
viharata radha vallabha ujhalata saurabha sara //
vaisa kalina si khilin lalita lalitadika vrinda //
tinaki nakha duti dekhata phikau lagata canda //
tinake jovana ulahata sukha sobha ki bhira //
sada hun pata pahirata hota jarakasi cira //
sahaja sugandhana tinaki bhayau madhukara gati bhula //
jinake mukha musikata jharain ujvala rasa ke phula //
tinake lakhata banavata upama lajata ananta //
jinake tana phulyau rahai nita hi madana vasanta //
tinamen milata ladili taba chabi aisi hota //
hari cakha kamalana chai rupa bhora ki jota //
karata kataksha drigana ki murata priya ki pitha /
gore hiya piya hvai rahyau milata ditha son ditha //
ura urajana ke bojhana lacaki-lacaki kati jata /
dekhata madana-mohana ki citavana lacakana panta //
bhulata palakana pritama priye prema ki punja /
ja tana citavata citavana bhai arasi kunja //
rijha kumvari ki raci rahi navala kumvara hiya manhi /
roma-roma yaun bandhi rahyau bhayau phirata braja chanhi //
sithila karata kou sahaja hi sanamukha cali gaja cala /
kou kasi bhuja men hamsi-hamsi masarata vadana gulala //

syama ki sainana saun kou ali mandata bhala /
kou anjana kaun anjata chuvata kapolana bala //
lakhi lalita dhiga ai kain kahata bacana mana cora /
jutha visakhadika uta hama mohana ki ora //
kou sakhi sakha bani hain sisa candrika dhara /
mili mridanga dapha talana gavata sarasa dhamara //
candana ki chintana saun chirake chaki nanda-nanda /
krishna jalada men jhalakai manu jasa udagana vrinda //
chirakin chaila bandanasaun te tiya saba badabhaga /
manahun mana ke bagana baye hain bija anuraga //
aragaja tiya lapatavata ura parasata musikata /
rasika hiye lapatai kain apuna lapati jata //
lapatavata mrigamada mukha alabelina kai lala
bane driga manon singara sara phule kamala visala //
bhurakata cura kapura kucana para opi vama /
samara sambhu manu puje khela vijai hita syama //
ramani bhurakata rori rangilau kinau hai phagu /
prita lata manu launi lahakata jharata paragu //
dhari bihari picakari lika dipin pacaranga /
mano ghana damini singari lahariya sari anga //
chati chaila takatu jaba durata murata rasadani //
phiri tari dai musikata kampata jaba dou pani //
race hain gulalana anana kavi yaun karata bakhana /
lali barasi manu kamalana sasi kiye amrita bhana //
ranga-ranga udata abirana pari hai laja ki gadha /
ghumadi suranga ati andhina phaguna kiyau asadha //
darasata anga dure jaba muthin uthata duhun ora /
manata janama saphalata dekhata nanda-kisora //
dhorata sisana kesara krishnagara /
badalata tana baranani kaun badhyau moda apara //
avalana ke bala men phamse lase hain jugala sujana /
kanha banae hain gori, gori kinhi hai kanha //
ganthajora kari kilakin saji mangala tihi thaura /
gati byaha ke gavata bandha duhunna siramaura //
aisehin hulasau vilasau amsa bhuja dou meli /
dularavata sahacari sukha kunja-mahala ki keli //

Translation: H. S. Mathur

It is the month Phālguna (February-March) and today Vaṃśīvaṭa is full of color and pleasure. Rādhā's Dear (Rādhāvallabha, Krishna) wanders and proudly enjoys the fragrant scents.

The girlfriends, including lovely Lalitā and others, blossom like flower buds. Even the moon appears graceless in comparison to the glow of their polished nails. Their lives are brimming with happiness and beauty. Even if they wear ordinary clothes, these seem woven with golden and silver threads (jari). The bees appear to have lost their way, having smelled the sweet fragrances. When the girls smile it appears as if bright-colored flowers are falling down from them. Seeing their beauty, the god of love has nothing to compare it with. In their bodies the spring season and the god of love blossom forever.

When Lādilījī (Rādhā) joins them, there is such splendor it appears as if the lotus eyes of Krishna have been brightened with morning's beauty. While turning her back towards Krishna, Rādhā winks at him with her eyes. But when their eyes meet it seems that Krishna has penetrated the lovely heart of Rādhā. Because of the burden of Krishna in her heart, Rādhā's slender waist bends frequently. And when she sees the eyes of the Love's Enchanter (Madanamohana, Krishna), her gait sort of totters. Rādhā, the acme of love, totally forgets herself when she sees her beloved. Wherever she looks in the bower, his image arises. In Krishna's heart, Rādhā also dwells as an emblem of love. With Rādhā entangled in his every limb, he wanders ainlessly in Braj.

Simulating the graceful movements of an elephant, some girlfriends further try to slow down Rādhā's listless pace. Other girlfriends embrace her and laughingly rub scented red powder on her face. One girl presses her forehead, seeing Rādhā's winking. Lalitā applies mascara to her eyes and touches her hair and cheeks. Just then, getting close to Rādhā, Lalitā tells her in a heart-soothing voice that a group of girlfriends headed by Viśākhā, have gone to where Mohana is. One girl, having decorated her head with an ornamental half-moon, has adopted the role of one of Krishna's cowherd friends. Others sing mellifluous Holi Dhamārs with drum, cymbals, and tambourine. The girls also thoroughly sprinkle Krishna with sandalwood paste. In this form he appears like a galaxy of stars (the beads of sandalwood) amidst a dark cloud (*śyāma*). Those maidens who sprinkle Krishna are fortunate. The beads of sandalwood are like seeds of love sown in the garden of the heart. Some girls smear Krishna with sweet-scented paste and smile while embracing him. Having thus embraced amorous Krishna, they cling to him. Some smear musk on their own red faces. If beauty is a pond, their eyes are like large lotus flowers in it. One girl spreads camphor on her breasts. It is as if Śambhū (Śiva) has playfully won a battle with Śyāma (the white camphor surrounds her dark nipples).

One cowherd girl spreads *rolī* (a scented red powder) everywhere, making Holi even more colorful. It appears as if the vine of love has blossomed and its pollen is floating there. Then the Player (Bihārī, Krishna), using a water syringe, drenches the cowherd girls. The multi-colored girls look like a combination of clouds; silver linings adorn all their dresses. When the amorous Krishna glances at the bosom of his pleasure-giving Beloved (Śrī Priyā, Rādhā), she turns away to hide herself. When she claps and smiles, both her hands tremble. The faces of all the Holi revelers are smeared with red powder, and the poet describes this scene as if the nectar-giving sun has reddened the moon-like faces of the maidens into lotuses.

There are no reservations in celebrating Holi. Colored powder and water flow freely, and with such a storm in the air the month of Phālguna has been turned into Āṣāḍh (the monsoon month). While the girls move their fists full of powder, their concealed body parts are exposed. When Kānhaiyā sees them, he deems it life's happiest moment. The enamored girls throw amber and saffron feverishly over the heads of the Holi revelers, so quickly, so thickly, that the colors change constantly, providing great merriment. Surrounded with maidens on all sides, Rādhā and Krishna look extremely attractive. Due to the colors of Holi, the dark Kānhā (Krishna) becomes fair and the fair Rādhā becomes dark. Symbolically, their personalities exchange in deep love. On this very spot, the cowherd girls happily tie their auspicious wedding knots. They also tie wedding garlands over their foreheads and sing marriage songs. The poet Sahacarī Sukhajī blesses them to remain joyful, to embrace each other, and to have nuptial merriment in the bower house eternally.

25. Gvalina saundhe (The Cowherd Girl's Wet, Fragrant Blouse), RV 1. 185-186, Ghanaśyāmajī

This forty-line poem of Ghanaśyāmajī is set to a combination of the *rāgas* Sarang and Kedar. It is played in a medium-fast Dīp Chandī with alternate faster sections. Very fast cymbal-playing begins on line thirty-four, the line beginning with "*tohi.*" Instead of starting at the beginning, this recording includes only the last section (set apart) beginning with line thirty-three, "*jo bhavai so lai.*" The same structure of melody and rhythm are maintained throughout the entire song. The singer here is Śrī Krishna Caitanya Bhatt ("Bhattaji") of the Vrindaban temple of Śrī Śrī Rādhāmadanamohana. While he is a member of the Gauḍīya Sampradāya, he uses the Rādhāvallabha Songbook in his daily temple music. His style of singing and accompaniment is a bit more lively and robust than the majority of Rādhāvallabha music. Note that all forty lines of the song end in the syllables "ari."

gvalina saundhe bhini angiya sohai kesara bhini sari /
lahanga chapedara chabilau china lanka chabi nyari //
adhika bara rijhavara phaga khilavara calata bhuja dari /
atara lagaye catura nari gavata hori ki gari //
badi badi baruni taruni karani rupa jovana matavari /
chabi-phulela alaken jhalaken lalaken lakhi chaila bihari //
hava bhava ke bhavana kidhau bhaunhana ki upama bhari /
vasikarana kaidhaun jantra mantra mohana mana ki phandavari //
ancala men na samata badi akhiyan cancala aniyari /
janon gansi gajabela kama ki sruta kharasana samvari //
besara ke moti ki latakana matakana ki balihari /

manon madana mohana ju kau mana ancavata adhara sudha ri //
biri mukha musikana dasana damakata cancala cauka ri /
kaundhi jata manon ghana men damini chabi ki punja chata ri //
syama bindu gori thodi men upama catura bicari /
janon aravinda cubhyau na calai macalyau ali kau cikula ri //
pota jota dulari tilari tarakuli sravana khutala ri /
khayana bane kancana bijayathe karana curi gajara ri //
campakali cauki gunja gajamohina ki mala ri /
karain catura cita ki cori dori ke jugala jhaba ri //
paine sukha daine kancana kuca khubhi kancuki kari /
kama kuti kara dini hai kini siva son phira yari //
edi lala mahavara jehara tehara bajana vari /
ghayala kiye pamya payala kara sayala nanda lala ri //
jora ditha son ditha itha majitha rangana ranga bhari /
lagi lala kai pagi khagi cita citavana ki picakari //
mohana madana gopala lala para padi gulala jaba dari /
sanga lagyau dolai rasiya vrindavana men banavari //
chabi daurana morana marora piya jaya bhare ankavari /
prema phanda pakare jakare gori nen giravara dhari //
china lai murali kara ten patuka pata pita utari //
gvalina adhara dhari vamsi varasi rasa sindhu sudhari /
jo bhavai so lai lalana kalana palana mohi pyari /
tohi dada ki saun hai gvalini dai vamsi ha-ha ri //
bamhana men bamhe cahen mukha canda-cakora piyari /
mohana syama tamala bala lapatani hema lata ri //
gantha jora gobinda canda son dini sakhina samvari /
tari dai-dai gari gaven gvala deta kilakari //
vasikarana baliyana rasa barasata barasane ki nari /
prabhu ghansyama diyau mana meva phaguva pranana pyari //

Translation: H. S. Mathur

The tight blouse of one of the cowherd girls is wet, and her *sārī* is perfumed with the light scent of saffron. She wears a lovely printed skirt around her waist which looks very charming. Many times her lover puts his arm around her in the play of Phāg, while she sings the abusive songs of Holi. Her big, big eyelashes denote her youth and beauty, and she is mad with excitement. With scented oil applied, her eyes seem to be enamored of Krishna. It is hard to find similes to match the Enchanter's (Mohana, Krishna) amorous movements. It seems as if the Enchanter lays traps for the girls' hearts with enticing *mantras* and magical diagrams (*jantra*).

One girlfriend cannot cover her darting big eyes with a veil, as if the pointed, sharp spears of the god of love can be stopped. While her pearl nosering swings hither and thither in a beautiful manner, the heart of the Enchanter wants to enjoy the nectar of her lips. She wears beautiful earrings, and when she smiles her teeth shine like bright lightning flashing in the clouds. On her fair chin there is a dark spot, like a baby bee attracted by a lotus but not wanting to move. She wears a garland of two stringed golden necklaces, a black dot, and two types of earrings. She also wears bangles, arm ornaments, and flower garlands, as well as wreaths of ivory, *campa* flowers, and *guñjā* seeds. She steals the hearts of everyone.

Like two tassles on a string, her breasts steal all hearts. Her golden breasts are tightly bound, even giving her some pain. It looks if the god of love has developed a friendship with Śiva. Her ankle bells produce a tinkling sound, but have wounded her feet. The Son of Nanda is enamored of all this. Joining eye to eye, their eyes appear reddish. One girl shot a powerful glance at the feet of Krishna as if with a watergun. And after she threw some red powder on Love's Enchanter along with an enchanting spell, amorous Krishna wandered behind her all over Vrindaban. And when Krishna rushed and tightly embraced the girl, the fair-skinned girl caught him in the net of love. She snatched his flute and took off his yellow scarf. When the garlanded one put the flute to her lips, extreme charm flowed. Krishna said, "Oh beloved, take anything from me, but swear by your brother that you will give me back my flute." Joining his arms with hers, he wanted to kiss his beloved's lips, like a *cakora* bird thirsting for the moon. The Enchanter looks like a young dark *tamāla* tree, and the girl clinging to him like a golden vine. Rādhā's girlfriends tie her knot with that of Krishna, and then cry out with joy, hurling abuses and singing taunts. Their voices have an enchanting effect on all the ladies of Barsana. The poet Ghanaśyāma gives those lovely ladies some dried fruit as a gift for the Phāg season.

26a and 26b. Dou rajata jugala kisora (Two Young Men Shine), RV 1.194-195, Gaṅgala Prabhu

As a comparison, we include recordings of this poem of Gaṅgala Prabhu by two different singers, Śrī Krishna Caitanya Bhatt and Śrī Rajendra Sharma. As in the previous track, the first example here is by Śrī Krishna Caitanya Bhatt, which is rendered in a quick Dīp Chandī. Example 26a by "Bhattaji" continues up to the line that ends on "*lagana laga.*" Example 26b, by Śrī Rajendra Sharma ("Masterji"), ends at the word "*bamsuri*" in line seven. Notice that in the Bhatt version the melody changes by the third line on "*uta sri madana gopala.*" Sharma's version is more conservative in keeping with his normal style. There are fast repeats on the verses.

dou rajata jugala kisora ati ananda bhare /
braja juvatina ke cita cora parama vicitra khare //dhru o//
uta sri madana gopala sakha ansana bhuj dine /
itahi kumvari radhika mela apanau sanga line //
kumvari kumvara son neha hai badhyau ati anuraga /
nikasi gamva ke goire hari khelana lage phaga //
bajata dapha bamsuri tala mili madhura mridangana /
gavata saranga raga sunata sukha upajata angana //
nara narinu kai nekahu laja rahi nahin gata /
kachu kahata kachu vai kahen ho, sabai syama ranga gata //
taba tina gvalana umangi lai hathana picakari /
juvatina ken mukha bharata deta horina ki gari //
ghata kiyain citavata phirai uta chailana ke baga /
savadhana saba gopika ho deta na lagana laga //
tavahi gvalina dhai gahyau sangi hari piya kau /
ankha anji mukha manda diyau sendura kau tikau /
kana ainthi gulaca diyau saba aru dinau mukarai /
calata apane jhunda kon vake khisala parata hain pani //
tabahi nanda ke lala kalapi ika bata vicari /
dharyau triyakau rupa jai bhentin brajanari //
pache te sakucin sabai jaba janyau yaha bhava /

tari dai hari hamsi cale hama liyau sakha kau dava //
tabahi sahacari bhesha eka haladhara kau kinau /
gokula tana hvai ai pahira nilau pata jhinon //
tahi milana kesau cale kari agraja ki kani /
ita citavata ducite bhaye uta gahe gvalini ani //
kou ali bhuja teki kou patuka jhakajhorai /
kou dhari hari milai kou mukha son mukha jorai //
kou naina ki saina dai kahai to garbhita bhai /
kahu batana lai lala ki murali lai chidai //
chutana paye tabahi daina phaguva jaba manyau /
ranga ranga basana mangaya diyau jahi jaisau banyau /
kahu bhushana pana dai kahu tana musikai /
ekana ankon bhari cale hari sabakau bhalau manai //
nana barana bilasa rasa kine vrindavana /
harakhita kari ballavi parama sukha saun ju gopagana //
madana lajanau dekhi kai sri kamala-naina ki keli /
gangala prabhu ae gharain ho saba sukha sagara jheli //

Translation: H. S. Mathur

The joyful young men, Krishna and Balarāma, are very graceful and capture the hearts of the young girls of Braj. On one side is Cowherd Cupid (Krishna), resting his arms on the shoulders of his friends. On the other side is Rādhā, along with her girlfriends. The mutual love of Prince and Princess (Krishna and Rādhā) increases. In the precincts of the village of Vrindaban, Hari (Krishna) starts celebrating Phāg (Holi). Drum, flute, and tambourine are played, creating a sweet sound together. Some people sing the *rāga* Saranga which gladdens the heart. Men and women have no hesitation of any sort: some say this and others that, but all are drenched in dark colors. Then, with great gusto the Gvālinas (cowherd women) take water syringes in their hands. The lips of these young maidens are full of Holi's teases and taunts.

Groups of young men wander about, cautiously waiting to pounce upon young ladies. But the girls are cautious, too, and don't give them any chance. Just then, the girls run and capture a companion of the beloved Remover of Sin (Hari,

Krishna). Smearing his eyes and blackening his face, they place colored powder on his forehead. They then pull his ears, push him and show him his funny face in a mirror. When he returns to his own group, his feet drag in embarrassment. Then the Son of Nanda (Nandalāla, Krishna) makes a plan of his own. Disguising himself as a woman, he meets with the maidens of Braj. When the maidens discover his deception, they become most ashamed. Nonetheless, Hari departs clapping and laughing, and saying that he takes revenge for their treatment of his dear friend.

Then, a girl disguises herself as Plow-bearer (Halādhara, Balarāma). She comes near Gokula wearing a thin blue veil. Showing respect to his elder brother, Fine-hair (Keśava, Krishna) goes forward to meet him. While he is confused by the disguise, some girls capture him. One girl holds his arm and another shakes his shawl. One girl holds Krishna down and another puts her face near his. Then some girls look him in the eye and speak proudly. Some others lure him by their sweet words and then snatch his flute. Krishna can free himself only by agreeing to present Phagwa (Phālguna) gifts to all of them. Procuring many things, he gives dresses (*sārīs*) of different colors according to their choices. He also gives ornaments and betel leaves to some, and lovingly smiles at others. He even embraces some of the girls. Having satisfied everyone, Krishna then departs. In this way, he performs all kinds of romantic pranks in Vrindaban, and in the end, makes all the cowherd boys and girls very happy and content. Seeing the wonderful amorous dalliances of Kānhaiyā (Krishna), even the god of love is put to shame. Having experienced this great ocean of pleasure, the poet Gaṅgala Prabhu returns home.

[CD 4]

27. Suranga hori khelai samvarau (Krishna Plays Colorful Holi), RV 1.196-198, Chīta Svāmī

This is a poem by the Vallabhite poet Chīta Svāmī. As mentioned before, several poems by members of the Ashtachap group (eight poets: Sūra Dāsa, Nanda Dāsa, Paramānanda Dāsa, Kumbhana Dāsa, Chīta Svāmī, Kṛṣṇa Dāsa, Govinda Svāmī, Caturbhuja Dāsa) are contained in the Rādhāvallabha Songbook. These are, however, rendered in the style of Samāj-Gāyan rather than the Rāga Saṅgīta style of Puṣṭi Mārg (Vallabhite) tradition. In this recording of only three lines, the *rāga* is Vrindabani Sarang and the *tāla* is Dīp Chandī. There are no cymbals.

suranga hori khelai samvarau sri-vrindavana manjha //surangi o//
braja ki nava-nava nagari ghiri ain saba samjha //surangi o//
sarasa vasanta suhavani ritu ai sukha daina //surangi o//
mate madhupani kokila kala kala baina //surangi o//
phule kamala kalindaja kesu kusuma suranga //suranga o//
campaka bakula gulaba ke saundhe sindhu taranga //surangi o//
subala subai sridama se pathaye sakha sikhaya //surangi o//
baje bajain nava rangi line dhola madhaya //surangi o//
runja muraja dapha bamsuri bherina kau bharapura //surangi o//
phunka naphiri pheri kai uncai gai sruti dura //surangi o//
braja kau prema kaha laun kahaun kesara son ghata puri //surangi o//
kancana ki picakariyan marata hain taki duri //surangi o//
andhi adhika abira ki coba ki maci kica //surangi o//
phaili rela phulela ki candana bandana bica //surangi o//
phula chari gahi hatha saun marata bamha uthai //surangi o//
ancala cancala pharaharain paine naina nacaya //surangi o//
braja ki navala ju nagari sundara sura udara //surangi o//
khelana ai sabai ghirin sri radha ke darabara //surangi o//
sri radha ki priya sakhi lalita lola subhai //surangi o//
chala kari chailahi chiraka kai hamsi bhaji daha kai //surangi o//
nari kau bhesha banai kain pathyau sakha sikhaya //surangi o//
ati hi adhika kahavati lalita bheti jaya //surangi o//
genduka niki phula ki dini sri radha hatha //surangi o//
aya acanaka aucaka taki mare brajanatha //surangi o//
braja ki bithi samkari uta jamuna kau ghata /surangi o//
baladau kaun bolikai dinen gadha kapata //surangi o//
haladhara hain ju kaha bali sance tuma balarasa //surangi o//
bala kau bala ju kaha bhayau, gahi bandhe bhuja pasa //surangi o//

nainana anjana anji kain saundhau upara dhara //surangi o//
pamya pari dvara pathai dae rasa ki rasi vicara //surangi o//
hamsi bhajin saba dai daga avana dine aura //surangi o//
madana gupala bulaya ken gahi lain barajora //surangi o//
giri dharyau kara vama son khara maryau gahi pamya //surangi o//
tinakau bhara kahan gayau lalita leta uthaya //surangi o//
ghara men gheri sabai calin sri radha kon sanga leta //surangi o//
dou jana khenca milai kain nainana kon sukha deta //surangi o//
taba lalita hamsi yon kahyau sri radha kaun sira naya //surangi o//
nilambara son dhampi kain mukha mundau musikyaya //surangi o//
uta sridama acapalau ita lalita ati lola //surangi o//
bica visakha sakha ki murali mangata ola //surangi o//
vasavasi vrishabhana kau madana sakha vakau nama //surangi o//
syama mate kau milaniyan vasa kiyau saba gama //surangi o//
pathyau madana basithai dhitha maha mada lola //surangi o//
china auren china aura saun chakyau chaila duchola //surangi o//
madana madana gulala kaun haladhara kaun lai ava //surangi o//
sri radha ki disa jaya ken campyau hai hamsi pamva //surangi o//
sridama hamsi yon kahyau meva dehu mangaya //surangi o//
nenka hamare syama kaun anana kau madhu pyaya //surangi o//
bhaga suhaga sabai badhau khelata phagu vinoda //surangi o//
sri radha madhava baithore braja-rani ki goda //surangi o//
bhushana deta jasomati pahunci pamya pachela //surangi o//
ghade tika tikavari hira hara hamela //surangi o//
sri vitthala pada padma ki pavana rainu pratapa //sngurangi o//
chitaswami giridhara mile mete tana ke tapa //surangi o//

Translation: H. S. Mathur

Krishna plays colorful Holi in Vrindaban [this line repeats after every verse]. All the young ladies of Braj gather together there in the evening. The pleasing and lovely Spring season has arrived, for the honeybees and cuckoos make pleasing sounds and are exhilarated. Flowers like the lotus and the *kesu* sprout in the river Yamunā, and other flowers like the *campaka*, *bakula* and rose float in the waves of the river. Krishna sends his friends Subāla, Subāhu, and Śrīdāma there and they make music. The *dholaka* drums, the *ruñja*, the *muraja*, the tambourine, the flute, and the trumpet are all in full play. The sound of the clarinet reaches quite far. How much of the bliss of Braj can I describe?

Clay pitchers are full of saffron. Holi celebrants holding golden waterguns aim them from a distance. Red powder flows as in a storm. There is so much colored Holi water that a hole has been dug in the earth. The smell of hair oil also spreads there amidst the aroma of sandalwood. The celebrants of Holi raise their hands and strike each other with sticks made of flowers. The scarves of the girls flap in the wind, and their sharp eyes squint. The beautiful young ladies of Braj are large-hearted and have come to celebrate Holi in the company of Rādhā. Among them, the dearest friend of Rādhā, Lalitā, is specially attractive. Through trick, Lalitā sprinkles Holi water on Krishna and, laughing, runs away making loud noises. After being advised for some time, one of Krishna's friends comes forth dressed like a woman. Lalitā, being very talkative, goes and meets him (her). A ball made of flowers is placed in the hands of Rādhā, and suddenly she aims and throws it at Krishna.

The lanes of Braj on the other bank of the Yamunā River are very narrow. Balarāma (Krishna's brother) is summoned. Closing the doors of their homes, the girls say, "You are called Plow-bearer. Let us see how strong you really are! What has happened to the so-called power of Balarāma?" Then they tie down both his hands, put black collyrium on his body and cover him with a sheet. They shower him with taunts and send him outside, considering this a prank of Holi season. The girls then run away, laughing mischievously, and allow others to come.

They grab at and catch Cowherd Cupid (Madanagopāla, Krishna) forcibly, bringing him along as well. The girls taunt, "Krishna lifted Govardhan Hill with his left arm and killed a demon with his foot. But what has happened to all those powers when Lalitā lifts Krishna up in the air?" Surrounding Krishna, the girls enter the house of Rādhā. They all hug each other and share great happiness. Then, smiling and enjoying,

Rādhā bends down pleadingly as if to cover Krishna's face with a blue cloth. On one side is Śrīdāma who is very naughty, and on the other side is Lalitā who is specially frolicsome. In between them is Viśākhā as a witness, requesting Krishna to pawn his flute.

Now there is another friend of Krishna named Madana who is well trusted and loyal, and who always supports Krishna. Having enchanted the entire village, Krishna sends him as an envoy to talk with this and that girl. Being very clever, Krishna urges him to bring Balarāma back to him. The envoy then goes to Rādhā and touches her feet in plea for her return. Śrīdāma laughs in the midst of this and, ordering some dried fruit, asks Rādhā to give a little of the nectar of her lips to our Krishna: "Let Krishna kiss you." In this way, their pleasure increases while celebrating Phāg. The girls then make Rādhā and Krishna sit on the lap of Mother Yaśodā (Brajarāṇī). Mother Yaśsodā distributes many ornaments like golden bangles, bracelets, and other beautifully crafted ornaments—even a necklace made of diamonds. Says the poet Chīta Svāmī, "having met Krishna by the grace of Śrī Viṭṭhala and by the dust of his lotus feet, all ailments and bodily pains are extinguished."

28. Nainana men picakari dai (You Squirt Water in My Eyes), RV 1.260, Śrī Śālagrāma Jī

This poem by Śrī Śālagrāma Jī is classified as a Holi Rasiyā, as is Song 20. The pace is moderately fast and steady throughout. It is set in the *rāga* Bhairavi (S R̲ G̲ M P D̲ N̲ s) in Keherva̅. As is found in this musical genre, there is a touch of R and D. The insertion of [*mohe*] in the first line is used as a filler. While this word does not appear in the original text, it has been supplied by the singers. Occasionally this device is used to round out a line or fill in a space. The most common filler is "*mai*" or "*eri mai*" at the end of a line. This is simply an exclamation like "O Dear," and generally fits in with the meaning of the poem. The term "*mohe*" here means "to me" or "with me," and gives some accent to the meaning of the line. The phrase "*hori kheli na jaya*" is repeated after the verses. Notice the faster hand cymbals in the repeats of this song.

nainana men picakari dai, [mohe] gari dai, hori kheli na jaya //teka//
kyonre langara langarai mote kinhin, kesara kica kapolana dinhin,
liye gulala thadau musakaya, hori kheli na jaya //
naika na kana karata kau ki, najara bacavai baladau ki,
panaghata saun ghara laun bataraya, hori kheli na jaya //
aucaka kucana kuma-kuma marai, ranga suranga sisa son dharai,
yaha udhama suni sasa risaya, meri nanada risaya, hori kheli na jaya //
hori ke dinana moson dunon-dunon arujhai,
saligarama kauna jaya barajai, anga lapata hamsi ha-ha khaya, hori kheli na jaya //

Translation: H. S. Mathur

"Naughty Krishna, you squirt water in my eyes. why do you play this game of mischief with me? I am unable to play Holi with you. You place a mixture of paste on my face, and now you smile with a handful of red powder. I am unable to play Holi with you. You have not the least restraint. You avoid the glance of Balarāma. You continue to talk all the way from the waterfront to the house, but I am unable to play Holi with you. You even throw balls of color upon my chest, and then you throw color on my head. Learning of this, my mother-in-law and sister-in-law become very angry. I am unable to play Holi with you." Krishna entangles Rādhā more and more during the Holi season and poet Śrī Śālagrāma says, who can stop him? He smiles and embraces her and then begs her pardon, but still she is unable to play Holi.

29. Gaunhana paryau ri mere (Oh Shame Surrounds Me), RV 1.262, Ghanaśyāma Jī

Another Holi Rasiyā, this poem by Ghanaśyāma Jī is played in medium Kehervā in an almost folk-like tune. The notes used comprise the basic major scale of Vilaval. There are fast repeats on the verses beginning with "*yaki ghali.*"

gaunhana paryau ri mere gaunhana paryau /
samvarau salaunau dhota mere gaunhana paryau //
yaki ghali meri ali kahau kita jaun /
bansuri men gavai vaha lai-lai merau naun //
samvare kamalanaina agen neku ai /
lajana ke mare mopai kahun gayaui na jai //
jo haun citaun adau dai-dai cira /
sennana men kahai cala kunja kutira //
angana men thadi hun ata cadhi avai /
mukata ko chahiyan mere paina chuvavai //
hita ghanasyama milongi dhai /
samvare salaune binu rahyaui na jaya //

Translation: H. S. Mathur

I cannot go out anywhere because of embarrassment. Krishna chases me constantly. This lovely, dark-eyed boy pursues me. He has smitten me with love. Now friend, where can I go? He plays the flute and calls me. O, lotus-eyed, dark Krishna, come in before me for a while. Out of shame, I cannot go out. Wherever I glance I see his scarf, and Krishna tells me with his eyes, "Let us go to the isolated grove together." When I stand in the courtyard, he climbs over the wall and touches my feet with his crown. The poet Ghanaśyāma Jī says that Rādhā will go quickly to meet Krishna, as she cannot live without that dark and beautiful Śyāma.

Hori Dol—The Swing Festival

30. Jhulata dou navala kisora (Two Fresh Youths Are Swinging), RV 1.269, Śrī Hita Harivaṃśa

This is a song by Śrī Hita Harivaṃśa commemorating the swing festival known as Dola Yātrā during the month of Holi. It is set in Tintāl to a variation of the *rāga* Gaud Malhar. Only the last portion of this poem is included on the recording, from the words "*dai nava uraja akora,*" in the sixth line, to the end. This charming tune is also used for several poems of the Rainy Season (Volume 2). The first line begins with "*dou navala kisora*" and ends with "*jhulata.*"

jhulata dou navala kisora /
rajani janita ranga sukha sucata anga-anga uthi bhora //
ati anuraga bhare mili gavata sura mandara kala ghora /
bica-bica pritama cita corata priya naina ki kora //
avala ati sukumara darata mana vara hindora jhakora /
pulaki-pulaki pritama ura lagata dai nava uraja akora //
urajhi vimala mala kankana son kundala son kaca dora /
bepatha juta kyaun banai vivecata ananda badhyau na thora //
nirakhi-nirakhi phulata lalitadika bibi mukha candra cakora /
dai asisa harivamsa prasansata kari ancala ki chora //

Translation: H. S. Mathur

Youthful Rādhā and Krishna are swinging. The night scene generates pleasure in every limb as they experience the enjoyment of their passion. They sing in the lower registers out of pure love, full of deep sound. Occasionally, he glances toward his beloved and steals her heart. With the fast swinging of the *jhulā* (swing), Rādhā is suddenly frightened. She embraces Krishna with great pleasure, holding him close to her breasts. But then her beautiful garland becomes entangled in his bracelet, and the string tying her hair is caught in his earring. The pleasures of their entanglement become very deep and are difficult to analyze. When the girlfriends, Lalitā and others, see the moon-like faces with their *cakora*-like eyes, they become very happy. Śrī Harivaṃśa blesses and praises the couple, veiling himself out of modesty.

31. Jamuna pulina suhavanau (The Yamunā's Beautiful Bank), RV 1.272-273, Śrī Dāmodara Dāsa

This poem describing the Dola Yātrā or Swing Festival of Holi by Śrī Dāmodara Dāsa (1613-1643) is performed in *rāga* Miśra Kafi with the inclusion of G and G̲. It begins in medium Dīp Chandī, and alternates with Tintāl in the verses. The fast repeats of the verses include very quick playing of the hand cymbals. The patterns resolve with the words, "*dola suhavanau.*" The portions included on this recording are the beginning up to line twelve, then a break that resumes with the penultimate line of "Damodara hita."

jamuna pulina suhavanau, ranga bhine jhulain /
tana mana moda badhai, dola suhavanaun ranga bhine jhulain //
kancana khambha jatita bane, ranga bhine jhulain /
dekhata mana lalacai, dola suhavanaun ranga bhine jhulain //
navala lala nava ladili //ranga //
mudita sakhi yaha bhai //dola //
manaun juga sasi ekathan //ranga//
kumudita phuli dinga ai //dola//
nila pita pata rajahin //ranga//
bhushana rahe chabi chai //dola//
yaha chabi kavi ko kahi sakai //ranga//
citavana mridu musikai //dola//
caraun driga cancala bane //ranga//
upama kachu thaharai //dola//
manaun rupa tadaga men //ranga//
khelata mina subhai // dola//
madhura-madhura sura gavahin //ranga//
khaga mriga rahe lubhai //dola//
adbhuta ranga badhyau tahan //ranga//
sarada bali-bali jaya //dola//
suranga gulala akhanda saun //ranga//
gagana rahyau ghamadai //dola//
manu hari upara kama nai //ranga//

racyau hai vitana banai //dola//
bada jhotana bhaya bhamini //ranga//
lagata piya tana dhai //dola//
manahu sundara megha saun //ranga//
chabili chata lapatai //dola//
sobha ke sagara dou //ranga//
china-china chabi adhikai //dola//
damodara hita rasika je //ranga//
jivata yaha jasa gai //dola//

Translation: Chandrakala Pandey

The bank of the Yamunā River is very pleasant to behold! Krishna sits on a swing, and the pillars on either side are gold and studded with many jewels. The picturesque beauty of this scene enchants everyone. Rādhā then joins Krishna on the swing and it seems that two moons are sitting together. Several girlfriends sit in front of them looking like lilies, all decked out in blue and yellow cloth with ornaments. No poet can describe their beauty, as they glance here and there, smiling. As their eyes move back and forth, the poet offers a simile—their eyes are like beautiful ponds in which two fish swim and play. All the girlfriends sing with sweet voices, and birds and animals are attracted to this spot upon hearing to them. The atmosphere is very difficult to express in language. It is amazing—even Sarasvatī is stunned. There are clouds above, and it seems like the sky is a canopy, giving shade to all. This ocean of beauty is boundless. The poet Dāmodara becomes immortal after singing this song, praising Rādhā and Krishna.

32. Mohana mohani suhelara gaun (I Sing a Happy Song for the Enchanter and Enchantress), RV 1. 306-307, Bihāriṇī Dāsa

This is a Rādhāvallabha rendition of the first four lines of a poem by Bihāriṇī Dāsa of the Haridāsī Sampradāya. It is performed in the *rāga* Misra Kafi (with addition of N) and in

Cautāl (12 *mātrās*: 4-4-4), the most common rhythmic cycle of Dhrupad. There is a fast repeat of lines three and four.

mohana mohani suhelara gaun /
ladili lala gahelara ladaun //
sri vrindabana ghana sahaja sobha mana lobha upajavai /
jinakon kripa karen sri syama tinahin sunyaun jasa bhavai /
vipina vilasina prema prakasina jo nija premahin paun /
jyonhin-jyonhin kunja vihara karau mili tyonhin-tyonhin tumahin ladaun //
sunahu saheli prema gaheli kautika eka dikhaun /
ancala jori citai trina toraun tana mana moda badaun //
rayabela satabarga sevati bica-bica campe ki kaliyan /
raci-raci causara hara gundai guhi pahiravana calin aliyan //
kusumita kunja gunja ali mala candana carcita galiyan /
sukhada samara bahata saurabha jala kamala virajata thaliyan //
sarasa hamsa cakora mora pika catraka bhasha bhaliyan /
gavata rasa jasa piya pyari kau sakhi suni paga prema na taliyan //
kabahun ka bala salajja sapiya tana kabahun hamsata mukha mori /
kabahun ka nipuna surata sukha sagara nagara navala kisori //
china-china prati dampati nava-nava rati anga-anga abhirama /
prathama samagama syama dinahin dina dulaha dulahini syama //
amsana amsa jori bhuja ballabha bhamini jamini jage /
vilasata hamsata hamsavata rasa vasa ati ananda anurage //
nautana tarala tamala lala mili lata lalita phala phaliyan /
deta asisa biharina dasi karahu navala nita raliyan

Translation: H. S. Mathur

For Enchanter and Enchantress, I sing a Suhelera (auspicious, joyful) song and for the boy and girl I arrange a Gahelera contest. The clouds of Vṛndāvana are a naturally beautiful sight and attract the heart. Only by the grace of Śrī Rādhā does one hear the fame of Cloud-dark Lord (Śyāma, Krishna). As you enjoy yourselves in a forest bower and express your love, how can I fathom your affection? The more you engage in love play in the forest groves, the more I will arrange your love-battles. O friend, immersed in love, I will show you some fun as I tie knots in your clothing, break a straw with my teeth (a sign of determination) and enjoy physical and mental pleasure. A certain type of vine has seven branches and the *campaka* bush has buds between them. Making a four-stringed garland the girlfriends offer it to Rādhā and Krishna. The forest bower is full of beautiful flowers, and the buzzing of black bees, and garlands of sandalwood fill the lanes. Full of fragrance, a soothing breeze blows and plenty of lotus flowers adorn the ponds. In pleasing tones, cranes, swans, *cakora* birds, and peacocks chatter. They sing of the famed love of Rādhā and Krishna and the affection of their girlfriends. Hearing all this brings boundless bliss. Sometimes Rādhā shyly embraces Krishna, and sometimes she turns her face away and smiles. Sometimes, though a young adolescent, Rādhā reveals her adeptness in amorous play. Moment by moment the couple expresses their mutual adoration. Each of their limbs is beautiful. From their first meeting and then, day after day, they look like bride and bridegroom, thoroughly joining their arms. Remaining awake the whole night, Rādhā and Krishna are full of love for one another as they smile and engage in love play, just like a young *tamāla* tree and a clinging vine that have joined to blossom and give fruit. Bihārinī Dāsī blesses them and wishes that they may play like this every day.

33. Dulaha dulahini adhika bani (Bride and Groom Fully Decorated), RV 1. 307, Bihāriṇī Dāsa

This is another poem by Bihāriṇī Dāsa of the Haridāsī Sampradāya. The first line is set in a slow Dhamār. By the second line, the tempo picks up to a fast Rūpak with very intricate hand cymbal playing. Specific to this song are the downward leaps in the melody. The third line resumes the Dhamār pattern again. The last two lines change over into a medium Keherva until the end, with repeat of the refrain.

dulaha dulahini adhika bani /
pujana cali kalpa taru sundara aurahi thamna thani //
kiyau sakhina gathajora sabana mili age dhana pache ju dhani /
gavata calin gita mangala ke sabahi sughara sajani //
runaka jhunaka paga dharata dharani para chabi pavata avani /

chiraki sugandha mula taru pujyau phulana mala ghani //
ancala jori yahai vara mangaun rchau yaha prema sani /
sri rasika biharina ho na mana chaka keli kala kamani //

Translation: Chandrakala Pandey

The bride and bridegroom are fully decorated. As they go to worship the *kalpataru*, a tree which fulfills all wishes, the girlfriends tie their clothes together with *dupaṭṭā*. Krishna is two steps behind Rādhā. All the cowherd girls sing songs, and Rādhā's anklets make beautiful sounds. Both Rādhā and Krishna offer scents and garlands of flowers along with their prayers to the base of the *kalpataru*. They pray for their love to become immortal. The poet Bihārinī Dāsa is enamored of Rādhā and Krishna who are masters of the arts of love.

Caitra—First Month of the Hindu Year

34. Pyari sahajahi mana hari leta (His Lover Easily Steals Hari's Heart), RV 1.319-320, Nāgarī Dāsī

This poem of Nāgarī Dāsī is rendered in slow Rūpak (7 *mātrās*). The scale is Vilaval with the addition of accidentals like upper g̱. The tune, like many in the Rādhāvallabha Songbook, is meandering and complex when compared with the normal *sthāyī* and *antarā* of classical songs. Significant here is the repeat of the word "*aho*" in the middle of the fourth and sixth lines. Only the first six lines are included in the recording.

pyari sahajahi mana hari leta /
tu mana mohani ri mohana heta //
tuma ati prema pravina ho (pyari) sughara siromani jnana /
mana krama bacana bilasini mere tuma bina gati nahin ana //
tu tana tu mana men basi (pyari) tu mama jivana prana /
tu sarvasa dhana manini dai mohi mana rati dana //
bhamini tuva bhuvachepa ho (pyari) mopai sahyau na jaya /

ancala pala alakavali ke antara mana akulaya //
mo mana aisi hota hai (pyari) to tana men mili jaun /
tuva mukha candra cakora lon naina pana karata na aghaun //
sravana suyasa rasana rasaun tuva karata rahon guna gana /
jancata jyon jala mina lon tuva darasa parasa aghrana //
tuma lavani guna nidhi agari (pyari) aba jina karahu nidana /
purana prema prakasani dai mohi adhara madhu pana //
taba lalita bacana suni syama ke (pyari) nainana men musikyaya /
vyakula viraha biloki ken pyari liye hain lala ura laya //
main mana kiyau tuma son kabai pyare kalapi-kalapi kita leta /
mere pritama prana hau piya jivana tumahin sameta //
(taba) lataki lagi ura syama ke (pyari) hulasata hamsata udara /
koka nipuna nava nagari barabasa kiye sukumvara //
bhaye madana matta rasa madhuri sukha barasata sukhana aghai /
nirakhi harakhi rasa phulahin sri-lalitadika sukha pai //
surata ranga men rangi rahyau (ho) kunja sadana sukha rasi /
sri-vipula-viharini dasi para bali navala nagari dasi //

Translation: H. S. Mathur

His Lover (Rādhā) effortlessly steals Hari's heart. The Enchanter (Mohana, Krishna) tells her, "You are adept in the arts of love, and I know you as a beautiful crown jewel. By your heart, words, and deeds, you are amorous and I cannot live without you. You reside in my body and in my heart; you are my very life breath. You have all the wealth and I beg that you give me the gift of love. I am unable to bear the closing of my eyes; even when you cover your eyes with a scarf I become desperate. O Dear! I feel in my heart as if I am joined with your body. Your face is like the moon, and I am like a *cakora* bird that is never sated, drinking in your appearance. I wish to compose a song in praise of your beauty, a song to attract the ear. Like a fish writhing for water, I thirst for you, enjoying your sight, touch, and sweet smell. Don't delay the climax—please give me a sweet kiss on my lips as a fulfillment of our love." Hearing these words of Krishna, Rādhā smiles with her eyes. Then, seeing that Krishna is pining in separation, she embraces him, saying, "I have never shown any annoyance, so why do you trouble yourself! You are my beloved, my life, and my life is for you." Then she falls into his arms, and becomes very happy and full of laughter. Rādhā, expert in sports of love, thus makes Krishna helpless. Then both of them become so engrossed in love play that there is no end to their pleasure—happiness flows everywhere. The girlfriends of Rādhā, Lalitā and others, are full of happiness when they witness this amorous play. The forest bower is colored by the play of love and joy. The poet Nāgarī Dāsī offers herself in the service of the great, vivacious beauty (Rādhā).

35. Kalinda nandini su tira (Bank of the Daughter of Kalinda), RV 1.333, Nāgarī Dāsa

This poem of Nāgarī Dāsa conforms to the Dhrupad pattern of Cautāl in the *rāga* Bhupali (derived from pentatonic scale of S R G P D s). The *Sam* is on the syllable "*-lind-*" of the word "*kalinda.*" The verses (*antarā*) begin with "*ubhaya kantha*" and "*sarasa surata,*" which each have fast repeats that continue with a repeat of the refrain. The second line of each verse requires that the singer maintain an upper *ga* as part of the melody, which he does admirably.

kalinda nandini su tira vilasata nava kumvara dhira,
nanda nandana mudita sri vrisabhanu-nandini /
ubhaya kantha bhujana dharain adhara sudha pana karain,
gaura syama anga manaun jalada candini /
komala janu kanaka beli rajata nava ranga naveli
piya ke gata lapata rahi ananda kandani /
sarasa surata sukhana bharain adhara sudha pana karain,
nagari dasa nyauchavara rasika bandini //

Translation: H. S. Mathur

On the bank of the Yamunā River, Nanda's Son (Nandanandana, Krishna) enjoys love play with Vṛṣabhānu's Daughter. As they embrace each other and kiss each others' lips, they resemble the joining of dark cloud with bright lightning during a thunderstorm—or a golden vine clinging to its beloved dark tree. Rādhā is a treasure house of bliss, and Krishna is radiant with enjoyment. Witnessing the amorous pleasure in their kissing, the poet Nāgarī Dāsa offers himself to Rādhā and Krishna.

Hitotsava Mangal Badhāi -- Appearance Day of Śrī Hita Harivaṃśa

The festival starts from full moon day with a chain of auspicious greeting songs.

36. Jai jai sri harivamsa vyasa kula mandana (Glory, Glory to Śrī Harivaṃśa, Ornament of the Vyāsa Family), RV 1.341-342, Sevaka Dāmodara Dāsa

This is one of the most important "signature songs" of the Rādhāvallabha Songbook, composed by Sevaka Dāmodara Dāsa (1577-1610). It commemorates the appearance day of the founder Śrī Hita Harivaṃśa. It is sung with great emotion and consistency within the tradition. Broken up into four large stanzas, these again are each subdivided into slow and faster sections of four lines each. The tune of the faster sections is one of the most unique and recognizable of the "Braj melodies," and is utilized by other *sampradāyas* in Vrindaban including the Gauḍīya (Caitanya) Sampradāya. The beginning sections are performed in a slow Dhamār *tāla*, and the faster sections are in a quick Dīp Chandī. In terms of *rāga*, it displays similarities with Shyam-Kalyan with its characteristic phrases (N S R, *M* P, G M R).

jai jai sri harivamsa vyasa kula mandana /
rasika ananyana mukhya guru jana bhaya khandana //
sri vrindavana vasa rasa rasa bhumi jahan /

kridata syama syama pulina manjula tahan //
pulina manjula parama pavana trividha tahan maruta bahai /
kunja bhavana vicitra sobha madana nita sevata rahai //
tahan santata vyasa nandana rahata kalusha vihangana /
jai jai sri harivamsa vyasa kula mandana //

jai jai sri harivamsa candra uddita sada /
dvija kula kumuda prakasha vipula sukha sampada //
para upakara vicara sumati jaga vistari /
karuna-sindhu kripal kala-bhaya saba hari //
hari saba kalikala ki bhaya kripa rupa ju vapu dharyau /
karata je anasahana nindaka tinahun pai anugraha karyau //
nirabhimana nirvaira nirupama nihakalanka ju sarvada /
jai jai sri harivamsa candra uddita sada //

jai jai sri harivamsa prasansata saba duni /
sarasara vivekata kovida bahu guni //
gupta riti acarana pragata saba jaga diye /
jnana dharma brata karma bhakti kinkara kiye //
bhakti hita je sharana aye dvanda dosha ju saba ghate /
kamala kara jina abhaya dine karma bandhana saba kate //
parama sukhada sushila sundara pahi svamini mama dhani /
jai jai sri harivamsa prasansata saba duni //

jai jai sri harivamsa nama guna gai hai /
prema lakshana bhakti sudridha kari pai hai //
aru badhai rasa riti priti cita na tarai /
jiti vishama samsara kirati jaga vistarai //
vistarai saba jaga vimala kirati sadhu sangati na tarai /
vasa vrinda vipina pavai sri radhikaju kripa karain //
catura jugala kishora sevaka dina prasadahi pai hai /
jai jai sri harivamsa nama guna gai hai //

Translation: H. S. Mathur

Glory, glory to Śrī Hita Harivaṃśa of the illustrious Vyāsa family. He is the remover of the fear of disciples, and chief of the *rasikas* (relishers of rasa). He resides in Vṛndāvana, the land of pleasure where Rādhā and Krishna play. Along the beautiful sacred sands of the Yamunā River, three types of wind blow—cool, slow, and sweet-smelling. There is an enchanting beauty in the bower which is being attended by the god of love. The son of Vyāsa, Hita Harivaṃśa, lives there blamelessly and constantly. Glory, glory to Śrī Hita Harivaṃśa of the illustrious Vyāsa family.

Glory, glory to Śrī Harivaṃśa, upon whom the moon is always shining, and around whom Brahmin families shine like lilies, full of pleasure. With the intention of benefiting others, he describes the glory of Krishna to the world. Hari has removed the fear of the world. Being so kind and benevolent, Krishna removed the dread of the Kali Yuga when he took birth and bestowed favor even on non-believers and those who speak ill of him. He is without pride, without enmity, without comparison, and without any blemish. Glory, glory to Śrī Harivaṃśa, upon whom the moon is always shining.

Glory, glory to Śrī Harivaṃśa, who is widely praised throughout the world. He is very learned and moral, and can always distinguish between right and wrong. Even his secret conduct is known to everybody. Knowledge, religion, vows, good deeds, devotion; all are subservient to him. He came to the protection of Lord Krishna out of love, and all his doubts and deficiencies have subsided. When Krishna gave him his blessings with his lotus hands, all the shackles of *karma* were cut away. Glory, glory to Śrī Harivaṃśa, who is widely praised throughout the world.

Glory, glory to Śrī Harivaṃśa, who is full of praise for Rādhā, who is very noble and beautiful, and a bestower of happiness. May she strengthen his feelings of devotion and love, so that they will go on increasing and never diminish. Having vanquished all obstacles, may his fame spread throughout the world, and may he always be in the company of noble people, *sādhus*. With the kindness of Rādhā, may Śrī Harivaṃśa always find his abode in Vṛndāvana and, being a servant of Rādhā and Krishna, always receive their grace. Glory, glory to Śrī Harivaṃśa, who is full of praise for Rādhā.

37. Sri dvija raja bhavana men rangili (A Celebration in the House of the King of the Twice-born), RV 1.370-371, Śrī Rūpa Kiśorīlāla

This is another poem celebrating the birthday of Śrī Hita Harivaṃśa. Only the first section is given in the recording, but it is an important song of the tradition that is set in a slow Tintāl to the *rāga* Miśra Kafi. The tempo changes with the third line, and the tune changes with the fourth line, which also has a very fast repeat.

sri dvija raja bhavana men rangili bajata aju badhai /
jagamani jani dvija rani jayau suta sukhadai // rangili o//teka//
sune eka rasa ki dvai murata gaura syama ranga bhine /
vrindavana ki sampati dampati nita nava neha navine //
tinakau hita vamsi tain hitamaya trividha eka vapu dhare /
sri harivamsa nama hvai pragate hita svarupa vistare //1//
nava nikunja jau maha madhura rasa adbhuta anga rasilau /
ujjvala rasa ki ujvalata laun jagamagata catakilau //
jakau dhyana dharata hain sripati aise veda bakhanai /
tahi ke ye udaya karana kaun udaya bhaye ruci manai //2//
lakhi aciraja son prathama vyasaju puni rishi-rava sudhi kinau /
taba tau phula uthe dvija nripaju mangala men mana dinau //
phulana mandapa dvara dhuja dhari-kesara ajira lipaye /
bandhi bandana-mala manohara motinu cauka puraye //3//
jala gulaba chirakaya cahu-disi kadali kalita rupaye /
dipavali dipata kari manimaya kancana kalasa bharaye //
tana vitana vividha racana ruci pancaun sabda karavain /
jaya-jaya kahi bajai dundubhi divi sura sumanana barasavain //4//
bhai chabili bhira dvara para kou gavain kou nacain /
magadha manjula vamsa bakhanata suta purанana bancai //
mahideva dhapi dhaye aye nigama ricana sunavain /
padhata kavitta vividha bandi jana aru guna guni dikhavain //5//
eka dharata sira hari duba kaun ika hamsi painu lagain /
ekana bhanta dhari lai age misra nirakhi anuragain //
ghora amola kumakuma candana chirakata saba chavi chaye /
manahun rupa saravara men sundara hema puhupa vikasaye //6//
deta sabacacha dhainu viprana kaun kanaka vasana mani mala /
gaji-gaji ghanalaun dhana barashata jacaka kiye nihala //
bandhu vadhu pahirai mana dai mevana goda bharai /
deta asisa sakala nara nari kirati dhuja phaharai //7//
praphulita rasika rangile bahuvidha ati ananda son dolai /
cita cahata phala paya prema sau sri hita-sri hita bolain //

nitya bihara bhajana-dayaka kau utsava hiyau siravai //
(jaya) sri hita rupa kisorilala yaha umagi-umagi jasa gavai //8//

Translation: H. S. Mathur

Today there are colorful festivities going on at the King of the Twice-Born's palace. His famed queen gave birth a pleasing son; we have heard that one bliss took two forms, one fair-skinned and the other dark-skinned, both are the treasured and lovely children of Vṛndāvana—Krishna and Balarāma. One of them loved his flute very much. His flute later reappeared on earth as Śrī Hita Harivaṃśa.

The bower is very beautiful and colorful, and with the brightness of the whole atmosphere, it scintillates. He is the one of whom the Vedas speak and whom the saints worship; because of his descent into the world, everything looks beautiful. First of all, Vyāsa looks at his son in great wonder. After that the king is full of joy, and gives the blessings of his heart. The courtyard is full of flowers; the king of the twice-born, overjoyed, hears the sound of the birth cry, and thinks of organizing celebrations. Then he arranges for the gateway to be decorated with flowers, and the courtyard is swept with saffron. Lovely garlands are hung, the yard is decorated with pearls, rose water is sprinkled everywhere, and pillars are made of banana plants. The earthen lamps are lit in rows everywhere, and golden ceremonial pitchers are filled. A large tent is constructed very intricately, inside which five different kinds of instruments, including drums, are played as if saying "Victory, victory!" The gods shower flowers from the sky. A great crowd and commotion arises at the main gate—some are singing and some are dancing. Bards describe the glory of the family. Brahmins hastily arrive and start reading the scriptures, including Vedas and ancient traditions. And the poets also begin reading poetical stanzas describing the qualities of the child. Ceremonially, one person places green grass at the head of the baby, and another smiles and touches his feet, while another brings a gift, placing it in front of him while smiling lovingly at baby boy. Someone else sprinkles red powder, sandalwood powder, and scented water all around. It appears as if golden flowers have blossomed in a pond of beauty. The king of the twice-born donates cows with calves to the Brahmins along with gold, new garments, and garlands of jewels. Wealth is even given to the beggars, fulfilling all their wishes. Nuts and dried fruit are distributed respectfully to all the relatives and ladies. All the men and women present are showered with blessings, and the fame of Vyāsa spreads far and wide. Happy, beautiful young boys wander around, receiving all the fruits they love. The poet Śrī Rūpa Kiśorīlāla says that this great celebration with beautiful music is very appealing, and he sings its praises again and again.

Chapter Two: The Rādhāvallabha Songbook, Volume II

[CD 6]

Pāvas Ritu—The Rainy Season

38. Dou jana bhinjata atake batana (The Couple While Being Soaked Talked On), RV 2.78 (SV 23), Śrī Hita Harivaṃśa

This poem of Śrī Hita Harivaṃśa opens our collection of songs sung during the Rainy Season (Pāvas Ritu). Its melody, unique to the Rādhāvallabha Songbook, is the same as Songs 44 and 46. It defies strict *rāga* classification, but the lower portion of the melody resembles *rāga* Dhani (S G̲ M P N̲ s) but with the added D̲. In the *antarā* (second line), there is an immediate breakaway from the *rāga* structure with the notes of s s s g̲ r̲ s s, on the words "*saghana kuñja.*" And then with D̲ in the remainder of the line, all ties with known *rāgas* are abolished. The rhythm is a slow and dignified Rūpak *tāla*. There are some moving fast repeats in the second half of the composition.

dou jana bhinjata atake batana /

saghana kunja ke dvara thade, ambara lapate gatana //
lalita lalita rupa rasa bhiji, bunda bacavata patana /
jaya Sri Hita Harivamsa paraspara pritama,
milavata rati rasa ghatana //

Translation: Charles S. J. White (1996, 99)

It is raining and the couple is entranced in talking.
Their clothes mold their bodies,
    As they stand in the door of the dense bower.
The leaves give raindrop shelter to Rādhā,
    Drenched in the Beloved's beauty.
Śrī Hita Harivaṃś says, the Lover mixes
    Tricks with the *rasa* of erotic pleasure.

39. Nayau neha nava ranga nayau rasa (New is the Love, Novel the Merriment and New the Delight), RV 2.78 (CP 54), Śrī Hita Harivaṃśa

This composition of Śrī Hita Harivaṃśa is one of the most beautifully set Dhrupads in all the Rādhāvallabha Songbook. The *rāga* is a variant of the Gaud Malhar *rāga* (S R G M P N̲ D N s, s D N̲ M P D M P G M R S) and the rhythm is a clearly defined Cautāl (12 beats). The *sam* of the *sthāyī* begins with the word "*nayau*," and the *antarās* (verses) begin with "*nava pitambara.*" These are rendered in fast repeats until the end. The *tanpura* sound adds to the effect, as it was recorded in the Satsanga Bhumi ("Hitashram"), where occasionally Swami Śrī Hita Dasji Maharaj played the *tanpura*. Many of the compositions in this volume were recorded under these circumstances.

nayau neha nava ranga nayau rasa
navala syama vrishabhanu kisori /
nava pitambara navala cunnari
nai - nai bundana bhijata gori //
nava vrindavana harita manohara
nava cataka bolata mora mori /
nava murali ju malara nai gati

sravana sunata aye ghana ghori //
nava bhushana nava mukuta virajata
nai - nai urapa leta thori - thori /
jai sri hita harivamsa asisa deta
mukha cirajivau bhutala yaha jori //

Translation: Rupert Snell (1991, 231-232)

New is the love, novel the merriment and new the delight
of young Śyāma and Vṛṣabhānu's daughter;
new is his yellow garment and new her many-coloured *sārī*,
and with ever new raindrops is the fair one drenched.
Fresh is Vṛndāvana, verdant and captivating,
where the young cuckoo calls with peacock and pea-hen;
new is the flute which [plays] the Malāra *rāga* with a novel lilt,
and hearing it massy clouds have gathered.
Resplendent with new ornaments and new diadems
they take ever new and dainty *urapa* steps;
Hita Harivaṃśa utters this benediction:
may this pair live long on the earth!

40. Suhavani bunda lagai mana bhai (The Rain of Love Pleases the Heart, Brother), RV 2.84, Śrī Rūpa Lāla

This poem of Śrī Rūpa Lāla (1718-1818) is played in a slow Tintāl, and begins with the words, "*bunda lagai.*" The charming melody is in the *rāga* Gaud Malhar. The lead voice is unfortunately a bit weak in the recording. However, the tune can be heard in the line of the harmonium (which almost always follows the melody), and the words can be comprehended in the choral repeats, which include the word "*suhavani*" at the tail end. There are fast repeats on the *antarās* beginning on the fourth line. Notice the fine interplay between the cymbals and the *pakhavāj* on the fast repeats, including a *tihāi* (triple repeated phrase) at the end after the refrain.

suhavani bunda lagai mana bhai /
uta camakana damini bhamini ita ghana ghanasyama durai //
neha nira varashata harasata driga cataka laun rata lai /
hiya abhilasha sarovara purita bana tana tapa mitai //
praphulita kumudavali ali gana mana priti lata sara-sai /
jai sri rupalala hita sahacari sevata dampati prema badai //

Translation: H. S. Mathur

The drizzling rain of love is very pleasing to the heart. On one side the flashes of lightning are like the fair Braj ladies, and on the other, the dark clouds are comparable to Ghanaśyāma (Krishna). The rain of love is very soothing to the eyes, and the Cāṭaka bird is constantly singing. All the desires of one's heart are fulfilled like a pond filled with water in the forest, and all the passions of the body are satisfied. Bunches of lotuses are blossoming, gladdening the bees, and the vine of love in the heart seems to blossom. The poet Śrī Rūpa Lāla notes that her girlfriends are serving Rādhā and Krishna, thus increasing their love.

41. Ya braja syama saghana ghana unaye (Dark Clouds Rise Up in Vraja), RV 2.84, Śrī Hita Cita Jī

This poem of Śrī Hita Cita Jī is rendered in a melody closely following the contours of the *rāga* Miya ki Malhar (S M R P N̲ D N s, s N̲ P M P G̲ M R S). It is set in a slow Tintāl, and includes fast repeats of the *antarās* from line two. The refrain begins with the words, "*syama saghana*," and ends with "*ya braja*." Even the *antarās* resort to ending with the closing "*ya braja*." This is a pattern that is found in several songs. The lead voice is again weak, and so the patient listener will have to be content with hearing the substance of the recording in the choral repeats. Notice again the strong *pakhavāj* playing including the *tihāi* at the end.

ya braja syama saghana ghana unaye /
capala camaki - camaki ura lavata pritama prema naye //
kuhukana mora papiha piyu - piyu madana bisasa daye /
jai sri hita cita rupa tribhangi rangi rangini mola laye //

Translation: H. S. Mathur

Dark clouds have arisen in the Braj skies. Frequent flashes of lightning are bringing new waves of love to the heart. The peacock and *papiha* birds are calling as if they have the confidence of Kāmadeva with them. The poet Śrī Hita Cita describes the triple-bending form of Krishna that has captivated Rādhā.

42. Nacata morana sanga syama (Śyāma Dances with the Peacocks), RV 2.91, Svāmī Haridāsa

This is a famous composition by Svāmī Haridāsa that is also sung in the Haridāsī Sampradāya in a similar tune. The rhythm of the refrain is in a slow Dhamār that picks up to a medium Rūpak speed as the second line progresses. The third line once again reverts back to the slow Dhamār. The melody is also unique, defying *rāga* classification, yet contains many elements of Kalyan parent scale, such as the sharpened *M*.

nacata morana sanga syama mudita syamahi rijhavata /
taisiye kokila alapata papiha deta sura taisoi megha garaja mridanga-bajavata //
taisiye syama ghata nisi-si kari taisiye damini kaundhi dipa dikhavata /
sri haridasa ke svami syama kunja vihari rijhi radhe hamsi kantha lagavata //

Translation: H. S. Mathur

Śyāma dances happily with the peacocks and entices Rādhā. *Kokila* birds (cuckoos) sing and *papiha* birds respond. Thunder in the sky sounds drums. Dark clouds recall the blackness of night, and flashes of lightning look like *ārati* lamps. Poet Svāmī Haridāsa observes that Kuñjavihārī (Enjoyer in the Bower, Krishna), enamored of Rādhā, smiles and embraces her.

43. Aja kachu kunjana men varasha-si (Today, a Little Rain in the Bower), RV 2.91-92, Śrī Harirāma Vyāsa

This composition of Śrī Harirāma Vyāsa (1511-1613 C.E.) is set to the same rhythmic and melodic pattern as Song 41, resembling the *rāga* Miya ki Malhar. In this recording, the lead voice is much clearer, making it a superior listening experience. The *tanpura* sound belies its setting in Śrī Satsaṅga Bhūmi, yet in this case *tabla* was used instead of the normal *pakhavāj*. The full force of the choral response is something quite unique in current Indian classical music, yet may offer an authentic window into past performance practices.

aja kachu kunjana men varasha-si /
badara dala men dekhi sakhi ri camakata hai capala-si //
nhani-nhani bundana kachu dhurava se pavana bahai sukharasi /
manda-manda garajana-si suniyata nacata mora-sabha-si //
indra dhanusha men vaga pankati dolata bolata kokila-si /
indravadhu chabi chai rahi manau giri para aruna ghata-si //
umaga mahiruha saun mahi phuli bhuli mriga mala-si /
ratata vyasa cataka ki rasana rasa pivata hu pyasi //

Translation: H. S. Mathur

Today, there has been slight rain in the bowers. Within the clouds, O friend, observe those flashes of lightning. Small drops of rain fall, and in the darkness and dampness, a cool breeze blows. Light thunder is audible, groups of peacocks dance, and a rainbow is visible. Flocks of geese fly overhead and the cuckoo bird sings. The beauty of the bride of Indra spreads over the mountain top like a red cloud, and the earth fills with blossoming flowers. Even the deer have lost their way. Poet Vyāsa says that he is narrating this scene as if he were a *cātaka* bird; having drunk this nectar, his tongue is still thirsty.

44. Kanaka patravali jhunmata (Golden Earrings Swing), RV 2.93, Nāgarī Dāsī

This composition of Nāgarī Dāsī follows the pattern of Song 38 above.

kanaka patravali jhunmata ghunghata /
lahanga pita kancuki kasumbhi tai saui gaura tana lasata nila pata //
kesara ki ada jarai kau bainda taisiya mukha para rurata lalita lata /
vara vanika chabi rahi piya nainana nagari dasi dhiraja na rahyau ghata //

Translation: H. S. Mathur

Golden earrings hang under Rādhā's veil. Her *sārī* is yellow and her blouse is the color of saffron; her fair body is beautiful, covered with a blue scarf. She has a decorated *bindi* of saffron on her forehead. In this manner, Rādhā's beauty is embedded within the eyes of Krishna, and the poet Nāgarī Dāsī says that no inhibition remains in this situation.[46]

[CD 7]

45. Bhinjata dou, ghana damini (Lovers Drenched, Cloud and Lightning), RV 2.93, Nāgarī Dāsī

This poem of Nāgarī Dāsī follows the patterns of Songs 41 and 43 above.

[46] Occasionally a *bhakti* poet will feminize his name, as in this case with Nāgarī Dāsī. This is a figurative method to suggest that he is a *gopī* or *sakhī*, a female companion of Rādhā, and is thus able to observe the intimate affairs of Rādhā and Krishna.

bhinjata dou, ghana damini tana herain /
catraka rata pika gana bheka rava sunata keki kala terain //
pulaka-pulaka lapatata gata gasa hamsa uroja ura bherain /
aruna vasana tana avani amita chabi ali lalitadika gherain //
pavasa sampati dampati vilasata kula kalindini nerain /
nagari dasi nava nagara nehi sada vasau ura merain //

Translation: H. S. Mathur

Drenched in rain, Rādhā and Krishna glance at each other's bodies. Together they look like a dark cloud and its bright lightning. A *cātaka* bird chirps and a peacock sings. Hearing the sounds of frogs, the peacocks start crying. Krishna and Rādhā happily embrace each other and massage each others' chests. Dressed in red, the grace of their bodies is immeasurable. Their girlfriends led by Lalitā surround them. The lovers enjoy themselves on the bank of the river Yamunā during the rainy season. The poet Nāgarī Dāsī wishes such youthful love will always dwell in his heart.

46. Savana prema sampada layau (The Rainy Season Brings Treasures of Love), RV 2.97, Kalyāna Pūjārijī

This poem of Kalyāna Pūjārijī (ca. 1700) follows the patterns of Songs 38 and 44 above. This one is the best of the three in terms of the quality of the recording.

savana prema sampada layau /
harita bharita phala phula vipina
ranga morana mangala gayau //
cataka piu-piu karata lalaki rata
kokila sabda sunayau /
yon jahan-tahan nirabhara hariyari
avani singara vanayau //
capala camaki-camaki ati laghava
cahun disi ten ghana chayau /
vilasata jugala seja sukha ki nidhi
dekhi kali jasa gayau //

Translation: H. S. Mathur

The rainy season ushers in a rich treasure of love. The groves are green and full of flowers and fruits, and peacocks sing auspiciously. The *cātaka* chirps `piu piu,' and the cuckoo calls. The earth is decorated here and there with greenery. Brief lightning flashes very lightly and clouds cover all four directions. Rādhā and Krishna enjoy themselves on a bed of pleasure. Seeing all of this, their girlfriends sing their praises.

47. Kunja bihari ho lala (O Boy, Enjoyer in the Bower), RV 2.121, Śrī Rūpa Lāla

This is a very unusual composition celebrating Luhar ("hot wind of summer") by Śrī Rūpa Lāla (1718-1818). It is set in slow Dhamār in a scale that resembles Asaveri with added notes. The ascending melody of the refrain, with the double on "*lala*," is unlike almost anything else in the repertoire. There are fast repeats beginning with the *antarā* in line two. There is also a nice ascending-descending melodic glide on the word "*samvare.*"

kunja bihari ho lala darasana dijau samvare /
thare gunarupa nihara saphala karain driga bhamvare //
lalita tribhangi ho lala latakata-latakata aiyau /
ranga mahala ri ho bata jaya sri lala rupa darasayau //

Translation: H. S. Mathur

Kuñjavihārī (Enjoyer in the Bower, Krishna), please bestow on me your *darśana* (vision)! May my eyes be blessed by seeing your virtuous beauty! You are enticing as you sway in your thrice-bent form (*tribhaṅgī*). On your way to Raṅga Mahala (the Palace of Pleasure), please reveal to me, the poet Rūpa Lāla says, your lovely form.

Śrī Lālajū kī Janama Badhāi—The Appearance Day of Śrī Krishna

48. Ananda aju nanda ke dvara (There is Joy Today at Nanda's Door), RV 2.254 (SV 11), Śrī Hita Harivaṃśa

This poem by Śrī Hita Harivaṃśa, from his work *Sphuṭa-Vāṇī*, marks the distinct change to the season of the Badhāis (Congratulations) of Krishna and Rādhā. The term *badhāi* usually refers to songs in celebration of the birth of a god or a saint, as in the previous *badhāi* to Śrī Hita Harivaṃśa. The setting of this poem involves a unique melody in Kalyan scale, with sharpened M (*M*), and the free-style rhythm of Keshervā. Yet there is a specific pattern of the hand cymbals in eight beats. If one listens closely, it goes like this: X xx X xx xx X X xx. The X signifies one strike per *mātrā*, and xx signifies two strikes per *mātrā*. This is quite a sophisticated pattern, especially in combination with the drum improvisations, and carries with it the singular spirit of Braj. There is such a beautiful bond between the melody, the rhythm, and the lyric that it almost seems as if the poem was written with this tune in mind.

ananda aju nanda ke dvara /
dasa ananya bhajana rasa karana pragate lala manohara //
candana sakala dhenu tana mandita kusuma dama ranjita agara /
purana kumbha bane torana para bica rucira pipara ki dara //
juvati jutha mili gopa virajata bajata panava mrdanga su tara /
jaya sri harivamsa ajira vara vithina dadhi madhi dudha harada ke khara //

Translation: Charles S. J. White (1996, 94-95)

There is joy today at Nanda's door:
Darling Krishna born a cowherd from the *bhajana rasa* of the *bhaktas'* songs.
Sandal paste adorns the bodies of the cows:

The houses elegant with flower garlands, arches beauteous there are, full of Pipal branches in the midst of jars.
How handsome are the maidens, met with cowherds,
Keeping time upon the drums, both long and small.
Śrī Hita Harivaṃśa says, in the courtyards and the lanes is the best of saffron-colored honey, milk, and curd!

49. Mohana janamata mai (Enchantment is Born, O Mother!), RV 2.260, Śrī Kiśorī Lāla

"*Mohana janamata mai*" by Śrī Kiśorī Lāla is performed in the same manner as Song 56, "*Sundara vraja ki bala.*" These are both classic examples of Samāj-Gāyan, beginning in slow Dhamār, then proceeding to medium Rūpak and Dīp Chandī (starting in line three), and then finally shifting to a faster Kehervā in the last two lines. The melody is set in a Misra Kafi, with additional notes of G and N. The second line of each verse is given a fast repeat.

mohana janamata mai, aju bajata badhai ghosha nripati ghara /
jasumati saba sukha phalana phali ki kaha kahaun bhaga nikai // //aju //teka//1//
nahin samatula saci rati rambha pannaga nahin kumvari /
krishna janama dina te maga gavanin kidhaun viranci samvari //2//
bagara-bagara ten bani-bani banita nikasi bhanti bhali ahin /
nanda sadana manu rupa udadhi chabi sarita milana cali hain //3//
ura driga arati kula vidarata suni suta janama sihani /
ruki gaye pathika amangala jaga ke sujasa nira sarasani //4//
varija vadana alaka ali sraini kati nata sabda marala /
nauka naina kataksa su khevaka kautika sarita bala //5//
mukha sasi joti candrika mandira atisai pa bhai hai /
lakhi hari dhanya kahata saba jasumati kula mani dayau dai hai //6//
puni-puni pada vandana kari gavata nirttata pulakita hiyen /
hari shishu rupa trishita driga bhari-bhari rahi-rahi sadara piyen //7//
bali hita rupa carita guna varidha kridata brajajana mahin /
jai sri kishori lala hita deva vimanana ja sukha kaun pachatahin //8//

Translation: H. S. Mathur

Today, on the occasion of the birth of Krishna, congratulatory songs are sung at the residence of Nanda Bābā. How can we describe the excellent fortune of Mother Yaśodā who has been granted all types of pleasure! Even Śacī (wife of Indra), Rati (wife of Kāmadeva), and Rambhā cannot compare in grace with Yaśodā, who is decorated with emeralds. Since the day of Krishna's birth, they have made themselves scarce. From every street decorated women come and proceed to the house of Nanda Bābā, like rivers of beauty going to meet the ocean of grace and loveliness. Hearing of the birth of Krishna, all the pain in their hearts and eyes is taken away, and they are very happy. And all inauspicious signs have disappeared. They are all delighted to hear the praises of Krishna. Their faces are like lotuses and the locks of their hair like black bees. Their jeweled girdles clink like a gaggle of geese. The amused glances of their eyes are like boats in the river of beauty. Their moon-like faces have a lovely glow of moonlight, and this gives them an elegant appearance. Seeing Krishna, all of them praise the good fortune which has given such a jewel of a boy to Yaśodā. With gladdened hearts, they go to the feet of Krishna, dancing and singing. Seeing the childlike beauty of Krishna, they imbibe his beauty with their eyes. Krishna, who is a sea of virtue, is very beautiful and handsome, and plays along with the residents of Braj. The poet Kiśorī Lāla says that even the gods who are sitting in their planes, are envious of this pleasure.

50. Terau mai cirujivau gopala (O Mother, May Your Gopāla Be Long-lived), RV 2.280, Sūra Dāsa

This poem of Sūra Dāsa (1478-1580) is set to the *rāga* Vrindabani Sarang (S R M P N s, s N P M R S), a pentatonic *rāga* that is believed to have originated in Vrindaban itself. The restless character of this *rāga* seems suitable for poems of Krishna, who is described as *cañcala* (restless) as he moves hither and thither in Braj to trick the girlfriends and cowherd girls. In this performance, there are traces of Dha and Ga in the *antarās*. The rhythm begins in Dīp Chandī, a "restless" *tāla*, and then changes to a Kehervā at the end that includes a repeat of the refrain.

terau mai cirujivau gopala /
begi badhau badhi hohu vriddha lata mahari manohara gvala //
upaji paryau ihi kukha kamala ten sindhu sipa jyon lala /
saba gokula ke prana jivana dhana bairinu ke ura sala //
sura kitau jiya sukha pavata hai nirakhata syama tamala /
araja raja lagau meri ankhiyana roga dosha janjala //

Translation: H. S. Mathur

O Mother Yaśodā, may your child Gopāla have a long life. May he quickly grow up to be a young man, and become the head of all the maidens and cowherd men. From a seashell he is born out of the womb like a red lotus. He is the very life of all the people in Gokula, yet he creates fear in the hearts of his enemies. Looking at Śyāma (Krishna) like a dark tree (*tamāla*), the poet Sūra Dāsa says that his heart feels great pleasure, saying, "May my eyes be cured of all defects by applying the dust of Krishna's feet."

[CD 8]

51. Baranyau cahata kachuka aba (I Describe a Little Today), RV 2.255-258, Śrī Rūpa Lāla

This poem by Śrī Rūpa Lāla (1718-1818 C.E.) commemorating Krishna's birth is structured like a long epic or ballad. One is reminded of the lengthy "*Asa Di Var*" poem of Guru Nānak of the Sikh tradition, with alternating recitation and *rāga* music. The recited portions, marked "*dohā*," consist of unaccompanied phrases in *rāga* Bhairav in the upper tetrachord (M P $\underline{D}$ N s $\underline{r}$ g) that resolve mostly on upper sa. These portions alternate with the parts marked "*cautuka*" that are performed in Tintāl with drums and cymbals in two different melodies resembling *rāga* Asaveri (S R M P $\underline{D}$ s, S $\underline{N}$ $\underline{D}$ P M $\underline{G}$ R S), except with G in the middle register. All sections involve group choral response in unison. This is a spectacular recording in that the poem has been captured in its entirety of about forty minutes in length. The numbering may appear strange at first. The "*dohās*" are numbered separately and add up to thirteen. The "*cautukas*" are also numbered as thirteen, with three in succession at the end. There is also an intervening section of three stanzas marked "*karasha*." Also, the poet's name is given in both the first and last stanzas.

doha - baranyau cahata kachuka aba krishna candra parivara /
dehu buddhi mati suddha ati sri harivamsa udara //1//
gana uddesa ju dipika madhya kahi kachu riti /
jai sri rupa lala hita saun likhata sunahu rasika dai priti //2//

cautuka - vimala jasa dhandhi karata bakhana /
vajata badhai nandarai griha pragata bhayau sukha dana //teka//
dhandhina sanga samaja saja lai singha pauri men nacai /
lai - lai nama gopavamsana ke sata sakha ten bancai //
aye simita sabai nara - nari kahata dehu jo jancai /
mohi cau jasuda suta nirakhana bata yahai suna sancai //1//

doha - sinha pauri brajaraja ki badi bhira bhai ani /
vividha bhanti saun gopa kula dhandhi kahata bakhani //3//

cautuka - tina bhanti ke gopa basain braja tinaki bata bakhanaun /
uttama vaisya dharama gau raksa kari viveka pahicanon //
tinahun ten ahira madhyama go gaya bhainsa dhana dhanaun /
braja ke chora basata je gujara inahun ten ghati janaun //2//

doha - sunata nanda upananda saba baithe sabha banai /
barana adi ten gopa kula dhandhi liyau bulai //4//

cautuka - baranana karata gopa vamsana kaun dhandhi mana hulasai /
devamidha jadukula naresa ki katha puratana gai //
jajana dana vraja chatra dharma saba vidhi saun karata sadai /
kumvara kanha ke paradade bhaye soma vamsa ke rai //3//

doha - devamidha ghara dvai bhai patibrata patarani /
ika kanya chatrina ki eka vaisya ki jana //5//

cautuka - chatri kanya ten upaje suta surasaina sukha data /
ati brahmanya sila subha karma veda artha ke jnata //
tina ten sri vasudeva bhaga ki kahata na abai bata /
nandaraya ke mitra piyare racipaci kiye hain vidhata //4//

doha - jadaba kula vasudeva laun dhandhi kahyau sunai /
aba baranaun kula gopa kau brajapati kaun sira nai //6//

cautuka - vaisya kanyaka ten ju bhaye parajanya dharma adhara /
narada kau upadesa pai laksmi-pati bhaje bhuvara //
nandisvara pura vasa karata tapa santati heta vicara /
bhai akasa vimala vani suni tana mana rahi na sambhara //5//

doha - bani bhai akasa suphala phalau abhilasha saba /
braja kau nihacala vasa panca putra hvai hain ju aba //7//

cautuka - panca putra vhai hain tumhare tinamen ati nanda piyarau /
takai lala pragata hai esau tina bhuvana ujiyarau //
yaha suni harashi bhayau mana men ju mahavana vasa vicaryau /
kesi ke dara darapi gamva saba jamuna para utaryau //6//

doha - panca putra parajanya ke raja karata braja mahin /
sata dipa ke bhupa je ina sama kahe na janhin //8//

cautuka - bada bhayau upananda sabana ten gaura subhaga anga takau //
harita vasana tana lambi dadhi nau lakha godhana jakau //
tungi triya subhaga laksana juta jasaun hita jasuda kau /
lai - lai goda nirakhi mukha hari kau dhani dhani bolana bakau //7//

doha - bada bhrata upananda ju tinaki sampati gai /
aba baranaun abhinanda kaun bhare krishna ke bhai //9//

cautuka - ika abhinanda nanda ten jethe gaura barana anga sohai /
bhare kharika sata gai laksa dasa dana samana na kohai //
krishna prema saun chakyau kahata yaun bata nanda suni hohai /
tihare suta ten ya braja men kachu pyarau nahina mohai //8//

doha - nandana eka sunanda ika kaka krishna ke gai /
rijhi - rijhi braja isa taba daihain dana bulai //10//

cautuka - eka sunanda nanda ten lahure bahuta deha ke bhare /
sodasa lakha godhana take ghara bakula nama triya re //
inahun ten lahure nandana ika dou krishna kaka re /
sata lakha godhana dhana jake nandahi bahuta piyare //9//

doha - sananda aru nandini bahinc nanda ki jana /
aba svarupa srinanda kau kahaun sunaun dhari dhyana //11//

karasha - dhandhi gai nandarai kau dhyana dhari kain /
dvara tke parin siddhi nava niddhi saba mangi tapai jahi daridra thari kain //1//
subhra candana khaura anga chabi jagamagata sajala ghana sama vasana tanahin sajain /

phabi sira paga saubhagya locana visada bhala para tilaka kesara virajain //2//

sravana mani jalaja ki joti jhalakata lasata seta aru syama dadi virajai /
bahu ajanu bada dana danesa kau dekhi mukha sakala dukha dura bhajai //3//

doha - saba gopana kau jasa kahata dhandhi mana n aghai /
aba vaibhava srinanda kau baranata rahyau lubhyai //12//

cautuka - sahasra kharika phirata saba sveta kari braja dharani //
jamuna tira nira pivata nita sada harita trina carani //
krishna kamala kara phirata pitha para kaha kari ina karani //10//

doha - ye gaiyan nandarai ki carata rahata braja mahin /
siva viranci mana cintavata pada raja parasata nahin //13//

cautuka - ina gaiyana ke kaja syama aisvarja sabai bisarayau /
amrita chandi goloka dhama ten braja kau gorasa bhayau //
muni mana dhyana gyana paci hare para na kyaunhun payau /
maha bhaga bada bhaga jasomati aisau suta jina jayau //11//

cautuka - adbhuta rupa nirakhi nakha sikha ten thake naina mana harau /
koti canda ki joti sara kau banyau indu ika nyarau //
cancala naina sarada ambuja manu maha manohara pyarau /
nandarai suni ai bhavana dhana banthata kholi bhandarau //12//

cautuka - taba rijhe braja isa nanda ju bhavana bhandara lutayau /
ratana jatita todara mani nupura dhandhi kaun pahirayau //
lahara-vidara diye vahu gopana bhayau vida ghara ayau /
jai sri rupa lala hita nava kisora kaun gai-gai sukha payau //13//

Translation: H. S. Mathur

[Dohā] Poet Rūpa Lāla wishes to describe the family of Śrī Krishna, and he prays to Śrī Hita Harivaṃśa to give him the ability. His objective is to illuminate the family traditions of Krishna, and he lovingly invites the listeners to hear his description. (1-2)

[Cautukā] The bard is full of praise for this family because the giver of pleasure and comfort to everybody is born in the house of Nanda Rāja, where greetings are given. The bards dance in the courtyard along with others, and they read out the names of the seven branches of *gopas* (cowherd men). All the men and women have gathered there, and they want to offer whatever the bards demand. Their only interest is in hearing about Krishna the son of Yaśodā. (1)

[Dohā] In the courtyard of Nanda Bābā there is a big crowd, and bards praise the *gopa* family members in different ways. (3)

[Cautukā] They say in Braj three types of cowherders reside. The highest are the Vaiśyas, who are recognized as protectors of cows and religion. Under the second category fall the Ahīras whose profession is to look after the cows and buffaloes and tend to agriculture. The third category is the Gūjaras who live at the edge of Braj. (2)

[Dohā] Nanda, Upananda, and all the others sit in an assembly. Before hearing the descriptions of the cowherd families, they call the bards. (4)

[Cautukā] The bards then begin to describe the pedigree of the cowherds. They first describe the story of the Yādava king Devamīḍha, who observed the *dharma* of Kṣatriyas with sacrifices, acts of charity, and vows (oaths). The grandfathers of Krishna were kings of the lunar dynasty. (3)

[Dohā] King Devamīḍha had two chaste principal queens. One of them was a daughter of Kṣatriyas and one was a daughter of Vaiśyas. (5)

[Cautukā] The protector of all Surasenas was born of the Kṣatriya queen. He had great respect for Brahmins, performed noble deeds, and was well versed in the Vedas. Vasudeva was his son, and his glory is beyond description. By god's grace he was a very dear friend of Nanda Rāja. (4)

[Dohā] In this manner the bards describe the Yādava dynasty and then commence the description of the particular cowherder family that led to Krishna. (6)

[Cautukā] Parjanya was born from the Vaiśya queen and he was intensely religious. Under the direction of Nārada, with a desire for a child, he started worshipping at Nandīśvara. He heard a divine voice from the sky and then could not control the pleasure of his mind and body. (5)

[Sorathā] The voice declared that his worship had born fruit and that he should go and stay in Braj where he will have five sons. (7)

[Cautukā] Later on, he had five sons of whom Nanda was very dear to him. The illuminator of all three worlds, Krishna, appeared in the house of Nanda Rāja. Hearing this, Nanda Rāja was very happy and decided to stay in Mahāvana. The whole of the village shifted to the other bank in fear of Keśī, the horse demon. (6)

[Dohā] The five sons of Parjanya governed the Braj region and even the kings of seven kingdoms could not compare with them. (8)

[Cautukā] The oldest of them was the fair-skinned Upananda. He had a long beard and wore green clothes and had nine hundred thousand cows. His wife was named Tuṅgī; she had auspicious qualities and was very helpful to Yaśodā. She took Krishna on her lap and, gazing at his face, spoke lovingly. (7)

[Dohā] The bards, having described the wealth of the older brother Upananda, now describe Abhinanda, who was an uncle of Krishna. (9)

[Cautukā] He was elder to Nanda and very fair-complexioned. He had seven hundred thousand cows, and no one could match him in charity. He was full of love for Krishna, and he told Nanda: "Apart from your son, Krishna, there is no one dearer to me in Braj." (8)

[Dohā] Another uncle of Krishna was named Sunanda. He was also greatly enamored of Krishna, and used to give a lot of charity. (10)

[Cautukā] Sunanda was younger than Nanda and had a bulky body. He had one million, six hundred thousand cows, and his wife was named Bakulā. Nanda had another younger brother who owned seven hundred thousand cows, and was very dear to Nanda Rāi. (9)

[Dohā] The sisters of Nanda Rāi were named Sānandā and Nandinī. Now hear attentively the glory of Nanda Rāi. (11)

[Karaṣā] All the successes and the nine treasures used to stay near his door. He used to feed all beggars. He applied white sandalwood paste to his body which was resplendent like a water-filled, dark cloud. He wore a turban and had big eyes, and his broad forehead was marked with *tilaka* of saffron (*kesar*). On his ears he wore shining pearls, and he had a black beard. He had long arms extending to the knees, and he gave such generous charity that just by seeing his face all misery vanished away. (1-3)

[Dohā] Describing the glory of the Gopas, the bard is not satisfied in his heart, and now he describes the great prosperity of Nanda with great interest. (12)

[Cautukā] Nanda had ten thousand cows which could not be counted by the cowherds. The cows were like desire-fulfilling cows (*kāmadhenu*), making all the land of Braj white with flowing milk. The cows would drink water from the river Yamunā and graze on green grass every day. Krishna caressed the cows on the back, as they must have done virtuous deeds in past lives. (10)

[Dohā] The cows of Nanda Rāja grazed and roamed all over Braj. Even Śiva and Brahmā desired to touch the dust raised by these cows. (13)

[Cautukā] Because of these cows, Krishna forgot about his heavenly prosperity and, leaving the nectar of the abode of Goloka, relished the cows' milk in Braj. Even in deep meditation, the sages could not fathom the mystery of Krishna, and they praised Yaśodā for her fortune in having a son like Krishna. (11)

[Cautukā] Seeing the beauty of Krishna from head to foot, the eyes and mind are exhausted. With the effulgence of thousands of moons concentrated in one moon, Krishna appears. And his flickering eyes are like a very lovely winter season flower. Having heard praise of Krishna, Nanda Rāja opened up his store and distributed money, and in this manner he gave away a lot of wealth. (12)

[Cautukā] Nanda Rāja decorated the bard with anklets and bangles adorned with gems. He also gave lots of ornaments to the cowherds, and then returned to his home. Śrī Rūpa Lāla says that, having sung the praise of Krishna, he has obtained oceans of satisfaction and pleasure. (13)

52. Moda vinoda aja ghara nanda (Rejoicing Today at Nanda's House), RV 2.282, Sūra Dāsa

This is a composition of Sūra Dāsa (1478-1580) that appears to be rendered in a *rāga* format. The *sthāyī* is sung in *rāga* Jai Jaivanti (S R G M P N s, s N̲ D P D M G R G̲ R S) yet the *antarās* offer some variations from what one normally hears in classical recitals. It is set in Tintāl throughout except for the last line and refrain which are played in a faster Kehervā. The melody begins on the tenth *mātrā* and the *sam* falls on the lower S, which coincides with the syllable "a" of "*aja.*"

moda vinoda aja ghara nanda /
krishnapaksha bhadaun nisa athain pragate hain gokula ke canda //
bhavana dvara gomaya vara mandita varashata kusuma umapati inda /
gopi gvala paraspara gavata pulakita viharata matta gayanda //
bandana varain vrinda manohara bica banyau pata kira suchanda /
sura dasa haradi dadhi madhu ghrita ranjita pana karata makaranda //

Translation: H. S. Mathur

Today there is much rejoicing at the residence of Nanda Bābā. Krishna, who is like a moon in Gokula, is born on the eighth of the month of Bhadon in the dark fortnight. The door of the residence is smeared with cowdung, and Śiva and Indra shower down flowers from above. The cowherd girls and men are singing together and wandering about like drunken elephants. There are many flowers, and in the middle there is a green-colored cloth. The poet Sūra Dāsa says that the bees are tasting turmeric, yoghurt, honey, and clarified butter.

[CD 9]

53. Vraja bhayau mahari ken puta jaba (In Vraja is Born the Son of the Queen), RV 2.278-280, Sūra Dāsa

In this poem of Sūra Dāsa, there is a description of the birth activities of Krishna in Mathurā. It is played in a slow Dīp Chandī with alternate fast repeats. Only the first eight stanzas have been recorded. The song begins with"*bhayau mahari*," with the word "*vraja*" inserted in closing the line. The tune patterns, variations of the *rāga* Kafi, resemble those in the second half of Song 6.

vraja bhayau mahari ken puta jaba yaha bata suni /
suni anande saba loka gokula gunita guni //
graha lagana nakshatra bala sodhi kini veda dhuni /
subha purava pure punya raci kula atala thuni //1//
suni dhain saba braja nari sahaja singara kiye /
kara kankana kancana thara mangala saja liye //
tana pahire nautana cira kajara naina diye /
kasi kancuki tilaka lilata sobhita hara hiye //2//
saba apane-apane mela nikasin bhanti bhali /
manaun lala muninu kip anti pinjarana curi cali //
hamsi gavata mangala gita mili dasa panca ali /
manu bhora bhaye ravi dekhi phulin kamala kali //3//
dou sobhita tarala taraunna baini sithila guhi /
mukha mande rori ranga saindura manga chuhi //
ura ancala udata na janain sari suranga suhi /
ati srama jala mukhahi prasveda manaun megha phuhi //4//
ika pahilain pahuncin ai ati ananda bharin /
lai bhitara bhavana bulai sabai sisu pani parin //
te vadana ughari nihari deta asisa kharin /
cirujiyau yasoda nanda purana kama Karin //5//
dhani-dhani dina dhani yaha rata dhani yaha pahara ghari /
dhuni dhanya mahari ki kukha bhaga suhaga bhari //
jina jayau aisau puta saba sukha phalana phari /
thiru thapyau saba parivara mana ki sula hari //6//
suni gvalina gai bahori balaka boli laye /
guhi gunja ghasi vana dhatu angina citra thaye //
sira dadhi makhana ke mata kamvara kandha laye /
ika jhanjha mridanga bajavata saba nanda bhavana gaye //7//
ika nacata karata kulahala chirakata harada dahi /
manu barashata bhadaun masa nadi ghrita dudha bahi //
jakau jahin-jahin mana jaya kautuka tahin-tahin /
ati ananda magana ju gvala kahu badata nahi //8//

ika dhai nanda pai jaya puni-puni pani parain /
ika apu apuhi manhi hamsi-hamsi anka bharain //
ika dadhi rocana aru duba sabana ke sisa dharain /
ika ambara aura mangai deta na sanka karain //9//
jaba nhai nanda bhaye thade aru kusa hatha dhare /
nandimukha pitara pujai antara soca hare //
vara guru jana dvija pahirai sabana ken pani pare /
ghasi vandana caru mangai sabana ken tilaka kare //10//
gana gaiyan gain na janya taruna te baccha badhin /
te carain jamuna ke kula dune dudha cadhin //
khura rupe tamen pitha saune singa madhin /
te dinin dvijana bulai harashi asisa padhi //11//
taba apane mitra subandhu hamsi-hamsi boli liye /
mathi mrigamada Malaya kapura mathain tilaka kiye //
uramani mala pahirai vasana vicitra diye /
manu varashata masa asadha dadura mora jiye //12//
vara bandi magada suta angina bhavana bhare /
te bole lai-lai nama hita kou nahin bisare //
te dana mana paridhana purana kama kare /
jina joi jancyau soi payau rasa nandarai dhare //13//
taba ambara aura mangai sari suranga ghani /
te dinin badhuna bulai jaisi jahi bani //
te ati ruci saun hita mani nija griha gopa dhani /
te nikasin deta asisa ruci apani-apani //14//
taba ghara-ghara bheri mridanga pataha nisana baje /
vara bandhi vandana mala kancana kalasa saje //
te ta dina ten ve loga sukha sampati na taje /
kahi sura sabana ki yaha gati jina hari carana bhaje //15//

Translation: H. S. Mathur

The good news spread in Braj that a son was born to Yaśodā Mahārāṇī. This gave great pleasure to all the learned and talented people of Gokula. Mantras were recited after due calculation of auspicious astrological signs and omens. By the grace of past pious deeds the family tree was constituted. Hearing this message, all the ladies of Braj hastened to the site, Nanda Bhavan, with simple adornments. Wearing golden bracelets on their arms, they carried golden plates with auspicious *pūjā* materials. They wore new clothes and had *kajal* (eyeliner) applied to their eyes. Their blouses (*kanchukis*) were tight.

They had applied *tilak* to their foreheads and wore garlands of flowers around their necks. They came out collectively in various groups. Viewing them all, it appeared as if *lālamuni* birds had suddenly broken out of their cages. Five to ten girl-friends were walking together smiling and singing auspicious songs. It appeared as if at the rising of the sun fresh lotus buds had blossomed. Their ears were adorned with lovely earrings and their hair was loosely tied. There were marks of *rolī* (red powder) on their faces and their hair was parted with marks of *sindur* (auspicious red powder for married ladies). Their bodies were edged with the flowing borders of their beautiful *sārīs*. The perspiration sprinkling from their faces appeared like drizzling rain from clouds. (1-4)

Full of joy, some guests reached Nanda Bābā's house earlier and were called inside. All of them touched the feet of the new baby and, uncovering his face, offered him blessings: "May Yaśodā and Nanda Bābā live forever! They have fulfilled the longings of all of us. Blessed is this night. Blessed is this day. Blessed is this moment. Blessed is Lady Yaśodā's lap which is full of good luck in that she has given birth to this son who will fulfill all pleasures, having established the immortality of the family and redressed the pain of all our hearts." (5-6)

The cowherd girls summoned called all the children. Making garlands of *guñja* (wild seed) and perparing a metalic compound, they painted a picture in the courtyard. Carrying butter and yogurt in earthen pitchers on their heads, they hung rope buckets over their shoulders to carry earthen pots. Someone played the *jhāñjh* (hand cymbals) while someone else played a drum. All of them proceeded to Nanda Bābā's house. While one person danced, another made noise as someone else sprinkled yogurt and tumeric. It seemed there was a rain of butter and milk, turning into a rivulet. Everyone was celebrating according to his or her choice. All the cowherd men and women were immersed in joy, and no one was left out. Someone was racing Nanda Bābā, while someone else was falling at his feet repeatedly. With great pleasure they embraced one another. Then someone placed auspicious signs of yogurt, red sandalwood and *darba* grass on others' heads. Someone else was busy decorating clothes and was not dilly dallying. (7-8)

When Nanda Bābā stood up after his bath, he held *kuśa* (auspicious grass) in his hands. He worshiped Nāndīmukha and relieved himself of all anxieties. He then adored the feet of all the *brāhmaṇas* and elders present and gave them exquisite clothes to wear. Making a paste of sweet-smelling sandalwood, he placed it on the foreheads of all of them. The countless numbers of cows with young calves that grazed on the banks of the river Yamunā had the capacity to yield a profuse quantity of milk. Their hooves were enlaid with silver, their backs bore copper, and their horns with gold. *Brāhmaṇas* were invited and came with great pleasure. Many cows were donated to them. The *brāhmaṇas* then showered their blessings. Nanda Bābā smilingly spoke to his friend Subandhu and put *tilaka* on his forehead with a mixture of *kasturi*, sandalwood, and camphor. He then placed a jeweled necklace on his neck and offered him unique varieties of new clothings. Just as in the rainy season frogs and peacocks are animated; similarly, Nanda Bābā's house was resonant with the constant recitations of poets and bards who sang praises of everyone name by name. No one was left out. Nanda Bābā fulfilled all their desires by honoring them with gifts of money and clothing. Filled with emotion, Nanda Bābā offered to everybody as per his wish. Afterwards he collected more clothing and beautiful *sārīs* and made suitable gifts to all of his relatives. The wives of the cowherd men returned happily to their homes with the blessings and assorted gifts from the house of Nanda Bābā. Then *bherī* (drums) and other musical instruments were sounded in all the homes. Buntings were tied and golden pitchers were decorated. There was no dearth of happiness and wealth after that day. The poet Sūra Dāsa observes, "This is the fate of all those who worship Hari's feet."

54. Pragati sri vrishabhanu gopa ke sobha (Śrī Vṛṣabhānu's Beauty is Born), RV 2.365-366, Śrī Kamala Naina

After a short prelude on the harmonium, this poem of Śrī Kamala Naina (1692-1754) glorifies the birth of Rādhā. It is out of sequence due to the circumstances of placement on the CDs. It belongs in the group of Śrī Rādhā Appearance Day songs beginning with Song 62. The melody and rhythm patterns are the same as Songs 49 and 56. The verses are in medium Dīp Chandī, with fast repeats after the characteristic "*eri ha.*" The last two lines are in a medium Kehervā. In this poem, each line ends with the filler syllable,"*ri.*"

pragati sri vrishabhanu gopa ke sobha ki nidhi ai ri /
dhanya bhaga kiratida rani jina yaha kanya jai ri //
sunata hi dhai sakhi saheli mana vanchita phala pai ri /
hathana kancana thara virajata mangala gavata ai ri //
maharani kirati adara dai bhitara bhavana bulai ri /
bhushana vasana vividha nana ranga nakha-sikha ten pahirai ri //
dadhi kadaun jhara layau angana kica macai ri /
radha mohana jori avicala jai sri kamala naina sukhadai ri //

Translation: Chandrakala Pandey

Rādhā has taken birth as the daughter of Vṛṣabhānu. She is a treasure-house of beauty. Everyone admires Queen Kīrtidā for giving birth to this girl. Hearing the news all of the girlfriends rush to the palace. They hold golden *thālis* full of many ornaments and colorful clothes and sing praises. Queen Kīrati receives them with great respect and adorns her daughter from head to toe with the ornaments and clothes brought by the girlfriends. Milk and curds are normally presented to mothers and new-born babies, and it was surely plentiful here, as the whole floor of the palace became slippery. The couple of Rādhā and Krishna provide constant joy to the poet Śrī Kamala Naina.

[CD 10]

55. Aju badhai gokula bajata (Today, a Celebration in Gokula), RV 2.285, Śrī Harikṛṣṇa Dāsa

This poem of Śrī Harikṛṣṇa Dāsa is set in a medium Tintāl and follows the basic contours of the *rāga* Madhuvanti (S G *M* P N s, s N D P *M* G R S). Beginning on the Khali of Tintāl, the refrain proceeds with the *Sam* falling on the syllable"*go*" of gokula. The third line resembles the first two lines, only that there is a slight variation in the melody for "*sajata.*" The *antarās* (verses proper) appear in the fourth, sixth, and eighth lines, which come back to repeat the melody of the refrain. There are fast repeats beginning with the fourth line.

aju badhai gokula bajata /
putra bhayau jasumati rani ken vipra veda dhuni gajata //
griha-griha ten ain sundari kara kancana tharana sajata /
pharaharata ancala cancala vara anga-anga chabi chajata //
vividha vasana todara ratanana ke dhare adhika dhinga rajata /
nandarai lai-lai pahiravata nacata sakala su bhrajata //
umagi kahata nara nari sabai bhaiya aju bhalau dina lagata /
harikrishna dasa prabhu kamalanaina ki chabi nirakhata dukha bhagata //

Translation: H. S. Mathur

Today is a day of great celebration in Gokula. A son has been born to Yaśodā, and *brāhmaṇas* chant the Vedas. From different homes, beautiful maidens arrive with decorated golden plates in their hands. As their scarves wave in the wind, there is grace in all the limbs of their bodies. And with their various kinds of colorful clothing and jewelry, the picture created is extremely beautiful. Nanda Rāi distributes new clothes and also dances all around. All the men and women are full of enthusiasm, proclaiming today a very auspicious day. The poet Harikṛṣṇa Dāsa says: "viewing the beauty of lotus-eyed Krishna, all grief vanishes."

56. Sundara vraja ki bala (The Beautiful Women of Vraja), RV 2.290, Nanda Dāsa

This beautiful poem of Nanda Dāsa describes the situation of Krishna's birth at the home of Nanda Rāj. It follows the same pattern and sequence as in Songs 49 and 54 above. Set in the *rāga* Kafi, it begins in slow Dhamār and then proceeds quickly to Rūpak and then to a medium Dīp Chandī by line three. The last two lines are in a medium Kehervā. This recording is complete, and is the best of the three examples.

sundara vraja ki bala, juri calin hain badhaye nanda mahara ghara /
kancana thara hara cancala chabi kahi na parata tihin kala // juri cali //teka //1//
dahadahe mukha kumakuma ranga ranjita rajata rasa ke aina /
kanjana para khelata juga khanjana anjana juta bane naina //2//
damakata kantha padika mani kundala navala prema rasa bori /
atura gati jaisain canda udai bhaye dhavata trishita cakori //3//
khasi-khasi parata kusuma sisana ten upama kauna bakhanaun /
carana calana para rijhi cikura vara barashata phulana manaun //4//
gavata gitapunita karata jaga jasumati mandira ain /
vadana viloki balaiyan lai-lai detc asisa suhai //5//
mangala kalasa nikata dipavali thani-thani dekhi mana bhulyau /
mannahun agama nanda suvana ke saune phula vraja phulyau //6//
ta pachain gana gopa opa saun aye atisai sohain /
paramanda kanda rasa bhine nikara purandara ko hain //7//
ananda ghana jyaun gajata rajata bajata dundubhi bheri /
raga ragini gavata harashata barashata sukha ki dheri //8//
parama dhama sukha dhama syama abhirama sugokula aye /
miti gaye dvanda nanda-dasana ke bhaye manoratha bhaye //9//

Translation: H. S. Mathur

The lovely women of Braj go together to the house of Nanda Bābā to sing songs of congratulation. It is difficult to describe their beauty as they carry garlands on golden plates. Each face shines with red *kumkum* and seems the epitome of beauty. Each pair of eyes are like two wagtail birds playing on their lotus-like faces. They are full of love, wearing new earrings and shining necklaces on their necks. And they are most eager, like Cakorī birds who spot the rising moon with thirsty eyes. Flowers fall down from their heads and it is difficult to describe their incomparable beauty. When they walk slowly, flowers are showered upon their heads. Yaśodā comes into the house singing songs and sanctifying the entire home. The cowherd ladies see the infant face of Krishna and pay homage and give blessings. There are auspicious pitchers, and nearby is a row of lamps. One's heart is enchanted by seeing all of this. It seems that with the birth of a son to Nanda Bābā the whole of Braj blossoms with golden flowers. Later on, the cowherders arrive, charming and graceful. They are so full of joy, that even a group of Indras could not match them. Many sorts of drums are played, spreading clouds of pleasure everywhere. When singers render many *rāgas* and *rāgiṇīs*, pleasure swells up all around. Lovely Krishna has come all the way from Vaikuntha heaven, which is full of pleasure, to Gokula. As a result, Nanda Dāsa says that all conflicts are over, and all wishes have been fulfilled.

57. Aju braja-raja kain (Today, Of the King of Vraja), RV 2.293, Nāgarī Dāsa

This short poem by Nāgarī Dāsa is set to the rhythm of Jhaptāl (10 mātrās: 2-3, 2-3) and to a variation of the *rāga* Kafi (i.e., a slight touch of G in the middle register in the *antarā*). It is straightforward and consistent, with *sthāyī* and *antarā* patterns and fast repeats. There are no long interjections of "eri ha." What still make it different from classical performances are the call and response format, the use of hand cymbals, and the emphasis on the clear articulation of the lyrics of the poem.

aju braja-raja kain suta bhayau suni sakhi
umaga upahara lai calyau maharavanaun /
thara kara hara bhara bhara lacakata lanka
vasana asamhara ura phabyau phaharavanaun //
itihin suni gana aru mangala nisana dhuni

utahin nikau lagata ghanana ghaharavanaun /
nagari dasa braja-canda pragatata bhayau
nanda hiya sindhu ananda laharavanaun //

Translation: H. S. Mathur

Listen, Dear Friend, a son is born to the King of Braj (Nanda Bābā), so let us go there with gifts! As the Braj women bring plates full of flower garlands, their hips are swaying; and they arrange their scarves to cover their beautiful breasts. On one side we hear graceful songs, and on the other, at Nanda Bābā's residence, there is the delightful drumming of drums. The poet Nāgarī Dāsa says, "Krishna is born like a moon in Braj, and the heart of Nanda Bābā is swaying with pleasure like the waves of the sea."

58. Nava rasa rupa lala (A Child of Fresh Delight and Beauty), RV 2.296, Prema Dāsa

Prema Dāsa was important for the Rādhāvallabha tradition as he wrote a commentary on the *Caurāśi-Pad* (ca. 1792) of Śrī Hita Harivaṃśa. This poem by him is set in a variety of the *rāga* Kalavati (S G P D N̲ s, s N̲ D P G S). Yet the melody is unique and stands on its own merit, as do the majority of songs in the Rādhāvallabha Songbook. The rhythm is a slow Tintāl, with a fast repeat only at the end (starting with "*gvalana ke*") that then includes the refrain. It is an excellent example of *rāga*-based Samāj-Gāyan.

nava rasa rupa lala pragatyau hai subhakala,
locana visala dekhau kaha nikau lala hai/
cala hai marala cala sohaigi gunja mala,
bairina kau ura sala santana kau pala hai //
kirati ki suta bala jori jura hai rasala,
jaise hema dala aura samvarau tamala hai /
sunaun nanda tatkala koi prema rupa jala,
gvalana ke nala khela karaigau nihala hai //

Translation: H. S. Mathur

On this auspicious occasion, a child is born with exceeding beauty, and with all nine *rasas* (emotions). His large eyes are most lovely. He will walk with the pace of a goose, and a garland of pearls will adorn him. He will strike terror in the hearts of his enemies and be a protector of the righteous. Under a mango tree, a pair of lovers will meet, one fair like gold (Rādhā), and the other of dark complexion like the *tamāla* tree (Krishna). They will be praised by everyone. The poet Prema Dāsa addresses Nanda Bābā and says, "there will be a love-play, and Krishna will play with the maidens of Braj."

59. Ihi braja ghara-ghara aju badhai (Here in Vraja Today in Each House a Celebration), RV 2.297, Cācā Vṛndāvana Dāsa

This poem of Cācā Vṛndāvana Dāsa (1708-1787) is performed in a popular *rāga* known as Shiva Ranjani (S R G̱ P D s, s D P G̱ R S), a pentatonic *rāga* with only five notes and G̱ flattened. Two other songs in this collection are in Shiva Ranjani, Songs 76 and 83, though in different rhythms. There are fast repeats beginning with the first *antarā* in the second line. This *rāga*, while not unknown in classical performances, is more commonly found in Bhajan, Sikh Kirtan, and lighter forms of music.

ihi braja ghara-ghara aju badhai /
nanda sadana nabha canda udai bhayau mithyau tapa tama jaga kau mai //
sukrita punja suta jasumati jayau baranaun kaha bada bhaga nikai /
praphulita gopi gopa kumuda gana tribhuvana sujasa candani chai //
dana mana dvija guru pada vande brajapati sabaki asa pujai /
bali hita rupa sakala sukha mandira vrindavana hita kumvara kanhai //

Translation: H. S. Mathur

Today, congratulatory songs are sung in every Braj household. Like a moon that has risen in the sky, a son is born at the residence of Nanda Bābā. With his birth all the heat and darkness of the world have been abolished. A son has been born to Mother Yaśodā who is the epitome of virtue. How can we praise her good luck! Her fame has spread over the world like lovely moonlight, and all the cowherd women and men have blossomed like lilies. The King of Braj (Nanda Bābā) has given respect and charity to the Brahmins, paid his homage to the gurus, and fulfilled the expectations of everyone. The poet Vṛndāvana Dāsa says that young Krishna with his beauty gives great pleasure to everyone in their homes.

[CD 11]

60. Rupa jalada kau ri heli (Like A Beautiful Cloud), RV 2.308, Cācā Vṛndāvana Dāsa

This poem of Cācā Vṛndāvana Dāsa begins in a slow Rūpak Tāl but then expands by the third line into a fast Dīp Chandī with a new melody. Both melodies are based on Gaud Malhar scale. By the seventh line (the stanza marked 2), the original melody and rhythm pattern is resumed. This format continues throughout the four stanzas. The melody of the faster portions is a standard Braj tune unique to the area. The subject matter is a description of the festivities at Nanda Bābā's house surrounding the birth of Krishna.

rupa jalada kau ri heli dhurava unayau /
vyoma manohara ri heli nanda bhavana bhayau //
vyoma nanda niketa barashata aju paramananda hai /
cahun ora maruta prema badyau pravala urana amanda hai //
keli kulahala suta magada garaja bahu baje manaun /
jana ghosha catraka mudita ati hiya laga sukha kahan //1//
rucira alankrita ri heli vraja taruni bhai /
indra badhu si ri heli mili mandira gain //

gain mandira gopa banita damini duti deha ki /
nadi sagara milata upama aju vrajapati greha ki //
romanca manaun mahiruha nara nari braja ekata bhaye /
barasha abhuta viloka vyauma vimana krishna janama chaye //2//
priti alaukika ri heli saba hiya dekhiye /
gagana mahitala ri heli saguna viseshiye //
viseshiye subha saguna disa-disa sampada baranaun kaha /
agamana gokula canda mangala nikara vraja pragate maha //
gopa sabha banai baithe nanda ati sobhita bhae /
muni deva durllabha sudhana payau vividha dana dvijana daye //3//
muri-muri gopi ri heli deta asisa hita /
vidhi tana godi ri heli otata jiyahu nita //
nita jiyahu deta asisa jasumati bandi pada sukha men jhilin /
gavata badhay vividha purita prema saba sadara milin //
vrindavana hita rupa niravadhi labha locana paiyau //
braja isa suta janamata simiti saba ghosha kautika aiyau //4//

Translation: H. S. Mathur

The Dhruva (North) star rises like rain clouds, and the sky around Nanda Bābā's house becomes beautiful, with happiness raining down. All around, love circles like the wind; boundless happiness is in the hearts of everyone. The sound of peacocks is like the bard and minstrel singing in praise. And acclamations made by the gathered crowd are like the sounds of *cātaka* birds (a kind of cuckoo) that only drink drops of rain. How can I describe this happiness? The ladies of Braj decorate themselves nicely, and they go to the temple looking like wives of Indra. The cowherd women's bodies flash like lightning, as they go to the temple. The house of Nanda Bābā is like the place where river and sea meet. The ladies and gents of Braj have gathered together and, due to their high emotional states, their bodily hairs rise like trees growing on the earth. At the time of the birth of Krishna, there is monsoon rain. One can thus observe unbounded pleasure in the hearts of everyone, and discover auspicious omens both in the sky and on the ground. How can I describe all of this? Krishna is born in Gokula at an auspicious time. When Nanda Bābā is surrounded by cowherd men, he looks most radiant. The ascetics received wealth not available even to the demigods, and Nanda gave various gifts to the Brahmins. The cowherd women turn around and give their blessings. Krishna is held in their laps and they give their blessings that he may live long. They bless Yaśodā with a long life, and she is immersed in pleasure as she receives their congratulatory songs. The poet Vṛndāvana Dāsa remarks that human eyes need an eternity to gaze at the full beauty of Krishna. As a beautiful son is born to Nanda and Yaśodā, all the assembled people make loud noises as they watch this rare and auspicious event.

61. Lala cirujivanaun rani (May Your Son Live Long, Queen), RV 2.329, Cācā Vṛndāvana Dāsa

This song about blessing Krishna's birth by Cācā Vṛndāvana Dāsa is set in similar fashion as Song 48. However, in this recording Tintāl is played on the *tabla* rather than Keherva.

lala cirujivani rani /
hita saun deta asisa vadhu jana ami sravata vani //
gokula pati mandira kau gahanau braja jana sukha dani /
vrindavana hita rupa kautiki hvai hai hama jani //

Translation: H. S. Mathur

"Queen Yaśodā, may your son have a long life." While the ladies of Braj bestow their blessings, it is as if nectar flows in their speech. Krishna is an ornament in the house of Nanda Bābā in Gokula and will give infinite pleasure to all in Braj. The poet Vṛndāvana Dāsa says that Krishna will perform miraculous feats, as we all know.

Śrī Priyā Jū kī Janama Badhāi—Appearance Day of Śrī Rādhā

62. Calau vrishabhana gopa ke dvara (Let's Go to the Door of Cowherd Vṛṣabhānu), RV 2.347 (SV 16), Śrī Hita Harivaṃśa

Likewise, this poem of Śrī Hita Harivaṃśa is also set as in the previous number and in Song 48. Both 48 and this one are poems of Hita Harivaṃśa. The sound of the *pakhavāj* and the larger choral response places this recording in the Śrī Satsaṅga Bhūmi. Only the *tabla* drums were played at Choti Sarkar, while the *pakhavāj*, and occasionally the *tabla*, were played at Satsaṅga Bhūmi. There is a beautiful fast repeat in the last line.

calau vrishabhana gopa ke dvara /
janama liyau mohana hita syama ananda nidhi sukumara //
gavata juvati mudita mili mangala ucca madhura dhuni dhara /
vividha kusuma komala kisalaya dala sobhita bandana vara //
vidita veda vidhi vihita vipravara kari svastinu uccara /
mridula mridanga muraja bheri dapha divi dundubhi ravakara //
magada suta bandi carana jasa kahata pukari-pukari /
hataka hira cira patambara deta samhari-samhari //
candana sakala dhainu tana mandita cale hai gvala singara /
jaya sri hita harivamsa dugdha-dadhi cirakata madhya haridragara //

Translation: H. S. Mathur

Let us go to the house of Vṛṣabhānu, for a treasure of bliss has been born, Śrī Rādhā. Blessed is Mahārāṇī Kīrti who gave birth to this baby girl. Hearing this news all the cowherd maidens arrive and receive gifts to their hearts' content. They come with golden plates in their hands, singing sweet melodious songs. Mahārāṇī Kīrti calls all of them respectfully to her palace and gives them ornaments and colorful clothes, covering them from head to foot. Vedic scholars recite *mantras* to the sound of sweet *mṛdaṅga* drum, kettledrum, tom-tom, tambourine and flute. Bards and mintrels sing Vṛṣabhānu's praises. Like raindrops in the month of Bhadon (the rainy season), yogurt and butter flows over the courtyard which becomes slippery. Poet Hita Harivaṃśa says, "May the couple, Rādhā and Krishna, so pleasant to our eyes, be immortal."

63. Lali cirajivani teri (Dear Girl, May You Be Long-lived), RV 2.360, Cācā Vṛndāvana Dāsa

This poem blessing the birth of Rādhā is patterned musically after Song 61 above. The small setting, and the use of the *tabla*, reveals its venue as Choti Sarkar.

lali cirajivani teri /
aba ya braja sukha sindhu badaigau suna asisa meri //
hon hun macala paryau ya pauri mukha dekhaun neri /
vrindavana hita rupa bhagyaphala daiva dayau eri //

Translation: H. S. Mathur

"Dear Rādhā, may you live long!" Hearing my blessings, the ocean of pleasure in Braj will rise all the more. I also do not want leave your doorstep, so that I may continue to see your face. Poet Vṛndāvana Dāsa says, "Because of your good fortune, God has given you such beauty."

64. Ranga barasai (Colors Rain Down), RV 2. 393, Rasika Dāsa

This poem by Rasika Dāsa is patterned after Song 60 above, in slow Rūpak at first, with faster sections in Dīp Chandī. The fast repeats, however, are not included here, as only the first four lines are given in this recording. The subject matter is the birth of Śrī Rādhā in the home of Vṛṣabhānu as well as in Gokula.

ranga barasai ri heli kirati mahala men /

jasa darasai ri heli rasa ki cahala men //
aju braja phulyau sabai ravala vinoda suhavanau /
udau suraja vamsa kau nandaraya mana kau bhavanau //1//
sukrita phulyau ri heli sri mahibhana kau /
ananda jhulyau ri heli srutinu bakhana kau //
gopi-gopa su vimala angina anuthi ati mani rali /
varata ratana mani deta bhushana nirakhi palana men lali //2//
rangilau badhavau ri heli jiya chaki daina kau /
mridanga bajavau ri heli mangala caina kau //
vrishabhana ghara kanya bhai maha moda gokula men chayau /
palana men kilakata samvarau rati-bija jasumati hiya bayau //3//
bade gumana ke ri heli dana bahuta daye /
jacaka jana pai ri heli ghana laun unaye //
ashta siddhi ju sang alai tahala men rama nihariye /
aju ballavaraja pai aisvarya kotika variye //4//
saunja sajavau ri heli kancana thara men /
vidhihi lajavau ri heli raci singara men //
calahu kautika dekhiye brajaraja jahan nacata khile /
sohila men dou samadhi anka bhari-bhari ken mile //5//
kesara bhinje ri heli saurabha saun sane /
harada dahi ke ri heli ghata dhorata ghane //
rasika varata naina ita-uta calata gaja ki cala pai /
caraun carana ki renu jhalakata sukha sakhi ke bhala pai //6//

Translation: H. S. Mathur

O friend! Colors are flowing in the palace of Kīrti, Rādhā's mother, and there is glory in the flow of this enormous pleasure. Today the entire region of Braj is immersed in pleasure and joy. At her house in Rāval, the joy is like that of the birth of Krishna in Nanda's house. It appears that the good deeds of Vṛṣabhānu have fructified. And it is very pleasing to the ear to hear the full description.

Cowherd women and men gather with pleasure in the courtyard of the palace. They offer jewels and ornaments after seeing the beautiful baby girl in her cradle. They make offerings to their hearts' content and the house is colorfully decorated. The girlfriends talk among themselves, saying that they should peacefully play on the barrel-drum. In Gokula there is also a lot of rejoicing because a daughter was born in the house of

Vṛṣabhānu. Krishna is playing in his crib, and this event created a seed of love in the heart of Yaśodā. With great pleasure lots of money is given; it is as if wealth rains down on the ascetics. The Goddess of Wealth (Lakṣmī) is in attendance along with the eight perfections (*siddhis*).

King Vallabha (Nanda) receives immense riches, golden plates filled with gifts. Everyone is such that even Lord Brahmā feels ashamed. The girlfriends say, "Let us go and see the fun of Krishna dancing." In the midst of birth songs (*sohila*), each side of the family embraces the other heartily. The girlfriends are drenched in saffron and give off sweet scents. Vessels full of tumeric and yogurt are brought forth. The poet Rasika sacrifices his eyes seeing the elephant-like gait of the girlfriends, offering the dust of those four feet to the foreheads of the girlfriends as signs of happiness.

65. Tu dekha suta (Behold the Daughter), RV 2. 398, Caturbhuja Dāsa

This poem of Caturbhuja Dāsa is rendered in a slow Dhamār in a variey of the *rāga* Chayanat (the major scale in the ascent, with N̲ in the descent). The same format will be found in Song 67 below, the poem opening Volume III. As in many of these poems, they seem to have been written specifically with the tune in mind. There is an almost perfect correspondence between rhythm, melody, and poetic diction.

tu dekha suta vrishabhana ki /
mriga naini sundara sobha nidhi anga-anga sundara thana ki //
gaura varana bahu kanti badana ki sarada-candra unamana ki /
visva mohani bala dasa men kati kehari bandhana ki //
vidhi ki srishti na hoi manu yaha banika aurai bana ki /
catrabhuja prabhu giridhara layaka braja pragati jota samana ki //

Translation: H. S. Mathur

Behold the daughter of Vṛṣabhānu, who has lovely eyes like a deer. Exceedingly beautiful and a treasure of grace, each part of her body is a treasury of loveliness. Her fair complexion is complemented by a unique glow in her body, comparable to the moons of winter. As the infant embodiment of universal beauty, her waist is slim and well-formed like that of a lion. It appears that she is not the product of normal human creation, but was born by some other process. Caturbhuja says that now a perfectly suitable spouse is born in Braj for Lord Mountain-lifter (Krishna).

66. Pyari, tuma kaun hau ri (Sweetheart, Who Are You?), RV 2.500-501, Sūra Dāsa

This poem of Sūra Dāsa (1478-1580) concludes Volume II in our Rādhāvallabha Songbook. It is placed in the group of songs celebrating the festival of Sāñjhī, in which sand paintings are made all over Vrindaban. It has a distinct tune which is not according to any *rāga*, but could be placed in a Gaud Malhar scale (see Song 60 above). The rhythm begins in Tintāl, but quickly changes in the second line to a faster pace as with the second part of the melody. The refrain is repeated between the verses (*antarās*).

pyari, tuma kaun hau ri phulava binana hari //
neha lagana kau banyau bagica phuli rahi phulavari /
apu krishna vanamali aye tuma bolau kyaun na piyari //
hamsi lalita jaba kahyau syama saun ye vrishabhanu dulari /
tumharau kaha lagai ya vana men rokata gaila hamari //
syama sakha sakhiyana samajhavain hatha na karau meri pyari /
phala druma vana vatika sughara ke hamahin hain rakhavari //
radheju phala phula liye hain vividha sugandha samhari /
Sura syama radha mukha nirakhata ekataka rahe nihari //

Translation: H. S. Mathur

"Dear girl, who are you to be collecting flowers here? This garden is made of love and devotion and its flowers are blossoming here." "Krishna, the gardener himself, has come to greet you. Rādhā, why don't you speak to him?" When her smiling friend Lalitā introduces her to Krishna as the daughter of Vṛṣabhānu, Rādhā says, "What business do you have blocking my way in this grove?" The Dark One, his friends, and her girlfriends, all tell Rādhā not to be obstinate. Krishna says, "I am the keeper of all the fruit trees in this beautiful forest grove." The poet Sūra says, "Dear Rādhā, your perfumes are spread through all these fruits and flowers, and Krishna intently gazes at your face."

Chapter Three: The Rādhāvallabha Songbook, Volume III

[CD 12]

Daśahāra

Daśahāra refers to the tenth day of the bright half of the month of Jyeṣṭha, and the tenth day of the bright half of the month of Āśvina.

67. Prata samaya dou rasa lampata (At Dawn, the Two Are Greedy for Love), RV 3.1 (CP 3), Śrī Hita Harivaṃśa

This poem of Śrī Hita Harivaṃśa is rendered in a slow Dhamār in a variety of the *rāga* Chayanat (the major scale in the ascent, with N̲ in the descent). The same format will be found in Song 65 in Volume II. There is a near perfect correspondence between rhythm, melody, and poetic diction.

prata samaya dou rasa lampata,
surata-juddha jaya-juta ati phula/
srama-varija ghana-vindu vadana para,
bhushana angahi anga vikula//
kachu rahyau tilaka sithila alakavali,

vadana kamala manaun ali bhula/
jai sri hita harivamsa madana-ranga rangi rahe,
naina-baina kati sithila dukula//

Translation: Rupert Snell (1991, 186)

At dawn the two are [still] greedy for love,
rejoicing greatly in their victory in the battle of passion;
heavy drops of perspiration are on their faces,
and the adornments on their various limbs are in disarray.
Of their tilakas but little remains:
curly locks like wayward bees are loose on lotus-faces;
Hita Harivaṃśa, their eyes and words are steeped in the colour of love,
and their clothes lie loose at their waists!

Rāsa ke Pada—Rāsa Dance Songs

The Rāsa Līlā or Rāsa Dance is a vibrant tradition in Braj, associated since time immemorial with the pastimes of Krishna. Rāsa Līlā specifically refers to the circular dance of the cowherd girls with Krishna, and as well, to playful pastimes in which the participants partake of different flavors (*rasas*) and thus savour the tastes of amorous love-games in the company of Krishna. This pertains specifically to the roles of Rādhā and Krishna and their confidantes, the girlfriends (cowherd girls who are friends) of Rādhā and Krishna.

The Rāsa Dance is in fact celebrated throughout India every year by Vaishnavas during the autumnal season of Śāradā Pūrṇimā; the full moon in the month of Āśvina, usually around mid-October. In Vrindaban, the Rādhāvallabha Sampradāya celebrates the Rāsa Dance with a plethora of beautiful songs in various *rāgas* and *tālas*. In fact, the Rāsa Dance songs comprise the largest single collection in the hymnal. This group of songs describes the nocturnal Rāsa Dance near the bank of the Yamunā river. The lyrics contain many references to music. These songs or hymns are performed in Samāj-Gāyan style, and several of them are only performed on particular days of the calendar, and at no other time. Some are rendered in traditional *rāgas* (melodic modes) like Sarang, Kedar and Kamod and *tālas* (rhythmic cycles), while others exhibit special melodies unique to the Rādhāvallabha Sampradāya.

The Rāsa Dance episode has been translated and analyzed relative to its principal Sanskrit source, the *Bhāgavata Purāṇa*, by Graham Schweig in his recent book, *Dance of Divine Love: India's Classic Sacred Love Story: The Rāsa Līlā of Krishna* (2005). The critical significance of the Rāsa Dance narrative is stated boldly by Schweig: "Among all scriptural texts of India, originating with the Vedas, the Rāsa Līlā episode becomes the most important revelation of supreme love. As a story, the Rāsa Līlā has a beginning and an end. As a sacred love story, however, it is the timeless dance in which God and the soul lose themselves forever in the rhythms, melodies, and movements of divine love. The drama of the *rasa* is a celebration of souls joining together to glorify God's unlimited power to love, and further, of God's capacity to love each soul intimately."[47]

The Rāsa Dance section is divided into the five "Acts," (*Bhāgavata Purāṇa*, 10. 29-33), indicated below.

1. Krishna plays beautiful music on his flute, and attracts the cowherd girls in Vrindaban. The girls abandon their homes and families and go out into the forest to find him. Some girls remain and meditate on Krishna. Krishna, after visiting with them, suddenly disappears.
2. The cowherd girls then search for Krishna and discover in the sand footprints of an unnamed girl who had accom-

[47] Graham Schweig (2005), 182

panied him. They follow the tracks and suddenly find her (i.e., Rādhā, though she is not named in the *Bhāgavata*) alone, and stop to share her grief.

3. The Song of the Cowherd Girls: *Gopī-gīta*. All of the girls then sit together and sing songs of separation and longing for Krishna.
4. Krishna suddenly reappears to them and explains that his disappearance was deliberate in order to strengthen their love for him. He lectures about intensity and the purity of their love.
5. The Rāsa Dance then begins. Krishna multiples himself to accommodate each girl as they all dance together swiftly through the night. The heavenly Gandharva musicians sing and play drums to accompany the already tumultuous sounds of the Rāsa Dance. After growing tired, the girls relax with Krishna in the waters of the Yamunā. The girls then return home exhausted and weary but satisfied. Their husbands, deluded by cosmic illusion (*māyā*, were none the wiser.

With this scenario in mind, it becomes clear how the vernacular Vaishnava poets adapted the themes and scenic moments from this story to be conveyed in poetry meant for performance in Samāj-Gāyan.

68. Mohana madana tribhangi (Enchanting, Intoxicating Threefold Form), RV 3.5 (CP 63), Śrī Hita Harivaṃśa

One of the most beloved songs composed by Śrī Hita Harivaṃśa, included in his work *Caurāśi-Pad* (63), is "Mohana Madana Tribhaṅgī." It is sung only once a year on the evening of the full-moon on Śāradā Pūrṇimā, and was said by Kisori Saran Ali to be one of the tradition's most prized musical arrangements. The complete song is recorded here as sung by Rajendra Prasad Sharma and company. The text contains four stanzas of five lines each. The first line of each is sung in one tune, while the next two couplets repeat another tune that is spread over two lines. The *rāga* mentioned above the song in the anthology, *Rādhāvallabhjī kā Varṣotsava* (3.5) is Gaurī. In classical music Gaurī has two types, both of which have flatted r̲ and d̲; the composition discussed here does not have these, but resembles Vilaval scale (i.e., major scale).

Each group of five lines are performed in a format whereby the *jhelās* or responsorial singers repeat the line of the lead singer, who occasionally repeats phrases interspersed with exclamatory words like "eri ha," ("O Sakhī") which are again repeated verbatim by the chorus. After a series of interactive phrases, there is a quick repetition of the last two lines of the stanza before beginning slowly with the next stanza again. The rhythm is a slow *tāla* of 16 beats similar to Tintāl (16 beats) that is divided up into four sections: cymbals are played on the first three beats of each section.

mohana madana tribhangi / mohana muni mana rangi //
mohana muni saghana pragata paramananda, guna gambhira gupala /
sisa kirita sravana mani kundala, ura mandita banamala //
pitambara tana dhatu vicitrita, kala kinkini kati cangi /
nakha mani tarani carana sarasi - ruha, mohana madana tribhangi //1//

mohana venu bajavai / ihi rava nari bulavai //
ai braja nari sunata vamsi rava, grihapati bandhu bisare /
darasana madana gupala manohara, manasija tapa nivare //
harashita badana banka avalokana, sarasa madhura dhvani gavai /
madhumaya syama samana adhara dhara, mohana venu bajavai //2//

rasa racyau bana mahin / vimala kalpataru chanhin //
bimala kalpataru tira supesala, sarada raina vara canda /
sitala - manda - sugandha pavana bahai, tahan khelata nanda-nanda //
adbhuta tala mridanga manohara, kinkini sabda karahin /
jamuna pulina rasika rasa sagara, rasa racyau vana mahin //3//

dekhata madhukara keli / mohe khaga mriga beli //
mohe mriga dhenu sahita sura sundari, prema magana pata chute /
udagana cakita thakita sasi mandala, koti madana mana lute //
adhara pana parirambhana ati rasa, ananda magana saheli /
jaya sri hita harivamsa rasika sacu pavata, dekhata madhukara keli //4//

Translation: Rupert Snell (1991, 240-242)

Madanamohana of thrice-bent stance!
—Mohana who impassions the hearts of sages!
Mohana is the highest bliss, manifest in concrete form,
Gopāla profound in qualities;
on his head a diadem, on his ear a jeweled ring,
and his chest is adorned with a garland of wild flowers.
His yellow-clad body is coloured with mineral pigments,
sweet bells are at his handsome waist;
the gems of his toenails are suns to the lotuses of his feet:
Madanamohana of thrice-bent stance!

Mohana plays the flute,
and with this sound he calls the women.
On hearing the sound of his reed-pipe the women of Vraja are come,
dismissing all thought of husbands and kinsmen;
a vision of the captivating Madanagopāla
checks the anguish of desire.
With gladdened face and oblique glance
he intones a joyous and delightful sound;
holding it to his lips, [with music] like honeyed words of persuasion
Mohana plays the flute.

He has contrived a round-dance in the forest,
in the shade of the pure tree of plenty.
On the fair riverbank with its pure tree of plenty,
an autumn night and a splendid moon,
a cool, gentle and fragrant wind blows,
and there plays Nandananda.
Wondrous cymbals, the enchanting drum
and girdle-bells resound;

on the Yamunā's sandy bank the lover, the ocean of *rasa*
has contrived a round-dance in the forest!
Watching the honeybee's sport,
birds, beasts and creepers are enchanted.
With the beasts and cattle, beautiful deities [too] are enchanted,
immersed in love with dress disordered;
the constellations are bewildered, the moon's orb stilled,
and the hearts of myriads of love-gods stolen.
With that most relishable kissing and embracing
the companion-girls are engrossed in bliss;
Hita Harivaṃśa the voluptuary finds joy
watching the honeybee's sport.

[CD 13]

69. Lala ki rupa madhuri (The Boy's Beauty and Sweetness), RV 3.5-6 (SV 22), Śrī Hita Harivaṃśa

This is a rare and valued song by Śrī Hita Harivaṃśa that has been handed down for many centuries within the Rādhāvallabha tradition. It is performed in Dhamār (fourteen beats), at first very slow but with alternating medium tempo sections. The first words are "*rūpa mādhurī*," which are then joined with "*lāla kī*." At first, the tune resembles the *rāga* Bhupali (or Malkauns) but contains different notes as it slowly unfolds, serving to declassify it as a pure Hindustani *rāga*. When analyzed, it appears as if two Kalyan scales are conjoined, one from S and the other from P. The recorded version is a marvelously beautiful rendition with heartfelt phrasing and responses by the singers. It was recorded in its entirety, October 1992, in a private sitting at the interior grave site (*samādhi*) shrine of Śrī Lalitacaran Goswami, former head of the community (*sampradāya*).

lala ki rupa madhuri nainana nirakha naika sakhi /
manasija mana harana hasi, sanmarau sukumara rasi,
nakha-sikha anga angana umangi saubhaga simva nakhi //
rangamagi sira suranga paga, lataki rahi vama bhaga,
campakali kutila alaka, bica - bica rakhi /
ayata driga aruna lola, kundala mandita kapola,
adhara dasana dipati ki chabi kyon hun na jata lakhi //
abhayada bhuja danda mula, pina ansa sanukula,
kanaka nikasha lasi dukula damini dharakhi /
ura pura mandara hara, muktalara vara sudara,
matta durada gati tiyana ki deha dasa karakhi //
mukalita vaya nava kisora, vacana racana cita ke cora,
madhuritu pika sava nuta manjari cakhi /
jaya sri natavata harivamsa gana, ragini kalyana tana,
sapta svarana kala ite para, muralika barakhi //

Translation: Charles S. J. White (1996, 98-99)

O Sakhi, steal a glance at the beauty of the Darling. His laughter plunders Kāmadeva's heart. He is a treasure of handsome tenderness. From head to toe his beauty is exciting. His beauty pierces the utmost limits. The red-colored turban hangs down at the left. *Campaka* buds nestle in his curly locks. His large, beautiful eyes are colored with love. Earrings grace his cheeks. The beauty of his lips and teeth is shining. Why don't you go and see? His strong arms and big shoulders will protect you. Gold as from the touchstone adorns his clothes Like the lightning flash. Very becoming to his chest is the necklace chain of *mamdar* flower pearls. His love-mad elephant gait arouses women's bodies. The elegance of the young lover's words of blooming youth steals the heart, like the sounds of baby cuckoos, after tasting new mango flowers in the time of spring. Śrī Hita Harivaṃśa says, there is song and dance in the rhythm of the *rāga* Kalyan. The flute rains the seven beautiful sounds.

70. Calahi radhike sujana (Come, Wise Rādhikā), RV 3.6 (CP 12), Śrī Hita Harivaṃśa

This number follows the pattern of the *rāga* Bageshri of the Hindustani tradition (S M $\underline{G}$ M D $\underline{N}$ s, s $\underline{N}$ D M P D M $\underline{G}$ R S). The refrain (*sthāyī*) is composed of the first two lines, which alternate with the additional two-line verses (*antarā*). These fit into the normal style of a Dhrupad composition in Cautāl of twelve beats. It begins with the syllable "*ca*" on the first beat (*sam*) on the upper octave note in the scale (s). Sometimes the filler "*mai*" (O Sakhī) is inserted in order to complete the line. This occurs in several of the Samāj-Gāyan renditions. It would be comparable to the addition of "O Lord" or "Amen" in some Western hymns. This poem has been analyzed by Rupert Snell (1983).

calahi radhike sujana, tere hita sukha nidhana,
rasa racyau syama tata kalinda-nandini /
nirtata yuvati samaha, raga ranga ati kutuha,
bajata rasamula muralika anandini //
vamsivata nikata jahan, parama ramani bhumi tahan,
sakala sukhada malaya bahai vayu mandini /
jati ishada vikasa, kanana atisaya suvasa,
raka nishi sarada masa vimala candini //
narabahana prabhu nihara, locana bhari ghosha-nari,
nakha-sikha saundarya kama-dukha-nikandini /
bilasahu bhuja griva meli, bhamini sukha-sindhu jheli,
nava nikunja syama keli jagata-bandini //

Translation: Rupert Snell (1991, 193)

Come, wise Rādhikā! For your sake Śyāma has arranged a round-dance,
a store of joy, on the banks of the Yamunā;
groups of young girls dance in great eagerness at the music and
merriment as the joyful flute, source of delight, is playing.
In that most pleasing place near the *vaṃśīvaṭa*

a soft breeze blows from the [sandal-clad] Malaya mountain,
yielding all joys.
the forest is strongly fragrant with half-blown jasmine,
and there is bright moonlight in the full-moon autumn night.
Cowherd girl, feast your eyes on Naravāhana's Lord,
whose head-to-toe beauty removes the agony of desire;
Lady! Experience this ocean of delight, rejoice with your arms
joined around his neck,
for Śyāma's sport in the fresh bower is worthy of the world's praise!

71. Aja gopala rasa rasa khelata (Today Gopāla Plays in the Delight of the Round-dance), RV 3.7 (CP 24), Śrī Hita Harivaṃśa

This beautiful slow composition of Śrī Hita Harivaṃśa stays within the major scale except for a flatted seventh. This coincides with the *rāga* Khammaj in the Hindustani system, with two types of N (S G M P D N s, s N̲ D P M G R S). The repeated rests on the third note (G) give it the *rasa* effect of *karuṇā* (compassion). The first two lines comprise the refrain (*sthāyī*), which alternate with the succeeding couplets as verses (*antarā*). The *sam* is on the extended syllable "*rā*" of the third word, *rasa*.

aja gopala rasa rasa khelata,
pulina kalpa taru tira ri sajani /
sarada vimala nabha candra virajata,
rocaka trividha samira ri sajani //
campaka bakula malati mukalita,
matta mudita pika kira ri sajani /
desi sudhanga raga ranga nikau,

braja juvatina ki bhira ri sajani //
maghava mudita nisana bajayau,
vrata chandyau muni dhira ri sajani /
jai sri hita harivamsa magana mana syama,
harata madana ghana pira ri sajani //

Translation: Rupert Snell (1991, 204)

Today Gopāla plays in the delight of the round-dance,
on the sandy riverbank near the tree of plenty, oh my companion;
the moon of the clear autumn sky is resplendent
and pleasant is the breeze of threefold nature, oh my companion.
Campaka, Bakula and jasmine are in bud
and cuckoo and parrot are impassioned and enthralled, oh my companion;
excellent is the music and merriment of the *desi sudhanga* dance,
in that throng of Vraja damsels, oh my companion.
Indra has sounded his kettledrum in delight
and the resolute sage has abandoned his vow, oh my companion;
Hita Harivaṃśa, Śyāma with enraptured heart
removes the deep pain of passion, oh my companion.

72. Aja bana nikau rasa banayau (Today in the Forest the Rāsa Dance is Performed), RV 3.7 (CP 36), Śrī Hita Harivaṃśa

This Rāsa Līlā poem of Śrī Hita Harivaṃśa is performed in the *rāga* Vrinda-bani Sarang, which uses two types of N but no G (S R M P N s, s N̲ P M R S). It is rendered here in the lilting rhythm of Dīp Chandī, in a quick succession of fourteen *mātrās* (3-2-2, 3-2-2). The tune begins with a double-note for the syllables "*Aja*" on the second note (R) and goes up to the seventh (N), and ends back on the tonic (S) after touching the R and the N, below the tonic. The first line is repeated by the *jhelās*, and the second line serves as the beginning of the *antarās* (verses). There are fast repeats in the *antarā* portions, and a medium Keherva̅ in the final two lines with double-time in the repeat of the refrain.

aja bana nikau rasa banayau /
pulina pavitra subhaga jamuna tata, mohana bainu bajayau //
kala kankana-kinkini nupura dhvani, suni khaga-mriga sacu payau /
juvatina mandala madhya syama ghana, saranga raga jamayau //
tala mridanga upanga muraja dapha, mili rasa-sindhu badhayau /
vividha visada vrishabhanu nandini, anga sudhanga dikhayau //
abhinaya nipuna lataki lata locana, bhrikuti ananga nacayau /
tata thei-ta thei dharata nautana gati, pati brajaraja rijhayau //
sakala udara nripati cudamani, sukha varida barashayau /
parirambhana cumvana alingana ucita juvati jana payau //
varashata kusuma mudita nabha nayaka, indra nisana bajayau /
jai sri hita harivamsa rasika radha pati, jasa bitana jaga chayau //

Translation: H. S. Mathur

Today, a beautiful Rāsa Dance is being performed in the forest. The wind is pure and the banks of Yamunā are lovely where Mohana plays on the flute. The sound of the anklets is simply charming, and the deer and birds are very happy hearing it. Among the bevy of young girlfriends Krishna is playing the *rāga* Sarang, and the ocean of pleasure increases with the sound of *mṛdaṅga, upāṅga,* tambourine and other percussion instruments. Rādhā, the daughter of Vṛṣabhānu, exposes her lovely and scented limbs. She is an expert in acting (drama) as her braided curls hung over her eyes, and the movement of her eyebrows makes even Kāmadeva dance. In a fast dancing movement *tatta thei tatta thei,* she entices her husband, Krishna the King of Vraja. With a rain of pleasure, he embraces and kisses all the girlfriends. From the sky flowers start raining and even Lord Indra plays upon a tom tom. Śrī Hita Harivaṃśa says that Krishna's fame spreads like the sky over the whole world.

[CD 14]

73. Madana mathana ghana (Dense Bower Which Churns Desire), RV 3.8 (CP 65), Śrī Hita Harivaṃśa

This song by Śrī Hita Harivaṃśa is rendered in the *rāga* Puriya, which has a flatted second and a sharpened fourth (S R G *M* D N s, s N D *M* G R S). The first syllable "*ma*" of the word "*madana*" begins on the *khāli* (9th beat) of the sixteen-beat Tintāl, with the *sam* on the syllable "*ni*" of *nikunja*. The first two lines make up the refrain, with the succeeding couplets as *antarā* verses. The final two lines are given a fast repeat that will include the refrain.

madana mathana ghana nikunja khelata hari,
raka rucira sarada rajani /
jamuna pulina tata sura taru ke nikata,
racita rasa cali mili sajani //
bajata mridu mridanga nacata sabai sudhanga,
tain na sravana sunyau benu bajani /
jai sri hita harivamsa prabhu radhika ramana,
mokaun bhavai mai jagata bhagata bhajani //

Translation: Rupert Snell (1991, 243-244)

Hari plays in the dense bower which destroys desire,
on the lovely full-moon night of autumn;
come, my friend, and join the round-dance
contrived near the *kalpa* tree on the Yamunā's sandy shore.
All dance a *sudhaṅga* as the sweet drum resounds,
and [only] you have not heard the flute-playing;
Hita Harivaṃśa's lord, Rādhikā's lover, is dear to me
as worthy of worship with the world's adoration, oh my companion

74. Mohini mohana range (The Enchantress and Enchanter in Sport), RV 3.9 (CP 69), Śrī Hita Harivaṃśa

This poem by Śrī Hita Harivaṃśa is played in a slow Tintāl in the scale of Khammaj. The first syllable "*mo*" falls on the *khāli* on the note D, and the *sam* on P coincides with "*raṅge.*" There are fast repeats in the *antarās* beginning with the third line. The song is nearly complete, with the last two lines omitted in the recording.

mohini mohana range prema surange,
matta mudita kala nacata sudhange /
sakala-kala pravina, kalyana ragini lina,
kahata na banai madhuri anga ange //
tarani-tanaya tira trividya sakhi samira,
manaun muni-vrata dharyau kapoti kokila kira /
nagari-navakishora mithuna manasi cora,
sarasa gabata dou manjula mandara ghora //
kankana kinkini dhuni, mukhara nupurana suni,
(jai sri) hita harivamsa rasa barasai nava-taruni /

Translation: Rupert Snell (1991, 248)

The enchantress and Mohana are joyful and flushed with love-
intoxicated and delighted, they dance sweetly in the *sudhaṅga* step.
Skilled in all the arts and engrossed in the Kalyana *rāginī*,
their sweetness in every limb cannot be put into words.
On the bank of the Yamunā with a breeze of threefold nature,
sakhi, it is as though pigeon, cuckoo and parrot have taken a sage's vow of silence.
Skillful lady and fresh youth, a pair to steal the mind,
sing sweetly in a lovely low tone.
Hita Harivaṃśa, hearing the sound of bracelets and bells and tinkling anklets,

joy showers down on the young maiden.

75. Syama sanga radhika (Rādhikā with Śyāma), RV 3.9 (CP 71), Śrī Hita Harivaṃśa

This poem by Śrī Hita Harivaṃśa is rendered in the *rāga* Kedar, which has a sharpened fourth in its descending scale (S M G P D P N D s, s N D P *M* P D P M R S). The rhythm of Jhaptāl (10 *mātrās*: 2-3, 2-3) prevails, beginning with the *sam* ("śyā" of Śyāma) on the first beat, and the *khāli* ("rā" of Rādhikā) on the sixth. The first line is the refrain, with each additional two-lines acting as a verse (*antarā*) with fast repeats. This is one of only two songs (see Song 79) in the collection in which Śrī Kuñja Bihārī Dās, one of the main responsorial singers, leads the refrain and verses. There are no cymbals, only tabla and harmonium. Notice that in the fifth line there are the letters of the *sargam*, the Hindustani do re me (S R G, etc).

syama sanga radhika rasa mandala bani /
bica nandalala brajabala campaka barana,
jyonva ghana tadita bica kanaka marakata mani //
leta gati mana tatta thei hastaka bheda,
sa-re-ga-ma-pa-dha-ni-ye sapta sura nandani /
nirttarasa pahira pata nila pragatita chabi,
vadana janon jalada men makara ki candani //
raga ragini tana mana sangita matta,
thakita rakesa nabha sarada ki jamini /
jai sri hita harivamsa madhuri anga-anga
barabasa liyau mohana cita cori //

Translation: Rupert Snell (1991, 250)

Rādhikā is decked out with Śyāma in the Rāsa circle;
in the middle are Nandalāla and the Vraja damsel of
campaka hue,
like gold and emerald amidst cloud and lightning.
She adopts dance-steps, [calling] the measure "tatta
thei"

[making] various hand movements and delighting
in the seven notes of the *gamut*;
In the joy of the dancing, her face with its splendour
seen against
the blue dress she wears is like Capricorn moonlight
against a cloud.
The moon in the sky of that autumn night is worn
out
by the musical precepts of *rāga* and *rāginī*, note sequences and rhythmic variations;
Hita Harivaṃśa's lord is a *haṃśa* (goose), while she
has a lion's waist;
he has destroyed Madana's pride and she has the gait
of an enraptured elephant.

76. Sudhanga nacata navala kisori (The Young Maiden Dances a Sudhaṅga), RV 3.9 (CP 78), Śrī Hita Harivaṃśa

This composition of Śrī Hita Harivaṃśa is in a medium-slow Tintāl of sixteen *mātrās*. The *sam* falls on the syllable "na" of *navala*, whereas the first syllable of the first word coincides with the *khāli* (ninth beat). The *rāga* is Shiva Ranjani which has five notes (S R G̲ P D s, s D P G̲ R S) with a flatted third on G̲. The first three lines make up the *sthāyī* (refrain), and then the *antarā* (verses) are sung in two lines each with alternation of the refrain in between. The last line is given a fast repeat that builds to a climax with the repetition of the refrain.

sudhanga nacata navala kisori /
thei-thei kahata cahata pritama disi,
vadana candra manau trishita cakori //
tana bandhana mana men nagari,
dekhata syama kahata ho-hori /
jai sri hita harivamsa madhuri anga-anga
barabasa liyau mohana cita cori //

Translation: Rupert Snell (1991, 256)

The young maiden dances a *sudhaṅga*;
"thei! thei!" she calls, looking towards her lover
like a *cakori*, thirsting for the moon of his face.
Seeing the one skilled in well-timed melodic passages
and in rhythmic measurement, Śyāma cries "Ho hori!";
Hita Harivaṃśa, the sweetness of her various limbs
has forcibly stolen Mohana's mind!

77. Vrishabhanu nandini madhura (Sweet Daughter of Vṛṣabhānu), RV 3.9-10 (CP 81), Śrī Hita Harivaṃśa

This poem of Śrī Hita Harivaṃśa appears to be set to the well-known *rāga* Darbari Kanhara. But that would not be the case since *rāgas* that owed their origin to Islamic or Moghul courts (darbars) were forbidden within Hindu temple music. In this case, it would be renamed as simply Kanhara, of which there are many varieties that predate these court situations. The pace is a slow to medium Tintāl of sixteen *mātrās*. The *antarās* begin with the fourth line of which there is a fast repeat. Occasionally, in this song and others, the well-adjusted ear might perceive the editor's voice in support of the singers.

vrishabhanu nandini madhura kala gavai /
vikata aughara tana carcari tala saun,
nanda-nandana manasi moda upajavai /
prathama majjana caru cira kajjala tilaka,
sravana kundala vadana candrani lajavai
subhaga naka bhesari ratana hataka jari
adhara bandhuka dasana kunda camakavai
valaya kankana caru urasi rajata haru
kativa kinkini carana nupura bajavai
hamsa kala gamini mathata mada kamini,
nakhani madathankita ranga ruci dyavai //
nirta sagara rabhasa rahasi nagari navala
candra cali vividha bhedani janavai
koka vidya vidita bhai abhinaya nipuna,

bhu-vilasani makara-ketana nacavai //
nibida kanana bhavana bahu ranjita khana
sarasa alapa sukha punja barasavai /
ubhaya sangama sindhu surata pushana bandhu,
dravata makaranda harivamsa ali pavai //

Translation: Rupert Snell (1991, 258)

Vṛṣabhānu's daughter sings in soft and mellow tone;
With exacting and wondrous melodic passages in the *tāla* of Carcari,
she creates delight in the mind of Nandanandana.
Firstly bathing, and charming with veil, collyrium and *tilaka*
And with rings on her ears, her face puts the moon-light to shame;
She has a blessed nose-ring of jewel-studded gold,
And her lips like *bandhuka* flowers make her jasmine teeth gleam.
Pretty bracelets and bangles, the necklace adorning her heart,
The bells at her waist and the anklets at her feet she makes resound;
The lady with the gait of a *kalahaṃsa* stirs desire
As the *madayāmtika* of her nails gives a colourful lus-tre.
Impetuous in this ocean of dance, in solitude the young accomplished lady
Demonstrates the various movements of *candracali*;
Knowledgeable in the amatory arts, skilled in gestic-ulation and
Dramatic gesture, with the sporting of her eyebrow she sets the god of love adancing.
In the house in the impenetrable forest, her lover delighted in her arms,
She makes fall a shower of joy with the sweet pre-

lude;
Harivaṃśa the *ali* enjoys the nectar oozing from the lotus of
amorous enjoyment on the two confluent oceans!

78. Aju mere kahe calau mriganaini (Come Today at My Bidding, Doe-eyed Lady), RV 3.10 (CP 16), Śrī Hita Harivaṃśa

This song, also in Tintāl, differs from other songs in the selection of the starting words of the refrain. The first words are "kahe calau" with the *sam* on the penultimate syllable "*nai*" of *mriganaini* (doe-eyed), followed by "*aju mere.*" It is in the *rāga* Bhimpalasi, with flatted third and seventh (N̲ S G̲ M P N̲ s, s N̲ D P M G̲ R S). The *antarās* begin with the second line, and alternate between slow and fast repeats.

aju mere kahe calau mriganaini /
gavata sarasa juvati mandala men,
pia saun milai bhalai pika vainni /
parama pravina koka vidya men,
abhinaya nipuna laga gati laini /
ruparasi suni navala kisori,
pala pala dyatati candani raini /
jai sri hita harivamsa cali ati atura
radha ramana surata sukha daini /
rahasi rabhasa alingana cumbana,
madana koti kula bhai kucaini /

Translation: Rupert Snell (1991, 198)

Come today at my bidding, deer-eyed lady;
He sings sweetly amidst the circle of damsels-
It is good that you join your lover, cuckoo-voiced one.
So well versed in the amatory arts,
Skillful of gesture, one who dances the laga step-

Young girl, amassment of beautiful form, heed my words:
The moonlit night passes by with every moment.
Hita Harivaṃśa, she went to him eagerly,
This giver of sensual joy to Rādhāramaṇa;
And countless dynasties of love-gods became ill-at-ease
With the ardour of their clandestine embracing and kissing.

79. Mohani madana gopala ki bamsuri (The Flute of Madana Gopāla is an Enchantress!), RV 3.10 (CP 26), Śrī Hita Harivaṃśa

This poem of Śrī Hita Harivaṃśa is set in a charming composition in the *rāga* Kamod to the rhythm of *jhaptāl* of ten beats. Kamod has all the pure notes of the major scale with an added touch of the sharpened fourth on *M*. (S R P *M* P D P N D s, s N D P *M* P D P G M R S). The *sthāyī* begins on the *sam* with the first syllable "*mo*," and follows with the *khāli* on the syllable "*ma*" of *madana*. The next five verses of two lines each begin also on the *sam*. Śrī Kuñj Bihari Dās, normally the principal response singer, renders the lead very well in this recording. This poem is analyzed linguistically by Rupert Snell (1983).

mohani madana gopala ki bamsuri /
madhuri sravana puta sunata suni radhike,
karata ratiraja ke tapa kau nasuri //
sarada raka rajani vipina vrinda sajani,
anila ati manda sitala sahita basuri /
parama pavana pulina bhringa - sevita nalina,
kalpataru tira balabira krita rasu ri //
sakala mandala bhalin tuma ju hari saun milin,
bani bara banita upama kahaun kasu ri /
tuma ju kancanatani lala markata mani
jai sri ubhai kala hamsa harivamsa bali dasuri //

Translation: Rupert Snell (1991, 205)

The flute of Madana Gopāla is an enchantress!-
Hear me, O Rādhikā; as one hears her sweetness
She destroys the anguish of Kāma.
A full-moon autumn night in the *vṛndā* forest, my friend,
And a very cool and gentle breeze, laden with fragrance;
On the most pure sandy riverbank with lotuses attended by bees
Is a round-dance performed by Balavīra under the tree of plenty.
Best of the whole dance-circle, you have joined Hari-
With what could I compare this bride and groom adorned?
You the golden-bodied one and Lāla the emerald
Are a pair of *kalahaṃsas* (geese), and Harivaṃśa their votive slave.

80. Bainnu mai baje bamsivata (O Friend, the Flute Resounds Under the *Vaṃśivaṭa*), RV 3.10-11 (CP 64), Śrī Hita Harivaṃśa

This composition is in the *rāga* Bageshri (as in Song 70 above), but instead of in Cautāl, it is rendered in a slow Tintāl that builds up to a fast pace in the final two lines and a repeat of the refrain. The *sam* falls on the syllable "*ba*" of *baje* after five *mātrās*. The song thus begins with the word "*bainnu*" on the 12th beat. The *sthāyī* is composed of the first two lines, while the verses (*antarā*) continue in three lines each.

bainnu mai baje vamsivata /
sada basanta rahata [sri] vrindavana,
pulina pavitra subhaga jamuna tata //
jatita krita makarakrita kundala
mukha aravinda bhamvara manaun lata /

dasanana kunda kali chabi lajjita,
sajjita kanaka samana pitapata //
muni mana dhyana dharata nahin pavata,
karata vinoda sanga balaka bhata /
dasa ananya bhajana rasa karana,
jai sri hita harivamsa pragata lila nata //

Translation: Rupert Snell (1991, 243)

O friend, the flute resounds under the *vaṃśivaṭa*;
Springtime endures forever in Vrindavana,
On the pure sandbanks of the blessed Yamunā shore.
A studded diadem, and earrings in crocodile's shape,
And curls I deem as bees on the lotus of his face;
The splendour of jasmine buds is put to shame by the teeth
[of him] adorned in yellow garments like gold.
Sages who meditate inwardly cannot attain him
--he frolics in the company of gallant boys;
a source of the sentiment of devotion for his devoted servants,
Hita Harivaṃśa, he is manifest as the *līlā* dancer!

81. Main ju mohana sunyau (When I Heard the Enticing Flute of Gopāla), RV 3.11 (SV 13), Śrī Hita Harivaṃśa

This song follows the same tune, *rāga*, and *tāla* patterns as "Mohani madana gopala" (Song 79), with the same *sthāyī* and *antarā* structures. The lead singer here is Śrī Rajendra Sharma, however.

mai ju mohana sunyau venu gopala kau /
vyoma muniyana sura nari vithakita bhai,
kahata nahin banata kucha bheda yati tala kau //
sravana kundala churitu rurata kuntala lalita,
rucira kasturi candana tilaka bhala kau /
canda gati manda bhai nirakhi chabi kama gai,
dekha harivamsa hita vesha nandalala kau //

Translation: Charles S. J. White (1996, 95)

When I heard the enticing flute of Gopāl,
The wives of gods and *munis* in heaven—filled with joy
Could not say a word nor tell rhythms from pauses.
The rings flashing in his ears, the beautiful
Hair falling down,
The enchanting sandal and musk *tilak*
On his forehead:
The moon saw all this and slowed down.
Harivaṃśa says, Kāmadeva's beauty fled
When he saw Nandalāl's garment.

82. Nacata mohana sanga radhika (Rādhikā Dances with Mohana), RV 3.11, Kṛṣṇa Dāsa

This poem of Kṛṣṇa Dāsa is performed in a moderately paced rhythm of Tintāl in the *rāga* Bhupali (S R G P D s). Only the first six lines are recorded here. There are fast repeats on the *antarās*. At the end of the second line of the refrain, there is a pleasing *tāna* pattern (sequence of notes in a vowel sound) on the syllable "*e*" of *liye*.

nacata mohana sanga radhika
braja juvatina ke jutha liye /
bahu paraspara jori prema basa,
mudita ganda para ganda diyen //
kankana kunita runita bara nupura,
sunata sravana khaga uparaniyen /
bajata tala rasala sarasa gati,
malava raga sudesa giyen //
sughara sangita prabina nagari,
tirapa leta ananda hiyen /
latakata sisa subhaga paga patakata,
vadata syama ho - hova kiyen //
sukha bhara bharita paraspara mandala,
susmita rasa locanana piyen /
jai sri krishna dasa hita vadata sada yaha,

vritha kaha sata kalpa jiyen //

Translation: H. S. Mathur

Rādhikā dances with Mohana (Krishna) along with a bevy of young maidens of Braj. Out of love, they have joined their arms together, raising one upon the other. The ornaments of *kaṅkana* (bracelets) on the arms and *nūpura* (ankle bells) on the ankles make a lovely sound. Hearing those beautiful sounds, birds begin circling overhead, singing the Malava *rāga* in a very sweet and enchanting rhythm. Rādhā is adept in beautiful singing and sings a *tāna* (vocal phrase), with a blissful heart. While she bends her head and moves her feet, Śyāma (Krishna) admires her movements. The entire group of dancers is filled with joy; each one's smiling eyes appear to be drinking nectar. What is the point in living for hundreds of years?—Enjoy this very moment, says poet Kṛṣṇa Dāsa.

[CD 15]

83. Aja nacata navala lala (Today a Young Boy Dances), RV 3.16, Śrī Rūpa Lāla

This poem of Śrī Rūpa Lāla (1718-1818) is also played in the *rāga* Shiva Ranjani (see Song 76 above), but in the more formal Cautāl rhythm of 12 *mātras* (4-4-4). The *sam* falls on the first syllable "*a*." The first line is the *sthāyī*, and the three two-line verses (*antarās*) follow. The words "*dhrika dhilama*," etc. refer to drum *bols* or word-phrases corresponding to drum rhythmic patterns, and add a unique flavor to the listening experience. There are fast repeats on the *antarās* which begin with line two.

aja nacata navala lala saji saja jhinna /
dhrika dhilama dhrika dhilama bajata takitaki dhilama,
nacata nayanabhirama dhakita-dhakita dhinna //
lacaki-lacaki gatina leta thumaki-thumaki carana deta,

kara ki karatara deta vadata thoma thinna /
lalita vadata bhule syama dhi dhi taki dhi dhilama,
pyari hita rupa lala nacyau chanana china //

Translation: H. S. Mathur

Today a young boy (*lāla*, Krishna) dances to the beat of several types of percussion instruments. He dances to the various phrases of the drum —*dhrika dhilama. takitaki dhilama.* Moving back and forth, he increases the speed and patter of his feet and the clapping of his hands, saying "thoma thinna." Sakhi Lalitā says, "O Śyāma, you have completely lost yourself singing these dance rhythms for Rādhā," as poet Śrī Rūpa Lāla reports.

84. Nacata gopala banai natavara bapu kachain (Gopāla Dances, Tying His Cloth Up at the Waist), RV 3.29, Śrī Harirāma Vyāsa

This poem by Śrī Harirāma Vyāsa (1511-1613) is performed in a different rhythm than most of the others, a medium Ektāl of 12 *mātrās*. The melody is a variation of the *rāga* Suddha Vilaval (major scale) with N̲. The first line is the *sthāyī*, which begins on the syllable "*na*," but is broken into two parts: *nacata gopala banai* is repeated with one melody, and the final two words, *natavara bapu kachain*, complete the melody by rising up to the upper ṡ and back down to G.

nacata gopala banai natavara bapu kachain /
gavata gati milavata ati radha ke pachain //
kinkini kancana nupura dhuni tala mridanga sohe /
manda hasa bhru-vilasa sainana mana mohe //
taruvara girivara mriga nada-bana pohe /
vrindaraka vrinda badhu taraka vidhu mohe //
samira nira pangu bhayau, balaka na paya pyavain /
vyasa sakala jiva jantu nada svada jyavain //

Translation: H. S. Mathur

Having tied his cloth up at the waist, Gopāla (Krishna) dances in the pose of a grand stylish dancer. While he sings and follows Rādhā with quick pace, the small bells accompanied by the sound of *mṛdaṅga* drum are very enticing. And with the brisk movement of his eyebrows and sweet smile, Krishna entices the hearts of everyone. Even the trees, the mountain, and the deer are captivated by his song. And beside the young maidens of Vrindaban, the stars and moon are enticed. The movement of air and water has stopped, and even children stop drinking their milk. Poet Vyāsa remarks that, "sipping the sounds of this music, all of creation is absorbed."

85. Sarada suhai ai rata (The Bright Night of Autumn Came), RV 3.30-37, Rāsa-pañcādhyāyī of 30 verses by Śrī Harirāma Vyāsa

While the theme of the Rāsa Līlā is woven throughout much of the literary output of *bhakti* poetry, it was only Nanda Dāsa and Harirāma Vyāsa who rendered full and separate vernacular versions of the Rāsa Līlā and labeled them "Rāsa Pañcādhyāyī." Literary analyses of the Rāsa Pañcādhyāyī texts of Nanda Dāsa and Harirāma Vyāsa are found in the work of R. S. McGregor (1973) and Heidi R. M. Pauwels (1996), respectively. From their observations, we can make some comparisons between the two texts. While the version of Harirāma Vyāsa predates that of Nanda Dāsa, Nanda Dāsa follows the above scenario, the *Bhāgavata Purāṇa* version, much more closely than Harirāma. True to the *Bhāgavata Purāṇa*, for example, Nanda Dāsa does not mention the name of Rādhā, Krishna's favorite consort, yet her name is found throughout Harirāma's version. Nanda Das includes the section on the separation (*viraha*) between Krishna and the Gopīs, i.e., his disappearance from the Gopīs' presence, which is absent in

Harirāma Vyāsa. These two vernacular renditions thus differ somewhat with regard to their parent model; Nanda Dāsa's is the more conservative version and Vyāsa's a much more liberal and intuitive work.[48]

Śrī Harirāma Vyāsa (ca. 1511-1613) is acknowledged as one of a trinity of early saints in Vrindaban, called "Hari-trayī" by contemporaries, along with Śrī Hita Harivaṃśa and Svāmī Haridāsa, and is believed by most to have been a prolific author in the Rādhāvallabha tradition. While there is a lingering controversy surrounding the sectarian affiliation of Harirāma Vyāsa (see Heidi R. M. Pauwels, 1996, 7-8), his model in the Sanskrit original provided him with the raw material upon which he creatively wove a more intense and "sweeter" rendition of the spiritual dance event that avoided much of the formality and theological pretensions of the *Bhāgavata Purāṇa*.

The rendering of this poem in Samāj-Gāyan style, as recorded in the Rādhāvallabha temple compound (October 15-21, 1992), is based on the *rāga* Kafi, in which two notes are flattened, the third and the seventh (S R G̲ M P D N̲ s, s N̲ D P M G̲ R S). It is set to a 16 *mātrā* (beat) Tintāl structure in medium tempo (*madhya laya*). A *tāla* in Indian music contains a specific number of *mātrās* or beats in a time-cyle (6, 8, 10, 12, 16, etc.). Tintāl is a very common rhythm of 16 beats, as found in this example. The 16 *mātrās* are divided into *tāli* (clap), *khāli* (open hand), or simply as a counted beat. The name "Tintāl" (*tin*—three, *tāl*—clap) refers to its three *tālis* or claps, spread out over the four divisions of four in the total number sixteen; it also has one *khāli* or open hand. There is a natural correlation between the notion of *mātrā* as "syllable, long or short" and rhythmic beat in music; thus in music a long vowel of a syllable would encompass two or more beats, while a short vowel is normally limited to one. When a short vowel

---

[48]Heidi R. M. Pauwels (1996), 63-79, discusses some of the principal differences between the Rāsa Pañcādhyāyī poems of Nanda Dāsa and Harirāma Vyāsa from a literary point of view.

is surrounded by two consonants, the syllable often counts as a long vowel, or two *mātrās*.

Tintāl consists of four sections of four *mātrās* each, with the first *mātrā* called the *sam*, and the ninth the *khāli*. The first line of the *tripadī* begins at the *khāli* to be resolved on the *sam* on the syllable "a" of the word *ai*. There are additional interpolated sections of "eri ha" in which extended vocal passages are rendered primarily on the syllable "ha," which is a means of expressing delight at the event by the musical participants as they imagine themselves to be spiritual voyeurs of the Rāsa Dance itself.

While the recording only presents the first *tripadī*, the first five of the thirty *tripadīs* (triple-lines) of Harirāma Vyāsa's work are given below.

sarada suhai ai rata /
dasa disi phuli rahi vana jati /
dekhi syama mana sukha bhayau //
sasi go mandita jamuna kula /
barashata vitapa sada phala phula /
trividya pavana dukha davana hai //
radharavana bajayau baina /
suni dhuni gopina upajyau maina /
jahan tahan ten uthi calin //
calata na dinaun kahu jababa /
hari pyare saun badyau bhava /
rasa rasika guna gaihaun //1//

ghara dara bisaryau badhyau uchahu /
mana cintyau payau hari nahu /
braja naika laika sunyau //
dudha puta ki chandi asa /
godhana bharata kiye nirasa /
sancyau hita hari son kiyau //
khana pana tana kin a sambhara /
hilagi chutayau griha byauhara /
sudha budha mohana hari lai //
anjana manjana anga singara /
pata bhushana sira chute bara /
rasa rasika guna gaihaun //2//

eka duhavata ten uthi bhagi /
aura cali sovata ten jagi /

utkantha hari son badhi //
uphanata dudha na dharyau uteri /
sijhi thuli culhain dari /
purusha tajyau jainvatahu tain //
paya pyavata balaka dhari cali /
pati seva kachu kari anabhali /
dharyau rahyau bhojana bhalau //
tela ubatanaun nhaivau bhula /
bhagyana pai jivana mula /
rasa rasika guna gaihaun //3//

anjata eka naina bisaryau /
kati kancuki lahanga ura dharyau /
hara lapetyau carana saun //
sravanana pahire ulate tara /
tirani para cauki singara /
catura caturata hari lai //
jakau mana mohana hari liyau /
takau kahu kachu na kiyau /
jyaun pati saun tiya rati karai //
syamahin sucata murali nada /
suni dhuni chute vishaya savada /
rasa rasika guna gaihaun //4//

mata pita pati rokin ani /
sahi na piya darasana ki hani /
sabahi kau apamana kai //
jakau manuba jasaun atakyau /
rahai na chinahu ta binu hatakyau /
kathina priti kau phanda hai //
jaise salita sindhuhi bhajai /
kotika giri bhedana nahin lajai /
taisi gati inaki bhai //
eka ju ghara ten nikasi nahin /
hari karuna kari aye tahin /
rasa rasika guna gaihaun //5//

Translation: Heidi R. M. Pauwels (1996, 79-87)

1.
The bright night of autumn came,
All over (the forest) lotuses bloomed open,
When Śyāma saw this, joy filled his heart.
The banks of the Yamunā with moonbeams adorned,

Trees dripping with nectar from flowers and fruit,
The breeze, thrice pleasant, burnt sorrow away.
Rādhā's lover (Rādhāramaṇa) played his flute,
The sound of the tune awoke passion in the milk-maids,
Wherever they were, they got up to go.
They left without telling anyone.
Their feeling grew stronger for Hari, the beloved.
I shall sing in praise of the lovers of the round dance.

2.

In their growing excitement, they forgot the honor of the family.
Their heart's wish fulfilled: the Lord for a husband.
The hero of Vraja [Braj] is reported to be worthy.
They gave up their interest in kine and in kin,
Causing frustration to husband and cattle,
True love they felt for Hari (alone),
Unconcerned with food and drink, with (the needs of) the body.
This frenzy freed them from domestic chores;
Mohana deprived them of (good) sense and judgement.
Application of collyrium and make-up,
Garments and jewelry, and their coiffure disheveled:
I shall sing in praise of the lovers of the round dance.

3.

One (girl) stopped milking and hurried away,
Another ran off, woken up from her sleep.
Their longing for Hari grew stronger.
Boiling milk was not taken off (the stove),
Cooked porridge was flung in the hearth.
Men were left in the midst of their meals,
Children taken down from the breast and abandoned.
Care for the husband was totally neglected,

And their (own) food left aside, untouched.
Forgotten their oil-massages and toilet.
Yet fortunate women they were: they had found the essence of life.
One should sing in praise of the lovers of the round dance.

4.

One forgot to apply kohl to her eyes,
(One) put her bodice on her hips and her skirt around her chest,
(Another) wound her necklace around her feet,
Earrings worn upside-down in their ears,
Amulets adorning the string of their skirt:
Clever (Hari) has taken their cleverness away.
People whose heart is stolen by Mohana,
Are not conscious of anyone or anything at all.
Similar to a woman who is devoted to her husband.
Syama makes the music flow from his flute,
Listen to the sound, and the link with the senses snaps.
One should sing in praise of the lovers of the round dance.

5.

Mother, father and husband stood in their way.
They could not bear (this) bar to meeting their lover,
And insulted each and every one of them.
Without the one on whom the mind is set,
No one can be restrained, not for a moment:
Unyielding is the snare of love.
Like rivers rushing to the sea,
Cleaving mountains by millions, without inhibitions,
That's what their (headlong) rush had become.
One (girl) could not slip away from home,
But the Lord took mercy and came to her.

One should sing in praise of the lovers of the round
dance.

86. Vamsivata mula khare (Under the Vaṃśivaṭa Tree They Stand), RV 3.38-39, Dhruva Dāsa

This Dhrupad-style composition of Dhruva Dāsa (1650-1775) is in the *tāla* of Cautāl (12 beats). It is sung in the *rāga* Vrindabani Sarang, with the *sam* on the first syllable of "*vam.*" There is a slight deviation from this *rāga* in the *antarās*, which begin to resemble those in Song 39. Only about nine lines of this poem are included in this recording.

vamsivata mula khare dampati anuraga bhare,
gavata hain saranga piya saranga vara naini /
umahi kumvari karata gana sikhavata piya vikata tana,
sapta svara saun madhura-madhura leta kokila baini //
citrita candana suanga bhushana phulana suranga,
dasana basana sahaja ranga besara chabi daini /
lasata kantha jalaja mala jhalaka sveda kana rasala,
diragha vara locana mashi rekha bani paini //
cahun disi sakhiyana bhira sakala prema rasa adhira,
ubhaya rupa raga ranga sukha abhanga laini /
umadyau jala prema naina rahita bhae rasana baina,
ihi gati rahau matta citta hita dhruva dina raini //

Translation: H. S. Mathur

The couple stand under the Vaṃśivaṭa tree full of love. They sing the *rāga* Sarang with a lovely tune, and in great enthusiasm the young lady teaches her lover a difficult *tāna* (vocal phrase). Her voice is like a cuckoo bird, and she sings beautifully all the seven notes. Her body is adorned with sandalwood paste and she wears ornaments of colorful flowers and a saffron-colored dress. She wears a garland of lotus-flowers around her neck, with the beads of perspiration shining. Her eyes are large and beautiful. She has applied collyrium so that her eyes are sharply defined and elongated.

Her girlfriends gather around the couple. Passionately in love with the couple, they all admire the beauty and decoration of the pair. Love flows in them so much that they are speechless. The poet Dhruva Dāsa prays that the girlfriends remain madly in love like this day and night.

87. Bhaja mana rasa rasika kisora (O Mind! Honor the Young Enjoyer of Rasa.), RV 3.43, Dāmodara Dāsa

A fast Dīp Chandī is the opening rhythm of this poem by Dāmodara Dāsa (1613-1643), which is also in the *rāga* Vrindabani Sarang. In this rendering the word order of two words in the refrain is switched to accomodate a smoother execution. It becomes "*bhaja mana rasika rasa kisora.*" The refrain is repeated at the end.

bhaja mana rasa rasika kisora /
gaura syamala sakala guna nidhi catura cita ke cora //
subhaga mandala para birajata jugala sundara vesha /
basana bhushana jagamagai ati anga-anga sudesa //
caru carana sudesa nirmala gati vilasa vinoda /
padana patakana nakhana damakana hota nava-nava moda //
jori kabahun kara paraspara badana sanmukha caru /
ghana ghata se calata dou bhramata karata vihara //
mukuta kabari lataka bhrikuti mataka madhuri hasa /
harashi barashata ranga bhinaun hita damodara dasa //

Translation: H. S. Mathur

The poet Dāmodara Dāsa addresses his heart saying that we should pray for the Rāsa Līlā of Krishna, who is fond of *rasa*. The fair one and the dark one are the epitome of all virtues, and steal everyone's hearts. Both are beautifully dressed and sit on a lovely swing. Their bodies are adorned with gorgeous clothes and ornaments. And they are in a playful, amorous mood. When they move their lovely feet their toenails shine and give off continuous pleasure. Sometimes they face each other and join hands, and sometimes they wander hither and thither looking like a cloud and lightning. With their crowns askew and their eyebrows quirking up and down, they laugh as they move back and forth. The poet Dāmodara Dāsa says that they are drenched in waves of overflowing pleasure.

88. Dekhau ri nagara nata (Behold Krishna, the Expert Dancer), RV 3.79, Nanda Dāsa

Nanda Dāsa (1530-1584) is the most celebrated poet of the Vallabha sect behind Sūra Dāsa. Nanda Dāsa was a member of the select Ashtachap group of eight poets who wrote and performed Braj Bhasha songs in honor of the Krishna deity of Śrī Nāthji in Govardhan. The first group of four, believed to have been disciples of Vallabha, include Sūra Dāsa (c. 1478-1580), Paramānanda Dāsa, Krishna Dāsa, and Kumbhana Dāsa. The second group, believed to have been disciples of Vallabha's son Viṭṭhalanātha (1516-1586), includes Caturbhuj Dāsa, Cit Svāmī, Nanda Dāsa, and Govinda Svāmī.

Nanda Dāsa "was born perhaps around 1530 and lived in a village called Rampur, east of Braj, possibly near Soron. He was initiated as a disciple by Viṭṭhalanātha of the Vallabha Sampradāya, probably in the early or mid-1560's, and may have composed poetry before this date. Thereafter he lived very largely at least at Gokul with a reputation as a poet and singer and upholder of the Puṣṭimārga. His active career as a poet is likely to have straddled the period of composition of Tulsidas's *Ramcaritmanas*. He died possibly within a few years of 1585, and by 1640 or earlier various traditions about him had arisen and been consolidated within his sect."[49] Among his many attributed works, his rendering of the *Rāsa Pañcādhyāyī* is viewed as his finest work along with the *Bhamara-gīta*, a poetic description, also taken from *Bhāgavata Purāṇa*, of the Gopīs conversation with Uddhava.

[49] R. S. McGregor (1973), 34.

This poem is performed in slow Cautāl (12 *mātrās*), the standard rhythm of Dhrupad singing. The song is performed in the *rāga* Kedar, with the *sam* falling on the first syllable of "*de.*" The first line (up until *lataka*) is the *sthāyī*, and the other three lines form the verses (*antarā*). There is a fast repeat in the last line, with the insertion of the syllable "*mai*" at the end.

dekhau ri nagara nata nirttata kalindi tata gopina ke madhya rajai mukata lataka /
kachini kinkini kati pitambara ki cataka kundala kirana ravi ratha ki ataka //
tatta thei tatta thei sabda sakala ghata urapa tirapa gati paga ki pataka /
rasa men radhe-radhe murali men yehi rata nanda dasa gavai tahan nipata nikata //

Translation: H. S. Mathur

Behold! Krishna who is an expert dancer dances on the bank of the river Yamunā along with the Gopīs, and his hanging headgear adorns his face. He has tied a yellow cloth around his waist. The tinkling sound of the small bells and the flashes from his earrings, have stopped the movement of the chariot of the sun. The patter of Krishna's feet and the sound of the drum "*tat thei tat thei*" engross the whole universe. In the Rāsa Līlā there is the singing of "Rādhe Rādhe," and the same tune appears on the flute. The poet Nanda Dāsa is also singing along nearby.

89. Bandana karaun kripa-nidhana (I Bow to Śuka, the Store of Grace), RV 3.80-100, Nanda Dāsa

Nanda Dāsa's poem, like the Sanskrit *Bhāgavata Purāṇa*, is divided into five parts, roughly corresponding to the *Bhāgavata Purāṇa* in subject matter. After a short introductory section in praise of Śrī Śuka, the narrator in the *Bhagavata Purāṇa*, and Krishna in Vrindaban, the poem begins with Krishna playing on his flute to attract the "herdgirls" (McGregor's translation of Gopīs). Sung in the style of Samāj-Gāyan, it is rendered in a variation of the *rāga* Asavari, in which three notes are flattened, the third, the sixth, and the seventh (S R M P $\underline{\text{D}}$ s, s $\underline{\text{N}}$ $\underline{\text{D}}$ P M $\underline{\text{G}}$ R S). Yet with many of these songs, there are accidentals, notes outside of the *rāga*; in this case the pure N is used in the second section of east stanza. It is set to the twelve-*mātrā* *tāla* called *ektāl* in medium tempo. The *sam* is on the syllable "pa" of "kripa."

While the recording presents only the first four stanzas, below are the text, Roman transliteration, and English translation of the first seven stanzas.

bandana karaun kripa-nidhana sri suka subhakari /
suddha joti maya rupa sada sundara avikari //1//
hari lila rasa matta mudita nita vicarata jaga men /
adbhuta gati katahun na ataka hoi nisarata maga men //2//
nilotpala dala syama anga nava jovana bhrajai /
kutila alaka mukha kamala manaun ali avail birajai //3//
sundara bhala bisala dipata manaun nikara nisakara /
krishna-bhakti-pratibandha timira kaun koti divakara //4//

kripa ranga rasa aina naina rajata ratanare /
krishna rasasaba pana alasa kachu ghumma ghummare //5//
sravana krishna rasa bhavana ganda mandala bhala darasai /
premananda mili su manda musikana madhu barasai //6//
unnata nasa adhara-bimba suka ki chabi chini /
tina madhi adbhuta bhanti lasata kachu ika masi bhini //7//

Translation: R. S. McGregor (1973)

I bow to Śuka, store of grace—
Beneficent and blest!
Whose form pure light pervades;
Who strays, by Hari's deeds obsessed,
Forever fair, and free
From fault, through the world delightedly:
No hill, nor other hazard stays
His passage—strange his ways!
His limbs glow fresh with youth—dark petals

Of some blue lotus—and his face their flower,
His trailing locks the bees that round it swarm:
His graceful brow--a host of moons—
Gleams broad and bright, its light
By his love for Krishna cast, that galaxy
Of suns, to banish night!
His eye, where compassion dwells,
Shines, somnolent and shot with red—
Heavy with the sweet draught of Krishna's sight;
His ear's a temple of delight
To Krishna; hair drawn back reveals
A graceful cheek, and honey's shed
In his slow smile, when love's bliss upon him steals!
Between his noble nose, and his lips of red,
Lies an elegant moustache, shining, shapely, and dark.
Between the two, demean
His namesake's shape and sheen;
At his throat, voluted lines
Unfold a parable of love for the divine—
Extinguish error, greed,
Anger, lust, and pride!
His breast defies art's power to praise—
But the beauty it affords
Is most of all in Kanha's light, the lord's,
Undying in his heart;
And on the broad torso gleams
A sleek, rich line of hair, that seems
A rivulet, to draw delight
From his heart, as from a lake,
To the navel: there it streams
Into a hollow, deep and bright,
Whose folds three ripples on it make!
The arms reach to the knees; the knees
Are hid; the lordly gait awakes
A joy, which as he takes his way

Re-sanctifies each holy site
And Ganges doubly sacred makes!

90. Suni dhuni murali bana (Listen to the Beautiful Sound of the Flute in the Forest), RV 3.100, Svāmī Haridāsa

Set in slow Dhamār, the refrain of this poem of Svāmī Haridāsa actually begins with the words, "*e hari rasa racyau.*" The song then proceeds to Rūpak by the second line, and Dīp Chandī in the fast repeat. In the very last line, there is the insertion of the word "*aja*" (today) after the word "*nikai.*"

suni dhuni murali bana bajai e hari rasa racyau /
kunja-kunja druma beli praphullita
mandala kancana maninu khacyau //
nirttata jugala kisora juvati jana
sruti ghura raga kedarau macyau /
sri haridasa ke svami syama kunjabihari
nikai [aja] pyarau lala nacyau //

Translation: H. S. Mathur

Listen! Hari has arranged a Rāsa Līlā in the forest grove, and the beautiful sound of his flute comes forth. In every grove, even the trees and creepers appear to be happy, and the whole dance circle is adorned with gold and jewels. The couple dances with all the young girls and the sweet tune of the *rāga* Kedar resounds everywhere. The poet Svāmī Haridāsa says that his chosen deity and beloved Kuñja Bihārī has performed an excellent dance.

91. Nava nikunja nava bhumi (Fresh Bower, Fresh Land), RV 3.101, Viṭṭhalavipula Dāsa

This poem by Viṭṭhalavipula Dāsa (1550-1635) of the Haridāsī Sampradāya is set in the same manner as Song 58.

nava nikunja nava bhumi rangamagi /
navala bihari lala ladilau navala sarada ki jonha jagamagi //
nava sata saji sakala anga sundara navala badana para alaka sagabagi /
sri vitthala vipula bihari ke anga ladata ladili sahaja ura lagi //

Translation: H. S. Mathur

The forest grove is fresh, and the land is new and colorful. A young boy and a young girl are there, and the rays of the new moon are shining. The nine young lady friends of the young girl have decorated all the parts of their lovely bodies, and the braids of their hair are beautiful. Then the poet Vitthalavipula Dāsa says "Behold, the girl fully embraces the boy."

Ujyari men Rāsa ke Pada—Songs for the Bright Half of the Lunar Month

92. Ari heli radha lala (O Rādhā, Reveal Your Love for Krishna), RV 3.115-116, Cācā Vṛndāvana Dāsa

The first line of this poem of Cācā Vṛndāvana Dāsa (1708-1787) is rendered in slow Dhamār in a combination of two *rāgas*: Vilaval and Kafi. This may seem to resemble the *rāga* Patdeep (S G̲ M P N s, s N D P M G̲ R S), but the opening phrase (s N D P) on *"radha lala,"* which then moves back up to N̲, is characteristic of Vilaval. The next phrase takes us down to flattened G̲ and then R S, which places us in the Kafi scale. As this is all there is to the recording, the remainder of the performance is uncertain.

ari heli radha lala suhaga kaun duaravau sukha lehu /
sarada saravari jagamagai heli jagamagai jugala sanehu //1//
kripa ujhali hama disa rahi heli dekhau naina nihari /
gunavanti-gunavanta pai heli dehu apanapau bari //2//
locana rakshaka palaka hai heli tajata na apani riti /
ihi vidhi nagara-nagari heli tumakaun poshata priti //3//

gaura syama saba guna nikara heli tuma parakhe saba anga /
tadyapi rijhata hama gunana heli bhare adhika rasa ranga //4//
purati nanda vari saun heli kanana sara abhirama /
kridata karata prasansa kaun heli nisi dina syama-syama //5//
lahanaun gahanaun sakhinu kau heli ye dou lalita kisora /
kunjana sobha gahara kaun heli barashata lahata na ora //6//
dai asisa trina tori kai heli baithe dhari bhuja amsa /
vrindavana hita rupa bali heli jivana sri harivamsa //7//

Translation: H. S. Mathur

The *sakhīs* address Śrī Rādhā, saying that she should reveal her true affections for Krishna and simply enjoy the moment. They say, "The nocturnal sky of the Śārada season shines just like your mutual love. Please open your eyes and glance toward us with kindness. You are virtuous, so therefore sacrifice your all to Krishna who is equally virtuous. As the eyelids protect the eye (without changing them), the style of mutual seduction causes your love to grow stronger. The fair one and the dark one are a storehouse of all qualities and we have seen all their features. Still, we are enamored of their loving nature, which is like the forest and the pond full of the water of pleasure. We thus admire the love-play of the fair and the dark one night and day." Circling the lovely girl and the young man, the *sakhīs* hold each other tightly. There is no end to the radiance of the forest groves, where the pair resides. The *sakhīs* offer their blessings to them with all their hearts. The poet Cācā Vṛndāvana Dāsa herein offers his life to Śrī Harivaṃśa.

[CD 16]

Annakūṭa—Festival of Govardhana Hill

Annakūṭa refers to the festival on the day following Diwali in which a large quantity of cooked food is offered to Krishna in Vaishnava temples and homes.

93. Bhojana kau samayau jaba janyau (When the Time for Eating Came), RV 3.162-164, Śrī Kamala Naina

This poem by Śrī Kamala Naina (1692-1754) is the quintessential description of the large quantites of cooked food offered to Rādhā and Krishna in the Rādhāvallabha tradition. While only the first line is recorded, we can get a glimpse of the devotion of this festival. The song begins in a slow and reverential Dhamār, then quickens to a fast Rūpak with an extended melisma on "*eriha.*" The scale is a major scale with a touch of *M*, signifying Kalyan.

bhojana kau samayau jaba janyau /
taba sakhiyana manimaya cauki para
patambara bichayau mana manyau //1//
jhari dhari bhari sitala jala kancana thara dhuvaye /
bela jani dhare bela avala nava lala bulaye //2//
kucha-kucha bhushana-vasana asana kau samayau jani utaryau /
ratana sucauka mundari pahunci dhari patuka pata nyaryau //3//
dai acamana parosata vyanjana barane kapai jai /
campaka lata catura saba vidhi son karai dharai mana lai //4//
paisa bura aru ghrita pura bara lucai roti /
bhata pita sita vara kamoda kau kadhi pakauri choti //5//
dhoba dara munga saje puni bari phulauri kini /
mithi kadhi murabba amarasa panau sikharani dini //6//
ela lavanga kapura suvasita puni meva madhi dari /
khicari thuli ghrita kari misrita khata adhika rucikari //7//
matha rayate bhanti-bhanti ke vividha sandhane ane /
patra phula phala phalli kanda tarakari dari jane //8//
salana bahuta kare besana ke jholc pitaura banaye /
phala dala saka sameta heta saun ika dadhi takra milaye //9//
sakhare vyanjana bahuta bhanti ke kanha lagi baranaun jete /
parasi bahuri mana ki ruci karana meva surasa samete //10//
nibu adau aru narangi surasa dadimi dane /
seva ama sarada bihi khira nasapata rasa sane //11//
surasa dacha meva ali jeti dali bhari-bhari keti /
kaiu lavanga kaiu bura son kaiu jyon kit yon teti //12//
puva puri jalebi ladu khaja khurma phaini /
candrakala papara aru ghevara amrita-puti sukha daini //13//

mohana bhoga dudha ki roti khova seva malai /
amrita guti aru amrita bundi matharinu leta sarai //14//
seva sidhare ke khuramajuta sakkarapure pera /
gujhiya aura paraka payari papara tare karera //15//
tali kancariya bhanti-bhanti ki nonna madhura rasa sane /
petha pista tali ciraunji page makhane dane //16//
eka-eka pakavana bahuta vidha parasi kacauri ani /
sakhijana deta leta piya pyari heta adhika jiya jani //17//
vyanjana kine cara bhanti ke shatarasa rasa kara sane /
bhakshya-bhojya aru coshya-lehya ye vividha prakara bakhane //18//
lavana kasaya tikta katu amlaru madhura vividha vidha kete /
ruci anusara banaye raci kara misrita nyare jete //19//
kaii ramatha jira son chaunke puni patraja son kete /
saunpha gandhela saunpha cini son kai ika launga samete //20//
ela lavanga kapura jayaphala javitri madhi nai /
kesara puta puni nagabela rasa atara kusuma adhikai //21//
giri chuare dacha ciraunji pista aru badama /
yatha yogya samigri milaye campaka catura subhama //22//
dulaha-dulahini radhavallabha bhojana karata virajain /
hamsata paraspara kaura deta mukha dasanana ki chabi chajain //23//
yahi prakara bhojana karai kain puni acamana divayau /
pani agaunchi khababata biri karata apa mana bhayau //24//
baithe jaya singhasana upara sakhiyana thara uthayau /
raja-bhoga ki karata arati jai Sri Kamala Naina yasa gayau //25//

Translation: Chandrakala Pandey

The *sakhīs* decided that it was time for the Annakūṭa festivities and started making arrangements. They spread a yellow carpet on a *cauki* (four-legged low-lying table) which was decorated with jewels. Golden plates were cleansed and a pitcher filled with cold water placed near. All the *sakhīs* then called for the handsome Śrī Krishna. As it was time for food, heavy clothes and ornaments were put aside, including a diamond ring and bangle that were removed. Everyone then washed their hands and started serving the food. At that time the *sakhīs* looked like creepers of *campa* flowers. Varieties of foods were served - *payas, bura*, ghee, *pura, bara, luchai, roti*, rice, yellow and white curries and small *pakodi.* Many items were made of moong *dāl* (lentil). Sweet curry, jam, mango juice, raw mango, *sarbat* and curd were given as a fragranced sweet drink. Cardamon, clove, camphor, and scented dried fruits were mixed into a sweet drink. *Khichadi* mixed with ghee was very tasty and appetizing. Salted whey and *raita* added richness to the food, as well as many vegetables and curries including green leaves and fruits mixed with gram flour. The curd and fried items were innumerable.

After the main course was served, dry fruits, limes, oranges, juicy pomegranates, apples, mangoes, guavas, cucumbers, pears, black grapes were placed in big buckets. The last course was a sweet dish. There were so many varieties of sweet dishes that one could not even count: *puva, puri, jalebi, laddu, khaja, khurma, pheni, chandrakala, ghewar, mohana bhoga, khoa, sew malai, sakkan para, ghujia, parag papadi,* and *petha.*

Dried fruits like *pista, chirrauri,* and *makhana* were divided into four categories and of six different tastes: the four categories were solid, liquid, semi-liquid and thick paste like (*puri*), and the six tastes were salty, bitter, sour, sweet, hot, and acidic.

All the food was cooked with special care. Many spices (*masālas*) were added like cumin seeds, *jaifal, javitri,* and saffron. Dried fruits, coconut, almond, and flower scents were also used. The *sakhīs* were very intelligent and good cooks. Rādhā and Krishna fully enjoyed the food as bride and bridegroom. They were smiling and feeding each other with their hands. While smiling their teeth were shining. After couple had finished eating, the *sakhīs* washed their hands and dried them with small towels. The last item offered was folded betel leaves (*pān*). After this, the pair sat upon the large lion-throne (*siṃhāsana*). The *sakhīs* cleaned everything and performed the Rāja-Bhoga Ārati. The poet Śrī Kamala Naina sings the glories of this event.

Vyahulau Utsava—Wedding of Rādhā and Krishna

In the Rādhāvallabha Sampradāya, Rādhā and Krishna are viewed as eternally married in the spiritual realm of Eternal Sport (*nitya-vihāra*). As part of their spiritual practice, the devotees re-imagine and re-experience the wedding of the divine couple by performing these wedding songs as part of the religious calendar. The two songs below in this category represent a very intimate part of the Rādhāvallabha worship tradition. These songs are sung annually at Rādhāvallabha temples during the festival of Vyahula (Wedding of Rādhā and Krishna), which is held on the first day of the bright half of the month (*śukla-pakṣa*) of Kārtika (Fall season), just after the new moon (*amāvasyā*), the time otherwise celebrated as Diwali in Hindu traditions.

94. Sakhiyana ke ura aisi ai (The Girlfriends Had an Idea Like This), RV 3.164, Dhruva Dāsa

This is a beautiful rendition of the poem by Dhruva Dāsa (1650-1775), an important *ācārya* in the Rādhāvallabha lineage. It is performed in slow Rūpak in the Kalyan scale. The structure resembles that of Song 36, in which the first two lines of each stanza are sung in a slow tempo, and then the melody changes in the fourth line as the rhythm also increases feverishly with faster repeats in Dīp Chandī. The slow melody takes form after the first words, "*sakhiyana ke*" are sung on the note P which then drops to R with a turnaround on "*ura*" to resolve on M on the word "*aisi.*" This same process repeats at the beginning of each stanza. This lengthy recording is complete in about fifty minutes.

sakhiyana ke ura aisi ai / byaha binoda racain sukhadai //
yahai bata saba ke mana bhai / ananda moda badhyau adhikai //
badhyau ananda moda sabakain maha prema suranga rangi /

aura kachu na suhai tinakaun yugala seva sukha pagi //
nisi dyausa janata nahin sajani eka rasa bhiji rahain /
gopa-gopinu adi durllabha tihi sukhahi dina prati lahain // 1 //

yaha nava dulahini ati sukumari / ye nava dulaha lala bihari //
ranga bhine dou prana piyare / nava sata angana anga singare //
nava sata singare anga angana jhalaka tana ki ati badi /
maura-mauri sisa sohain maina panipa mukha cadi //
jalaja sumana su sehare raci ratana hire jagamagain /
dekhi adbhuta rupa manamatha koti rati panyana lagain // 2 //

sobha mandapa kunjana dvarain / hita ki bandhi bandana varen //
kumakuma saun lai ajira lipayau / adbhuta motinu cauka purayau //
puraya adbhuta cauka motinu citra racana bahu kari /
aya dou thade bhaye tahan sabana ki gati-mati hari //
suranga mahadi ranga race carana kara ati rajahin /
vividha ragani kinkini aru madhura nupura bajahin // 3 //

vedi seja sudesa suhai / mana drga ancala granthi jurai //
riti bhanti vidhi ucita banai / neha ki devi tahan pujai //
puji devi neha ki dou rati-binoda biharahin /
tihi samai sakhi lalitadi hita saun heri pranana varahin //
eka baisa subhava eka sahaja jori sohani /
eka dori prema ki dhruva bandhe mohana-mohani // 4 //

Translation: H. S. Mathur

The girlfriends thought of arranging a cheerful marriage ceremony. The idea was appreciated by everyone, and it greatly enhanced their joy. The girlfriends were happily drenched in the colors of divine love. Being immersed in the joy of serving the couple, they could not relish any other worldly object. Being absorbed in this single thought they lost all sense of time, and the cowherd men and women enjoyed unattainable bliss everyday.

The new bride is young and tender, and the groom is a playful boy. Dearest to each other's heart, they are both colorful and their bodies are decorated with sixteen kinds of embellishments; and thus the beauty of their forms has increased immensely. With radiant faces, they are wearing wedding crowns. The veil of garlands worn by the groom is made of lotus flowers, with jewels and diamonds shining through it. Thousands of gods and goddesses of love would feel vanquished by their wondrous beauty.

The gate of the lovely canopy in the grove is adorned with buntings tied around. The inner courtyard is painted with red powder and is decorated with designs of pearls, with many paintings made on it. When the couple arrives everyone is wonderstruck. Their feet and palms are beautifully and artfully colored with hena (*mehandi*). The trinkets on their waists and feet produce various musical sounds.

The platform for the marriage ceremony looks lovely. The hearts, eyes and ends of clothing of the couple are tied together. All the marriage ceremonials have been performed properly with worship of the goddess of love. After the worship the couple becomes engrossed in amorous play. At that time the girlfriend Lalitā and others fervently wish for the couple's well-being. The couple appears very natural, being of the same age and temperament. The poet Dhruva Dāsa observes, the delightful girl and boy are tied to each other with an eternal cord of love.

95. Sri vrindabana dhama rasika mana mohai (Vṛndāvana Captivates the Hearts of the Tasteful), RV 3.165-166, Dhruva Dāsa

In this second poem by Dhruva Dāsa on the subject of the wedding of Rādhā and Krishna, we are transported to new heights of beauty by means of a totally unique and exquisite melody. In terms of both melody and rhythm, each line alternates throughout the twenty-nine two-line stanzas. The first line of each stanza, in slow *tintāl*, begins on the note M in what appears to be a Vilaval scale pattern, but then offers a change in the repeat with a flattened G̲. At the beginning of the second line of each stanza, the tempo picks up to Kehervā with soaring melismas on a double "*eriha*," and a continued faster pace until the first line of the next stanza. The occasional sound of fireworks gives this otherwise fantastic recording some local flavor. Only eight and one-half stanzas (17 lines) are preserved here, however.

sri vrindavana dhama rasika mana mohai /
dulaha dulahini byaha sahaja tahan sohai // 1 //
nitya sahane pata aru bhusana sajahin /
nitya navala sama baisa eka rasa rajahin // 2 //
sobha kau sira-maura candrika mora ki /
barani na jai kachu chabi navala kisora ki // 3 //
subhaga manga ranga rekha manon anuraga ki /
jhalakata mauri sisa suranga suhaga ki // 4 //
maninu khacita nava kunja rahi jagamaga jahan /
chabi kau banyau bitana soi mandapa tahan // 5 //
bedi seja sudesa raci ati bani kai /
bhanti-bhanti ke phula suranga bahu ani kai // 6 //
gavata mora marala suhae gita ri /
sahacari bharin ananda karata rasa riti ri // 7 //
alabele sukumvara phirata tihi thamvari /
drga ancala pari granthi leta mana bhamvari // 8 //
kangana prema anupa kabahun nahin chutahi /
poyau dori rupa sahaja so na dutahi // 9 //
raci rahe komala kara aru carana suranga ri /
sahaja chabile kumvara nipuna saba anga ri // 10 //
nupura kankana kinkini baje bajahin /
nirttata koti ananga nari saba lajahin // 11 //
badhyau hai mana mahin adhika ananda ri /
phule phirata kisora vrindavana canda ri // 12 //
sakhiyana kiye bahu cara aneka binoda ri /
dudha bhati heta badhyau mana moda ri // 13 //
lalita lala ki bata jabahi sakhiyana kahi /
laja sahita sukumari ota pata dai rahi // 14 //
namita griva chabi simva kumvari nahin bolahin /
budhi bala karata upaya ghunghata pata kholahin // 15 //
kanaka kamala kara nila kalaha ati kala bani /
hansata sakhi sukha heri sahaja sobha ghani // 16 //
bama carana saun sisa lala kau lavahin /
pani vari kumvari para piyahi piyavahin // 17 //
meli sugandha ugara so biri khabavahin /
samajhi kumvari musikai adhika sukha pavahin // 18 //
aura hasa-parihasa rahasi rasa ranga rahyau /
nitya vihara binoda yathamati kachu kahyau // 19 //
ancala ota asisa sakhi saba dehin ri /
pala-pala badau suhaga naina sukha lehin ri // 20 //

jaisen navala visala navala navala karain /
mana-mana ki ruci jana neha bidhi anusarain // 21 //
baithi hain nija kunja kumvari mana mohani /
jhalakata rupa apara sahaja ati sohani // 22 //
chahi-chahi so rupa rasika sira-maura ri /
bhari aye dou naina bhai gati aura ri // 23 //
ati ananda kau moda na urati samata ri /
rijhi-rijhi rasa bhiji apu bali jata ri // 24 //
arujhe mana aru naina badhyau anuraga ri /
eka prana dvai deha nagara aru nagari // 25 //
yaun rajata dou pritama hamsi musikata ri /
nirakhi paraspara rupa na kabahun aghata ri // 26 //
tinahi ke sukha ranga sakhi dina ranga magin /
aura na kachu suhai eka rasa saba pagin // 27 //
ubhaya rupa-rasa sindhu magana jahan saba bhae /
durlabha sripati adi soi sukha dina nae // 28 //
hita dhruva mangala sahaja nitya jo gavahi /
sarvopara soi hoi prema rasa pavahi // 29 // II

Translation: H. S. Mathur

Vṛndāvana captivates the hearts of all connoisseurs, and is the natural site for the performance of the wedding ceremony of the bridegroom and bride. Every day they are adorned with new garments and ornaments and, being of the same age and tastes, they are drawn to each other. The head ornament of Krishna made of peacock feathers is the peak of loveliness, and the grace of the Fresh Youth is beyond description. The red powder (*sindur*) in the parting of Rādhā's hair is an emblem of love, and the brilliance of the crown on her head is a token of the auspicious marriage.

The new grove is shining with jewels and the canopy is permeated with loveliness all around. The wedding platform has been designed very artfully with various types of flowers. Even the peacocks and swans are singing merrily. Their girlfriends have joyously performed all the rites. The graceful couple has wandered there. Like the ends of the marriage ceremony clothes, their eyes are tied to each other and their hearts thump with joy. Their bangles, strengthened with unique love and entwined with the thread of love, will never break. Their tender feet and palms are painted with beautiful colors, and Krishna has a natural grace and perfect figure. The small bells of their ornaments, on their feet, waists and arms, jingle, and it seems as if thousands of Kāmadevas (gods of love) are dancing there, making women feel shy. His heart full of great joy, the glory of Vrindavan, roams about in extreme delight.

The girlfriends have arranged many plays for fun, and the ceremony of feeding milk and rice to each other greatly enhanced the couple's joy. When the girlfriends conveyed a message from Krishna, Rādhā hid her face behind the veil because of shyness. With her neck bent in shyness, she does not speak and the girlfriends use all their wits to get her to remove her veil. With his bluish hands Krishna struggles to hold the golden, tender hands of Rādhā, and the friends enjoy this lovely scene. They make Krishna bow his head at Rādhā's feet and drink the sacrificial water given first to her. They offer the boy scented betel leaf to eat and the girl smiles.

There was more frolic and fun, but only some of the eternal pleasure and play has been described here. All the girlfriends bless the couple behind the veil and view the ever increasing good fortune with gladness. Both seducer and seductress with knowledge of mutual tastes and likings, make newer and newer plays of love. Extremely lovely Rādhā, with dazzling and indescribable beauty, is sitting in her bower. The great connoisseur Krishna admires her beauty again and again. His eyes are filled and he is drawn into himself. He is unable to contain the great effusion of pleasure. Being submerged in the waves of enchantment, he gives himself to Rādhā. With intense enchantment of mutual love their hearts and eyes are entangled; the lover and beloved have two bodies but one soul. Both of them smile and laugh and never grow tired of viewing each other's beauty. The girlfriends, too, are submerged in their joys and do not relish anything else. Everyone drowns in a sea of love and in pleasure everyday such as is not easily available even to Viṣṇu Bhagavān. Poet Dhruva Dāsa says: one who sings about this auspicious ceremony everyday gets the supreme nectar of love.

[CD 17]

Murali Nada men Rasa ke Pada—The Sacred Sound of Krishna's Flute

96. Rata ri murali meri radhe-radhe (O My Flute! Sing Rādhe Rādhe!), RV 3.131, Cācā Vṛndāvana Dāsa

This short poem by Cācā Vṛndāvana Dāsa captures the essence of the Rādhāvallabha theology. Krishna is constantly thinking of Rādhā and chanting her name in various ways. This performance is in a medium Tintāl and in the *rāga* Bhupali (S R G P D s). The refrain begins on the twelfth *mātrā* with the *sam* falling on the syllable "*ra*" in "*murali.*" There are fast repeats on the *antarās* and the repeat of the refrain at the end.

rata ri murali meri radhe radhe /
yei mere sadhana aradhana rasa simva guna rupa agadhe //
ja karana main mridu mukha dhari so bisarai jina tu pala adhe /
vrindavana hita mantra mohini japau nirantara pujai sadhe //

Translation: H. S. Mathur and Guy L. Beck

O my flute, go on chanting "Rādhe Rādhe." This flute is the means of my worship. It is the epitome of pleasure, beauty and good qualities. Therefore, I put this sweet flute to my lips and do not forget it even for half a moment. This flute is an mantra of enchantment, and poet Vṛndāvana Dāsa says we should always worship it.

Khicari Utsava—Festival with Khicari (a dish containing rice and dāl mixed together)

97. Aju dekhi braja sundari (Behold, today, the Beauty-of-Vraja), RV 3.184-185 (CP 17), Śrī Hita Harivaṃśa

As with Song 96 above, this poem of Śrī Hita Harivaṃśa is set to the *rāga* Bhupali. The rhythm is Cautāl (12 *mātrās*) with the first word falling on the *sam* at upper s. There are also fast repeats on the *antarās* and a repeat of the refrain at the end.

aju dekhi braja sundari mohana bani keli /
amsa amsa bahu dai kisora jora rupa sasi /
manau tamala arujhi rahi sarasa kanaka beli /
nava nikunja bhramara kunja manju ghosha prema punja,
gana karata mora pikani apane sura son meli /
madana mudita anga anga bica bica surata ranga,
pala pala harivamsa pivata naina cashaka jheli //

Translation: Rupert Snell (1991, 198)

See the forest-sport of the Beauty-of-Vraja and Mohana!
Each with an arm on the other's shoulder, the youthful pair is a
Congest of form, as though a lovely golden creeper were entwining a *tamāla* tree.
With a sweet tumult of the humming of bees in the fresh bower,
This amassment of love sings, blending the voices of peacocks and parrots
With its own;
They are impassioned in every limb in the recurring joy of love-making,
As at every moment Harivaṃśa drinks it in through the chalices of his eyes.

Mohan Bhog—Offering of Sweets

98. Ballabi su kanaka vallari (The Cowherdess is a Creeper of Gold), RV 3.197 (CP 80), Śrī Hita Harivaṃśa

Set to an early morning *rāga*, Bhairava, this poem of Śrī Hita Harivaṃśa is in Cautāl (12 *mātrās*). The first word is on the *sam* at the upper s. Fast repeats appear in the *antarās* and build to the repeat of the refrain.

ballabi su kanaka vallari tamala syama sanga
lagi rahi anga-anga manobhiramini (mai)
badana joti manon mayanka alaka tilaka chabi kalanka
chapata syama anka manaun jalada damini (mai)
bigata-basa hema khambha, manon bhuvanga beni-danda
piya ke kantha prema-punja kunja kamini (mai)
jai Sri Sobhita Harivamsa natha satha surata alasa vanta
uraja kanaka kalasa radhika sunamini (mai)

Translation: Rupert Snell (1991, 257)

Enchanting in every limb, the cowherdess is a creeper of fine gold
Clinging to the *tamāla* tree of Śyāma;
The brightness of her face is like the moon, her locks and *tilaka* the
Blemishes on its brightness, as she lurks in Śyāma's embrace like lightning in cloud.
Unclad are the golden pillars [of her thighs], as a serpent her staff-like braid —
The lady of the grove is a mass of love in the lover's embrace;
Ornamented with her lord, Harivaṃśa, and wearied by amorous dalliance
Is she with breasts like golden pitchers, the prettily-named Rādhikā.

99. Kaha kahau ina nainana ki bata (What Can I Say of Those Eyes?), CP 60, Śrī Hita Harivaṃśa

Set in the *rāga* Bahar (S G̱ M P Ṉ D N s, s Ṉ P M P G̱ M R S), this poem of Śrī Hita Harivaṃśa is played in a medium Tintāl. The *sthāyī* begins with "*ina nainana ki*" with the *sam* on Ṉ and on the first syllable of the word "*bata*." There is a fast repeat on the last *antarā* (line six), and a repeat of the refrain.

> *kaha kahaun ina nainana ki bata /*
> *ye ali priya badana-ambuja-rasa atake anata na jata //*
> *jaba-jaba rukata palaka samputa lata ati atura akulata /*
> *lampata lava nimesha antara tain alapa kalapa sata-sata //*
> *sruti para kanja, driganjana, kuca bica mrigamada hvaina samata /*
> *(jai sri) hita harivamsa nabhi sara-jalacara jancata samvala gata //*

Translation: Rupert Snell (1991, 238)

What can I say of those eyes?
They are like bees engrossed in the nectar of the
    beloved's lotus face,
and do not stray elsewhere!
Whenever obstructed by an eyelid or a covering curl,
They are quite restless and confounded;
Seven hundred aeons seem less long to these greedy
    ones
Than the duration of that momentary blinking.
They cannot be accommodated as the lotus at her
    ear,
Her collyrium, or the musk between her breasts;
Hita Harivaṃśa, they beg to be a dark-bodied fish in
    the pool of her navel!

[CD 18]

Sain ke Pada—Evening Songs

These songs are performed in the evening when the deitiy of Rādhāvallabha is being prepared for rest. They are usually sung during the final *ārati* ceremony in the temple, at any time during the year.

100. Chandi dai manini mana (Cease this Holding of Proud Anger in the Mind), RV 3.221 (CP 83), Śrī Hita Harivaṃśa

This poem of Śrī Hita Harivaṃśa is rendered here in a very poignant manner. It was recorded at Śrī Satsaṅga Bhūmi and so there is the larger choral response group. The rhythm is slow Jhaptāl (10 *mātrās*: 2-3, 2-3) in the *rāga* Shobhavari (S R M P D sa, sa D P M R S) with a touch of N̲. The *antarās*, beginning with the second line and appearing again in line six and ten, are especially poignant with the falling interval, r̲ - D̲, (i.e, on the word "*sughara*" in the second line). The performance retains the same slow pace until the last *antarā* in the tenth line, which rises to a very fast Jhaptāl in the repeat and in the reprise of the refrain.

chandi dai manini mana mana dharibau /
pranata sundara sughara prana ballabha navala,
bacana adhina saun itau kata karibau //
japata hari vivasa tava nama pratipada vimala,
manasi taba dhyana tain nimisha nahin taribau /
ghatata pala pala subhaga sarada ki yamini,
bhamini sarasa anuraga disi daribau //
haun ju kachu kahata nija bata suni mana sakhi,
sumukhi bina kaja ghana viraha dukha bharibau /
milata Harivamsa Hita kunja kisalaya sayana,
karata kala keli sukhasindhu men taribau //

Translation: Rupert Snell (1991, 260)

Cease this holding of proud anger in your mind, haughty lady;

Why act thus towards your young dear-as-life,
Who is humble, handsome, adroit, and dependent on your word?
Helplessly Hari constantly recites your perfect name,
His mind straying from contemplation of you not for a second;
The blessed autumn night slips by with every moment,—
Lovely lady, set yourself towards joyous love!
Listen to what I say, heed your *sakhi*:
Fair-faced one, vain is your suffering in the deep pain of separation,
Hita Harivaṃśa, they meet on a bed of leaves in the grove,
And make sweet sport, swimming in an ocean of pleasure.

101. Nagari nikunja aina (The Bower Bed is Made), RV 3.221, Śrī Hita Harivaṃśa

With this poem of Śrī Hita Harivaṃśa, there is the more relaxed mood of the deities preparing for their eternal rest in the bower (*kuñja*). The melody is attractive in the *rāga* Desh (S R M P N D P N s, s N D P M G R G S), but with added g, and in its *tāla* of Dadra (6 *mātrās*). In Western terms, it is like a fast waltz or 6/8. The melody is complete in two lines, with the two-line *antarās* complementing the *sthāyīs*.

nagari nikunja aina kisalaya dala racita saina,
koka kala kusala kumvari ati udara ri /
surata ranga anga-anga hava-bhava bhrukuti bhanga,
madhuri taranga mathata koti mara ri //
mukhara nupurana subhava kinkini bicitra rava,
birama-birama natha vadata bara vihara ri /
ladili kisora raja hamsa-hamsini samaja,
sincata harivamsa naina surasa sara ri //

Translation: H. S. Mathur

The pleasure bed for the amorous love-sports has been plentifully decorated with lotus flowers by an expert *sakhi* in the bower. As they make love all of their arms and legs are dancing wildly. The movements of their eyebrows and the pulsing of their love have overcome even Kāmadeva. The tinkling sound of their waist belts and anklets is extremely beautiful as they enjoy their amorous play. The boy and girl look like king and queen swans, and poet Hita Harivaṃśa watches this love-game, drenched by his own tears of love.

102. Rati rana jiti paudhi bala (The Bold Girl Wins the Battle of Love), RV 3.223, Śrī Hita Vinoda

This poem by Śrī Hita Vinoda is rendered in medium Rūpak *tāla* and in the *rāga* Desh. There is fast repeat on the last line and in the repeat of the refrain.

rati rana jiti paudhi bala /
koka davana hava bhavana vivasa kine lala //
sithila bhushana vasana anga-anga marajagi ura mala /
(jai sri) hita vinoda ali carana sevata krishna dasa tihikala //

Translation: H. S. Mathur

The bold girl wins the battle of love. With her body's movements and the fire of her passion, she overcomes the boy and renders him helpless. His ornaments and clothing are all loose, and in the press of their bodies the flower garland tears. The poet Hita Vinoda says that, at that time, Krishna massages the girl's feet like a servant.

103. Rajata nikunja mahal thakurani (The Queen Rules the Bower Palace), RV 3.223-224, Śrī Harirāma Vyāsa

This song is the first recording of the Rādhāvallabha musicians that the editor made back in March, 1975. The poem is by Śrī Harirāma Vyāsa (1511-1613), and was sung by Śrī Damodar Das Mukhiya in the main Rādhāvallabha Temple. The quality is marred by monophonic equipment, but the arresting nature of the singing style and performance is unmistakable. It follows the *rāga* Desh, with a touch of g. One enchanting feature is the irregular pattern of the hand cymbals combined with Keherva *tāla*. If you listen closely, you will hear the hand cymbals playing X xx X xx xx X X xx alongside the 8 *mātrās* of Kehervā, a truly magical effect.

rajata nikunja mahal thakurani
kusuma seja para paudi syama / raga sunata mrdu vani //
lalita carana palotana lagi / lala drsti lalacani //
panha parata sajani ke mohana / hita saun ha-ha khani //
bhai kripala lala para lalita / dau ajna musikani //
avahu mohana carana palotau / jaise kumari na jani //
ajna dai kumvari lalita kaun / mukha upara pata tani //
bina bajaya gaya kachu tanana / jyaun upajai sukha sani //
gavana lage rasika mana mohana / taba jani maharani //
uthi baithi sri vyasa ki svamini / vrindavana ki rani //

Translation: H. S. Mathur and Guy L. Beck

The queen adorns the bower palace, lying on a bed of flowers and listening to a lovely *rāga*. Her friend Lalitā starts massaging her limbs, and a young man looks on, allured. Mohana then besieges Lalitā, pleading with her and touching her feet. Lalitā takes pity on Mohana and smilingly gives him permission to join in, but tells him to come and massage Rādhā's feet in a manner that she does not notice that it is him. The young lady, her face covered with a cloth, doesn't suspect anything. But when he starts to play the *vīṇā* and sing melodies, giving her much pleasure, she hears his voice and is suddenly aware of his presence. Up she sits, the lord of poet Vyāsa, the queen of Vrindaban.

104. Lalana ki batiyan coja sani (Amorous Talk With Wit), RV 3.224, Śrī Harirāma Vyāsa

This poem of Śrī Harirāma Vyāsa is set to the *rāga* Bihag (S G M P N s, s N D P *M* P G M G R S) in a slow Tintāl. This *rāga* is especially appropriate for the later evening.

lalana ki batiyan coja sani /
parama kripala citai karunamaya locana kora ani //
umagi dhare dou surata seja pai tutin taraki tani /
parama udara vyasa ki svamini bakasata mauja ghani //

Translation: H. S. Mathur

Krishna indulges in amorous talk with Rādhā, full of compassion and looking with benevolent eyes. Both have laid themselves on the love-couch, and her garments are loosened. The queen of poet Vyāsa's heart thoroughly enjoys herself.

Phutkar Pada—Assorted Songs

105. Nahin surajhai urajhana prema ki (There is No Untangling the Tangles of Love), RV 3.226, Nāgarī Dāsa

This is a poem by Nāgarī Dāsa which is set in slow Dhamār, but which has fast repeats in the *antarās* beginning on the second line.

nahin surajhai urajhana prema ki, rahi roma-roma men bhoya /
radheju mohana hvai rahin mohana radhe hoya //
lalita latana tara rangamage, dou maina sanamana /
nainana saun naina mile, page prana son prana //
cibuka tare piya kara diye sobhita hain ihi bhaya /
nila kamala para aruna kamala manau khile hain parama sacu paya //
nagariya rajani ghatai uta canda malina duti hoya /
tyon-tyon alasa rupa duhuna kau itai caugunon hoya //

Translation: H. S. Mathur

The parts of their bodies are entangled in love and cannot be separated. Rādhā has turned into Mohana and Mohana has become Rādhā. They are entwined in love under the beautiful creepers. Their eyes are interlocked and so also their breaths. Mohana lifts her chin with his hand and that looks as lovely as if a red lotus were blossoming over a blue lotus. The poet Nāgarī Dāsa says that while the wee hours of the night pass away and the moon loses its luster, the fatigued beauty of the divine couple increases fourfold.

106. Cali kumvari radhika (Young Rādhikā Goes), RV 3.226, Nāgarī Dāsa

This poem by Nāgarī Dāsa follows the same melody and rhythm as Song 101 above.

cali kumvari radhika nikunja bhavana ravana pasa
saji suvasa matta bhamvara sanga-sanga-sanga /
aya rasika raya nikata lai bhujana jheli meli
karata keli parasata sukha anga-anga-anga //
jurata naina tutata hara ancala ura chutata bara,
cala kataksa bhrikuti bhanga ranga-ranga-ranga /
ta ghariya dekhi duhuna nagariya latana ota
tana mana gati sravana naina panga-panga-panga //

Translation: H. S. Mathur

Rādhikā comes from her home to the nearby grove, her body so fragrant that bees follow her. When she approaches the king of *rasikas*, he hugs her and starts his love-play, giving joy to every limb of her body. Their garlands are breaking, breaking, breaking; her scarf is slipping, slipping, slipping, and the movements of her eyebrows give him pleasure, pleause, pleasure. Yet their eyes stay locked to one another's. The poet Nāgarī Dāsa observes them from behind the tangled creepers—his mind, body, ears, and eyes all immobilized.

107. Kunja padharau radhe ranga (Rādhā Comes to the Bower), RV 3.227, Rasika Vihārī

This poem by Rasika Vihārī follows the same pattern as Song 103 above, except that in this version the *tabla* player has employed Tintāl instead of the appropriate Kehervā.

kunja padharau radhe ranga bhari raina /
ranga bhari dulahini ranga bhare piya syama sundara sukha daina //
ranga bhari seja sakhiyana nen ranga bharyau ulahata maina /
rasika vihari piya-pyari dou mili karau seja sukha saina //

Translation: H. S. Mathur and Guy L. Beck

Rādhā comes to the bower because the night is so colorful. The precious girl and her lover Śyāmasundara appear bursting with beautiful color, delighting everybody. Rādhā's girlfriends have decorated their pleasure bed, giving enchantment to the heart. The poet Rasika Vihārī blesses the lover and his beloved—"you two sleep very peacefully on this bed."

Jade men Sain ke Pada—Winter Evening Songs

108. Lala ki nida jhapata ankhiyan (The Boy's Eyes Are Sleepy), RV 3.230, Cācā Vṛndāvana Dāsa

This poem by Cācā Vṛndāvana Dāsa (1708-1787) follows the same melody and rhythm as Song 104 above.

lala ki, nida jhapata ankhiyan
khanjana suta ara barata udana manu
ulahin nai pankhiyan
pyari rupa chakin kai ghumata
matavari lakhiyan
vrindavana hita rupa rasasava
pivata jivata sakhiyan

Translation: H. S. Mathur

The boy's eyelids are getting heavy. They flutter like the new wings of a young bird that is trying to fly. The sweetheart's girlfriends, drenched with her beauty as she sleeps, appear crazy. The poet Vṛndāvana Dāsa says that the girlfriends seem to live by drinking the nectar of love with their eyes.

The Songs: श्री राधावल्लभजी का वार्षोत्सव

First Volume: प्रथमविभाग

(१)

[गोस्वामी श्रीहितहरिवंशचन्द्रजी महाप्रभु के पद—राग वसन्त।]

मधुरितु वृन्दावन आनन्द न थोर।
राजत नागरी नव कुशल किशोर॥
जूथिका युगल रूप मञ्जरी रसाल।
विथकित अलि मधु माधवी गुलाल॥
चम्पक बकुल कुलविविध सरोज।
केतकी मेदनी मद मुदित मनोज॥
रोचक रुचिर बहै त्रिविध समीर।
मुकलित नूत नदत पिक कीर॥
पावन पुलिन घन मञ्जुल निकुञ्ज।
किसलय शयन रचित सुख पुञ्ज॥
मञ्जरी मुरज डफ मुरली मृदङ्ग।
बाजत उपङ्ग वीना वर मुखचङ्ग।
मृगमद मलयज कुमकुम अबीर।
बन्दन अगरसत सुरङ्गित चीर॥
गावत सुन्दरि-हरि सरस धमार।
पुलकित खग मृग बहत न वारि॥
जय श्रीहित हरिवंश हंश-हंशिनी समाज।

ऐसेहो करहु मिल जुग-जुग राज॥ (१.१)

(२)

राधे, देख बनकी बात।
रितु बसंत अनन्त मुकलित कुसुम अरु फल पात॥
वेनु धुनि नन्दलाल बोली सुनिव क्यों अरसात।
करत कतव विलम्ब भामिनि वृथा औसर जात॥
लाल मरकत मणि छबीलौ तुम जु कंचन गात।
बनी जै श्रीहित हरिवंश जोरी उभै गुन गन मात॥ (१.१)

(३)

[स्वामी श्री हरिदासजी कृत—]
कुच गड्डवा जोवन मौर कंचुकी वसन ढाँपि लै राख्यौ वसंत।
ये गुन मंदिर रूप बगीचा में बैथी हैं मुख लसंत॥
कोटि काम लावन्य बिहारी जाहि देखत सब दुख नसन्त।
एसे रसिक श्री हरिदास के स्वामी काकौं भरन आइं मिल हसंत॥ (१.५)

(४)

[श्री नागरीदासजी कृत—]
विहरत विपिन फिरत रंग ढरकी।
हरखि गुलाल उडाय लाड़िली सम्पति कुसमाकर की॥
कसूंभी सारी सौंधे भीजी उपर बंदन भुरकी।
चोली नील ललित अञ्चल चल झलक उजागर उर की॥
मृदुल सुहास तरल दृग कुण्डल मुख अलकावलि रुरकी।
श्रीनागरीदासि केलि सुख सनि रहे मैन ललक नहीं मुरकी॥ (१.५-६)

(५)

रितु वसंत में लसंत मूरत दोऊ बैठे निकसि निकुञ्ज बाग।
ललित गुञ्ज मंजुल लतान पर अलि पुञ्जन की सुनि सुनि गुनगुन पुनि पुनि
रस कौ चढत पाग॥
मौरे आमन चढि चढि बौरे जुग जुग व्है कुहकत कोकिल कुल रीझत सुनि
कलरव विभाग।

प्रफुलित गुललाला की क्यारी, पवन लगत महकत लहकारी पिय प्यारी चख लगन लाग॥
रँग रँग रतन सतन के कूजे जतनन गुल नरगिस सों गँसि ताखन बिच राखन सलाग।
नवल लाल नव बाल परस्पर फूलि फूलि फूलन के झौरा राखे पेंचन बिच अलाग॥
लालन कर नरगिस की डांडी अति इतराय धरत किय उरपर अथ मननथ उर होत जाग।
बाला गुललाला की बेंदी कर उचाइ धरि लाल भाल पर यों करत रंग दोऊ रस तडाग॥
ललिता ललित रंग रँग भीने लखि लखि रीझी भीजी तान बजायौ है मधुर वसंत राग।
रति रस झेली सबै सहेली नव रङ्ग भीने झीने बागे रागे सुगल जुगलसुहाग॥
एकन कर बिच रँग रँग सीसी रतन पियाले लिये ससी सी हुलसीं अलि आनन्द याग।
दसन अरुणई वसन अरुणई दसन वसन अरुणई नई लखि पोहि लई पिय प्रेम धाग॥
अलि संकुलित लता हलिहलि नेति नेति कहत सी रहत सी थकि थकि सिखवत दिखवत अनङ्ग राग।
आनन्द चिक दै दै अलबेली के अधर कुसुम कौ अनुपम लंपट मधुप मीत मुसिकन पराग॥
सौंधे सनी बनी चोली तें छनि छनि छवि की छता छबीली छुटत छैल छलक्यौऽनुराग।
छलकि छलकि छलछल रतिपति की छकन छके लखि छिपि छिपि छिनु छिनु वल्लभ रसिक सखि चख सभाग॥ (१.३७-८)

(६)

[गोस्वामी श्रीहितहरिवंशचन्द्र महाप्रभुजी कृत—राग गौरी (यह पद नित्य होय है)]

प्रथम यथामति प्रणउँ श्रीवृन्दावन अति रम्य।
श्री राधिका कृपा बिनु सबके मनन अगम्य॥
वर यमुना जल सींचन दिन ही शरद वसंत।
विविध भांति सुमनस के सौरभ अलि कुल मंत॥
अरुण नूत पल्लव पर कूजत कोकिल कीर।

निर्त्तन करत शिखी कुल अति आनन्द अधीर॥
बहत पवन रुचिदायक शीतल मंद सुगंध।
अरुण नील सित मुकलित जहाँ तहाँ पूषनबंधु॥
अति कमनीय विराजत मंदिर नवल निकुंज।
सेवत सगन प्रीत जुत दिन मीनध्वज पुञ्ज॥
रसिक रासि जहाँ खेलत श्यामा स्याम किशोर।
उभय बाहु परिरंजित उठे उनींदे भोर॥
कनक कपिस पट शोभित सुभग साँवरे अङ्ग।
नील बसन कामिनि उर कंचुकी कँसूभी सुरंग॥
ताल रबाब मुरज डफ बाजत मधुर मृदङ्ग।
सरस उकत गति सूचत वर बँसुरी मुख चंग॥
दोऊ मिलि चाँचर गावत गौरी राग अलाप।
मानस मृग बल बेधत भृकुटी धनुष दृग चाँप॥
दोउ कर तारिन पटकत लटकत इत उत जात।
हो-हो-होरी बोलत अति आनन्द कुलकात॥
रसिक लाल पर मेलत कामिनि बंदन धूरि।
पिय पिचकारिनु छिरकत तकि-तकि कुमकुम पूरि॥
कबहुँ कबहुँ चदन तरु निर्मित तरल हिंडोल।
चढि दोऊ जन झूलत फूलत करत कलोल॥
वर हिंडोर झकोरन कामिनी अधिक डरात।
पुलकि-पुलकि वेपथ अँगे प्रीतम उर लपटात॥
हितचिंतक निज चेरिनु उर आनन्द न समात।
निरखि निपट नैनन सुख तृण तोरत बलि जात॥
अति उदार विवि सुन्दर सुरत सूर सुकुमार।
जय श्रीहित हरिवंश करौ दिन दोऊ अचल विहार॥ (१.८१)

(७)

[श्रीभगवान हित रामरायजी कृत—राग विहागरौ (फागुन वदी १ परवाकौ)]

रंग हो-हो-हो-हो होरी खेलै लाड़िलौ व्रजराज कौ।
साँवरे गात कमल दल लोचन नाइक प्रेम समाज कौ॥
प्रथमहिं रितु वसंत विलसे हुलसे होरी डाँडौ रोप्यौ।
मानों फाग प्रान जीवन धन आनंदन सब व्रज ओप्यौ॥
मृगमद मलय कपूर अगर केसर व्रजपति बहु जोर धरे।

सरस सुगंध सँवारि संग दै रंगन कंचन कलस भरे॥
प्रेम भरी खिलवारन के हित सुख कौ सार सिंगार कियौ।
भाग अपार जसोमति मैया बार बार जल वारि पियौ॥
फेंट भराइ लइ जननी पै आज्ञा लइ व्रज ईस सौं।
नन्दराइ तब रतन पेच रचि बाँध्यौ गिरधर सीस सों॥
तापर मोर चंद्रिका सोभित ग्रीव डुलन लहकात है।
मदन जीत कौ बानों मानौं रूप ध्वजा फहरात है॥
भइ रँगीली भीर दुवारें प्रीतम दरसन कारनें।
अब बन ठनि निकसे मंदिर तें कोटि काम किये वारनें॥
तैसेइ सखा संग रंग भीने हरखि परस्पर मन मोहैं।
बरन बरन ज्योति के कमल मानौं अमृत दिनमणि संग सोहैं॥
आनन्द भरि बाजे बाजत नाचत मधु मंगल रंग कियौ।
हरि की हेंसन दसनन की किरन नैनन की ढुरन मन मोह लियौ॥
अबीर गुलाल उड़ाइ चले खेलत जैसें सब कोऊ हरषैं।
छिरकत भरत छैल नवरंगी कहा कहियै रस घन वरषैं॥
कोउ द्वारन कोउ चढ़ी अटारिन कोऊ खिरकिन बदन सुहाये।
गोकुल चंद्रमा देखन कौं मनौं इन्दु विमानन चढ़ि आये॥
श्रीराधाजू दृष्टि परत ही मोहन फूलि-फूलि नैनन घूम्यौ।
सनमुख ह्वै पिय कलप तरोवर महाभाग फल रस झूम्यौ॥
प्रमदागनमणि स्यामा रसिक सिरोमणि सों खेलन आई।
दुहुँ दिसि सोभा उमँगि रंग मच्यौ गान वेनु धुन धुनि लाई॥
नैनन बैनन खेल मच्यौ गैंदुक नवलासिन मार मची।
कमल नैन कर लई पिचकारी मृग नैनिन की भौंह नची॥
छिरकीं छैल छबीली भाँतिन मनहरनी जोवन वारी।
रँग-रँग छींट बनी तिय वसनन फूल रही छवि फुलवारी॥
पुहुप पराग उड़ाइ दाइ रचि अछन-अछन नियरें आईं।
दौरि दामिनिनु घन घेरयौ पिय बात बनी सब मन भाई॥
कोउ मुख माड़त दै गरबहियाँ कोऊ पौंछत आछी छवि सों।
अलकन भौंहन—मूल रंग रह्यौ शोभा कही न जाइ कवि सौं॥
कोऊ रचि पान खबावत पुलकित सुन्दर अधरन परम कियें।
कोऊ भुज गहि लड़काइ फाग माँगत पिय नैनन चैन दियें॥
(श्री) राधाजू नागर स्याम सुन्दर पर प्रीत उमग केसर ढोरी।

महा मनोहरता कौ राज अभिषेक कियौ कहि हो-होरी॥
सर सुती सहित महामुनि मोहे यह सोभा संपति हेरें।
कहि भगवान हित रामराय प्रभु हँसि चितवन बसि जिय मेरे॥ (१.८४)

(८)

[श्रीनन्ददासजी कृत—राग गौरी—फागुन वदी अष्टऽमी ८ कौ]
राधा रवनी रंग भरी।
रंग होरी खेलें॥
अपने प्रीतम के संग।
अहो हरि होरी खेलें॥
इक पहिलें ही रँगमगी।
रंग होरी खेलें॥
पुनि भीनी रंग रंग।
अहो हरि होरी खेलें॥
रँग रँग की सँग सहचरी। [रंग ०]
बनी रँगीली के साथ॥ [अहो ०]
पहिरें वसन रँग रंग के। [रंग ०]
रँन्ग भरे भाजन हाथ॥ [अहो ०]
रँग रँग की कर पिचकई। [रंग ०]
सोहत एक समान॥ [अहो ०]
मनों मैन शिव पर सज्यो। [रंग ०]
हाथन तुपी कमान॥ [अहो ०]
काहू पै कुसुम गूंथित छरी। [रंग ०]
काहू पै नये नये नौर॥ [अहो ०]
काहू पै कुसुम गेंदुक चलैं। [रंग ०]
काहू पै नूतन मौर॥ [अहो ०]
काहू पै अरगजा रंग कौ। [रंग ०]
काहू पै केसर कौ रंग॥ [अहो ०]
कोऊ गौरा मृगमद लियें। [रंग ०]
होत भँवर जहाँ पंग॥ [अहो ०]
तिनमें मुकटमनि लाड़िली। [रंग ०]
सोहत अति सुकुँवार॥ [अहो ०]
लटक चलति जनु पवन ते। [रंग ०]
कोमल कंचन डार॥ [अहो ०]

पिय कर पिचका देखि कें। [रंग ०]
तिय नैना छवि सों डराहिं॥ [अहो ०]
खंजन से मनौ उड़हिंगे। [रंग ०]
ढरकि मीन ह्वै जाहिं॥ [अहो ०]
छिरकत पिय जब तियन कौं। [रंग ०]
यों मन उपजै आनंद॥ [अहो ०]
मनहुँ इंदु सींचत सुधा। [रंग ०]
अपनी कुमुदिन के वृन्द॥ [अहो ०]
भीजि वसन तन लपटाने। [रंग ०]
बरनत बरनी न जाइ॥ [अहो ०]
उपमा दैन न दैंहि नैन। [रंग ०]
गहि राखत हा-हा खाइ॥ [अहो ०]
रंग रँगीली राधिका। [रंग ०]
रँगीलो गिरधर पीय॥ [अहो ०]
ये रँग भीने नित बसौ।
रँग होरी खेलें॥
नंददास के हीय।
अहो हरि होरि खेलें॥ (१.९५-९६)

(९)

[चाचा श्रीवृन्दावनदासजी कृत। राग गौरी। फागुन वदी १४ शिवरात्री कौ]
यह जोगी बसत कहाँ है।
मैं परख्यौ बड़ी बेर ते यामें जुक्ति जोग की ना है॥ टेक॥
कौन गुरू उपदेश ते इन घर छाँड़्यौ तातालिलिता निकट बुलायकै यासों बूझ मरम की बात॥
चितवन भरी सनेह की हियें ललक कछू और।
घर-घर प्यासौ सौ फिरै याके चित की वृत्ति न ठौर॥
यह जोगी भयौ तर्क सों नहीं ज्ञान कौ अंग।
जोग जवाहर ज्यौं दिपै जो कियौ होहि गुरू संग॥
कै जोगी जादू जु करि मोह्यौ राजकुमार।
सुन्दरता पै रीझ कै लै आयौ अपने लार॥
बाहु सौं विरच्यौ जु अब पुर कौतुक कियौ हेत।
रूप सवादी सौ लगै यह फिर-फिर फेरी देत॥

जिहि देखै तन ऊजरी तहाँ उरझावै नैन।
यह औगुन है जोग में सत्य कहत हौं बैन॥
वह जोगी तुम नृपसुता घटती कही न जाय।
जो सण्देह सो बूझिये तौ अबही लैहुँ बुलाय॥
ललिता काचे जोग बल जिन त्याग्यौ परिवार।
विधि प्रतिकूल तहाँ भयौ यह जान परी निरधार॥
जोगी लियौ बुलाय कैं बैठ्यौ सन्मुख आइ।
हिय के हिय फूले सखी कछु वस्तु डरी सी पाइ॥
सींगी नाद बजाइ तू कछु राग रँगीलौ गाय।
वास भानुपुर दैहिंगी प्यारी सुन्दर कुटी छबाय॥
सिंगी अधरन धारि कैं रुचिर अलाप्यौ राग।
विद्या फुरी जु मोहिनी अति उर उझल्यौ अनुराग॥
रीझी कीरति नंदिनी विद्या अखिल निधान।
जो कछु इच्छा रावरी अब विरमौ पुर बृषभान॥
कौन मनोरथ करि भये तुम जु परम अवधूत।
अलख पुरुष परच्यौ नहीं लई हिये जु रावरी कूत॥
ग्रीव ढोर रावल कही तुम भाषत जु अनीत।
परदा में की भामिनी क्यों लखैं जोग की रीत॥
जोगी कौ घर दूर है को भाषन समरत्थ।
गुरु गम सौं पहुँच्यौ तहाँ जहाँ नाथ गह्यौ दृढ़ हत्थ॥
हाथ गहन कौं को कहाँ सूनसान सौ देश।
जोग ध्यान नाहिंन सुन्यौ हम कारौ गोरौ भेष॥
सब वाही के बरन हैं सब वाही के रूप।
सकल पसारौ अलख कौ सुनि बेटी रावल भूप॥
अलख-अलख जाकौं कहत बरनौ ताके अंग।
जैसे फूल अकास के किन देखे कैसे रंग॥
दिन दस नगरी विरमते समझि तुम्हारौ नेह॥
अब चरचा ऐसी करी पग धरैं न तुम्हरे गेह॥
जोगी कुल जनमे नहीं जोग लियौ सुनि ज्ञान।
राज विभौ हमने तजी ताकौ तुम जु करत अभिमान॥
कौन देश और कौन कुल कौन नाम, को ग्राम।
रावल बदन प्रकाशियै हम सब मिल करैं प्रनाम॥

भली भई तुम आप मुख कही आपनी आदि।
यह संदेह निवारिये बलि और बात सब बादि॥
निरखत प्यारी बदन दिस हिय में धकपक होत।
जैसे परसत पवन के झकुरात जु दीपक जोत॥
देस रँगीलौ कुल बड़ौ नाम धाम सुख मूल।
विदित लोक सब जानिये प्रेमिन कुल अनुकूल॥
सब प्रानी निर्भय बसैं सब कौ पालन होय।
हम सुख लाड़ तहाँ पले यामें संदेह न कोय॥
हम जोगी बन बन फिरत काहू सौं न चिन्हार।
सुखित भये गुरु ज्ञान सौं सब बिरस गन्यौ संसार॥
ये गुन ब्रजमंडल सबै तुम ठहरायौ कौन।
बूझत कीरति नंदिनी मुख रावल गहि रह्यौ मौन॥
रहि-रहि कैं बोलत सखी हँसत नैन की कोर।
जोगी कैधौं कौतुकी तन सिमटत जैसे चोर॥
जोग छदम सौ गिनत ये सखी न मानत आन।
कैसें तुम ढिंग विरमिये सुनि निंदा अपने कान॥
तुम मूरत जु सनेह की बचन अमी की धार।
श्रवन न तृपत जु होत हैं श्यामा सुनिये बारंबार॥
चित्रा नेरैं आउ तू लक्षण परख निराट।
रावल-रावल कहा कहै जाकी चरचा औरै घाट॥
केश ढपे सिर बसन सौं जे भीजे जु फुलेल।
जोगी नहिं भोगी सखी ये नंदसुवन के खेल॥
सुन गहवर बन कौं भजे सुख जु अपूरव लूट।
मन बाजी ह्याहीं रह्यौ गई बाग हाथ सों छूट॥
खेल बिबिध नित-नित रचैं भीजैं उर अहलाद।
वृंदावन हित रूप जस गायौ श्रिहरिवंश प्रसाद॥ (१.१०८-११०)

(१०)

[श्री माधौदासजी कृत राग काफी। फागुन वदी चौदस १४ कौ (छदम)।]
वाधंवर ओढ़े साँवरौ हो यामें योगी कौ हुनर कौन॥ टेक॥
ग्वाल बाल कोऊ संग नहीं हो अंग विभूत रमाइ।
कमलनैन सुख दैंन कुँवरि कौं आये हैं भेष बनाइ॥

शंख शब्द् सुनि सुनि जित तित तें घिर आइ ब्रज नारि।
वदन विलोक कुँवरि राधे कौ बैठे हैं आसन मार॥
दण्ड कमण्डल धरें मन मोहन कटि बाँधें मृगछाल।
भौंह अनियारी नेंन कमल दल मोहिं लइ ब्रज बाल॥
कौंन दिसा तें आये हो रावल कहाँ तेरी मनसा जाइ।
आपनु मौन गही मेरे स्वामी दक्षिण दिसा बताइ॥
हँसि बूझत वृषभानुनंदिनी रावल उत्तर देहु।
कारन कौन भेष तपसी कौ वन तजि डोलत गेह॥
सींगी पत्र विभूत न बटुआ सिर चन्दन की खौर।
मेरे मन एसी आवत है कंत विसारी गौर॥
चंचल चपल चतुर दिखयत अति मुख मधुरी मुसकान।
जोगी नहीं कोऊ बड़ौ है वियोगी भोगी है भँवर निदान॥
चटुकीविभूत दई राधे कों चले हैं वाघंबर झार।
मन हरि लियौ तनक चितवन में गोहन लगी है कुँवरि॥
नगर बगर अरु भवन-भवन प्रति निस दिन फिरत उदास।
नैन चकोर भये राधे के हरि दरसन की प्यास॥
मन हुतौ रतन जतन हरि लीनौ चपल नैन की कोर।
श्रीजगन्नाथ जीवन धन माधौ प्रीत लगी दुहूँ ओर॥ (१.१०७-१०८)

(११)

[श्रीनागरीदासजी कृत॥ राग धनाश्री॥ फागुनवदी १५ अमावस्या कौ]
रूप अनूपम मोहनी।
रंग राचे लाल॥
मोहे कुँवर किशोर।
लाड़ गहेलरी, रंग राचे लाल॥ ध्रु०॥
बदन सुधा रस श्रवत री॥ रंग०॥
पीवत नैन चकोर॥ लाड़०॥
नैन कमल मुख कमल के॥ रंग०॥
चरन कमल कर लाल॥ लाड़०॥
तन मन फूले कमल री॥ रंग०॥
मोहन मुदित मराल॥ लाड़०॥
हास कुसुम जोबन लता॥ रंग०॥
अलि आसक्त तमाल॥ लाड़०॥

वचन रचन सुर शब्द कै॥ रंग०॥
मृग मन मोहे रसाल॥ लाड़०॥
ये घन तुम दुति दामिनी॥ रंग०॥
मिलि विलसौ प्रेम सुहाग॥ लाड़०॥
आलस क्यौं बलि कीजिये॥ रंग०॥
हिलमिल खेलहु फाग॥ लाड़०॥
सुनत भयौ चित चाउ री॥ रंग०॥
सुघर सिरोमनि जान॥ लाड़०॥
सहचरी संच सुरन लियें॥ रंग०॥
करत मधुर कल गान॥ लाड़०॥
श्रीकुंजबिहरी खेलहीं॥ रंग०॥
प्रेम भरे रस रंग॥ लाड़०॥
बूका बंदन मेलहीं॥ रंग०॥
कुमकुम कुसुम सुरंग॥ लाड़०॥
मदन मुदित अँग अंगरी॥ रंग०॥
सुरत सुखद कल केलि॥ लाड़०॥
उर करवर परसैं हँसें॥ रंग०॥
जुगल नवल रस झेल॥ लाड़०॥
पिवत सुधा रस माधुरी॥ रंग०॥
चित्रित पीक कपोल॥ लाड़०॥
अंग-अंग अनुराग री॥ रंग०॥
कहत मधुर मृदु बोल॥ लाड़०॥
राग रंग अति रंग रह्यौ॥ रंग॥
श्रीहरिदासि बिनोद॥ लाड़०॥
विचित्र विहारिन दास री। रंग०॥
विपुल बढ़ावत मोद॥ लाड़०॥
छिन-छिन प्रति रति साजहीं॥ रंग०॥
कुंज सदन सुख रासि॥ लाड़०॥
मधुर प्रेम रस बिलसहीं॥ रंग०॥
बलि-बलि नागरी दासि॥
लाड़ गहेल री रंग राचे लाल॥(१.११०)

(१२)

[श्रीव्यासजी कृत॥ राग गौरी॥ फागुन सूदी १ (परवा) कौ]

ए चलि ललन भरें मिलि।
चलि हो चलि अलि बेगि गिरिधरन भरहिं मिलि॥ टेक॥
अलीं चलीं गिरिधरन भरन कौं पहिरें सुरंग दुकूल।
नवसत अभरन साजि चलीं सब अंगन-अंगन फूल॥ गिरिधरन॥
सनमुख आवत होरी गावत सखन सहित बलवीर।
उभै मदन दल उमड़े मानहुँ जुरे हैं सुभट रनधीर॥
महुवर चंग उपंग बाँसुरी बीन मुरज मृदंग।
ढोलक ढोल झाँझ डफ बाजत कह्यौ न परत सुख रंग॥
ब्रजजन बाला रसिक गुपाला खेलत रँग भरे फाग।
तान तरंगन मुनि गन मोहे छाइ रह्यौ अनुराग॥
रतन जटित पिचकारिन भरि-भरि छिरकत चतुर सुजान।
कनक लकुट छैलन पर टूटत फिरत कुँवरिजू की आन॥
छुटत बसन उर टूटत माला धरत भरत भुज पेलि।
लाल गुलाल आनन पर तकि-तकि करत चपल कल केलि॥
इक भानपुरा की अमान गूजरी हरखी अङ्ग न माइ॥
छैलन खेद कहूँ लौं आई हलधर पकरे धाइ॥
आई सिमिट सबै ब्रजवाला लेत आपनौं दाइ।
मानौं ससि अवनी पर घेर्यौ उड़गन पहुँचे आइ॥
एकै धाइ धरत आँकौ भरि एक मरोरत कान।
इक सनमुख ह्वै साजि आरतौ बहु पूजा सनमान॥
जोरि सखन मन मोहन धाये दाऊजू की भीर।
जुवतिन जूथ सनमुखै उमड़े कूकें देत अभीर॥
जुवतिन नैन सैन भेदन में मोहन लीने घेरि।
मधुमंगल हँसत दूर भयौ ठाड़्यौ सुबल बजाबत भेरि॥
मोहन पकरि जूथ में ल्याईं पूजा रचत बनाइ।
दधि अक्षत रोरी कौ टीकौ गनपति गौर मनाइ॥
एकै कुच बिच लेत लाल कौं लाइ रहत उर झेल।
मानहुँ तरुन तमालहिं लपटी कनक लता बहु बेलि॥
गौर लेप मोहन मुख लेप्यौ लिखी छबीली भौंह।
ये ढोटा वृषभान राइ के सुबल तुम्हारी सौंह॥
पकरि श्रीदामा चोबा सों माड़्यौ लै आई भरि बाथ।
नन्दराइ यह ढोटा जायौ दयौ है हमारे साथ॥

भजि मनसुख जसुमति पै आयौ कहत आतुरे बोल।
वृषभान पुरा की जोर गूजरी भैयन लै गई ओल॥
चली महरि तब यह सुख देखन जोर आपने वृन्द।
सुर नर मुनि जन एक भये हैं थकित भये रवि चन्द॥
देखत सोभा ब्रजपति रानी आनँद मन मन होइ।
आज रोहिनी भाग हमारे ताहि न पूजै कोइ॥
तब रोहिनी ललिताजू बोलीं आगें आवहु भाम।
कर जोरें हम करत बीनती चलहु हमारे धाम॥
तब ललिता राधा पै आई बात सुनहु दै कान।
बड़ी महरि अपने घर बोलत पायौ चाहत मान॥
तब राधा सखियन पै आई लगत सबन के पाँइ।
गावत खेलत हँसत हँसावत चलहु महरि कैं जाँइ॥
इतनौं सुनत सबै जुर आईं चली महरि जू के द्वार।
ब्रजपति रानी दृष्टि परी तब भाजि गये सब ग्वार॥
आगें ह्वै रोहिनी तब आई अरघ पाँवड़े देत।
कंचन थार उतार आरतौ बारि बलैयाँ लेत॥
रतन जटित सिंहासन आन्यौं दियौ किशोरी राज।
बाबाजू अब करत बीनती मोल लिये हम आज॥
अगनित मेवा गनौं कहाँ लौं भूषन बसन अमोल।
प्रेम मगन नन्दरानी वरषत कहत बचन मधु बोल॥
नौतन भूषन खुले सबन तन उपजत कोटिक भाइ।
प्रथम उतीरन दिये व्यास कौं विमल विमल जस गाइ॥ (१.१११-११३)

(१३)

[श्री अचलदासजी कृत—राग विहागरौ—फागुन सुदी ४ चौथ कौं]
अहो रंग हो-हो-हो-होरी खेलैं सकल कुंवरि बरसाने की।
तिनमें रसिक सिरोमनि स्यामा एकहि वैस समाने की॥
रंग हो-हो-हो होरी ० ॥ तेक॥
नव निधि साजि सिंगार विविध रँग नख सिख बनीं इक बाने की।
कीरत प्रान अधार लली जीवन सब देस भयाने की॥
गागर लई भराइ माइ पै केसर मृगमद साने की।
कोमल करन कनक पिचकारी मनि नग रचित खचाने की॥

बाजत ताल मृदंग झाँझ डफ ढोल ढमक सहदाने की।
गावत घोर जील स्वर तानन कोकिल कंठ समाने की॥
आई हैं वट संकेत सघन वन सुभग सींब सरसाने की।
श्रवन सुनत आये मनमोहन सैना सखा अमाने की॥
दुहुँ दिसि ख्याल मच्यौ जु परस्पर चोखचाख अति ठाने की।
इत उत अहुट न मानत कोऊ कमलन मार मचाने की॥
बढ़ी है रेलपेल बीथिन में सोहै रंग बरसाने की।
उड़त अबीर कपूर धूर मिलि गगन मध्य मँड़राने की॥
चंपक लता गहे मनमोहन कर सारत कुंज बसाने की।
चंद्रावलि पकरे बल जू धपि धाइ धन्य मरदाने की॥
लिये दमामे छीन लड़ैती जीती है रावल राने की।
बिचरे सखा भजे जित तित कौं हार मान महराने की॥
बलजू की आँख आँजि मुख माँड़्यौ कान न करी बड्याने की।
हा-हा खाइ पाँइ परि छुटे रही न कछु विरद बाने की॥
गहि गहि चिबुक उठाबत ललिता दृष्टि न जुरत खिस्याने की।
रहे जू कहा नार नीची करि अङ्ग अङ्ग सकुच लज्याने की।
सकल सिमिट आईं कान्हर ढिंग करि-करि बात बखाने की॥
परे आइ बस नवल बधुन के ह्याँ नहि चलत सयाने की॥
जानत हौ मन में लालाजू छलबल करि भज जाने की।
परौ पाँइ श्रीराधजू के और न कछू बस्याने की॥
गावत नारि गारि होरी की अंचल गाँठ जुराने की।
कोटि-कोटि सुख बारिये इन पर हो-हो कहि हँसि जाने की॥
रसना एक कहाँ लगि बरनौ यह सुख सिंधु समाने की।
नगर बगर घर गली गल्यारे प्रेम हिलोर छकाने की॥
ब्रह्मा शिव मुनि करत प्रसंसा गोपिन भाग बड़ाने की।
अचलदास गिरिधरन भये बस प्रेम के हाथ बिकाने की॥ (१.११७-११८)

(१४)

[श्रीराघवदासजी कृत॥ राग गौरी॥ फागुन सुदी ६ छट को]
ए चलि जाँहि जहाँ हरि खेलत गोपन सङ्गा।
आनक बहु बाजे ताल मुरज मुखचङ्गा॥
गावत सुनि भावत मंद मधुर मुख बानी।
जनु हरखि परस्पर मनहु मदन गति ठानी॥

चलि जाँहि जहाँ॥ ठेक॥
चलि जाँहि जहाँ क्रीडत नन्दनंदन झाँझ पणव डफ भारी।
बीन मृदङ्ग उपङ्ग चङ्ग बहु देत परस्पर गारी॥ १॥

कर पिचक विकच मुख कटि पट भेष बनायौ।
जनों गुदर दैन कौं बनि बसंत ब्रज आयौ॥
हाटक मणि नग खचित विविध कर जेरी साजैं।
रुञ्ज मुरज नीसान ढोल ढोलक डफ बाजैं॥
आवझ अति आतुर बजैं ब्रज जन खेलत फाग।
तान तरंगन वायु बँध्यौ छाय रह्यौ अनुराग॥ २॥

धुनि सुनत पियारिनु कुमकुम भूषन कीने।
बहु रंग बसन तन जावक चरनन दीने॥
कवरी करज सँवार निरखि उपमा कौं हारी।
मानों हाटक लता रही खग पन्नग नारी॥
श्रवन तार उर हार छवि अरु मुक्ता सरस सुढार।
जनों जुग गिरि बिच देखि कैं धसी सुरसरी धार॥ ३॥

रचि तिलक भाल पर मृगमद रेख सँवारी।
जनु जुगल जीभ धरि पन्नग पिवत सुधारी॥
खञ्जन मीन अधीन देखि दृग सारंग लाजै।
बदन चंद भ्रुव चाप स्वातिसुत नासा राजै॥
उपमा कौं अवलोकि कवि या सम नाहिन और।
मनौं कीर उडगन गहैं चुगत नहीं सुनि बौर॥ ४॥

अति अधर अरुन छवि अरु दसनन दुति पाइ।
मानों बिज्जुल बीजन बिद्रुम बार बनाइ॥
कंठ कपोत लज्यात करन अङ्गद जगमगियौ।
मानौं जलज मृनाल सरद ससि बालक लगियौ॥
पहुँचन में पहुँची सघन संदर स्याम सुपास।
मनहुँ कंज के कंठ लगि भृङ्ग रहे मधु आस॥ ५॥

बनि चली हैं सकल तिय पग नूपुर सुर भारी।
मनों विविध काम कलहंस करत किलकारी॥
साख जबादि सुगंध कुमकुमा केसर घोरी।
भाजन भरि लै चलीं सकल तिय गावत होरी॥
नख सिख तें अबलोकि छबि नागर मोहे गान।

मनों संगीतसाला पढ़ीं घटबढ़ परत न तान॥ ६॥

छबिसिंधु ललन तन देखत लोचन भूले।
चितवत चित चोरत अङ्ग-अङ्ग अनुकूले॥
बरन-बरन सिर पाग श्रवन कुंडल मनिमय अति।
मनहुँ स्याम नग सिखर तरनि जुग रमत तरल गति॥
उर वनमाल बिशाल छबि विविध सुमन बहु वेख।
मनहुँ जलद् में प्रगट अति सतमख सारंग रेख॥ ७॥

रचि तिलक मलय कौ पिय कर खौर बनाइ।
मनु जुगल अहिन शशि घन पर दई हैं दिखाइ॥
घन तन देखि लज्यात कंज दृग क्यौं सम पावहिं।
मुख ससि स्याम भुजान देख अहि वपुहिं लज्यावहिं॥
नख सिख तें अवलोक छबि कटि पट पीत सुदेश।
मनहुँ जलद् धुरवा सखी दामिनि रही परवेश॥ ८॥

छबि श्रीमोहन तन लघु मति बरनी न जाई।
चितवत चित चोरत मनमथ रह्यौ है लज्याई।
तियन परस्पर हरखि हरित कर डगे निवाजे।
उठे गोप किलकार लागि दुहुँ दिसि तें बाजे॥
एकन कर कुमकुम लियौ एकन घोरि गुलाल।
चलीं सकल ब्रज सुन्दरी पकरन मदन गुपाल॥ ९॥

सैनन ही मोहन हलधर दियें है बताइ।
गहि नील वसन तन द्वै बिन्दु दिये छिटकाइ॥
बहुर्‌यौं मोहन पकरि सबै राधा पै लाई।
तबहि तरुनि मुसिक्याइ साख भाजन लै धाई॥
छींटत छिरकत भरत बहु प्रेम छकी नँदनंद।
मनहुँ अवनि पर मेघकौं घेरि रहे बहु चंद॥ १०॥

निरख़त विथकित नभ जहाँ तहाँ अमर विमान।
वरसत सुर सुमनन अरु बजाइ नीसान॥
रह्यौ परस्पर रंग सकल तिय भवनन आइ।
तबहि तिनहिं ब्रजराज विविध पट दई है मिठाई॥
आइ तरनितनया सलिल मज्जन कियौ बलबीर।
पहरि वसन आये भवन संग सकल आभीर॥ ११॥

परिवा श्रीमोहन राजत पीत सुवास।

बैठे सिंघासन बलि बलि राघौदास॥ १२॥ (१.१२१-१२३)

(१५)

[गो० श्रीसदानन्दजी कृत॥ राग काफी॥ फागुन सुदी ७ कौ॥ निकुञ्ज की॥]

श्रीवृन्दावन रानी राधा सुन्दर रूप निधान।
बनितन गन चूड़ामनि मंदन मोहन जीवन प्रान॥
अंग अंग छवि मन भाँवती हो सजनी देखहु नैन निहार॥ टेक॥
ललित अलक कुसुमन सों गथित सेंदुर रचित सीमंत।
मनों रतिपति मृग-क्रीड़ा कारन कियो सखी उदित बसंत॥
सीस फूल रस मूल बदन छवि नव-नव सोभा होत।
मनों नव ग्रह उडपति ढिंग बैथे जगमग अपनी जोत॥
सुन्दर मस्तक बेंदी राजत लखि सुख पावत लाल।
प्रगटित भाग सुहाग मनों मणि दिपत मनोहर भाल॥
कानन बर ताटंकन की दुति झलक कपोल अभंग।
कनक कमल में मनु प्रतिबिंबित छवि सों प्रात पतंग॥
दीरघ सुन्दर नैन सु चंचल अंचल पट न समाहिं।
मानों श्रवन करी मरजादा ज्यौं बढ़ि अधिक न जाहिं॥
अरुन अधर मिलि मखि सुठि लोचन बिच मोती बहु भाँति।
दुहुँ ठाँ की दुति परस त्रिवेनी भइ कल गुंजा कांति॥
चिबुक सुदेश दिठौना लौना छवि सों सुभग सुहात।
मनों अलिछौंना पी मकरंदहिं बैठ्यौ ढिंग जलजात॥
गौर मनोहर भुजा विराजत बलय बलित छवि जाल।
मानौं भूषन भूषित सोभित कोमल कनक मृनाल॥
उदित उजागर उर पर मंजुल रुरकत मुक्ता हार।
मानौं मूरतिवंत सुभगता करत सुदेस बिहार॥
नाभि सरोवर त्रिवली लहरी प्यारी परम प्रवीन।
तामें रंग भयौं डोलत सखी संतत पिय मन मीन॥
कंकन किंकिनि नूपुर बाजत राजत छबि विस्तार।
मानों कंचन बेलि बिलंवित मदन मुनी धुनि चारु॥
तनसुख सारी सुभग विराजत अतरौटा अति रंग।
ऐसी छवि सों गोरी होरी खेलत पिय के संग॥
सखी समाज मध्य पिय प्यारी बरषत अमी आनन्द।

उड़गन कोटि कलोलत मानौं विच डोलत बिबि चंद॥
बाजे बाजत घन ज्यों राजत बरषत रंग अपार।
भीजत तन मन हरि जुवती जन प्रेम विहार उदार॥
अरुन अबीर गगन में घुमड़्यौ मनु घन उमड्यौ लाल।
रंग भरी चमकत चंचल तन दामिनि सी नव बाल॥
वदन छवीले नैन रँगीले घुमड़ गुलाल सुरंग।
मानौं भोर दिनेश्वर के मधि मीन फिरत ससि संग॥
भरत परस्पर प्रीतम प्यारी हिय भारी अनुराग।
निरखि-निरखि सुख हरखि कहत यों बड़भागी यह फाग॥
श्रीवृन्दावन कालिंदी तट खेल बढ्यौ सुख सार।
जै श्रीसदानंद हित व्यास सुवन बल गावत जुगल विहार॥ (१.१२३-५)

(१६)

[श्रीबिहरिनदासजी कृत॥ बना॥ राग धनाश्री॥ फागुन सुदी ८ कौ]
श्रीवृन्दावन सहज सुहावनौं॥
नव नागरि ए॥
अरी एरी नवल नव नागरि ए॥
नव नागरि नेह निधान॥
बना॥ हाँ हाँ हंबै॥ बना हंबै॥ टेक॥
होरी खेलन के मते॥ नव०॥
बन बैठे करि ठान॥ बना०॥
मान मनावत प्रथम ही॥ नव०॥
ए दोउ करत परस्पर आन॥ बना०॥
रोंट मेटि मिलि खेलहीं॥ नव०॥
हँसि दिये हैं दुलहिनी पान॥ बना०॥
नवल निकुंज बिराजहीं॥ नव०॥
रवि तनया के तीर॥ बना०॥
भृङ्ग विहंग कुलाहला॥ नव०॥
नव जुवतिन की भीर॥ बना०॥
स्याम ओर की साँवरी॥ नव०॥
गोरी के गोरे गात॥ बना०॥
उमगि चलीं चित चौंप सों॥ नव०॥
अपनी-अपनी गहि घात॥ बना०॥
सब सखि मन अनुसारानी॥ नव०॥

उन सजि लीनी सब सौंज॥ बना०॥
लाल रतन मणि की कुँड़ी॥ नव०॥
केसर की ओजाओज॥ बना०॥
कस्तूरी कर्पूर सों॥ नव०॥
साख कुमकुमा आदि॥ बना०॥
चंदन मलयागिर घसे॥ नव०॥
घसि गौरा मेद जवादि॥ बना०॥
बाजे बाहैं अनभतीं॥ नव०॥
सब मिले हैं संच सुर तार॥ बना०॥
बीन अमृती आवझी॥ नव०॥
वर किन्नर कठतार॥ बना०॥
गावत चैत सुहावनौं॥ नव०॥
मेरी पिय प्यारी कौ हेत॥ बना०॥
खेलत मेलहि मिलवहीं॥ नव०॥
उन बद्यौ है सबन संकेत॥ बना०॥
लै लावन लाँगें कसीं॥ नव०॥
बैनी कटि सों लपटाइ॥ बना०॥
आधे कुच कंचुकी कसी॥ नव०॥
अति आनंद उर न समाइ॥ बना०॥
आज्ञा लै सनमुख भई॥ नव०॥
उन दीनी है जुक्ति बनाइ॥ बना०॥
अरगजा पिचकारी चलीं॥ नव०॥
सब भरत परस्पर धाइ॥ बना०॥
चोबा के चहले मचे॥ नव०॥
भये अंबर अरुन अबीर॥ बना०॥
हार जीत नहिं समझहीं॥ नव०॥
अति मन मगन गंभीर॥ बना०॥
फागु खिलावत फूल सों॥ नव०॥
दैं सैनन ही सनकार॥ बना०॥
नैन कमल कज्जल भरे॥ नव०॥
मची है कटाक्षन मार॥ बना०॥
इक झुकि बैठीं पीठ दै॥ नव०॥
इक मानिन ह्वै मुख मोरि॥ बना०॥
एक मनावत दीन ह्वै॥ नव०॥

इक पाइन परत निहोरि॥ बना०॥
दिन दुलहिन कौं दुलरावहीं॥ नव०॥
दिन दूलह कौं दै गारि॥ बना०॥
गावत सुख दै रुख लियें॥ नव०॥
मुख चूँवत भरि अँकवारि॥ बना०॥
सौंधे में सौंधीं सबै॥ नव०॥
कौन पिछानें काहि॥ बना०॥
सबै प्रेम रस रँग रँगी॥ नव०॥
रहे हैं रसिक मुख चाहि॥ बना०॥
मेरौ कुंजविहारी कौतुकी॥ नव०॥
इहि कौतिक रहे लुभाइ॥ बना०॥
मत्त भये रस माधुरी॥ नव०॥
रस पीवत सुख दै धाइ॥ बना०॥
होरी खेलत रंग रह्यौ॥ नव०॥
सब गोरी लई हैं बुलाइ॥ बना०॥
को गोरी को साँवरी॥ नव०॥
मोसों कहौ स्याम समझाइ॥ बना०॥
स्याम कहौं गोरी सबै॥ नव०॥
गोरी के तन मन स्याम॥ बना०॥
निरखि बदन तनमय भये॥ नव०॥
यों सफल किये सब काम॥ बना०॥
बातन रहसि बहस बढ़ी॥ नव०॥
इहि विधि खेलैं फाग॥ बना०॥
(अपने) रसिकन की रस रीति कौ॥ नव०॥
प्रगट कियौ अनुराग॥ बना०॥
सखी सहेली सहचरी॥ नव०॥
श्रीहरिदासी सुख रासि॥ बना०॥
श्रीविपुल विहारिनि दासि कों॥ नव०॥
रीझि दई स्यामासि॥ बना०॥
हाँ हाँ हंवै॥ (१.१२५-७)

(१७)

[श्रीनंददासजी कृत धमार॥ राग गौरी॥ फागुन सुदी ९ नौमी कौ]

अरी चलि नवन किशोरी गोरी भोरी, होरी खेलन जाँहि॥ टेक॥
अरी ऐसी मधु जामिनि देखि भामिनि, क्यौं तोहि भवन सुहाहि॥
अरी उहाँ (सब) ब्रज वर वर नारिनु के, जूथ जुरे हैं आइ।
अरी उहाँ नँदनँदन पुनि आये, रँगीले रसिक मनि राइ॥
अरी आली तिनमें तू नहीं देखी, रहि गये नैना नाइ।
अरी तब इत उत तकि मोहन पिय, मो तन तक्यौ अरगाइ॥
सखी मोसौं सैनन ही में कह्यौ कहाँ, मैं कहयौ ग्रीव ढुराइ।
तबतौ री छबीले कुँवर तो पहियाँ, सैनन दई पठाइ॥
तू अब न करि गहरु नागरि तिय, आनि बन्यौ भलौ दाइ।
यह सुनि नवल लाडिली सहचरि तन, मुसिकी नैंन ढुराइ॥
इतने ही परम चतुर सखी जिन तिन, भुज भरि लई उठाइ।
गहि नव कंचुकी सौंधे बोरी, बोरी दई बनाइ॥
पुनि पद पीठ पटोरा पोंछि कें, आगें धरी समुहाइ।
चली नवसत सजि स्वामिनि कामिनि, सखी के अंस भुज लाइ॥
मानों कनक धातु पर्वत पर, तड़ित लता चमकाइ।
नव गुन नवल रूप नव जोवन, नवल नेह हुलसाइ॥
झूमक सारी प्यारी पहिरें, चलत लंक लचकाइ।
जनु यह रूप जोति जगमग-सी, पवन लगे झकुराइ॥
कमल फिरावत करवर बाला, माला उरसि रुराइ।
पुनि इक लट छबि सों जु छबीली के, बेसर रही अरुझाइ॥
मनु प्रीतम मन मीन की बनसी, भख मुकता लटकाइ।
ललितादिक सखियन में सुन्दरि, सोभित हैं इहि भाइ॥
जनु नव कुमुदिन के मंडल में, इन्दु पगन चल्यौ जाइ।
कबहुँक बदन दुराइ उघारत, पुनि हँसि लेत दुराइ॥
मंजुल मुकर मरीचिन सी मनु, छिन-छिन छवि अधिकाइ।
अरु जैसे नव मद मत्त गयंदनि, मल्हकत बाहु ढुराइ॥
सोभित श्रवनन स्वेद सुदंति के, मानों पटे चुचाँइ।
नीवी-बन्धन फुँदवा घंटा, किंकिनि घन घुँघराइ॥
नूपुर ऊपर चूरा रूरा, मनु संकल झनकाइ।
चंचल अंचल चँवर विराजत, नैंकु चलत जब धाइ॥
सखियन के कर कुसुम छरी ते, अगढ़ बने चहूँ घाइ
मदन महावत कौ बल नाहीं, अंकुस देत डराइ॥

सखियन में हितू विशेष विसाखा, ज्यौं तन की परछाँइ।
सो नंदनंदन नियरें जानि कें, सहज उठी कछु गाइ॥
सबहिन जान्यौं श्रीराधाजू आईं, भये चौगुने चाइ।
जे हुतीं नवल किशोरी की साथिन, ते दौरीं समुहाइ॥
तिन संग मोहन धाये आये, ज्यों रंक महानिधि पाइ।
पहिलैं ही लाल जुहार कह्यौ मृदु, मुरली माँहि बजाइ॥
इतनें कुटिल कटाक्षन पिय तन, चितयौ मुरि मुसिकाइ।
सो सुख पिय नैना ही जानै मो मन में न समाइ॥
चाँचर देंन लगीं ब्रज वीथिनु, रँगीले रंग उपजाइ।
गावन लागीं ग्वालिन गारी, सुन्दर ललहिं लगाइ॥
राधाजू गारी सुनि-सुनि हँसि-हँसि, हरि तन हेरि लज्याँइ।
ललनु अबीर भरत ग्वालिन कौं, (अपनी) प्राण प्रियाहिं बचाइ॥
और जु प्रेम विवस रस कौ सुख, कहत कह्यौ नहिं जाइ।
जेहि सुख कहिवे कौं कोटिक सरसुती की सुमति हिराइ॥
सेस महेस सुरेस न जानें, अज अजहूँ पछिताइ।
सो रस रमा तनक नहिं पायौ, जदपि पलोटत पाँइ॥
श्रीवृषभानुसुता पद अंबुज, जिनके सदा सहाइ।
इहि रस मगन रहत जे तिन पर, नंददास बलि जाइ॥ (१.१२७-१२९)

(१८)

[श्रीवृन्दावनदासजीकृत॥ सजनी असीस कौ॥ फागुन सुदी ११ कौ है॥]
सजनी लाल फाग फल पायौ।
रंग भरि-भरि कें घेरि कुंज मधि गहि-गहि बाँह नचायौ॥
पिय किये प्रिया प्रिया करीं प्रीतम बढ़ि गयौ रंग सबायौ।
भाँवरि दै बैठारे मंडल लखि दृग भाग्य मनायौ॥
ललित घूंघटी स्याम बदन पर रचि कौतुक उपजायौ।
वारि-वारि पहुपांजलि सबहिन अति हित सौं दुलरायौ॥
गौर स्याम अंगन जु रंग चौंपन चाइन छिरकायौ।
तन भींजन मन भींजन कौ सुख आनन उझल जु आयौ॥
कुसुम छरी दै हाथ बहुरि झूमक कौ खेल खिलायौ।
दूलह दुलहिन प्रेम माहिलौ छंदन रचि-रचि गायौ॥
न्यौछावर किये प्राण परम कौतिक होरी मन भायौ।

यह जु अपूरव लाड़ झूमका बना-बनी दरसायौ॥
औरै चाह समझि कै दोऊन कुंज सदन पधरायौ।
वृन्दावन हित रूप घुमड़ि रस कौ अम्बुद बरसायौ॥ (१.१३२-३)

(१९)

[गो० श्रीकिशोरीलालजी कृत॥ राग जोगिया आसावरी॥ नित्य होय॥]
होरी रंग रँगीली आई।
खेलौंगी ब्रजमोहन सोंहन सो अतिहो मन भाइ।
सुनहु सहेली ललित आदि रंगन घोरौ बहु चाइन चाई।
जै श्रीकिशोरीलाल हित सौं मिल खेलौं करि हौं अपनी ही दाइ॥ (१.१४१)

(२०)

[रसिया —]
ब्रज कौ दिन दूलह रंग भयौं।
हो-हो-होरी बोलत डोलत हाथ लकुट शिर मुकट धर्यौं॥
गाढ़े रंग रँग्यौ ब्रज सगरौ फाग खेल कौ अमल पर्यौं।
वृन्दावन हित नित सुख वर्षत गान तान सुन मन जु हर्यौं॥ (श्रृङ्खला समाप्त) (१.१४१)

(२१)

[गोस्वामी श्रीकिशोरीलालजी कृत (फा० शु० ११ से पूर्णिमा तक खेल में सन्ध्या आरती के बाद नित्य गाया जाता है।)]
रंग रँगीले दोऊ नव निकुंज मधि प्रेम रंग भरे खेलत होरियाँ, हो हो हो।
स्याम वरन सखी स्याम संग भई गोरी के संग सहेली सब गोरियाँ, हो हो हो॥
पैंटन भरे गुलाल विविध रंग तक-तक मेलत नवल किशोरियाँ, हो हो हो।
जै श्रीकिशोरीलाल हित सौं गहि आन्यौ मुख माँड्यौ करि-करि बर जोरियाँ, हो हो हो॥ (१.१४६)

(२२)

अरी चलि बेग छबीली! हरि सों खेलें जाहिं॥ ध्रु०॥
निकस्थौ है मोहन साँवरौ बलि फाग खेलन ब्रज माँझ।

उमड़्यौ है अबीर गुलाल गगन बिच मानौ माई फूली है साँझ॥
बाजत ताल मृदंग मुरज डफ कही न परत कछु बात।
रँग-रँग भीने ग्वाल बाल सँग मानों माई मदन बरात॥
आई हैं इतते जुरि सुन्दरि सब करि-करि अपनौ ठाट।
खेलत नहिं कोऊ कान्ह कुँवर सों चाहत तुम्हरी बाट॥
बिनु राजा दल कौन काज बलि उठिये छाँड़िये ऐंड।
उमड़्यौ है निधि ज्यौं नवल नन्द कौ रुकत रावरी मैंड़॥
उठी है विहँसि वृषभानु कुँवरि वर कर पिचकारी लेत।
सहि न सकत कोऊ महा सुभट लौं सुनत समर संकेत॥
आई हैं रूप अगाधा राध छबि बरनी नहिं जाइ।
नवल किशोर अमल चंदहि मनों मिली है चन्द्रिका आइ॥
खेल मच्यौ ब्रज बीथिन माँहियाँ बरषत प्रेमानन्द।
दमकत भाल गुलाल भरे मनौ बंदन भुरके चन्द॥
और रंग पिचकारिन छबि सों छिरकत हरि तन तीय।
कुटिल कटाक्ष प्रेम रंग भरि-भरि भरत पीय कौ हीय॥
दुर मुरि भरन बचावन छबि सों बाढ्यौ है रंग अपार।
मैंन मुनी सी बोलत डोलत पग नूपुर झनकार।
सिब सनकादिक सारद नारद बोलत जै-जै-जै।
नंददास अपने ठाकुर की जियौ बलैयाँ लै॥ (१.१५६-७)

(२३)

चली है कुँवरि राधे खेलन होरी।
पंकज पराग वर लियें भरि झारी॥
रँग रँग रली सँग सोहें गन अलीं।
सफल करी हैं सब गोकुल की गलीं॥
बाजें डफ ताल मृदंग झाँझ सुहाए।
मदन सदन मानों मंगल बधाए॥
गावत सरस सुर ऐसी मीठी धुनि।
हरजू जायौ मनोज जियौ जाइ सुनि॥
सो हैं मुख कछु-कछु अंवर दुराए।
आधे-आधे विधु मनों बदरन छाए॥
अबीर धूँधर मधि राजैं रंग भीनी।
मानों डीठ डर मार सार ढाँपि लीनी॥

उततें आये मोहन भीनें रंगरंगा।
चरन लुठत आवैं कोटिक अनंग॥
रँगिल्ली गलिनु बिच खेल मच्यौ भारी।
उत हरि इत वृषभान की दुलारी॥
छिरकीं छबीले आन प्यारी तीय गन।
रंगन बरसै मानों नूतन सघन॥
छूतें पिचकारी रंग भरी सोभा भरी।
छबि सौं छूटत मानों मैन फुलझरी॥
तियन के अंग रंग कन गन सोहैं।
कंचन जराइ जरी छरी छवि कोहै॥
इततें रंग की धार साँवरे पै मेली।
अबहीं उलही मानों नव प्रेम बेली॥
अबीर गुलाल मिलि मंदित गगन।
मानों अबहीं रवि चाहत उगन॥
हँसत-हँसत उत चन्द्रावलि गई।
लाल सों कहत हौं तिहारी दिसि भई॥
बाँसुरी छिड़ाइ लीनी छलकै किसोरी।
तारी दै-दै हसैं सब कहैं हो-हो होरी॥
राधाजू अधर धरी बाँसुरी विराजी।
ऐसी कबहूँ साँवरे पिय पै न बाजी॥
बंसी दैन मिस प्यारी राधिका बुलाए।
हँसत-हँसत लाल इकले ही आए॥
कामिनी के वृन्द स्याम घेर लीने ऐसें।
दामिनी निकर मानों नव घन जैसें॥
साँवरे के अंग संग सोहैं तिय ऐसी।
सिंगार कलप तरु छवि लता जैसी॥
नंददास और सुख कहाँ लों बखानौ।
विधि हूँ कह्यौ है सोई जानों सोई जानौ॥

(२४)

[श्रीसहचरीसुखजी कृत॥ राग राइसौ —]
रंग आज वंशीवट फागुन विविध विहार।
विहरत राधा वल्लभ उझलत सौरभ सार॥

वैस कलिन सी खिलीं ललित ललितादिक वृन्द॥
तिनकी नख दुति देखत फीकौ लागत चंद॥
तिनके जोवन उलहत सुख सोभा की भीर॥
सादा हूँ पट पहिरत होत जरकसी चीर॥
सहज सुगंधन तिनकी भयौ मधुकर गति भूल॥
जिनके मुख मुसिकत झरैं उज्वल रस के फूल॥
तिनके लखत बनावन उपमा लजत अनंत॥
जिनके तन फूल्यौ रहै नित ही मदन वसंत॥
तिनमें मिलत लाड़िली तब छबि ऐसी होत॥
हरि चख कमलन छाई रूप भोर की जोत॥
करत कटाक्ष दृगन की मुरत प्रिया की पीठ।
गोरे हिय पिय ह्वै रह्यौ मिलत दीठ सों दीठ॥
उर उरजन के बोझन लचकि-लचकि कटि जात।
देखत मदनमोहन की चितवन लचकन पाँत॥
भूलत पलकन प्रीतम प्रिये प्रेम की पुंज।
जा तन चितवत चितवन भई आरसी कुंज॥
रीझ कुँवरि की रचि रही नवल कुँवर हिय माँहि।
रोम-रोम यौं बँधि रह्यौ भयौ फिरत ब्रज छाँहि॥
सिथिल करत कोऊ सहज ही सनमुख चलि गज चाल।
कोऊ कसि भुज में हँसि-हँसि मसरत वदन गुलाल॥
स्यामा की सैनन सौं कोऊ अलि माँडता भाल।
कोऊ अंजन कौं आँजत छुवत कपोलन बाल॥
लखि ललिता ढ़िग आइ कैं कहत बचन मन चोर।
जूथ विसाखादिक उत हम मोहन की ओर॥
कोऊ सखी सखा बनी हैं सीस चंद्रिका धार।
मिलि मृदंग डफ तालन गावत सरस धमार॥
चंदन की छींटन सौं छिरके छकि नँदनंद।
कृष्ण जलद में झलकै मनु जस उडगन वृन्द॥
छिरकीं छैल बंदनसौं ते तिय सब बड़भाग।
मनहुँ मन के बागन बये हैं बीज अनुराग॥
अरगजा तिय लपटावत उर परसत मुसिकात।
रसिक हिये लपटाइ कैं आपुन लपती जात॥
लपटावत मृगमद मुख अलबेलिन कै लाल।

बने दृग मनों सिंगार सर फूले कमल विशाल॥
भुरकत चूर कपूर कुचन पर ओपी वाम।
समर शंभु मनु पूजे खेल विजै हित स्याम॥
रमनी भुरकत रोरी रँगीलौ कीनौ है फागु।
प्रीत लता मनु लौनी लहकत झरत परागु॥
ढारी बिहारी पिचकारी लीक दिपीं पचरंग।
मनो घन दामिनी सिंगारी लहरिया सारी अंग॥
छाती छैल तकतु जब दुरत मुरत रसदानि॥
फिरि तारी दै मुसिकत कँपत जब दोऊ पानि॥
रचे हैं गुलालन आनन कवि यौं करत बखान।
लाली बरसि मनु कमलन ससि किये अमृत भान॥
रंग-रंग उड़त अबीरन परी है लाज की गाढ़।
घमड़ि सुरँग अति आँधीन फागुन कियौ असाढ़॥
दरसत अंग दुरे जब मुठीं उठत दुहूँ ओर।
मानत जनम सफलता देखत नंदकिशोर॥
ढ़ीरत सीसन केसर कृष्णागर रिझवार।
बदलत तन बरननि कौं बाढ्यौ मोद अपार॥
अवलन के बल में फँसे लसे हैं जुगल सुजान।
कान्ह बनाए हैं गोरी, गोरी कीन्ही है कान्ह॥
गँठजोरा करि किलकीं सजि मंगल तिहि ठौर।
गीत ब्याह के गावत बांध दुहुँन सिरमौर।
ऐसेहीं हुलसौ विलसौ अंस भुजा दोऊ मेलि।
दुलरावत सहचरि सुख कुंजमहल की केलि॥ (१.१६१-३)

(२५)

[श्रीघनश्याम जी कृत॥ राग सारङ्ग]
ग्वालिन सौंधे भीनी अँगिया सोहै केशर भीनी सारी।
लहुँगा छापेदार छबीलौ छीन लंक छवि न्यारी॥
अधिक बार रिझवार फाग खिलवार चलत भुज डारी।
अतर लगाये चतुर नारि गावत होरी की गारी॥
बड़ी बड़ी बरुनी तरुनी करनी रूप जोवन मतवारी।
छवि-फूलेल अलकें झलकें ललकें लखि छैल बिहारी॥
हाव भाव के भवन किधौं भौंहन की उपमा भारी।

वसीकरन कैधौं जन्त्र मन्त्र मोहन मन की फँदवारी॥
अंचल में न समात बड़ी अखियाँ चंचल अनियारी।
जनों गाँसी गजबेल काम की श्रुत खरसान सँवारी॥
बेसर के मोती की लटकन मटकन की बलिहारी।
मनों मदन मोहन जू कौ मन अँचवत अधर सुधा री॥
बीरी मुख मुसिकान दसन दमकत चंचल चौका री।
कौंधि जात मनों घन में दामिनि छबि की पुंज छटा री॥
स्याम बिंदु गोरी ठोड़ी में उपमा चतुर बिचारी।
जनों अरविंद चुम्यौ न चलै मचल्यौ अलि कौ चिकुला री॥
पोत जोत दुलरी तिलरी तरकुली श्रवन खुटला री।
खयन बने कंचन बिजायठे करन चुरी गजरा री॥
चंपकली चौकी गुंजा गजमोतिन की माला री।
करैं चतुर चित्त की चोरी डोरी के जुगल झबा री॥
पैने सुख दैने कंचन कुच खुभी कंचुकी कारी।
काम कुटी कर दीनी है कीनी शिव सों फिर यारी॥
एड़ी लाल महावर जेहर तेहर बाजन वारी।
घायल किये पाँय पायल कर सायल नंद लला री॥
जोर दीठ सों दीठ ईठ मजीठ रँगन रँग भारी।
लगी लाल कै पगी खगी चित चितवन की पिचकारी॥
मोहन मदन गोपाल लाल पर पढ़ि गुलाल जब डारी।
संग लग्यौ डोलै रसिया बृन्दावन में बनवारी॥
छवि दौरन मोरन मरोर पिय जाय भरे अँकवारी।
प्रेम फंद पकरे जकरे गोरी नें गिरवर धारी॥
छीन लई मुरली कर तें पटुका पट पीत उतारी॥
ग्वालिन अधर धरी बंशी वरसी रस सिंधु सुधारी।
जो भावै सो लै ललना कलना पलना मोहि प्यारी।
तोहि ददा की सौं है ग्वालिनि दै वंशी हा-हा री॥
बाँहनमें बाँहें चाहें मुख चंदचकोर पियारी।
मोहन स्याम तमाल बाल लपटानी हेम लता री॥
गाँठ जोर गोबिंद चंद सों दीनी सखिन सँवारी।
तारी दै-दै गारी गावें ग्वाल देत किलकारी॥
वशीकरन बतियन रस बरसत बरसाने की नारी।
प्रभु घनश्याम दियौ मन मेवा फगुवा प्रानन प्यारि॥ (१.१८५-६)

(२६)

[श्री गंगल प्रभु जी कृत॥ राग सारंग॥]

दोऊ राजत जुगल किशोर अति आनंद भरे।
ब्रज जुवतिन के चित चोर परम विचित्र खरे॥ ध्रु०॥
उत श्री मदन गोपाल सखा अंसन भुज दीने।
इतहि कुँवरि राधिका मेल अपनौ संग लीने॥
कुँवरि कुँवर सों नेह है बाढ़यौ अति अनुराग।
निकसि गाँव के गोइरे हरि खेलन लागे फाग॥
बाजत डफ बाँसुरी ताल मिलि मधुर मृदंगन।
गावत सारंग राग सुनत सुख उपजत अंगन॥
नर नारिनु कै नेकहू लाज रही नहिं गात।
कछू कहत कछु वै कहें हो, सबै स्याम रंग गात॥
तब तिन ग्वालन उमँगि लई हाथन पिचकारी।
जुवतिन कें मुख भरत देत होरिन की गारी॥
घात कियैं चितवत फिरै उत छैलन के बाग।
सावधान सब गोपिका हो देत न लागन लाग॥
तवही ग्वालिन धाइ गह्यौ संगी हरि पिय कौ।
आँख आँजि मुख माँड़ दियौ सेंदुर कौ टीकौ॥
कान ओंठि गुलचा दियौ सब अरु दीनौ मुकराइ।
चलत आपने झुंड कों वाके खिसल परत हैं पाँइ॥
तबहि नंद के लाल कलपि इक बात विचारी।
धर्यौं त्रियाकौ रूप जाइ भेटीं ब्रजनारी॥
पाछे ते सकुचीं सबै जब जान्यौ यह भाव।
तारी दै हरि हँसि चले हम लियौ सखा कौ दाव॥
तबहि सहचरी भेष एक हलधर कौ कीनौ।
गोकुल तन ह्वै आइ पहिर नीलौ पट झीनों॥
ताहि मिलन केसौ चले करिअग्रज की कानि।
इत चितवत दुचिते भये उत गहे ग्वालिनी आनि॥
कोऊ अली भुज टेकि कोउ पटुका झकझोरै।
कोऊ धरि हरि मिलै कोऊ मुख सों मुख जोरै॥
कोऊ नैन की सैंन दै कहै तो गर्भित भाइ।
काहू बातन लाइ लाल की मुरली लई छिड़ाइ॥

छूटन पाये तबहि दैन फगुवा जब मान्यौ।
रँग रँग बसन मँगाय दियौ जाहि जैसौ बान्यौ॥
काहू भूषन पान दै काहू तन मुसिकाइ।
एकन आँकों भरि चले हरि सबकौ भलौ मनाइ॥
नाना बरन बिलास रास कीने वृन्दावन।
हरखित करि बल्लवी परम सुख सौं जु गोपगन॥
मदन लजानौ देखि कै श्रीकमलनैन की केलि।
गंगल प्रभु आए घरैं हो सब सुख सागर झेलि॥ (१.१९४-५)

(२७)

[श्रीछीतस्वामीजी कृत॥ राग सारंग॥]
सुरंग होरी खेलै साँवरौ श्री वृन्दावन माँझ॥ सुरंगी०॥
ब्रज की नव-नव नागरी घिरि आईं सब साँझ॥ सुरंगी०॥
सरस वसंत सुहावनी रितु आई सुख दैन॥ सुरंगी०॥
माते मधुपा मधुपनी कोकिल कल कल बैन॥ सुरंगी०॥
फूले कमल कलिंदजा केसू कुसुम सुरंग॥ सुरंगी०॥
चंपक बकुल गुलाब के सौंधे सिंधु तरंग॥ सुरंगी०॥
सुबल सुबाहु श्रीदाम से पठये सखा सिखाय॥ सुरंगी०॥
बाजे बाजैं नव रंगी लीने ढ़ोल मढ़ाय॥ सुरंगी०॥
रुंज मुरज डफ बाँसुरी भेरिन कौ भरपूर॥ सुरंगी०॥
फूँक नफीरी फेरि कै ऊँचै गई श्रुति दूर॥ सुरंगी०॥
ब्रज कौ प्रेम कहा लौं कहौं केसर सों घट पूरि॥ सुरंगी०॥
कंचन की पिचकारियाँ मारत हैं तकि दूरि॥ सुरंगी०॥
आँधी अधिक अबीर की चोबा की मची कीच॥ सुरंगी०॥
फैली रेल फुलेल की चन्दन बन्दन बीच॥ सुरंगी०॥
फूल छरी गहि हाथ सौं मारत बाँह उठाइ॥ सुरंगी०॥
अंचल चंचल फरहरैं पैने नैन नचाय॥ सुरंगी०॥
ब्रज की नवल जु नागरी सुन्दर सूर उदार॥ सुरंगी०॥
खेलन आइ सबै घिरीं श्रीराधा के दरबार॥ सुरंगी०॥
श्रीराधा की प्रिय सखी ललिता लोल सुभाइ॥ सुरंगी०॥
छल करि छैलहि छिरक कैं हँसि भाजी डहकाइ॥ सुरंगी०॥
नारी कौ भेष बनाइ कैं पठयौ सखा सिखाय॥ सुरंगी०॥

अति ही अधिक कहावती ललिता भेटी जाय॥ सुरंगी०॥
गेंदुक नीकी फूल की दीनी श्रीराधा हाथ॥ सुरंगी०॥
आय अचानक औचका तकि मारे ब्रजनाथ॥ सुरंगी०॥
ब्रज की बीथी साँकरी उत जमुन कौ घाट॥ सुरंगी०॥
बलदाऊ कौं बोलिकै दीनें गाढ़ कपाट॥ सुरंगी०॥
हलधर हैं जु कहा बली साँचे तुम बलरास॥ सुरंगी०॥
बल कौ बल जु कहा भयौ, गहि बाँधे भुज पास॥ सुरंगी०॥
नैनन अंजन आँजि कैं सौंधौ ऊपर ढ़र॥ सुरंगी०॥
पाँय परि द्वार पठै दए रस की रासि विचार॥ सुरंगी०॥
हँसि भाजीं सब दै दगा आवन दीने और॥ सुरंगी०॥
मदन गुपाल बुलाअय कें गहि लाई बरजोर॥ सुरंगी०॥
गिरि धार्यौ कर वाम सों खर मार्यौ गहि पाँय॥ सुरंगी०॥
तिनकौ भार कहाँ गयौ ललिता लेत उठाय॥ सुरंगी०॥
घर में घेरि सबै चलीं श्रीराधा कों संग लेत॥ सुरंगी०॥
दोऊ जन खेंच मिलाई कैं नैनन कों सुख देत॥ सुरंगी०॥
तब ललिता हँसि यों कह्यौ श्रीराधा कौं सिर नाय॥ सुरंगी०॥
नीलाम्बर सों ढाँपि कैं मुख मूँदौ मुसिक्याय॥ सुरंगी०॥
उत श्रीदाम अचपलौ इत ललिता अति लोल॥ सुरंगी०॥
बीच विसाखा साख की मुरली माँगत ओल॥ सुरंगी०॥
वसवासी वृषभान कौ मदन सखा वाकौ नाम॥ सुरंगी०॥
स्याम मते कौ मिलनियाँ वस कीयौ सब गाम॥ सुरंगी०॥
पठयौ मदन बसीठई ढ़ीठ महा मद लोल॥ सुरंगी०॥
छिन औरें छिन और सौं छाक्यौ छैल दुछोल॥ सुरंगी०॥
मदना मदन गुपाल कौं हलधर कौं लै आव॥ सुरंगी०॥
श्रीराधा की दिस जाय कें चाँप्यौ है हँसि पाँव॥ सुरंगी०॥
श्रीदामा हँसि यों कह्यौ मेवा देहु मँगाय॥ सुरंगी०॥
नैंक हमारे स्याम कौं आनन कौ मधु प्याय॥ सुरंगी०॥
भाग सुहाग सबै बढ़ौ खेलत फागु विनोद॥ सुरंगी०॥
श्री राधा माधव बैठारे ब्रजरानी की गोद॥ सुरंगी०॥
भूषन देत जसोमती पहुँची पाँय पछेल॥ सुरंगी०॥
घड़े टीक टिकावरी हीरा हार हमेल॥ सुरंगी०॥

श्री विट्ठल पद पद्म की पावन रैनु प्रताप॥ सुरंगी०॥
छीतस्वामी गिरिधर मिले मेटे तन के ताप॥ सुरंगी०॥ (१.१९६-१९८)

(२८)

[श्री सालिगरामजी कृत]
नैनन में पिचकारी दई, [मोहे] गारी दई, होरी खेली न जाय॥ तेक॥
क्योंरे लँगर लँगराई मोते कीन्हीं, केसर कीच कपोलन दीन्हीं,
लिये गुलाल ठाड़ौ मुसकाय, होरी खेली न जाय॥
नैक न कान करत काऊ की, नजर बचावै बलदाउ की,
पनघट सौं घर लौं बतराय, होरी खेली न जाय॥
औचक कुचन कुकुमा मारै, रंग सुरंग सीस सों ढारै,
यह ऊधम सुनि सास रिसाय, मेरी ननद रिसाय, होरी खेली न जाय॥
होरी के दिनन मोसों दूनों-दूनों अरुझै, सालिगराम कौन जाय बरजै,
अंग लिपट हँसि हा-हा खाय, होरी खेली न जाय॥ (१.२६०)

(२९)

[श्रीहित घनश्यामजी कृत]
गौंहन पर्यौ री मेरे गौंहन पर्यौ,
साँवरौ सलौनौ ढाटा मेरे गौंहन पर्यौ॥
याकी घाली मेरी आली कहौ कित जाउँ।
बाँसुरी में गावै वह लै-लै मेरौ नाउँ॥
साँवरे कमलनैन आगें नेकु आइ।
लाजन के मारे मोपै कहूँ गयौई न जाइ॥
जो हौं चितौउँ आड़ौ दै-दै चीर।
सेंनन में कहै चल कुंज कुतीर॥
अँगना में ठाड़ी हूँ अटा चढ़ि आवै।
मुकट की छहियाँ मेरे पाइन छुवावै॥
हित घनश्याम मिलोंगी धाइ।
साँवरे सलौने बिनु रह्यौई न जाय॥ (१.२६२)

(३०)

[गोस्वामी श्रीहित हरिवंश महाप्रभु जी के पद॥ राग देव गंधार॥]
झूलत दोऊ नवल किशोर।

रजनी जनित रंग सुख सूचत अंग-अंग उठि भोर॥
अति अनुराग भरे मिलि गावत सुर मंदर कल घोर।
बीच-बीच प्रीतम चित चोरत प्रिया नैन की कोर॥
अवला अति सुकुमार डरत मन वर हिंडोर झकोर।
पुलकि-पुलकि प्रीतम उर लागत दै नव उरज अकोर॥
उरझी विमल माल कंकण सों कुंडल सों कच डोर।
बेपथ जुत क्यौं बनै विवेचत आनंद बढ्यौ न थोर।
निरखि-निरखि फूलत ललितादिक बिबि मुख चन्द्र चकोर।
दै असीस हरिवंश प्रसंसत करि अंचल की छोर॥ (१.२६९)

(३१)

[श्री दामोदर स्वामीजी कृत॥ राग धनश्री॥]
जमुना पुलिन सुहावनौ, रंग भीने झूलैं।
तन मन मोद बढ़ाइ डोल सुहावनौं, रंग भीने झूलैं॥
कंचन खंभ जटित बने, रंग भीने झूलैं।
देखत मन ललचाइ, डोल सुहावनौं रंग भीने झूलैं॥
नवल लाल नव लाड़िली॥ रंग०॥
मुदित सखी यह भाइ॥ डोल०॥
मानौं जुग ससि एकठाँ॥ रंग०॥
कुमुदिन फूली ढिंग आइ॥ डोल०॥
नील पीत पट राजहीं॥ रंग०॥
भूषण रहे छवि छाइ॥ डोल०॥
यह छवि कवि को कहि सकै॥ रंग०॥
चितवन मृदु मुसिकाइ॥ डोल०॥
चारौं दृग चंचल बने॥ रंग०॥
उपमा कछु ठहराइ॥ डोल०॥
मानौं रूप तड़ाग में॥ रंग०॥
खेलत मीन सुभाइ॥ डोल।०।
मधुर-मधुर सुर गावहीं॥ रंग०॥
खग मृग रहे लुभाइ॥ डोल०॥
अद्भुत रंग बढ्यौ तहाँ॥ रंग०॥
सारद बलि-बलि जाय॥ डोल०॥

सुरंग गुलाल अखंड सौं॥ रंग०॥
गगन रह्यौ घमड़ाइ॥ डोल०॥
मनु हरि ऊपर काम नै॥ रंग०॥
रच्यौ है वितान बनाइ॥ डोल०॥
बड़ झोटन भय भामिनी॥ रंग०॥
लागत पिय तन धाइ॥ डोल०॥
मानहु सुन्दर मेघ सौं॥ रंग०॥
छबीली छटा लपटाइ॥ डोल०॥
सोभा के सागर दोऊ॥ रंग०॥
छिन-छिन छबि अधिकाइ॥ डोल०॥
दामोदर हित रसिक जे॥ रंग०॥
जीवत यह जस गाइ॥ डोल०॥ (१.२७२-२७३)

(३२)

मोहन मोहिनी सुहेलरा गाऊं।
लाड़िली लाल गहेलरा लड़ाऊं॥
श्रीवृन्दाबन घन सहज सोभा मन लोभा उपजावै।
जिनकों कृपा करें श्रीस्यामा तिनहिं सुन्यौं जस भावै॥
विपिन वलासिन प्रेम प्रकासिन जो निज प्रेमहिं पाऊं।
ज्योंहीं-ज्योंहीं कुंज विहार करौ मिलि त्योंहीं-त्योंहीं तुमहिं लड़ाऊं॥
सुनहु सहेली प्रेम गहेली कौतिक एक दिखाऊं।
अंचल जोरि चितै तृन तोरौं तन मन मोद बड़ाऊं॥
रायबेल सतवर्ग सेवती बिच-बिच चम्पे की कलियाँ।
रचि-रचि चौसर हार गुँदै गुहि पहिरावन चलीं अलियाँ॥
कुसुमित कुंज गुँज अलि माला चन्दन चर्चित गलियाँ।
सुखद समीर बहत सौरभ जल कमल विराजत थलियाँ॥
सारस हंस चकोर मोर पिक चात्रक भाषा भलियाँ।
गावत रस जस पिय प्यारी कौ सखि सुनि पग प्रेम न टलियाँ॥
कबहुँक बाल सलज्ज सपिय तन कबहुँ हँसत मुख मोरी।
कबहुँक निपुन सुरत सुख सागर नागर नवल किशोरी॥
छिन-छिन प्रति दम्पति नव-नव रति अङ्ग-अङ्ग अभिरामा।
प्रथम समागम श्याम दिनहिं दिन दूलह दुलहिनि श्यामा॥
अंसन अंस जोरि भुज बल्लभ भामिनि जामिनि जागे।

विलसत हँसत हँसावत रस वस अति आनंद अनुरागे॥
नौतन तरल तमाल लाल मिलि लता ललित फल फलियाँ।
देत असीस बिहारिन दासी करहु नवल नित रलियाँ॥ (१.३०६-३०७)

(३३)

दूलह दुलहिनि अधिक बनी।
पूजन चली कल्प तरु सुन्दर औरहि ठाँन ठनी॥
कियौ सखिन गठजोर सबन मिलि आगे धन पाछे जु धनी।
गावत चलीं गीत मंगल के सबहि सुघर सजनी॥
रुनक झुनक पग धरत धरनि पर छबि पावत अवनी।
छिरकि सुगन्ध मूल तरु पूज्यौ फूल्लन माल घनी॥
अञ्चल जोरि यहै वर माँगौं रहौ यह प्रेम सनी।
श्रीरसिक बिहारिन हो न मान छक केलि कला कननी॥ (१.३०७)

(३४)

[श्रीनागरीदासजी कृत॥]
प्यरी सहजहि मन हरि लेत।
तू मन मोहिनी री मोहन हेत॥
तुम अति प्रेम प्रवीन हो (प्यारी) सुघर सिरोमनि जान।
मन क्रम बचन बिलासनी मेरे तुम बिन गति नहिं आन॥
तू तन तू मन में बसी (प्यारी) तू मम जीवन प्रान।
तू सर्वस धन मानिनी दै मोहि मान रति दान॥
भामिनि तुव भुवछेप हो (प्यारी) मोपै सह्यौ न जाय।
अंचल पल अलकावली के अन्तर मन अकुलाय॥
मो मन ऐसी होत है प्यारी तो तन में मिलि जाऊँ।
तुव मुख चन्द्र चकोर लों नैना पान करत न अघाऊँ॥
श्रवन सुयश रसना रसौ तुव करत रहों गुन गान।
जाँचत ज्यों जल मीन लों तुव दरस परस अघ्रान॥
तुम लावनि गुन निधि आगरी (प्यारी) अब जिन करहु निदान।
पूरन प्रेम प्रकासनी दै मोहि अधर मधु पान॥
तब ललित बचन सुनि श्याम के (प्यारी) नैनन में मुसिक्याय।
व्याकुल विरह बिलोकि कें प्यारी लिये हैं लाल उर लाय॥

मैं मान कियौ तुम सों कबै प्यारे कलपि-कलपि कित लेत।
मेरे प्रीतम प्रान हौ पिय जीवन तुमहिं समेत॥
(तब) लटकि लगी उर स्याम के (प्यारी) हुलसत हँसत उदार।
कोक निपुन नव नागरी बरबस किये सुकुँवार॥
भये मदन मत्त रस माधुरी सुख बरषत सुखन अघाइ।
निरखि हरखि रस फूलहीं श्रीललितादिक सुख पाइ॥
सुरत रंग में रँगि रह्यौ (हो) कुंज सदन सुख रासि।
श्रीविपुल विहारिनि दासि पर बलि नवल नागरीदासि॥ (१.३१९-२०)

(३५)

कलिंद नंदिनी सु तीर विलसत नव कुँवर धीर,
नंद नँदन मुदित श्री वृषभानुनंदिनी।
उभय कंथ भुजन धरैं अधर सुधा पान करैं,
गौर श्याम अंग मानौं जलद चंदनी।
कोमल जनु कनक बेलि राजत नव रँग नवेलि
पिय के गात लपट रही आनंद कंदनी।
सरस सुरत सुखन भरैं अधर सुधा पान करैं,
नागरीदास न्यौछावर रसिक बंदिनी॥ (१.३३३)

(३६)

[श्रिसेवक (दामोदरदासजी) कृत॥ मंगल राग सुहौ बिलाचल॥ यह मङ्गल नित्य होय है।]

जै जै श्री हरिवंश व्यास कुल मंडना।
रसिक अनन्यन मुख्य गुरु जन भय खंदना॥
श्रीवृन्दावन वास रास रस भूमि जहाँ।
क्रीड़त श्यामा स्याम पुलिन मंजुल तहाँ॥
पुलिन मंजुल परम पावन त्रिविध तहाँ मारुत बहै।
कुंज भवन विचित्र शोभा मदन नित सेवत रहै॥
तहाँ संतत व्यास नंदन रहत कलुष विहंडना।
जै जै श्रीहरिवंश व्यास कुल मंडना॥
जै जै श्रीहरिवंश चन्द्र उद्दित सदा।
द्विज कुल कुमुद प्रकाश विपुल सुख संपदा॥

पर उपकार विचार सुमति जग विस्तरी।
करुणासिंधु कृपाल कालभय सब हरी॥
हरी सब कलिकाल की भय कृपा रूप जु वपु धर्यौ।
करत जे अनसहन निंदक तिनहुँ पै अनुग्रह कर्यौ॥
निरभिमान निर्वैर निरुपम निहकलंक जु सर्वदा।
जै जै श्रीहरिवंश चन्द्र उद्दित सदा॥
जय जय श्रीहरिवंश प्रशंसत सब दुनी।
सारासार विवेकत कोविद बहु गर्नी॥
गुप्त रीति आचरण प्रगट सब जग दिये।
ज्ञान धर्म ब्रत कर्म भक्ति किंकर किये॥
भक्ति हित जे शरण आये द्वन्द दोष जु सब घटे।
कमल कर जिन अभय दीने कर्म बंधन सब कटे॥
परम सुखद सुशील सुन्दर पाहि स्वामिनि मम धनी।
जय जय श्रीहरिवंश प्रसंसत सब दुनी॥
जय जय श्रीहरिवंश नाम गुन गाइहै।
प्रेम लक्षणा भक्ति सुदृढ करि पाइहै॥
अरु बाढ़ै रस रीति प्रीति चित ना टरै।
जीति विषम संसार कीरति जग विस्तरै॥
विस्तरै सब जग विमल कीरति साधु संगति ना टरै।
वास वृन्दा विपिन पावै श्रीराधिकाजू कृपा करैं॥
चतुर जुगल किशोर सेवक दिन प्रसादहि पाइ है।
जय जय श्रीहरिवंश नाम गुण गाइ है॥ (१.३४१-४२)

(३७)

श्री द्विज राज भवन में रँगीली बाजत आजु बधाई।
जगमानी जानी द्विज रानी जायौ सुत सुखदाई॥ रँगीली०॥ टेक॥
सुने एक रस की द्वै मूरत गौर स्याम रँग भीने।
वृन्दावन की सम्पति दम्पति नित नव नेह नवीने॥
तिनकौ हित वंशी तैं हितमय त्रिविध एक वपु धारे।
श्रीहरिवंश नाम है प्रगटे हित स्वरूप विस्तारे॥ १॥
नव निकुंज कौ महा मधुर रस अद्भुत अंग रसीलौ।
उज्वल रस की उज्वलता लौं जगमगात चटकीलौ॥

जाकौ ध्यान धरत हैं श्रीपति एसे वेद बखानै।
ताही के ये उदय करन कौं उदय भये रुचि मानै॥ २॥
लखि अचिरज सों प्रथम व्यासजू पुनि ऋषि-रव सुधि कीनौ।
तब तौ फूल उठे द्विज नृपजू मंगल में मन दीनौ॥
फूलन मंडप द्वार धुजा धरि-केसर अजिर लिपाये।
बाँधी बंदनमाल मनोहर मोतिनु चौक पुराये॥ ३॥
जल गुलाब छिरकाय चहूदिशि कदली कलित रुपाये।
दीपावलि दीपन करि मणिमय कंचन कलश भराये॥
तान वितान विविध रचना रचि पाँचौं शब्द करावैं।
जय-जय कहि बजाइ दुंदुभि दिवि सुर सुमनन बरसावैं॥ ४॥
भई छबीली भीर द्वार पर कोउ गावैं कोउ नाचैं।
मागध मंजुल वंश बखानत सूत पुरानन बाँचै॥
महीदेव धपि धाये आये निगम रिचान सुनावैं।
पढ़त कवित्त विविध बंदी जन अरु गुन गुनी दिखावैं॥ ५॥
एक धरत सिर हरी दूब कौं इक हँसि पाइनु लागैं।
एकन भेंट धरी लै आगे मिश्र निरखि अनुरागैं॥
घोर अमोल कुमकुमा चण्दन छिरकत सब छवि छाये।
मनहुँ रूप सरवर में सुन्दर हेम पुहुप विकसाये॥ ६॥
देत सबच्छ धैनु विप्रन कौं कनक वसन मणि माला।
गाजि-गाजि घनलौं धन बरषत जाचक किये निहाला॥
बंधु वधू पहिराइ मान दै मेवन गोद भराई।
देत असीस सकल नर नारी कीरति धुज फहराई॥ ७॥
प्रफुलित रसिक रँगीले बहुविध अति आनंद सों डोलै।
चित चाहत फल पाय प्रेम सौ श्री हित श्री हित बोलैं॥
नित्य बिहार भजन-दायक कौ उत्सव हियौ सिरावै।
(जय) श्रीहित रूप किशोरी लाल यह उमगि-उमगि जस गावै॥ ८॥
(१.३७०-१)

Second Volume: द्वितीयविभाग

(३८)

[गोस्वामी श्रीहित हरिवंशचन्द्रजी महाप्रभुजी कृत—राग मलाह]

दोऊ जन भींजत अटके बातन।
सघन कुंज के द्वारे ठाड़े अम्बर लप्टे गातन॥
ललिता ललित रूप रस भीजी बूँद बचावत पातन।
जय श्रीहित हरिवंश परस्पर प्रीतम मिलवत रति रस घातन॥ (२.७८)

(३९)

नयौ नेह नव रंग नयौ रस, नवल श्याम वृषभानु किशोरी।
नव पीतांबर नवल चूँनरी, नई-नई बूँदन भीजत गोरी॥
नव वृन्दावन हरित मनोहर, नव चातक बोलत मोर मोरी॥
नव मुरली जू मलार नई गति श्रवन सुनत आये घन घोरी॥
नव भूषन नव मुकुट विराजत, नई-नई उरप लेत थोरी-थोरी॥
जै श्रीहितहरिवंश असीस देत मुख चिरजीवौ भूतल यह जोरी॥ (२.७८)

(४०)

सुहावनी बूँद लगैं मन भाइ।
उत चमकन दामिनि भामिनि इत घन घनस्याम दुराई॥
नेह नीर वसषत हरसत दृग चातक लौं रट लाई।
हिय अभिलाष सरोवर पूरित बन तन ताप मिटाई॥
प्रफुलित कुमुदावलि अलि गन मन प्रीति लता सरसाई।
जै श्रूपलाल हित सहचरि सेवत दंपति प्रेम बढ़ाई॥ (२.८४)

(४१)

या ब्रज स्याम सघन घन उनये।
चपला चमकि-चमकि उर लावत प्रीतम प्रेम नये॥
कुहुकन मोर पपीहा पियु-पियु मदन बिलास दये॥
जै श्रीहित चित रूप त्रिभंगी रंगी रंगिनि मोल लये॥ (२.८४)

(४२)

नाचत मोरन संग स्याम मुदित स्यामाहि रिझावत।
तैसीये कोकिला अलापत पपीहा देत सुर तैसौई मेघ गरज मृदङ्ग बजावत॥
तैसीये स्याम घटा निशि-सी कारी तैसीये दामिनी कौंधि दीप दिखावत।
श्रीहरिदास के स्वामी स्यामा कुंज विहारि रीझि राधे हँसि कंठ लगावत॥
(२.९१)

(४३)

[श्रीव्यासजी कृत—राग मलार]
आज कछु कुंजन में वरषा-सी।
बादर दल में देखि सखी री चमकत है चपला-सी॥
न्हानी-न्हानी बूँदन कछु धुरवा से पवन बहै सुखरासी।
मंद-मंद गरजन-सी सुनियत नाचत मोर-सभा-सी॥
इन्द्र धनुष में वग पंकति डोलत बोलत कोकिला-सी।
इन्द्रवधू छवि छाइ रही मानौ गिरि पर अरुन घटा-सी॥
उमग महीरुह सौं महि फूली भूली मृग माला-सी।
रटत व्यास चातक की रसना रस पीवत हू प्यासी॥ (२.९१-२)

(४४)

[श्रीनेहि नागरीदासजी कृत—मलार, ताल रूपक]
कनक पत्रावलि झूँमत घूँघट।
लहँगा पीत कंचुकी कसूँभी तैसौइ गौर तन लसत नील पट॥
केसर की आड़ जराइ कौ बैंदा तैसीय मुख पर रुरत ललित लट।
वर वानिक छवि रही पिय नैनन नागरीदासि धीरज न रह्यौ घट॥ (२.९३)

(४५)

भींजत दोउ घन दामिनि तन हेरैं।
चात्रक रट पिक गान भेक रव सुनत केकि कल टेरैं॥
पुलक-पुलक लपटात गात गस हँस उरोज उर भेरैं।
अरुन वसन तन अवनि अमित छवि अलि ललितादिक घेरैं॥
पावस संपति दंपति विलसत कूल कलिंदिनि नेरैं।
नागरिदासि नव नागर नेही सदा वसौ उर मेरैं॥ (२.९३)

(४६)

सावन प्रेम संपदा लायौ।
हरित भरित फल फूल विपिन रँग मोरन मंगल गायौ॥
चातक पिउ-पिउ करत ललकि रट कोकिल शब्द सुनायौ।
यों जहाँ-तहाँ निरभर हरियारी अवनि सिंगार वनायौ॥
चपला चमकि-चमकि अति लाघव चहुँ दिसि तें घन छायौ।
विलसत जुगल सेज सुख की निधि देखि कली जस गायौ॥ (२.९७)

(४७)

[अथ लूहर (टेर)]
कुंज बिहारी हो लाल दरसन दीजौ साँवरे।
थारे गुनरूप निहार सफल करैं दृग भाँँवरे॥
ललित त्रिभंगी हो लाल लटकत-लटकत आईयौ।
रंग महल री हो वाट जय श्री लाल रूप दरसाईयौ॥ (२.१२१)

(४८)

[गो० श्री हित हरिवंशचन्द्र महाप्रभुजी कृत—(बधाई) राग बिलावल]
आनन्द आजु नंद के द्वार।
दास अनन्य भजन रस कारन प्रगटे लाल मनोहर ग्वार॥
चंदन सकल धेनु तन मंडित कुसुम दाम रंजित आगार।
पूरन कुंभ बने तोरन पर बीच रुचिर पीपर की डार।
जुवति जूथ मिलि गोप विराजत बाजत पणव मृदङ्ग सु तार।
जय श्री हित हरिवंश अजिर वर वीथिन दधि मधि दूध हरद केए खार॥ (२.२५४)

(४९)

[गो० श्रीकिशोरीलालजी कृत—राग आसावरी ताल रूपक]
मोहन जनमत माइ, आजु बजत बधाइ घोष नृपति घर।
जसुमति सब सुख फलन फली की कहा कहौं भाग निकाइ॥ आजु०॥ टेक॥ १॥
नहिं समतूल सची रति रंभा पन्नग नाहिं कुँवारी।
कृष्ण जनम दिन ते मग गवनीं किधौं विरंचि संवारी॥ २॥
बगर-बगर तें बनि-बनि बनिता निकसी भाँति भली हैं।
नन्द सदन मनु रूप उदधि छबि सरिता मिलन चली हैं॥ ३॥
उर दृग आरति कूल विदारत सुनि सुत जनम सिहानी।
रुकि गये पथिक अमङ्गल जग के सुजस नीर सरसानी॥ ४॥
वारिज वदन अलक अलि श्रैनी कटि तट शब्द मराला।
नौका नैन कटाक्ष सु खेवक कौतिक सरिता बाला॥ ५॥
मुख ससि जोति चंद्रिका मंदिर अतिसै ओप भई है।
लखि हरि धन्य कहत सब जसुमति कुल मणि दयौ दई है। ६

पुनि-पुनि पद वंदन करि गावत निर्त्तत पुलकित हीयें।
हरि शिशु रूप तृषित दृग भरि-भरि रहि-रहि सादर पीयें॥ ७॥
बलि हित रूप चरित गुन वारिध क्रीड़त ब्रजजन माहीं।
जै श्री किशोरी लाल हित देव विमानन जा सुख कौं पछताहीं॥ ८॥ (२.२६०)

(५०)

तेरौ माइ चिरुजीवौ गोपाल।
बेगि बढ़ौ बढ़ि होहु वृद्ध लट महरि मनोहर ग्वाल॥
उपजि पर्यौ इहि कूख कमल तें सिंधु सीप ज्यों लाल।
सब गोकुल के प्राण जीवन धन बैरिनौ के उर साल॥
सूर कितौ जिय सुख पावत है निरखत श्याम तमाल।
आरज रज लागौ मेरी अँखियन रोग दोष जंजाल॥ (२.२८०)

(५१)

[गो० श्रीरूपलालजी कृत—राग मारू—दोहा (वंशावली वरनन) दोहा—]
[दोहा] बरन्यौं चाहत कछुक अब कृष्ण चंद्र परिबार।
देहु बुद्धि मति सुद्ध अति श्री हरिवंश उदार॥ १॥
गन उद्देश जु दीपिका मध्य कही कछु रीति।
जै श्री रूप लाल हित सौं लिखत सुनहु रसिक दै प्रीति॥ २॥
[चौतुका] विमल जस ढाँढ़ी करत बखान।
वजत बधाई नंदराइ गृह प्रगट भयौ सुख दान॥ टेक॥
ढाँढिन संग समाज साज लै सिंघ पौरि में नाचै।
लै-लै नाम गोपवांशन के सात साख तें बाँचै॥
आये सिमिट सबै नर-नारी कहत देहु जो जाँचै।
मोहि चाउ जसुदा सुत निरखन बात यहै सुन साँचै॥ १॥
[दोहा] सिंह पौरि ब्रजराज की बड़ी भीर भई आनि।
विविध भाँति सौं गोप कुल ढाँढी कहत बखानि॥ ३॥
[चौतुका] तीन भाँति के गोप बसैं ब्रज तिनकी बात बखानौं।
उत्तम वैश्य धरम गौ रक्षा करि विवेक पहिचानौं॥
तिनहूँ तें अहीर मध्यम गो गाय भैंस धन धानौं।
ब्रज के छोर बसत जे गूजर इनहूँ तें घटि जानौं॥ २॥
[दोहा] सुनत नंद उपनंद सब बैठे सभा बनाइ।

बरन आदि तें गोप कुल ढाँढी लियौ बुलाइ॥ ४॥
[चौतुका] बरनन करत गोप वंशन कौं ढाँढी मन हुलसाई।
देवमढ़ जदुकुल नरेस की कथा पुरातन गाई॥
जजन दान व्रत छत्र धर्म सब विधि सौं करत सदाई।
कुँवर कान्ह के परदादे भये सोम वंश के राई॥ ३॥
[दोहा] देवमीढ घर द्वै भई पतिव्रता पटरानि।
इक कन्या छत्रीन की एक वैश्य की जान॥ ५॥
[चौतुका] छत्री कन्या तें उपजे सुत सूरसैन सुख दाता।
अति ब्रह्मन्य सील सुभ कर्मा वेद अर्थ के ज्ञाता॥
तिन तें श्री वसुदेव भाग की कहत न आबै बाता।
नंदराय के मित्र पियारे रचिपचि किये हैं विधाता॥ ४॥
[दोहा] जादब कुल वसुदेव लौं ढाँढी कह्यौ सुनाइ।
अब बरनौं कुल गोप कौ ब्रजपति कौं सिर नाइ॥
[चौतुका] वैश्य कन्यका तें जु भये परजन्य धर्म आधार।
नारद कौ उपदेश पाइ लक्ष्मीपति भजे भुवारा॥
नंदीश्वर पुर वास करत तप संतति हेत विचारा।
भई अकास विमल बानी सुनि तन मन रही न सँभारा॥ ५॥
[सोरठा] बानी भइ अकास सुफल फलौ अभिलाष सब।
ब्रज कौ निहचल वास पाँच पुत्र है हैं जु अब॥ ७॥
[चौतुका] पाँच पुत्र है हैं तुम्हरे तिनमें अति नंद पियारौ।
ताकैं लाल प्रगट है एसौ तीन भुवन उजियारौ॥
यह सुनि हरषि भयौ मन में जु महावन वास विचार्यौ।
केशी के डर डरपि गाँव सब जमुना पार उतार्यौ॥ ६॥
[दोहा] पाँच पुत्र परजन्य के राज करत ब्रज माहिं।
सात दीप के भूप जे इन सम कहे न जाँहिं॥ ८॥
[चौतुका] बड़ भैया उपनंद सबन तें गौर सुभग अँग ताकौ।
हरित वसन तन लाँबी दाढ़ी नौ लख गोधन जाकौ॥
तुंगी त्रिया सुभग लक्षन जुत जासौं हित जसुदा कौ।
लै-लै गोद निरखि मुख हरि कौ धनि धनि बोलन बाकौ॥ ७॥
[दोहा] बड़ भ्राता उपनंद जू तिनकी संपति गाइ।
अब बरनौ अभिनंद कौं भरे कृष्ण के भाइ॥ ९॥

[चौतुका] इक अभिनंद नंद तें जेठे गौर बरन अँग सोहै।
भरे खरिक सत गाइ लक्ष दस दान समान न कोहै॥
कृष्ण प्रेम सौं छक्यौ कहत यौं बात नंद सुनि होहै।
तिहारे सुत तें या ब्रज में कछु प्यारौ नाहिन मोहै॥ ८॥
[दोहा] नंदन एक सुनंद इक कका कृष्ण के गाइ।
रीझि-रीझि ब्रज ईश तब दैहैं दान बुलाइ॥ १०॥
[चौतुका] एक सुनंद नंद तें लहुरे बहुत देह के भारे।
षोडस लख गोधन ताके घर बकुला नाम त्रिया रे॥
इनहूँ तें लहुरे नंदन इक दोऊ कृष्ण कका रे।
सात लाख गोधन धन जाके नंदहि बहुत पियारे॥ ९॥
[दोहा] सानंद अरु नंदिनी बहिन नंद की जात।
अब स्वरूप श्रीनंद कौ कहौं सुनौं धरि ध्यान॥ ११॥
[करषा] ढाँढी गा[]इ नन्दरा[]इ कौ ध्यान धरि कैं।
द्वार ताके परीं सिद्धि नव निद्धि सब माँगि तापै जाहि दरिद्र टरि कैं॥ १॥
सुभ्र चंदन खौर अंग छबि जगमगत सजल घन सम वसन तनहिं साजैं।
फबी सिर पाग सौभाग्य लोचन विशद भाल पर तिलक केसर विराजै.॥ २॥
श्रवन मणि जलज की जोति झलकत लसत सेत अरु स्याम दाढी विराजै।
बाहु आजानु बड दान दानेश कौ देखि मुख सकल दुख दूर भाजै॥ ३॥
[दोहा] सब गोपन कौ जस कहत ढाँढी मन न अधाइ।
अब वैभव श्रीनंद कौ बरनत रह्यौ लुभ्याइ॥ १२॥
[चौतुका] सहस्र खरिक दस सहस्र ग्वाल पै गैया जाँइ न बरनी।
कामधेनु पय श्रवत फिरत सब स्वेत करी ब्रज धरनी॥
जमुना तीर नीर पीबत नित सदा हरित तृन चरनी।
कृष्ण कमल कर फिरत पीठ पर कहा करी इन करनी॥ १०॥
[दोहा] ये गैयाँ नंदराइ की चरत रहत ब्रज माहिं।
शिव विरंचि मन चिंतवत पद रज परसत नाहिं॥ १३॥
[चौतुका] इन गैयन के काज स्याम ऐस्वर्ज सबै बिसरायौ।
अमृत छाँडि गोलोक धाम तें ब्रज कौ गोरस भायौ॥
मुनि मन ध्यान ग्यान पचि हारे पार न क्यौं हूँ पायौ।
महा भाग बड भाग जसोमति ऐसौ सुत जिन जायौ॥ ११॥
अद्भुत रूप निरखि नख सिख तें थके नैन मन हारौ।

कोटि चंद की जोति सार कौ बन्यौं इंदु इक न्यारौ॥
चंचल नैन सरद अंबुज मनु महा मनोहर प्यारौ।
नन्दराइ सुनि आइ भवन धन बाँटत खोलि भंडारौ॥ १२॥

तब रीझे ब्रज ईश नन्द जू भवन भंडार लुटायौ।
रतन जटिल टोडर मणि नूपुर ढाँढी कौं पहिरायौ॥
लहरविडार दिये वहु गोपन भयौ विदा घर आयौ।
जै श्रीरूपलाल हित नव किशोर कौं गाइ-गाइ सुख पायौ॥ १३॥ ४ (२.२५५-२५८)

(५२)

मोद विनोद आजु घर नन्द।
कृष्णपक्ष भादौं निस आठैं प्रगटे हैं गोकुल के चंद॥
भवन द्वार गोमय वर मंडित वरषत कुसुम उमापति इंद।
गोपी ग्वाल परस्पर गावत पुलकित विहरत मत्त गयंद॥
बंदनवारैं वृंद मनोहर बीच बन्यौ पट कीर सुछंद।
सूर्दास हरदी दधि मधु घृत रंजित पान करत मकरंद॥ (२.२८२)

(५३)

[श्रीसूरदास कृत—राग आसावरी (नौमी के दिन कौ)]

व्रज भयौ महरि कें पूत जब यह बात सुनी।
सुनि आनन्दे सब लोक गोकुल गुनित गुनी॥
ग्रह लगन नक्षत्र बल सोधि कीनी वेद धुनी।
सुभ पूरव पूरे पुन्य रची कुल अटल थुनी॥ १॥

सुनि धाइ सब ब्रज नारि सहज सिंगार किये।
कर कंकन कंचन थार मंगल साज लिये॥
तन पहिरे नौतन चीर काजर नैन दिये।
कसि कंचुकी तिलक लिलाट शोभित हार हिये॥ २॥

सब अपने-अपने मेल निकसीं भाँति भली।
मनौ लाल मुनिनु की पाँति पिंजरन चूरि चली॥
हँसि गावत मंगल गीत मिलि दस पाँच अली।
मनु भोर भये रवि देखि फूलीं कमल कली॥ ३॥

दोऊ शोभित तरल तरौंना बैनी सिथिल गुही।

मुख माँऋ्ए रोरी रंग सैंदुर माँग छुही॥
उर अंचल उऋअत न जानैं सारी सुरङ्ग सुही।
अति श्रम जल मुखहि प्रस्वेद मानौं मेघ फुही॥ ४॥
इक पहिलैं पहुँचीं आइ अति आनन्द भरीं।
लईं भीतर भवन बुलाइ सबै शिशु पाँइ परीं॥
ते वदन उघारि निहारि देत अशीश खरीं।
चिरुजियौ यशोदा नन्द पूरन काम करीं॥ ५॥
धनि-धनि दिन धनि यह रात धनि यह पहर घरी।
धनि धन्य महरि की कूख भाग सुहाग भरी॥
जिन जायौ ऐसौ पूत सब सुख फलन फरी।
थिरु थाप्यौ सब परिवार मन की सूल हरी॥ ६॥
सुनि ग्वालिन गाइ बहोरि बालक बोलि लये।
गुहि गुंजा घसि वन धातु अंगन चित्र ठये॥
सिर दधि माखन के माट काँवर कन्ध लये।
इक झाँझ मृदङ्ग बजावत सब नन्द भवन गये॥ ७॥
इक नाचत करत कुलाहल छिरकत हरद दही।
मनु बरषत भादौं मास नदी घृत दूध बही॥
जाकौ जहीं-जहीं मन जाय कौतुक तहीं-तहीं।
अति आनन्द मगन जु ग्वाल काहू बदत नही॥ ८॥
इक धा[]इ नन्द पै जाय पुनि-पुनि पाँइ परैं।
इक आपु आपुही माँहि हँसि-हँसि अंक भरैं॥
इक दधि रोचन अरु दूब सबन के सीम धरैं।
इक अंबर और मँगाइ देत न संक करै.॥ ९॥
न्हाइ नन्द भये ठाऋ्ए अरु कुश हाथ धरे।
नाँदीमुख पितर पुजाइ अंतर सोच हरे॥
वर गुरु जन पहिराइ सबन कें पाँइ परे।
घसि चंदन चारु मँगाइ सबन कें तिलक करे॥ १०॥
गन गैयाँ गनि न जाँय तरुन ते बच्छ बऋहीं।
ते चरैं जमुन के कूल दूने दूध चऋहीं॥
खुर रूपे तामें पीठ सौने सींग मऋहीं।
ते दीनीं द्विजन बुलाइ हरषि अशीस पऋही॥ ११॥
तब अपने मित्र सुबन्धु हँसि-हँसि बोलि लिये।

मथि मृगमद मलय कपूर माथैं तिलक किये॥
उरमणि माला पहिरा[]इ वसन विचित्र दिये।
मनु वरषत मास असाढ़ह दादुर मोर जिये॥ १२॥
वर बंदी मागद सूत आँगन भवन भरे।
ते बोले लै-लै नाम हित कोऊ नहिं बिसरे॥
ते दान मान परिधान पूरन काम करे।
जिन जोई जाँच्यौ सोई पायौ रस नँदराइ ढरे॥ १३॥
तब अंबर और मँगाइ सारी सुरंग घनी।
ते दीनीं बधुन बुलाइ जैसी जाहि बनी॥
ते अति रुचि सौं हित मानि निज गृह गोप धनी।
ते निकसीं देत असीस रुचि अपनी-अपनी॥ १४॥
तब घर-घर भेरि मृदंग पटह निसान बजे।
वर बाँधी वंदन माल कंचन कलश सजे॥
ते ता दिन तें वे लोग सुख संपति न तजे।
कहि सूर सबन की यह गति जिन हरि चरन भजे॥ १५॥ (२.२७८-८०)

(५४)

प्रगती श्रीवृषभान गोप के सोभा की निधि आई री।
धन्य भाग कीरतिदा रानी जिन यह कन्या जाई री॥
सुनत ही धाई सखी सहेली मन वांछित फल पाई री।
हाथन कंचन थार विराजत मङ्गल गावत आई री॥
महारानी कीरति आदर दै भीतर भवन बुलाई री।
भूषण वसन विविध नाना रँग नखसिख तें पहिराई री॥
दधि कादौं भादौं झर लायौ आँगन कीच मचाई री।
राधा मोहन जोरी अविचल जै श्रीकमलनैन सुखदाई री॥ (२.३६५-३६६)

(५५)

[श्रीहरिकृष्णदासजी कृत—राग देवगंधार]
आजु बधा[]ई गोकुल बाजत।
पुत्र भयौ जसुमति रानी कें विप्र वेद धुनि गाजत॥
गृह-गृह तें आई सुंदरि कर कंचन थारन साजत।
फरहरात अंचल चंचल वर अंग-अंग छबि छाजत॥

विविध वसन टोडर रतनन के धरे अधिक ढिंग राजत।
नंदराइ लै-लै पहिरावत नाचत सकल सु भ्राजत॥
उमगि कहत नर नारि सबै भैया भलौ दिन लागत।
हरिकृष्णदास प्रभु कमल नैन की छबि निरखत दुख भागत॥ (२.२८५)

(५६)

[श्रीनन्ददासजी कृत—राग आसावरी (नौमी के दिन)]
सुंदर व्रज की बाला, जुरि चलीं हैं बधाये नन्द महर घर।
कंचन थार हार चंचल छबि कही न परत तिहिं काला॥ जुरि चली० ॥ठेक॥ १॥
डहडहे मुख कुमकुम रँग रँम्जित राजत रस के ऐना।
कंजन पर खेलत जुग खंजन अंजन जुत बने नैना॥ २॥
दमकत कंठ पदिक मणि कुंडल नवल प्रेम रस बोरी।
आतुर गति जैसैं चंद उदै भये धावत त्रिषित चकोरी॥ ३॥
खसि-खसि परत कुसुम सीसन तें उपमा कौन बखानौं।
चरन चलन पर रीझि चिकुर वर बरषत फूलन मानौं॥ ४॥
गावत गीत पुनीत करत जग जसुमति मंदिर आई।
वदन विलोकि बलैयाँ लै-लै देत असीस सुहाई॥ ५॥
मंगल कलश निकट दीपावलि ठाइँ-ठाइँ देखि मन भुल्यौ।
माँनहुँ आगम नन्द सुवन के सौने फूल व्रज फूल्यौ॥ ६॥
ता पाछैं गन गोप ओप सौं आये अतिसै सोहैं।
परमानंद कंद रस भीने निकर पुरंदर को हैं॥ ७॥
आनन्द घन ज्यौं गाजत राजत बाजत दुन्दुभी भेरी।
राग रागिनी गावत हरषत बरषत सुख की ढेरी॥ ८॥
परम धाम सुख धाम स्याम अभिराम सुगोकुल आये।
मिटि गये द्वंद नन्ददासन के भये मनोरथ भाये॥ ९॥ (२.२९०)

(५७)

आजु ब्रजराज कैं सुत भयौ सुनि सखी,
उमग उपहार लै चल्यौ महरावनौं।
थार कर हार भर भार लचकत लंक,
वसन असम्हार उर फब्यौ फहरावनौं॥
इतहिं सुनि गान अरु मंगल निसान धुनि,

उतहिं नीकौ लगत घनन घहरावनौं॥
नागरीदास ब्रजचंद प्रगटत भयौ,
नंद हिय सिंधु आनन्द लहरावनौं॥ (२.२९३)

(५८)

[श्रीप्रेमदासजी कृत—कवित्त]
नव रस रूप लाल प्रगट्यौ है शुभकाल,
लोचन विशाल देखौ कहा नीकौ लाल है।
चल हैं मराल चाल सोहैगी गुंज माल,
बैरिन कौ उर साल संतन कौ पाल है॥
कीरति की सुता बाल जोरी जुर है रसाल,
जैसे हेम डाल और साँवरौ तमाल है।
सुनौं नन्द तत्काल कोई प्रेम रूप जाल,
ग्वालन के नाल खेल करैगौ निहाल है॥ (२.२९६)

(५९)

[चाचा श्रीवृन्दावनदासजी कृत—राग विलावल]
इहि ब्रज घर-घर आजु बधाई।
नंद सदन नभ चंद उदै भयौ मिट्यौ ताप तम जग कौ माई॥
सुकृत पुंज सुत जसुमति जायौ बरनौ कहा बत्रॄअ भाग निकाई।
प्रफुलित गोपी गोप कुमुद गन त्रिभुवन सुजस चाँदनी छाई॥
दान मान द्विज गुरु पद वंदे ब्रजपति सबकी आस पुजाई।
बलि हित रूप सकल सुख मंदिर वृन्दावन हित कुँवर कन्हाई॥ (२.२९७)

(६०)

रूप जलद कौ री हेली धुरवा ऊनयौ।
व्योम मनोहर री हेली नन्द भवन भयौ॥
व्योम नन्द निकेत वरषत आजु परमानन्द है।
चहुँ ओर मारुत प्रेम बाढ्यौ प्रवल उरन अमंद है॥
केकी कुलाहल सूत मागद गरज बहु बाजे मनौं।
जन घोष चात्रक मुदित अति हिय लाग सुख कहाँ लौं भनौं॥ १॥
रुचिर अलंकृत री हेली व्रज तरुनी भई।

इंद्र वधू सी री हेली मिलि मन्दिर गई॥
गई मन्दिर गोप बनिता दामनी दुति देह की।
नदी सागर मिलत उपमा आजु व्रजपति ग्रेह की॥
रोमांच मानौं महीरुह नर नारि ब्रज एकत भये।
बरषा अभूत विलोक व्यौम विमान कृष्ण जनम छये॥ २॥

प्रीति अलौकिक री हेली सब हिय देखिये।
गगन महीतल री हेली सगुन विशेषिये॥
विशेषिये सुभ सगुन दिस-दिस संपदा वरनौं कहा।
आगमन गोकुल चंद मंगल निकर व्रज प्रगते महा॥
गोप सभा बनाइ बैठे नन्द अति सोभित भए।
मुनि देव दुर्ल्लभ सुघन पायौ विविध दान द्विजन दये॥ ३॥

मुरि-मुरि गोपी री हेली देत असीस हित।
विधि तन गोदी री हेली ओटत जियहु नित॥
नित जियहु देत असीस जसुमति बंदि पद सुख में झिलीं।
गावत बधाये विविध पूरित प्रेम सब सादर मिलीं॥
वृन्दावन हित रूप निरवधि लाभ लोचन पाईयौ।
ब्रज ईस सुत जनमत सिमिटि सब घोष कौतिक आईयौ॥ ४॥ (२.३०८)

(६१)

लला चिरुजीवनौं रानी।
हित सौं देत असीस वधू जन अमी श्रवत वानी॥
गोकुल पति मंदिर कौ गहनौ ब्रज जन सुख दानी॥
वृन्दावन हित रूप कौतिकी द्वै है हम जानी॥ (२.३२९)

(६२)

[श्रीहित हरिवंशचन्द्र कृत—राग सारङ्ग (नित्य होय है)]

चलौ वृषभान गोप के द्वार।
जनम लियौ मोहन हित स्यामा आनन्द निधि सुकुमार॥
गावत जुवति मुदित मिलि मङ्गल उच्च मधुर धुनि धार।
विविध कुसुम कोमल किशलय दल सोभित बंदन वार॥
विदित वेद विधि विहित विप्रवर करि स्वस्तिनु उच्चार।
मृदुल मृदंग मुरज भेरी डफ दिवि दुन्दुभि रवकार॥

मागद सूत बंदी चारन जस कहत पुकारि-पुकारि।
हाटक हीर चीर पाटम्वर देत सम्हारि-सम्हारि॥
चंदन सकल धैंनु तन मंडित चले हैं ग्वाल सिंगार।
जय श्रीहित हरिवंश दुग्ध-दधि छिरकत मध्य हरिद्रागार॥ (२.३४७)

(६३)

लली चिरजीवनी तेरी।
अब या ब्रज सुख सिंधु बढ़ैगौ सुन असीस मेरी।
हौं हूँ मचल पर्यौ या पौरी मुख देखौं रहौं नेरी।
व,न्दांवन हित रूप भाग्यफल दैव दयौ एरी॥ (२.३६०)

(६४)

रंग बरसै री हेली कीरति महल में।
जस दरसै री हेली रस की चहल में॥
आजु ब्रज फूल्यौ सबै रावल विनोद सुहावनौ।
उदौ सूरज वंश कौ नँदराय मन कौ भावनौ॥ १॥

सुकृत फूल्यौ री हेली श्रीमहीभान कौ।
आनंद झूल्यौ री हेली श्रुतिनु बखान कौ॥
गोपी-गोप सु विमल आँगन अनूठी अति मानी रली।
वारत रतन मणि देत भूषन निरखि पलना में लली॥ २॥

रँगीलौ बधावौ री हेली जिय छकि दैन कौ।
मृदंग बजावौ री हेली मंगल चैन कौ॥
वृषभान घर कन्या भई महा मोद गोकुल में छयौ।
पलना में किलकत साँवरौ रति-बीज जसुमति हिय बहौ॥ ३॥

बढ़ए गुमान के री हेली दान बहुत दये।
जाचक जन पै री हेली घन लौं ऊनये॥
अष्ट सिद्धि जु संग लै टहल में रमा निहारिये।
आजु बल्लवराज पै एश्वर्य कोटिक वारिये॥ ४॥

सौंज सजावौ री हेली कंचन थार में।
विधिहि लजावौ री हेली रचि सिंगार में॥
चलहु कौतिक देखिये ब्रजराज जहाँ नाचत खिले।
सोहिल में दोऊ समधी अंक भरि-भरि कें मिले॥ ५॥

केसर भींजे री हेली सौरभ सौं सने।
हरद दही के री हेली घट ढोरत घने॥
रसिक वारत नैन इत-उत चलत गज की चाल पै।
चारौं चरण की रेनु झलकत सुख सखी के भाल पै॥ ६॥ (२.३९३)

(६५)

[श्रीचतुर्भुजदासजी कृत—]
तू देख सुता वृषभान की।
मृग नैनी सुन्दर शोभा निधि अँग-अँग सुन्दर ठान की।
गौर वरन बहु कान्ति वदन की शरदचन्द्र उपमान की।
विश्व मोहिनी बाल दशा में कटि केहरि बंधान की॥
विधि की सृष्टि न होई मनु यह बानिक औरै बान की।
चत्रभुज प्रभु गिरिधर लायक ब्रज प्रगटी जोट समान की॥ (२.३९८)

(६६)

[श्रीसूरदासजी कृत—पद]
प्यारी, तुम कौंन हौ री फुलवा बीनन हारी॥ प्यारी०॥
नेह लगन कौ बन्यौ बगीचा फूलि रही फुलवारी।
आपु कृष्ण वनमाली आये तुम बोलौ क्यौं न पियारी॥
हँसि ललिता जब कह्यौ स्याम सौं ये वृषभानु दुलारी।
तुम्हरौ कहा लगै या वन में रोकत गैल हमारी॥
श्याम सखा सखियन समझावैं हठ न करौ मेरी प्यारी।
फल द्रुम वन वाटिका सुघर के हमहीं हैं रखवारी॥
राधेजू फल फूल लिये हैं विविध सुगंध सम्हारी।
सूरस्याम राधा मुख निरखत एकटक रहे निहारी॥ (२.५००-५०१)

Third Volume: तृतीयविभाग

(६७)

[श्रीहित हरिवंशमहाप्रभुजी कृत—]
प्रात समय दोऊ रस लंपट,
सुरत-जुद्ध जय-जुत अति फूल।

श्रम-वारिज घनविन्दु वदन पर,
भूषण अङ्गहि अङ्ग विकूल॥
कछु रह्यौ तिलक शिथिल अलकावलि,
वदन कमल मानौ अलि भूल।
जै श्रीहित हरिवंश मदन-रङ्ग रँगि रहे,
नैन-बैन कटि शिथिल दुकूल॥ १॥ (३.१)

(६८)

[श्रीहित हरिवंशचन्द्रमहाप्रभुजी कृत—राग गौरी (त्रिभगी छंद चारी)]
मोहन मदन त्रिभंगी। मोहन मुनि मन रंगी॥
मोहन मुनि सघन प्रगट परमानंद, गुण गंभीर गुपाला।
शीर किरीट श्रवण मणि कुंडल, उर मंडित बनमाला॥
पीतांबर तन धातु विचित्रित, कल किंकिणि कटि चङ्गी।
नख मणि तरणि चरण सरसी-रुह, मोहन मदन त्रिभंगी॥ १॥
मोहन वेणु बजावै। इहि रव नारि बुलावै॥
आईं ब्रज नारि सुनत वंशी रव, गृहपति बंधु बिसारे।
दरसन मदन गुपाल मनोहर, मनसिज ताप निवारे॥
हरषित बदन बंक अवलोकन, सरस मधुर ध्वनि गावै।
मधुमय श्याम समान अधर धर, मोहन वेणु बजावै॥ २॥
रास रच्यौ बन माहीं। विमल कल्पतरु छाँहीं॥
विमल कल्पतरु तीर सुपेसल, शरद रैन वर चंदा।
शीतल-मंद-सुगंध पवन बहै, तहाँ खेलत नँदनंदा॥
अद्भुत ताल मृदङ्ग मनोहर, किंकिणि शब्द कराहीं।
जमुना पुलिन रसिक रस सागर, रास रच्यौ वन माहीं॥ ३॥
देखत मधुकर केली। मोहे खग मृग बेली॥
मोहे मृग धेनु सहित सुर सुन्दरि, प्रेम मगन पट छूटे।
उडगन चकित थकित शशि मण्डल, कोटि मदन लूटे॥
अधर पान परिरंभन अति रस, आनँद मगन सहेली।
जय श्रीहित हरिवंश रसिक सचु पावत, देखत मधुकर केली॥ ४॥ (३.५)

(६९)

लाल की रूप माधुरी नैनन निरख नैक सखी।

मनसिज मन हरन हारि, साँमरौ सुकुमार रासि,
नख-सिख अङ्ग अङ्गन उमँगि सौभग सींव नखी॥ १॥
रँगमगी सिर सुरँग पाग, लटकि रही वाम भाग,
चंपकली कुटिल अलक, बीच-बीच रखी।
आयत दृग अरुण लोल, कुण्डल मंडित कपोल,
अधर दसन दीपति की छबि क्यों हूँ न जात लखी॥ २॥
अभयद भुज दण्ड मूल, पीन अंस सानुकूल,
कनक निकष लसि दुकूल दामिनी धरखी।
उर पुर मंदार हार, मुक्तालर वर सुढार,
मत्त दुरद गति तियन की देह दसा करखी॥ ३॥
मुकलित वय नव किशोर, वचन रचन चित्त के चोर.
मधुरितु पिक शाव नूत मंजरी चखी।
जय श्री नटवत हरिवंश गान, रागिणी कल्याण तान,
सप्त स्वरन कल इते पर, मुरलिका बरखी॥ ४॥ (३.५-६)

(७०)

चलहि राधिके सुजान तेरे हित सुख निधान,
रास रच्यौ श्याम तट कलिंद नन्दिनी।
निर्तत जुवती समूह राग रंग अति कुतूह,
बाजत रस मूल मुरलिका अनन्दिनी॥ १॥
बंसीवट निकट जहाँ, परम रमनि भूमि तहाँ,
सकल सुखद मलय बहै वायु मन्दिनी।
जाती ईषदी विकास कानन अतिशय सुवास,
राका निशि शरद मास विमल चन्दिनी॥ २॥
नरबाहन प्रभु निहार लोचन भरि घोष नारि,
नख-सिख सौंदर्य काम दुख निकंदिनी।
बिलसहु भुज ग्रीव मेलि भामिनि सुखसिंधु झेलि,
नव निकुंज श्याम केलि जगत बन्दिनी॥ ३॥ (३.६)

(७१)

आज गोपाल रास रस खेलत,
पुलिन कल्प तरु तीर री सजनी।
शरद विमल नभ चन्द्र विराजत,

रोचक त्रिविध समीर री सजनी॥
चंपक बकुल मालती मुकलित,
मत्त मुदित पिक कीर री सजनी।
देसी सुधंग राग रंग नीकौ,
ब्रज जुवतिन की भीर री सजनी॥
मघवा मुदित निसान बजायौ,
व्रत छाँड्यौ मुनि धीर री सजनी।
जै श्रीहित हरिवंश मगन मन श्यामा,
हरत मदन घन पीर री सजनी॥ ५॥ (३.७)

(७२)

आज बन नीकौ रास बनायौ।
पुलिन पवित्र सुभग जमुना तट, मोहन बेनु बजायौ॥
कल कंकन-किंकिनि नूपुर ध्वनि, सुनि खग-मृग सचु पायौ।
जुवतिन मंडल मध्य श्याम घन, सारँग राग जमायौ॥
ताल मृदङ्ग उपंग मुरज डफ, मिलि रससिंधु बढायौ।
विविध विशद वृषभानु नन्दिनी, अङ्ग सुधंग दिखायौ॥
अभिनय निपुन लटकि लट लोचन, भृकुटि अनंग नचायौ।
तता थेइ-ता थेइ धरत नौतन गति, पति ब्रजराज रिझायौ॥
सकल उदार नृपति चूडामणि, सुख वारिद बरषायौ।
परिरंभ चुम्बन आलिंगन उचित जुवति जन पायौ॥
वरषत कुसुम मुदित नभ नायक, इन्द्र निसान बजायौ।
जै श्रीहित हरिवंश रसिक राधा पति, जस बितान जग छायौ॥ ६॥ (३.७)

(७३)

मदन मथन घन निकुंज खेलत हरि,
राका रुचिर शरद रजनी।
जमुना पुलिन तट सुरतरु के निकट,
रचित रास चलि मिलि सजनी॥
बाजत मृदु मृदंग नाचत सबै सुधंग,
तैं न श्रवन सुन्यौ बैनु बजनी।
जै श्रीहितहरिवंश प्रभु राधिका रसन,
मोकौं भावै माइ जगत भगत-भजनी॥ ८॥ (३.८)

(७४)

मोहिनी मोहन रंगे प्रेम सुरंगे,
मत्त मुदित कल नाचत सुधंगे।
सकल कला प्रवीन कल्याण रागिनी लीन,
कहत न बनै माधुरी अङ्ग अङ्गे॥
तरनि तनया तीर त्रिविध सखी समीर,
मानों मुनि व्रत धर्यौ कपोती कोकिला कीर।
नागरी नव किशोर, मिथुन मनस चोर,
सरस गावत दोऊ मंजुल मन्दर घोर॥
कंकन किंकिनि धुनि मुखर नूपुरन सुनि,
जै श्री हित हरिवंश रस बरषै नव तरुनि॥ १०॥ (३.९)

(७५)

श्याम संग राधिका रास मंडल बनी।
बीच नंदलाल ब्रजबाल चंपक वरन,
ज्यौंव घन तडित बिच कनक मर्कत मनी॥
लेत गति मान तत्त थेई हस्तक भेद,
सा-रे-ग-म-प-ध-नि ये सप्त सुर नंदनी।
निर्तरस पहिर पट नील प्रगटित छबी,
वदन जनों जलद में मकर की चाँदनी॥
राग रागिनि तान मान संगीत मत,
थकित राकेश नभ शरद की जामिनी।
जैं श्रीहित हरिवंश पभु हंस कटि केहरी.
दूरि कृत मदन मद मत्त गज गामिनी॥ ११॥ (३.९)

(७६)

सुधङ्ग नाचत नवल किशोरी।
थेई-थेई कहत चहत प्रीतम दिशि,
वदन चन्द्र मनौ त्रिषित चकोरी॥
तान बंधान मान में नागरि,
देखत श्याम कहत हो-होरी।
जै श्रीहित हरिवंश माधुरी
अँग-अँग बरबस लियौ मोहन चित्त चोरी॥ १२॥ (३.९)

(७७)

वृषभानु नंदिनी मधुर कल गावै।
विकट औधर तान चर्चरी ताल सौं,
नन्दनंदन मनसि मोद उपजावै॥
प्रथम मज्जन चारु चीर कज्जल तिलक,
श्रवन कुंडल बदन चंदन लजावै।
सुभग नक बेसरी रतन हाटक जरी
अधर बंधूक दसन कुंद चमकावै॥
वलय कंकण चारु उरसि राजत हारु,
कटिव किंकिणि चरण नूपुर बजावै।
हंस कल गामिनी मथत मद कामिनी,
नखन मदयंतिका रंग रुचि द्यावै॥
निर्त्त सागर रभस रहसि नागरि नवल
चंदचाली विविध भेदन जनावै॥
कोक विद्या विदित भाइ अभिनय निपुन,
भ्रू विलासन मकरकेतन नचावै॥
निविड कानन भवन बाहु रंजित रवन,
सरस आलाप सुख पुंज बरषावै।
उभय संगम सिंधु सुरत पूषनबंधु
द्रवत मकरंद हरिवंश अलि पावै॥ १३॥ (३.९-१०)

(७८)

आज मेरे कहे चलौ मृग नैनी।
गावत सरस जुवति मंडल में,
पिय सौं मिलैं भलैं पिक बैनी॥
परम प्रवीन कोक विद्या में,
अभिनय निपुन लाग गति लैनी।
रूप रासि सुनि नवल किशोरी,
पल-पल घटत चाँदनी रैनी॥
जै श्रीहित हरिवंश चली अति आतुर,
राधा रवन सुरत सुख दैनी।
रहसि रभसि आलिंगन चुम्बन,
मदन कोटि कुल भइ कुचैनी॥ १४॥ (३.१०)

(७९)

मोहिनी मदन गोपाल की बाँसुरी।
माधुरी श्रवण पुट सुनत सुनि राधिके,
करत रतिराज के ताप कौ नासुरी॥
शरद राका रजनि विपिन वृन्दा सजनि,
अनिल अति मंद शीतल सहित बासुरी।
परम पावन पुलिन भृंग-सेवित नलिन,
कल्पतरु तीर बलबीर कृत रासु री॥
सकल मंडल भलीं तुम जु हरि सौं मिलीं,
बनी बर बनित उपमा कहौं कासु री।
तुम जु कंचनतनी लाल मर्कत मनी,
जै श्रीउभै कल हंस हरिवंश बलि दासुरी॥ १५॥ (३.१०)

(८०)

बैंनु माइ बाजै बंशीवट।
सदा बसंत रहत वृन्दावन,
पुलिन पवित्र सुभग जमुना तट॥
जटिल क्रीट मकराकृत कुंडल
मुख अरविन्द भँवर मानौं लट।
दसनन कुन्द कली छबि लज्जित,
सज्जित कनक समान पीतपट॥
मुनि मन ध्यान धरत नहिं पावत,
करत विनोद संग बालक भट।
दास अनन्य भजन रस कारन,
जै श्रीहित हरिवंश प्रगट लीला नट॥ १६॥ (३.१०-११)

(८१)

मैं जु मोहन सुन्यौ वेणु गोपाल कौ।
व्योम मुनियान सुर नारि विथकित भईं,
कहत नहिं बनत कुछ भेद यति ताल कौ॥
श्रवण कुंडल छुरितु रुरत कुंतल ललित,
रुचिर कस्तूरि चन्दन तिलक भाल क।

चंद गति मंद भई निरखि छबि काम गई,
देख हरिवंश हित वेष नँदलाल कौ॥ १८॥ (३.११)

(८२)

नाँचत मोहन संग राधिका
ब्रज जुवतिन के जूथ लिये।
बाहु परस्पर जोरि प्रेम बस,
मुदित गंड पर गंड दियें॥
कंकन कुनित रुनित बर नूपुर,
सुनत श्रवन खग उपरनियें।
बाजत ताल रसाल सरस गति,
मालव राग सुदेस गियें॥
सुघर संगीत प्रबीन नागरी,
तिरप लेत आनन्द हियें।
लटकत सीस सुभग पग पटकत,
वदत श्याम हो-होव कियें॥
सुख भर भरित परस्पर मंडल,
सस्मित रस लोचनन पियें।
जै श्री कृष्णदास हित वदत सदा यह,
वृथा कहा सत कल्प जियें॥ १९॥ (३.११)

(८३)

आज नचत नवल लाल साजि साज झिन्ना।
ध्रिक धिलाम ध्रिक धिलाम बाजत तकितकि धिलाम,
नाचत नयनाभिराम धकिट-धकिट धिन्ना॥
लचकि-लचकि गतिन लेत ठुमकि -ठुमकि चरन देत,
कर की करतार देत वदत ठोम ठिन्ना।
ललिता वदत भूले श्याम धी धी तकि धी धिलाम,
प्यारी हित रूपलाल नच्यौ छनन छिन्ना॥ ३१॥ (३.१६)

(८४)

नाँचत गोपाल बनै नट.वर बपु काछैं।
गावत गति मिलवत अति राधा के पाछैं॥
किंकिनि कंकन नूपुर धुनि ताल मृदंग सोहे।

मंद हास भ्रू-विलास सैनन मन मोहे॥
तरुवर गिरिवर मृग नाद-बान पोहे।
वृन्दारक वृन्द बधू तारक विधु मोहे॥
समीर नीर पंगु भयौ, बालक न पय प्यावैं।
व्यास सकल जीव जंतु नाद स्वाद ज्यावैं॥ ७३॥ (३.२९)

(८५)

[श्री हरिराम व्यासजी कृत : छन्द-त्रिपदी]
सरद सुहाई ऐई रात।
दस दिसि फूलि रही वन जाति।
देखि श्याम मन सुख भयौ॥
ससि गो मण्डित जमुना कूल।
बरषत विटप सदा फल फूल।
त्रिविध पवन दुख दवन है॥
राधारवन बजायौ बैन।
सुनि धुनि गोपिन उपज्यौ मैन॥
जहाँ तहाँ तें उठि चलीं॥
चलत न दीनौं काहु जबाब।
हरि प्यारि सौं बाढ्यौ भाव।
रास रसिक गुन गाइहौं॥ १॥

घर डर बिसर्यौ बढ्यौ उछाहु।
मन चिन्त्यौ पायौ हरि नाहु।
ब्रज नाइक लाइक सुन्यौ॥
दूध पूत की छाँडी आस।
गोधन भरता किये निरास।
साँच्यौ हित हरि सों कियौ॥
खान पान तन की न सम्भार।
हिलगि छुटायौ गृह ब्यौहार।
सुध बुध मोहन हरि लई॥
अञ्जन मञ्जन अङ्ग सिंगार।
पट भूषण सिर छूटे बार।
रास रसिक गुन गाइहौं॥ २॥

एक दुहावत तें उठि भगी।
और चली सोवत तें जगी।
उत्कण्ठा हरि सों बढी॥
उफनत दूध न धर्यौ उतारि।
सीझी थूली चूल्हौं डारि।
पुरुष तज्यौ जैंवतहु तैं॥
पय प्यावत बालक धरि चली।
पति सेवा कछु करी अनभली।
धर्यौ रह्यौ भोजन भलौ॥
तेल उबटनौ न्हैवौ भूल।
भाग्यन पाई जीवन मूल।
रस रसिक गुन गाइहौं॥ ३॥

अञ्जत एक नैन बिसर्यौ।
कटि कंचुकी लहँगा उर धर्यौ।
हार लपेट्यौ चरन सौं॥
श्रवनन पहिरे उलटे तार।
तिरनी पर चौकी सिंगार।
चतुर चतुरता हरि लई॥
जाकौ मन मोहन हरि लियौ।
ताकौ काहू कछू न कियौ।
ज्यौं पति सौं तिय रति करै॥
श्यामहिं सूचत मुरली नाद।
सुनि धुनि छूटे विषय सवाद।
रास रसिक गुन गाइहौं॥ ४॥

मात पिता पति रोकीं आनि।
सही न पिय दरसन की हानि।
सबही कौ अपमान कै॥
जाकौ मनुबा जासौं अटक्यौ।
रहै न छिनहू ता बिनु हटक्यौ।
कठिन प्रीति कौ फन्द है॥
जैसे सलिता सिंधुहि भजै।
कोटिक गिरि भेदत नहिं लजै।

तैसी गति इनकी भई॥
एक जु घर तें निकसी नहीं।
हरि करुना करि आये तहीं।
रास रसिक गुन गाइहौं॥ ५॥ (३.३०-३७)

(८६)

वंशीवट मूल खरे दंपति अनुराग भरे,
गावत हैं सारँग पिय सारँग वर नैनी।
उमहि कुँवरि करत गान सिखवत पिय विकट तान,
सप्त स्वर सौं मधुर-मधुर लेत कोकिल बैनी॥
चित्रित चंदन सुअङ्ग भूषण फूलन सुरंग,
दसन बसन सहज रंग बेसर छबि दैनी।
लसत कंठ जलज माल झलक स्वेद कन रसाल,
दीरघ वर लोचन मषि रेख बनी पैनी॥
चहुँ दिसि सखियान भीर सकल प्रेम रस अधीर,
उभय रूप राग रंग सुख अभंग लैनी।
उमड्यौ जल प्रेम नैन रहित भए रसन बैन.
इहि गति रहौ मत्त चित्त हित ध्रुव दिन रैनी॥ ३३॥ (३.३८-३९)

(८७)

भज मन रास रसिक किशोर।
गौर स्यामल सकल गुन निधि चतुर चित के चोर॥
सुभग मण्डल पर विराजत जुगल सुन्दर वेष।
बसन भूषन जगमगैं अति अंग-अंग सुदेस॥
चारु चरन सुदेस निर्मल गति विलास विनोद।
पदन पटकन नखन दमकन होत नव-नव मोद॥
जोरि कबहूँ कर परस्पर बदन सन्मुख चारु।
घन घटा से चलत दोऊ भ्रमत करत विहार॥
मुकुट कबरी लटक भृकुटी मटक मधुरी हास।
हरषि बरषत रंग भीनौं हित दामोदर दास॥ ४६॥ (३.४३)

(८८)

[श्रीनन्ददासजी कृत—राग केदारौ—]

देखौ री नागर नट निर्त्तन कालिंदी तट गोपिन के मध्य राजै मुकुट लटक।
काछिनी किंकिनी कटि पीतांवर की चटक कुंडल किरन रवि रथ की अटक॥
तत्ता थेई तत्ता थेई शब्द सकल घट उरप तिरप गति पग की पटक।
रास में राधे-राधे मुरली में येही रट नन्ददास गावैं तहाँ निपट निकट॥
१३३॥ (३.७९)

(८९)

[श्रीनन्ददासजी कृत—राग छन्द (प्रथम अध्याय)]
बन्दन करौं कृपानिधान श्री शुक सुभकारी।
सुद्ध जोति मय रूप सदा सुंदर अविकारी॥ १॥
हरि लीला रस मत्त मुदित नित विचरत जग में।
अद्भुत गति कतहूँ न अटक होइ निसरत मग में॥ २॥
नीलोत्पल दल स्याम अङ्ग नव जीवन भ्राजै।
कुटिल अलक मुख कमल मनौं अलि अवलि बिराजै॥ ३॥
सुंदर भाल बिसाल दिपत मनौं निकर निसाकर।
कृष्ण-भक्ति-प्रतिबन्ध तिमिर कौं कोटि दिवाकर॥ ४॥
कृपा रङ्ग रस ऐन नैन राजत रतनारे।
कृष्ण रसासब पान अलस कछु घूँम घुँमारे॥ ५॥
श्रवन कृष्ण रस भवन गंड मंडल भल दरसै।
प्रेमानंद मिली सु मन्द मुसिकन मधु बरसै॥ ६॥
उन्नत नासा अधरबिम्ब सुक की छबि छीनी।
तिन मधि अद्भुत भाँति लसत कछु इक मसि भीनी॥ ७॥ (३.८०-१००)

(९०)

[श्रीस्वामी हरिदासजी कृत—राग सारङ्ग व केदारौ]
सुनि धुनि मुरलि बन बाजै ए हरि रास रच्यौ।
कुंज-कुंज द्रुम बेलि प्रफुल्लित
मंडल कंचन मणिनु खच्यौ॥
निर्त्तत जुगल किशोर जुवति जन
श्रुति घुर राग केदारौ मच्यौ।
श्रीहरिदास के स्वामी स्यामा कुंजबिहारी
नीकै [अज] प्यारौ लाल नच्यौ॥ ६॥ (३.१००)

(९१)

श्रीबीठलविपुलजी कृत—राग कान्हरौ
नव निकुञ्ज नव भूमि रँगमगी।
नवल बिहारी लाल लाड़िलौ नवल सरद की जोन्ह जगमगी॥
नव सत साजि सकल अँग सुन्दर नवल बदन पर अलक सगबगी।
श्रीबीठलविपुल बिहारी के अँग लाड़त लाड़िली सहज उर लगी॥ १२॥
(३.१०१)

(९२)

अरी हेली राधा लाल सुहाग कौं दुलरावौ सुख लेहु।
सरद सरवरी जगमगै हेली जगमगै जुगल सनेहु॥ हेली०॥ १॥
कृपा उझलि हम दिस रही हेली देखौ नैन निहारि।
गुनवंती-गुनवंत पै हेली देहु अपनपौ बारि॥ २॥
लोचन रक्षक पलक हैं हेली तजत न अपनि रीति।
इहि विधि नागर-नागरी हेली तुमकौं पोषत प्रीति॥ ३॥
गौर स्याम सब गुन निकर हेली तुम परखे सब अंग।
तद्यपि रीझत हम गुनन हेलि भरे अधिक रस रंग॥ ४॥
पूरित आनन्द वारि सौं हेली कानन सर अभिराम।
क्रीडत करत प्रसंस कौं हेली निसि दिन स्यामा-स्याम॥ ५॥
लहनौं गहनौं सखिनु कौ हेली ये दोऊ ललित किशोर।
कुंजन सोभा गहर कौं हेली बरषत लहत न ओर॥ ६॥
दै असीस तृन तोरि कैं हेली बैठे धरि भुज अंस।
वृन्दावन हित रूप बलि हेली जीवन श्रीहरिवंश॥ ७॥ १७॥ (३.११५-११६)

(९३)

भोजन कौ समयौ जब जान्यौ।
तब सखियन मणिमय चौकी पर
पाटम्बर बिछयौ मन मान्यौ॥ १॥
झारी धरी भरी शीतल जल कंचन थार धुवाये।
बेला जानि धरे बेला अवला नव लाल बुलाये॥ २॥
कुछ-कुछ भूषण-वसन असन कौ समयौ जानि उतार्यौं।

रतन सुचौक मूँदरी पहुँची धरि पटुका पट न्यायौं॥ ३॥
दै आचमन परोसत व्यंजन बरने कापै जाई।
चम्पक लता चतुर सब विधि सों करै धरै मन लाई॥ ४॥
पाइस बूरा अरु घृत पूरा बरा लुचई रोटी।
भात पीत सित वर कमोद कौ कढ़ि पकौरी छोटी॥ ५॥
धोबा दार मूंग साजे पुनि बरी फुलौरी कीनी।
मीठी-कढ़ी मुरब्बा अमरस पनौ सिखरनी दीनी॥ ६॥
एला लवङ्ग कपूर सुवासित पुनि मेवा मधि डारी।
खिचरी थूली घृत करि मिश्रित खात अधिक रुचिकारी॥ ७॥
मठा रायते भाँति-भाँति के विविध सँधाने आने।
पत्र फूल फल फली कंद तरकारी डारी जाने॥ ८॥
सालन बहुत करे बेसन के झोल पिटौर बनाये।
फल दल शाक समेत हेत सौं इक दधि तक्र मिलाये॥ ९॥
सखरे व्यंजन बहुत भाँति के कँह लगि बरनौ जेते।
परसि बहुरि मन की रुचि कारण मेवा सुरस समेते॥ १०॥
नीबु आदौ अरु नारङ्गी सुरस दाड़िमी दाने।
सेव आम सरदा बीही खीरा नासपात रस साने॥ ११॥
सुरस दाख मेवा अलि जेती डाली भरि-भरि केती।
कैऊ लवंग कैऊ बूरा सों कैऊ ज्यों की त्यों तेती॥ १२॥
पूवा पूरी जलेबी लाडू खाजा खुरमा फैनी।
चन्द्रकला पापर अरु घेवर अमृतपुटी सुख दैनी॥ १३॥
मोहन भोग दूध की रोटी खोवा सेव मलाई।
अमृत गुटी अरु अमृत बूँदी मठरिनु लेत सराई॥ १४॥
सेव सिधारे के खुरमाजुत सक्करपारे पेरा।
गुझिया और पराक पायरी पापर तरे करेरा॥ १५॥
तली कचरिया भाँति-भाँति की नोन मधुर रस साने।
पेठा पिस्ता तली चिरौंजी पगे मखाने दाने॥ १६॥
एक-एक पकवान बहुत विध परसि कचौरी आनी।
सखिजन देत लेत पिय प्यारी हेत अधिक जिय जानी॥ १७॥
व्यंजन कीने चार भाँति के षटरस रस कर सानि।
भक्ष्य-भोज्य अरु चोष्य-लेह्य ये विविध प्रकार बखाने॥ १८॥
लवण कसाय तिक्त कटु अम्लरु मधुर विविध विध केते।

रुचि अनुसार बनाये रचि कर मिश्रित न्यारे जेते॥ १९॥
कैई रामठ जीरा सों छौंके पुनि पत्रज सों केते।
सौंफ गंधेल सौंफ चीनी सों कै इक लौंग समेते॥ २०॥
एला लवङ्ग कपूर जायफल जावित्री मधि नाई।
केशर पुट पुनि नागबेल रस अतर कुसुम अधिकाई॥ २१॥
गिरी छुआरे दाख चिरौंजी पिस्ता अरु बादामा।
यथा योग्य सामिग्री मिलये चम्पक चतुर सुभामा॥ २२॥
दूलह-दुलहिनि राधावल्लभ भोजन करत विराजैं।
हँसत परस्पर कौर देत मुख दसनन की छबि छाजैं॥ २३॥
यहि प्रकार भोजन कराइ कैं पुनि आचमन दिवायौ।
पानि अगौंछि खबाबत बीरी करत आप मन भायौ॥ २४॥
बैठे जाय सिंघासन ऊपर सखियन थार उठायौ।
राजभोग की करत आरती जै श्रीकमलनैन यश गायौ॥ २५॥ (३.१६२-१६४)

(९४)

[श्रीध्रुवदासजी कृत—राग विहागरौ (कार्तिक सुदी परवा कौ)]
सखियन के उर ऐसी आई। ब्याह बिनोद रचैं सुखदाई॥
यहै बात सब के मन भाई। आनन्द मोद बढ़्यौ अधिकाई॥
बढ़्यौ आनंद मोद सबकैं महा प्रेम सुरङ्ग रँगी।
और कछु न सुहाइ तिनकौं युगल सेवा सुख पगी॥
निशि द्यौस जानत नाहिं सजनी एक रस भीजी रहैं।
गोप-गोपिनु आदि दुर्लभ तिहि सुखहि दिन प्रति लहैं॥ १॥
यह नव दुलहिनि अति सुकुमारी। ये नव दूलह लाल बिहारी॥
रँग भीने दोऊ प्राण पियारे। नव सत अंगन अंग सिंगारे॥
नव सत सिंगारे अंग अङ्गन झलक तन की अति बढ़ी।
मौर-मौरी सीस सोहैं मैन पानिप मुख चढ़ी॥
जलज सुमन सु सेहरे रचि रतन हीरे जगमगैं।
देखि अद्भुत रूप मनमथ कोटि रति पाँयन लगैं॥ २॥
सोभा मंडप कुंजन द्वारैं। हित की बाँधी बंदन वारैं॥
कुमकुम सौं लै अजिर लिपायौ। अद्भुत मोतिनु चौक पुरायौ॥
पुराय अद्भुत चौक मोतिनु चित्र रचना बहु करी।

आय दोऊ ठाढ़े भये तहाँ सबन की गति-मति हरी॥
सुरङ्ग महदी रङ्ग राचे चरण कर अति राजहीं।
विविध रागनि किंकिनी अरु मधुर नूपुर बाजहीं॥ ३॥
वेदी सेज सुदेश सुहाई। मन दृग अञ्चल ग्रन्थि जुराई॥
रीति भाँति विधि उचित बनाई। नेह की देवी तहाँ पुजाई॥
पूजि देवी नेह की दोऊ रति-विनोद बिहारहीं।
तिहि समै सखी ललितादि हित सौं हेरि प्राणन वारहीं॥
एक बैस सुभाव एकै सहज जोरी सोहिनी।
एक डोरी प्रेम की ध्रुव बँधे मोहन-मोहनी॥ ४॥ १॥ (३.१६४-१६५)

(९५)

श्री वृन्दाबन धाम रसिक मन मोहई।
दूलह दुलहिनि ब्याह सहज सोहई॥ १॥
नित्य सहाने पट अरु भूषण साजहीं।
नित्य नवल सम बैस एक रस राजहीं॥ २॥
सोभा कौ सिरमौर चन्द्रिका मोर की।
बरनी न जाइ कछू छबि नवल किशोर की॥ ३॥
सुभग माँग रङ्ग रेख मनों अनुराग की।
झलकत मौरी सीस सुरङ्ग सुहाग की॥ ४॥
मणिनु खचित नव कुंज रही जगमग जहाँ।
छबि कौ बन्यौ बितान सोई मंडप तहाँ॥ ५॥
बेदी सेज सुदेस रची अति बानि कै।
भाँति-भाँति के फूल सुरङ्ग बहु आनि कै॥ ६॥
गावत मोर मराल सुहाए गीत री।
सहचरि भरीं आनंद करत रस रीति री॥ ७॥
अलबेले सुकुँवार फिरत तिहि ठाँवरी।
दृग अञ्चल परी ग्रन्थि लेत मन भाँवरी॥ ८॥
कँगना प्रेम अनूप कबहुँ नहिं छुटही।
पोयौ डोरी रूप सहज सो न टूटही॥ ९॥
रचि रहे कोमल कर अरु चरण सुरङ्ग री।
सहज छबीले कुँवर निपुन सब अङ्ग री॥ १०॥
नूपुर कंकण किंकिणी बाजे बाजहीं।

निर्त्तन कोटि अनङ्ग नारि सब लाजहीं॥ ११॥
बाढ़्यौ है मन माहिं अधिक आनन्द री।
फूले फिरत किशोर वृन्दावन चंद री॥ १२॥
सखियन किये बहु चार अनेक बिनोद री।
दूधा भाती हेत बढ़्यौ मन मोद री॥ १३॥
ललित लाल की बात जबहि सखियन कही।
लाज सहित सुकुमारि ओट पट दै रही॥ १४॥
नमित ग्रीव छबि सींव कुँवरि नहिं बोलहीं।
बुधि बल करत उपाय घूँघट पट खोलहीं॥ १५॥
कनक कमल कर नील कलह अति कल बनी।
हँसत सखी सुख हेरि सहज सोभा घनी॥ १६॥
बाम चरण सौं सीस लाल कौ लावहीं।
पानी वारि कुँवरि पर पियहि पियावहीं॥ १७॥
मेलि सुगन्ध उगार सो बीरी खबावहीं।
समझि कुँवरि मुसिकाइ अधिक सुख पावहीं॥ १८॥
और हास-परिहास रहसि रस रङ्ग रह्यौ।
नित्य विहार बिनोद यथामति कछु कह्यौ॥ १९॥
अंचल ओट असीस सखी सब देहिं री।
पल-पल बढ़ौ सुहाग नैन सुख लेहिं री॥ २०॥
जैसें नवल बिलास नवल नवला करैं।
मन-मन की रुचि जान नेह विधि अनुसरैं॥ २१॥
बैठी हैं निज कुंज कुँवरि मन मोहनी।
झलकत रूप अपार सहज अति सोहनी॥ २२॥
चाहि-चाहि सो रूप रसिक सिरमौर री।
भरि आये दोऊ नैन भई-गति और री॥ २३॥
अति आनंद कौ मोद न उरहि समात री।
रीझि-रीझि रस भीज आपु बलि जात री॥ २४॥
अरुझे मन अरु नैन बढ़्यौ अनुराग री।
एक प्राण द्वै देह नागर अरु नागरी॥ २५॥
यौं राजत दोऊ प्रीतम हँसि मुसिकात री।
निरखि परस्पर रूप न कबहूँ अघात री॥ २६॥
तिनही के सुख रंग सखी दिन रँग मगीं।
और न कछू सुहाइ एक रस सब पगीं॥ २७॥

उभय रुप्प-रस सिंधु मगन जहाँसब भए।
दुर्लभ श्रिपति आदि सोई सुख दिन नए॥ २८॥
हित ध्रुव मंगल सहज नित्य जो गावही।
सर्वोपर सोई होइ प्रेम रस पावही॥ २९॥ (३.१६५-१६७)

(९६)

रट री मुरली मेरी राधे राधे।
येई मेरे साधन आराधन रस सींवा गुण रूप अगाधे॥
जा कारन मैं मृदु मुख धारी सो बिसरै जिन तू पल आधे।
वृन्दावन हित मंत्र मोहनी जपौ निरन्तर पूजै साधे॥ २०॥ (३.१३१)

(९७)

आजु देखि ब्रज सुन्दरी मोहन बनी केलि।
अंस-अंस बाहु दै किशोर जोर रूप रासि,
मनौ तमाल अरुझि रही सरस कनक बेलि॥
नव निकुंज भँवर गुंज मंजु घोष प्रेम पुंज
गान करत मोर पिकन अपने सुर सों मेलि।
मदन मुदित अङ्ग-अङ्ग बीच-बीच सुरत रँग,
पल-पल हरिवंश पिवत नैन चषक झेलि॥ १६॥ (३.१८४-१८५)

(९८)

बल्लवी सु कनक वल्लरी तमाल स्याम सङ्ग
लागि रही अङ्ग-अङ्ग मनोभिरामिनी॥
वदन जोति मनों मयंक अलक तिलक छबि कलंक,
छपत श्याम अङ्क मनौं जलद दामिनी॥
विगत वास हेम खम्भ मनों भुवंग बैनी दंड
पिय के कंठ प्रेम पुंज कुंज कामिनी।
जै श्रीशोभित हरिवंश नाथ साथ सुरत आलस वंत,
उरज कनक कलश राधिका सुनामिनी॥ १२॥ (३.१९७)

(९९)

कहा कहौं इन नैनन की बात॥ १॥
ये अलि प्रिया बदन-अम्बुज-रस,

अटके अनत न जात॥ २॥
जब-जब रुकत पलक सम्पुट लट,
अति आतुर अकुलात॥ ३॥
लम्पट लव निमेष अन्तर तैं.
अलप कलप सत-सात॥ ४॥
श्रुति पर कंज, दृगंजन, कुच बिच,
मृग मद ह्वै न समात॥ ५॥
(जै श्री) हित हरिवंश नाभि सर-
जलचर जाँचत साँवल गात॥ ६॥

(१००)

छांड़ि दै मानिनी मान मन धरिबौ।
प्रणत सुन्दर सुघर प्राण बल्लभ नवल,
बचन आधीन सौं इतौ कत करिबौ॥
जपत हरि विवस तव नाम प्रतिपद विमल,
मनसि तब ध्यान तैं निमिष नहिं टरिबौ।
घटत पल-पल सुभग शरद की यामिनी,
भामिनी सरस अनुराग दिशि ढरिबौ॥
हौं जु कछु कहत निज बात सुनि मान सखि,
सुमुखि बिन काज घन विरह दुख भरिबौ।
मिलत हरिवंश हित कुंज किशलय शयन,
करत कल केलि सुखसिंधु में तरिबौ॥ १॥ (३.२२१)

(१०१)

नागरी निकुंज ऐंन किशलय दल रचित सैन,
कोक कला कुशल कुँवरि अति उदार री।
सुरत रङ्ग अङ्ग-अङ्ग हाव-भाव भृकुटि भङ्ग,
माधुरी तरङ्ग मथत कोटि मार री॥
मुखर नूपुरन सुभाव किंकिणी बिचित्र राव,
बिरम-बिरम नाथ वदत बर विहार री।
लाड़िली किशोर राज हंस-हंसिनी समाज,
सींचत हरिवंश नैन सुरस सार री॥ २॥ (३.२२१)

(१०२)

रति रण जीति पौढ़ी बाल।
कोक दावन हाव भावन विवस कीने लाल॥
शिथिल भूषण वसन अँग-अँग मरगजी उर माल।
(जै श्री) हित विनोद अलि चरण सेवत कृष्ण दस तिहिकाल॥ ७॥ (३.२२३)

(१०३)

राजत निकुञ्ज महल ठकुरानी।
कुसुम सेज पर पौढ़ी स्यामा राग सुनत मृदु वानी॥
ललिता चरण पलोटन लागी लाल दृष्ति ललचानी।
पाँइ परत सजनी के मोहन हित सौं हा-हा खानी॥
भई कृपाल लाल पर ललिता, दै आज्ञा मुसिकानी।
आवहु मोहन चरन पलोटौ जैसे कुँवरि न जानी॥
आज्ञा दई कुँवरि ललिता कौं मुख ऊपर पट तानी।
बीन बजाय गाय कछु तानन ज्यौं उपजै सुख सानी॥
गावन लगे रसिक मन मोहन तब जानी महारानी।
.□थि बैठी श्रीव्यास की स्वामिनि वृन्दावन की रानी॥ ९॥ (३.२२३-२२४)

(१०४)

ललन की बतियाँ चोज सनी।
परम कृपाल चितै करुनामय लोचन कोर अनी॥
अमगि ढरे दोऊ सुरत सेज पै टूटीं तरकि तनी।
परम उदार व्यास की स्वामिनि बकसत मौज घनी॥ १०॥ (३.२२४)

(१०५)

नहीं सुरझै उरझन प्रेम की, रही रोम-रोम में भोय।
रधेजू मोहन ह्वै रहीं मोहन राधे होय॥
ललित लतन तर रङ्ग्मगे, दोऊ मैंन सनमान।
नैनन सौं नैना मिले, पगे प्रान सों प्रान॥
चिबुक तरे पिय कर दिये सोभित हैं इहि भाय।
नील कमल पर अरुन कमल मानौ खिले हैं परम सचु पाय॥
नागरिया रजनी घटै उत चंद मलिन दुति होय।
त्यौं-त्यौं आलस रूप दुहुँन कौ इतै चौगुनों होय॥ १८॥ (३.२२६)

(१०६)

चली कुँवरि राधिका निकुँज भवन रवन पास
सजि सुवास मत्त भँवर सङ्ग-सङ्ग-सङ्ग।
आय रसिक राय निकट लई भुजन झेलि मेलि
करत केलि परसत सुख अङ्ग-अङ्ग-अङ्ग॥
जुरत नैन टुटत हार अञ्चल उर छुटत बार,
चल कटाक्ष भृकुटि भंग रंग-रंग-रंग।
ता घरिया देखि दुहुन नागरिया लतन ओट
तन मन गति श्रवन नैन पंग-पंग-पंग॥ १९॥ (३.२२६)

(१०७)

कुंज पधारौ राधे रंग भरी रैन।
रँग भरी दुलहिनि रंग भरे पिय श्याम सुन्दर सुख दैन॥
रंग भरी सेज रची सखियन नें रंग भयौ उलहत मैंन।
रसिक विहारी पिय-प्यारी दोऊ मिलि करौ सेज सुख सैंन॥ २२॥ (३.२२७)

(१०८)

लाल की नींद झपत अँखियाँ।
खंजन सुत अरबरत उड़न मनु उलहीं नई पँखियाँ॥
प्यारी रूप छकीं कैं घूँमत मतवारी लखियाँ।
वृन्दावन हित रूप रसासव पिवत जिवत सखियाँ॥ ८॥ (३.२३०)

A Note About the Way the Words Sound

From Song 24

ranga aja vamsivata phaguna vividha vihara
viharata radha vallabha ujhalata saurabha sara
vaisa kalina si khilin lalita lalitadika vrinda
tinaki nakha duti dekhata phikau lagata canda.

In these four lines we see an enormous number of musical sounds coming from the words themselves. Assonance, for example. In the first line, twelve of the seventeen vowels are "a." In the second line, it's fifteen of eighteen. There's a change in the third line, with only eight of eighteen being "a" and eight being "i." And the fourth line is mixed, though ten of its seventeen vowels are "a." That's 45 vowel sounds out of 70. It's smooth and mellow at start and end, with a bit of excitement in the middle. Repetition also abounds, as for example in the sequence "*vividha vihara viharata*" or "*kalina si khilin*" or "*lalita lalitadika*" or "*tinaki nakha duti.*" It's more than mere alliteration, though there's plenty of that too.

Mathur translates the passage thus:

> It is Phāgun month and today Vaṃśīvaṭa is full of color and pleasure. Rādhāvallabha (Krishna) wanders and proudly enjoys the fragrant scents. The girlfriends, including lovely Lalitā and others, blossom

like flower buds.

Translators differ in the amount of emphasis they give to sound, the way they treat repetition, and the degree of ambiguity they expect readers to accept. I don't know that this is a better translation, but it has a bit more of the sound repetitions than Mathur's more streamlined versions.

> As Phāgun arrives, essence of springtime, Vaṃśīvaṭa's grove overflows with fragrance. Rainbows of rich colors touch Rādhā's proud lover while he wanders, while he lingers, lighting Lalitā, lighting all the lovely lasses in whom sweet pleasures blossom, blossom like the energy in buds, bursting petals apart.

Song 25: You Must Return My Flute (Alternative Version)

The blouse of one of the cow-herding girls[50] is wet
  and her *sārī* is perfumed with the light scent of saffron.
She is wearing a lovely printed skirt,
  tied to show off her perfect smooth hips.
Many times her lover puts his arm around her: it's holiday; it's Spring
  and she's singing high-spirited taunts for Holi.
Long long eyelashes and lush luscious hair enhance her young figure,
  and she's mad with excitement.
Scented oils applied to her eyes accent their adoration of Krishna.
  It's hard to find similes to match Mohan's movements.
It's as if, with a magical jantra and an enticing *mantra*,
  he has laid a trap for the cow-tending girls' tender hearts.

And the way one special girl can't cover her huge, darting eyes with her veil—
  it's as if the sharp, pointed, spear of the love god has stopped in mid-flight.
When her pearl nose-ring swings round and round, so gracefully,
  Mohana's heart craves nectar from her lips.

[50]This girl is Rādhā, though the poet does not name her at any point in this poem

She is wearing beautiful earrings, and when she smiles,
her teeth shine like bright lightning flashes shine in the clouds.

On her fair chin, there is one dark spot, small and black,
like a baby bee attracted by a lotus, not wanting to move.
She is wearing a garland of two-strand golden necklaces,
one black dot, and two types of earrings.
She is wearing bangles, arm ornaments, and flower garlands—
wreaths of ivory, *campa* flowers, and *guñja* seeds.
She's a thief of all hearts. Like a pair of intricately gold-netted tassels
swaying on one cord, her two breasts steal hearts.
Her golden breasts are tightly bound, so tightly that they cause her pain,
so tightly that Kāmadeva seems to have befriended Shiva.
Her ankle bells tinkle beautifully, but they've wounded her feet.
Nanda's son loves her suffering beauty; they lock eyes 'til their eyes redden.

When she shot her powerful glance at the feet of her lover,
it was as if her glance were a gun.
When she tossed her red powder on Madanamohana and sang her magic spell,
he wandered behind her all over Vrindaban.
And when he rushed forward and tightly embraced the fair-skinned girl,
she caught him in the net of love, snatched his flute and took his yellow scarf.
When she, the much-garlanded girl, put his flute to her lips,
the essence of charm flowed from it.
"Oh, Beloved, take anything from me," he said,
But swear by your brother that you'll give back my flute."
Joining his arms with hers, he sought to kiss her lips,
like a *cakora* bird thirsting for the moon.

The cloud-dark lord looks like a young *tamāla* tree,
and the girl clings to it like a golden vine.
Her friends tie her cloth's knot to his, then cry for joy,
toss high their teasing words, sing their seductive taunts.
Their voices enchant all the ladies of Barsana.
Poet Ghanaśyāma gave dried fruit to those lovely ladies,
as a gift for the season of Spring.

Song 27: Ever Fresh, the Playful Boy of Braj (Alternative Version)

Ever fresh, the playful boy of Braj delights in Holi!
The Braj girls gather, gather in the gloaming; sweet Spring has come;
Bees buzz, cuckoos chirp, the evening atmosphere exhilarates.
O ever-fresh delight!

Flowers like the lotus and the *kesu* sprout in the river Yamunā
and flowers like the *campaka, bakula,* and rose float in the waves of the river.
O ever-fresh delight!

Krishna sends his friends Subala, Subāhu, and Śrīdāma to the river; they make music.
They pound drum, play *ruñja,* finger flute, shake tambourine and blow trumpet.
O ever-fresh delight!

The sound of the clarinet reaches quite far. How much of the bliss of Braj can I describe?
Ever fresh, the playful boy of Braj delights in Holi!

Clay pitchers are full of saffron. Holi celebrants aim golden waterguns
from a distance. Red powder swirls like a storm.
O ever-fresh delight!

There is so much colored Holi water that its streams dig holes in the earth.
The sweet smell of coconut hair oil spreads, blends with sandalwood scents.
O ever-fresh delight!

Boys and girls raise their hands and strike one another with sticks made of flowers.
The scarves of the girls flap in the wind, and their eager eyes squint.
O ever-fresh delight!

The large-hearted girls of Braj are lovely; they've come to celebrate with Rādhā.
Among them, her dearest friend Lalitā is especially beautiful.
O ever-fresh delight!

Through a clever trick, Lalitā sprinkles colors on Krishna, laughs, runs away, hooting loudly.
After sly chat and a change of clothing, one of Krishna's friends comes out--cross-dressed.
O ever-fresh delight!

Lalitā, loquacious, runs out to meet this lovely new lass. Suddenly Rādhā is holding
A large ball of flowers; she aims it and throws it at Krishna.
Ever fresh, the playful boy of Braj delights in Holi!

The lanes of Braj on the far bank of the Yamunā are very narrow.
The girls beckon, beckon Balarāma to that bank.
O ever-fresh delight!

Closing the doors of their houses, they taunt, "You are called the Plowman.
Let us see how strong you really are! What has happened to the Power of the Plowman?"
O ever-fresh delight!

Then they tie both his hands, blacken his body with collyrium, and cover him with a cloth.
They shower him with taunts, then send him off, gleefully pranking in Holi.
O ever-fresh delight!

The mischievous girls run away laughing, making room for more.
Ever fresh, the playful boy of Braj delights in Holi!

The girls grab the Intoxicating Cowherder, forcibly bring him along, taunting:
"Krishna lifted Mount Govardhan with his left arm and killed a demon with his foot.
O ever-fresh delight!

"But what has happened to that strength when Lalitā can lift him in the air?
Surrounding him, they enter Rādhā's house, hugging and sharing great happiness.
O ever-fresh delight!

Smiling, enjoying the game, Rādhā bends as though supplicating—but she's holding a blue cloth.

On one side is naughty Śrīdāma, on the other frolicsome Lalitā, with
Viśākhā between them.
O ever-fresh delight!

When Krishna's been taunted and trussed, she offers him freedom, if
he'll lend her his flute.
Ever fresh, the playful boy of Braj delights in Holi!

Now, Krishna's friend, Madana, is well trusted and loyal; he always
stands by his friend.
The Enchanter sends him as envoy to talk with this girl and that girl.
O ever-fresh delight!

Planning cleverly, he asks Madana to bring back his brother, Bala-
rāma.
Madana goes to Rādhā, touches her feet, and begs her to return.
O ever-fresh delight!

Śrīdāma giggles at this, asks for dried fruit, tells Rādhā, "Offer lips'
nectar to Krishna.
"Let him kiss you," she says. Thus the pleasure increases of those who
celebrate Spring.
O ever-fresh delight!

The girls make the couple sit on the lap of Braj's queen, Mother Yaśodā,
who gifts
the playful ones with gold bangles, bracelets, beautifully crafted—even
a necklace of diamonds.
O ever-fresh delight!

By the grace of Śrī Viṭṭhala, and by the dust of his lotus feet, says poet
Chīta Svāmī,
Having met the Mountain Lifter, all illnesses and bodily pains are ex-
tinguished.
Ever fresh, the playful boy of Braj delights in Holi!

Elizabeth Delmonico

Musical Aspects

Rāgas

While the Rādhāvallabha hymnals mention the names of the *rāgas* above the poems, these references appear, judging by the experience of extended listening to the songs performed, to be suggestions, or simply repetitions of previous conventions, that are not necessarily binding on the performers. As such, there is a certain degree of latitude when comparing text with recording. This is further confounded by the fact that the music that one hears in the temples has been handed down orally for many generations. In truth, many of the *rāgas* that are heard on the recordings are approximations or modifications of the strict Hindustani *rāgas* as currently performed by classical and professional musicians today. The differences in note emphasis and melodic phrasing in the *rāgas* as performed by the Rādhāvallabha musicians is accounted for by adjustments to the words of the text and the breaking down of sections of the poem for purposes of clarity in repetition and response. Accordingly, the precise identification of some of the *rāgas* by an outsider is often hampered by these modifications as well as frequent combinations of phrases from different *rāgas*, and even the changing of *rāgas*, within single compositions. As some of the songs extend in duration from thirty minutes to an hour, the employment of multiple *rāgas* within a single poem is not surprising. In several examples, only the bare modal frame of a *rāga* can be assessed with certainty, and these often with a few accidentals (notes outside the strictly defined classical *rāga*). In singular instances, a rare combination may be found like "Nat-Kedar." The search for the purity of a *rāga* is complicated further by the fact that there are slight disagreements about the grammar of a *rāga* between the various *gharāṇās* ("family") or lineages of Hindustani music. In sum, most of the lengthy renditions in this collection represent melodic compositions that are unique to the Rādhāvallabha Sampradāya and thus are often difficult to square with the performances of Hindustani *Rāgas* as heard by classical artists.

Nonetheless, as an aid to listening and understanding the deep connection between Hindustani music and the Samāj-Gāyan tradition of Vrindāban, an annotated description of the roughly three dozen *rāgas* that have been identified within the performance–recordings of the Rādhāvallabha Songbook are presented below, with their corresponding ascending and descending notes (separated by a comma) as they are defined in the Hindustani music canon. The Indian diatonic scale is generally written as Sa Re Ga Ma Pa Dha Ni sa (ascending), and sa Ni Dha Pa Ma Ga Ri Sa (descending). In this work, and in the description of the *rāgas* below, they appear as S R G M P D N sa. Upper Sa and notes above it are written in lowercase, and notes below lower Sa are in parentheses. The Western C-scale note equivalents for the Indian diatonic scale letter-notes correlate as follows:

> Sa = C, Re = D, Ga = E, Ma = F, Pa = G, Dha = A, Ni = B, sa = upper C.

When a note is flattened (*komala*), it is underlined ($\underline{\text{G}}$, $\underline{\text{N}}$), and when sharpened (*tīvra*), it is italicized (*M*). This system covers all of the principal notes used in *rāga* music, yet some ornaments (*alaṅkāra*) used by musicians in certain *rāgas* employ semitones for aesthetic effect. Diacritics have been left out of the *rāga* names because of the lack of uniformity in English transliteration.

Alahiya Vilaval – Morning: S G R G P N D N s, s N D P D $\underline{N}$ D P M G M R G P M G M R S

Asaveri — Morning: S R M P $\underline{D}$ $\underline{N}$ s, s $\underline{N}$ $\underline{D}$ P M $\underline{D}$ M P $\underline{G}$ R S

Bahar – Midnight: S M P $\underline{G}$ M D N s, r N s D $\underline{N}$ P M P $\underline{G}$ M R S

Bageshri – Midnight: S $\underline{G}$ M D $\underline{N}$ s, s $\underline{N}$ D M P D M $\underline{G}$ R S

Basant – Late Night, Spring Season: S G *M* $\underline{D}$ N s, s N $\underline{D}$ P *M* G *M* G $\underline{R}$ S, with addition of M is ascent from S in the melody of the composition.

Bhairav – Early Morning: S $\underline{R}$ G M P $\underline{D}$ N s, s N $\underline{D}$ P G M $\underline{R}$ S

Bhairavi – Early Morning: S $\underline{R}$ $\underline{G}$ M P $\underline{D}$ $\underline{N}$ s, s $\underline{N}$ $\underline{D}$ P M $\underline{G}$ $\underline{R}$ S

Bhimpalasi – Afternoon: ($\underline{N}$) S $\underline{G}$ M P $\underline{N}$ s, s $\underline{N}$ D P M P M $\underline{G}$ R S

Bhupali – Early Evening: S R G P D s, s D P G R (D) S

Bihag – Late Evening: (N) S G M P N s, s N D P *M* G M G R S

Chayanat – Early Evening: S R G M P D P s, s N D $\underline{N}$ D P R G M P M G M R S

Desh – Late Evening: S R M P N s, s $\underline{N}$ D P D M G R G (N) S

Gaud Malhar – Rainy Season: S R G M G M M P D N s, s D $\underline{N}$ P G M G R G R S

Jai Jaiyanti – Late Evening: S R G M D N s, s $\underline{N}$ D P M G R $\underline{G}$ R s (N) S (D) ($\underline{N}$) R

Jhinjhoti – Late Night: S (D) S R M G G M P D N s, s $\underline{N}$ D P M G R S ($\underline{N}$) (D) (P) (D) S

Kafi (Misra Kafi) – Midnight: S R $\underline{G}$ M P D $\underline{N}$ s, s $\underline{N}$ D P M $\underline{G}$ R S (N) S. Misra Kafi may display the addition of a few accidentals like *M*, G, and N.

Kalavati – Midnight: S G P D $\underline{N}$ D s, s $\underline{N}$ D P G P G S

Kalyan – Evening: S R G *M* P D N s, s N D P *M* G R S (N) S

Kamod – Early Night: S M R P D P s, s D *M* P M R P G M P G
M R S

Kanhara (Darbari Kanhara) – Midnight: S R G̱ M P Ḏ Ṉ s, s
Ḏ N P M P G̱ M R S

Kedar – Early Night: S M P D N s, s N D P *M* P D Ṉ D P *M* P
D P M R S

Khammaj – Night: S G M P D N s, s Ṉ D P M G R S

Kirwani – Night: S R G̱ M P Ḏ N s, s N Ḏ P M G̱ R S (N) S

Madhuvanti – Evening: S G̱ *M* P N s, s N D P *M* G̱ M G̱ R S

Malkauns – Late Night: S G̱ M Ḏ Ṉ s, s Ṉ Ḏ M G̱ M G̱ S

Miya ki Malhar – Rainy Season: S M R P Ṉ D N s, s D Ṉ M P
D M P G̱ M P M R S

Patdip – Evening: (N) S G̱ M P N s, s N D P M G̱ R S (N) S G̱
R S

Puriya – Evening: (N) Ṟ G *M* G *M* D N ṟ s, s N ṟ N D *M* G (N)
Ṟ S

Shobhavari – Late Morning: S R M P Ḏ s, ṟ s Ḏ P M R S

Shyam Kalyan – Evening: S R *M* P N s, s N D *M* P M P G M
R G (N) S

Shiva Ranjani – Midnight: S R G̱ P D s, s D P G̱ R S

Vilaval (Suddha) – S R G M P D N s, s N D P M G R S

Vrindabani Sarang – Noon: S R M P N s, s Ṉ P M R S

Source:
Patvardhan, Vinayak Rao. *Rāga-Vijñāna*. 7 volumes. Poona:
Sangeet Gaurav Granthamala, 1961-1974.

Tālas

The rhythmic cycles known as *tālas* are equally important
in rendering the compositions of Samāj-Gāyan in the Rādhāvallabha Songbook. The aesthetic combinations of *rāga* and

tāla, along with the words of the poems, is what is genuinely unique about the Indian musical tradition. In the case of Samāj-Gāyan, the use of cymbals along with the drums provides the added effect of marking musical time. The names of the important *tālas* in Samāj-Gāyan are given below, with the play of the cymbals denoted with an X or x. For example, X denotes the strike of the cymbals (one *mātrā*), xx the double strike (which also counts as one *mātrā*), with the dashes for the un-played *mātrās* or beats:

Cautāl (12 mātrās): X - - - X - - - X - X –

Dhamār (14 mātrās): X X – X X X - , X X – X X X –

Dīp Chandī (14 mātrās): X X – X – X -, X X – X – X-

Rūpak (7 mātrās): X xx xx X xx X xx

Jhaptāl (10 mātrās): X xx X xx xx X xx X xx xx

Tintāl (16 mātrās): X X X – X X X – X X X – X X X -

Kehervā (8 mātrās): X xx X xx xx X X xx

Glossary

ācārya (acharya) great spiritual teacher or founder of a lineage.

adṛṣṭa (adrishta) the unseen spiritual merit accrued through the chanting of Vedic mantras, performance of ritual, and the marking of musical time. Similar to *apūrva*.

ālāp introductory presentation of a Rāga in Indian music without percussion accompaniment.

āḻvār a group of twelve Tamil poet-saints from ca. fifth century to ninth century CE. who produced roughly 4000 songs and poems that have been collected by the tenth century.

Apabhraṃśa an early class of Prakrit language that developed into Braj Bhasha and Hindi.

ārati the ceremony of making a series of offerings as part of the *pūjā* ritual service, including flowers, incense, water, food, etc.

Aṣṭachāp a group of eight poet-saints associated with the Puṣṭi Mārga or Vallabha Sampradāya, the most famous being Sūra Dāsa. They were among the forerunners of northern Hindustani classical music as they wrote and sung compositions in the genre of Dhrupad and Dhamar. Their poems comprise the bulk of the Puṣṭi Mārga hymnals in use, of which there are many.

Balarāma the elder brother of Krishna who was also an incarnation of Vishnu.

basant (vasanta) the Spring season.

Bhagavad Gītā a Sanskrit text: famous discourse by Krishna in eighteen chapters that formed part of the epic *Mahābhārata.* Many pious Hindus consider this work to be the best summation of Hindu teachings, especially with regard to *bhakti.*

Bhāgavata Purāṇa a Sanskrit text: the most famous of the Vaishnava Purāṇas, as it describes in detail the various *avatāras* of Vishnu and presents the entire life of Krishna in the Tenth Book.

bhakti saṅgīta Devotional music, especially that which has incorporated the classical traditions. Music as part of temple worship from medieval times to the present, including the sub-categories of *kīrtana* and *bhajana.*

bhajana a sub-category of *bhakti saṅgīta,* referring to "worship music" or music as an offering to God.

bhāva an emotional state or experience derived from witnessing drama or music.

Brahmā the Creator God of Hindu tradition, part of the Trimūrti.

Braj (Vraja) the geographic and mythic region in northern India where Krishna took birth and performed his childhood pastimes.

Braj Bhasha the language of Braj; a medieval dialect of Hindi used by the *bhakti* poets.

Caurāsi-Pad a Braj Bhasha text: eighty-four verses composed by Hita Harivaṃśa, founder of the Rādhāvallabha Sampradāya.

cautāl the most prevalent rhythm in Dhrupad music, consisting of twelve beats.

dadra a rhythm (*tāla*) of six beats (*mātrās*).

devī the word for female divinity or goddess in Sanskrit.

dhamār a rhythm used in Dhrupad music, consisting of fourteen beats.

dhrupad the oldest surviving form of classical music in northern India, originally Dhruvapada ("fixed verse").

dhruva a class of vernacular songs in Prakrit that are described in the ancient musical texts of Bharata.

dīp chāndi a *tāla* of fourteen beats (*mātrās*), usually in faster tempo.

Gandharvas a class of heavenly musicians who sing in the court of Indra.

Gandharva Saṅgīta the ancient classical music of India as described in the *Nāṭya-śāstra* and the *Dattilam*.

Gauḍīya Sampradāya the Vaiṣṇava tradition founded by Śrī Caitanya in Bengal.

gītī/gītā song or musical composition in Indian tradition.

Gīta-govinda a Sanskrit text: famous devotional work of the twelfth century by Jayadeva.

Gopāla name for Krishna as a cowherd boy.

gopī cowherd woman, a wife or daughter of a cowherder (*gopa*).

Haridāsī Sampradāya one of the Krishna *sampradāyas* founded in Braj by Svāmī Haridāsa.

Harivaṃśa a Sanskrit text: an early work attached to the *Mahābhārata* that contains descriptions of Krishna's life and pastimes.

harmonium a small portable hand-driven reed organ used for devotional singing in India. Adopted from European prototypes.

Havelī Saṅgīta the Dhrupad-influenced *bhakti saṅgīta* of the Vallabha Sampradāya.

Hita Harivaṃśa the founder of the Rādhāvallabha Sampradāya.

Holi (Horī) Hindu spring festival of colors.

Janmāṣṭamī the birthday celebrations of Krishna in August-September.

japa the low-volume solitary muttering or chanting of divine names or *mantras*, often with the counting of beads or rosary.

jhāñjh hand cymbals used in *bhakti saṅgīta*, especially Havelī Saṅgīta and Samāj-Gāyan.

jhaptāl a rhythm in Indian classical music consisting of ten beats.

jhelā singers that accompany Samāj-Gāyan performance.

Karttika (Kartik) fall season of devotional observances.

khāli the point corresponding to a wave of the hand when counting a *tāla*, in opposition to the clap (*tāli*).

khyāl the most prevalent form of Hindustani vocal music, derived partially from Dhrupad.

kīrtan "praise song"; devotional music, *bhakti saṅgīta*.

laya tempo in Indian music.

Mahābhārata a Sanskrit text: the famous epic of India describing the feud between the Pāṇḍavas and the Kauravas culminating in an eighteen-day battle. The *Bhagavad Gītā* is the sermon of Krishna to his friend and disciple Arjuna that was delivered just before the battle commenced.

Mahāvāṇi a Braj Bhasha text: the hymnal of the Nimbārka Sampradāya, compiled by Harivyāsadevācārya.

mantra Sanskrit word or phrase used in Vedic ritual or Hindu piety.

Mathurā the town where Krishna was born in northern India.

mātrā a single beat in Indian music. The term is cognate with the English word meter and measure.

mokṣa liberation from *saṃsāra* or the cycle of rebirth.

mukhiyā song leader, respected title among musicians of the Rādhāvallabha Sampradāya.

Nāda-brahman the concept of sacred sound in Hindu tradition, encompassing both linguistic and non-linguistic sound (music). The cosmic sound of creation, both manifest (*āhata*) and unmanifest (*anāhata*).

Nāda-śakti the feminine potencies of sacred sound attached to the letters of the Sanskrit alphabet which are released when chanted or sung.

Nāda-yoga a form of *yoga* concentrating on sound and the perception of Nāda-brahman through chant and music.

nāma-kīrtan chanting the names of God in a musical setting.

Nārada Ṛṣi the son of Brahmā who brought music to earth and taught it to the human race.

nikuñja-vihāra the eternal pastimes of Rādhā and Krishna taking place in the forest grove of Vṛndāvana.

Nimbārka Sampradāya the Vaiṣṇava tradition founded by Nimbārka in the twelfth century.

nṛtya dance

Oṃ/AUM the cosmic sound of creation, reiterated at the beginning of Vedic rituals, *mantras*, and most Hindu recitations of scripture, believed to encapsulate all the letters of the Sanskrit alphabet and contain spiritual properties.

pada-kīrtan a musical composition involving sung poetry and verse.

pakhāvāj long barrel-drum used in northern Hindustani music and *bhakti saṅgīta*.

Prakrit the vernacular counterpart of Sanskrit, believed to encompass the many indigenous languages and vocabularies that influenced the development of Sanskrit through its many stages. Braj Bhasha belongs to this family.

pūjā ritual worship or divine service that replaced the Vedic fire sacrifice (*yajña*) as the center of temple Hinduism.

Puṣṭi Mārga the worship and musical tradition established by the Vallabha Sampradāya.

Rādhā the dearmost lover and wife of Krishna, often described as a goddess.

Rādhāṣṭamī celebrations of the birthday or appearance of Rādhā.

Rādhāvallabha Sampradāya the tradition founded by Hita Harivaṃśa in the sixteenth century in Braj.

rāga a special set of notes from a musical scale; a "mood" in Indian music, first described in the *Bṛhaddeśī*.

rasa an emotional state or mood, as in the eight (or nine) *rasas* described in the *Nāṭya-śāstra*.

Rāmāyaṇa a Sanskrit text: the second great epic of Hindu tradition, describing the descent of Viṣṇu as Rāma and his heroic recovery of his wife and the destruction of evil in the world.

rūpak a musical rhythm cycle of seven beats.

Śabda-brahman the concept of sacred sound or sonic absolute as presented in the Upaniṣads. While Śabda-brahman is associated with linguistic meaning, Nāda-brahman as outlined in the *Āgamas* also includes non-linguistic sound and music.

śakti power, the feminine principle or goddess.

Śaktism the traditions of goddess worship or veneration.

sam the point coinciding with the first *mātrā* of a *tāla*.

Sāma-gāna the performance of Sāman, the hymns of the Sāma-Veda.

Samāj-Gāyan the unique style of collective singing as found in Braj, especially in the Rādhāvallabha, Haridāsī, and Nimbārka *sampradāyas*.

Samāj-śṛṅkhalā a Braj Bhasha text: the hymnal used by the Haridāsī Sampradāya.

sampradāya a tradition, community, or scholastic lineage in the Hindu tradition.

saṅgīta the designation of classical music as delineated in the Sanskrit texts; i.e., Gandharva Saṅgīta.

Saṅgīta-ratnākara a Sanskrit text: musical work by Śārṇgadeva in the thirteenth century.

Sanskrit the classical and liturgical language of India, used by priests and scholars. The language of the Vedas and successive literature; the counterpart to the vernacular Prakrit.

Sāraṅgī a bowed chordophone musical instrument.

Sarasvatī the goddess of learning and music in the Hindu tradition.

sevā "divine service;" an expanded version of *pūjā* that involves a total experience and commitment to a deity.

śṛṅgāra the first of the eight *rasas* outlined by Bhārata; passionate love.

Shiva one of the great gods of the Trimūrti: the destroyer of the cosmos.

śloka a verse in Sanskrit, arranged in one of a variety of meters.

Śrī Rādhāvallabhajī kā Varṣotsava the three-volume hymnal of the Rādhāvallabha Sampradāya currently in use by the members for the purpose of Samāj-Gāyan.

tablas a pair of small drums used in Hindustani music.

tāla rhythm or rhythmic cycle used in Indian classical music, comprised of *tāli* (claps) and *khāli* (waves).

tāli the point corresponding to a clap when counting a *tāla*, in opposition to a wave (*khāli*).

tāna a series of musical notes arranged in phrases of ascending and descending passages. It may also refer to "fixed-tone" in Vedic chant.

Trimūrti the three great gods of Hindu tradition: Brahmā the Creator, Vishnu the Preserver, and Shiva the Destroyer.

vādya a musical instrument.

Vāsudeva a name of Krishna as the son of Vasudeva.

Vallabha the founder and *ācārya* of the Puṣṭi Mārga tradition, also known as the Vallabha Sampradāya.

Vṛndāvana the spiritual residence of Krishna. The spelling of Vrindaban is often used for the earthly town of Krishna's pastimes in India.

Bibliography

Agraval, Ramnarayan, ed. 1981. *Dhrupad-Samrāt Śrī Candanjī Caturvedī Smṛtī Granth.* 1st. Mathurā: Kṛṣṇarī Candanjī Caturvedī Śatābdi Samāroha Samīti.

Ālī, Śrī Kiśorī Śaraṇ. 1950. *Śrī Hita Rādhāvallabhīya Sāhitya-Ratnāvalī.* 1st. Bombay, India: Bombay Nivāsī Katipaya Rādhāvallabhīya Vaiṣṇava.

———. n.d. "Vṛndāvana kī Samāja Saṅgīta Paramparā." *Hitvāṇī,* pp. 29--32, 137--144.

Beck, Guy L. 1993. *Sonic Theology: Hinduism and Sacred Sound.* 1st. Columbia, SC: University of South Carolina Press.

———. Spring, 1996. "Vaishnava Music in the Braj Region of North India." *Journal of Vaisnava Studies* 4.2:115--147.

———. Fall, 1998. "Samāj-Gāyan for Rādhā and Krishna: Devotional Music in the Rādhāvallabha Sampradāya." *Journal of Vaisnava Studies* 7.1:85--100.

———. 2000. "Religious and Devotional Music: Northern Area." In *Garland Encyclopedia of World Music,* edited by Alison Arnold, Volume 5, 1st, 246--258. New York and London: Garland Publishing. Vol. 5, South Asia.

———, ed. 2005a. *Alternative Krishnas: Regional and Vernacular Variations on a Hindu Deity.* 1st. Albany: State University of New York Press.

———. 2005b. "Krishna as Loving Husband of God: The Alternative Krishnology of the Radhavallabha Sampradaya." In *Alternative Krishnas: Regional and Vernacular Variations on a Hindu Deity*, 1st, 65--90. Albany: State University of New York Press.

———. 2011a. "Radhavallabha Sampradaya." In *Brill's Encyclopedia of Hinduism*, Volume III, 1st, 467--477. Leiden, The Netherlands: Brill Academic Publishers.

———. 2011b. *Sonic Liturgy: Ritual and Music in Hindu Tradition*. 1st. Columbia, SC: University of South Carolina Press.

Bryant, Edwin. 2005. *Krishna: The Beautiful Legend of God*. 1st. New York: Penguin. Translation of the Tenth Book (Skandha) of the *Bhāgavata Purāṇa*.

Brzezinski, Jan. Fall, 1998. "Prabodhananda, Hit Harivamsa and the Radha-rasa-sudha-nidhi." *Journal of Vaisnava Studies* 7.1:19--61.

Chakrabarty, Ramakanta. 1988. "Vaisnava Kirtan in Bengal." In *The Music of Bengal: Essays in Contemporary Perspective*, edited by Jayasri Banerjee, 1st, 12--30. Bombay and Baroda: Indian Musicological Society. Reprinted in *Journal of Vaisnava Studies*, 4.2 (Spring, 1996): 179-99.

Entwistle, A. W. 1987. *Braj: Centre of Krishna Pilgrimage*. 1st. Groningen: Egbert Forsten.

Gaston, Anne-Marie. 1997. *Krishna's Musicians: Musicians and Music Making in the Temples of Nathdvara, Rajasthan*. 1st. New Delhi: Manohar Publishers.

Goswami, Lalita Caran. 1957. *Śrī Hita Harivaṃśa Gosvāmī: Sampradāya aura Sāhitya*. 1st. Vṛndāvana: Veṇu Prakāśana. In Hindi.

———, ed. 2028 Vikram [1970]. *Śrī Bayalis Līlā by Śrī Hita Dhruvadāsa Jī Mahārāja*. 1st. Vṛndāvana: Bābā Tulasīdāsa.

———. 1981. "Radhavallabhiya-Samaj ki Gayan-saili." In *Dhrupad-Samrāt Śrī Candanjī Caturvedī Smṛtī Granth*, edited by Ramnarayan Agraval, 1st, 227--228. Mathurā: Kṛṣṇarī

Candanjī Caturvedī Śatābdi Samāroha Samīti. Translated in Guy L. Beck (1996), 136-137.

———, ed. 1978-80. *Śrī Rādhāvallabhjī kā Varṣotsava (RV)*. 1st. Volume 1-3. Radhakunda, India: Śrī Rādhāvallabha Mandira Vaiṣṇava Committee. Based on *Śṛṅgāra-rasa-sāgara* in 4 volumes, 1956-62, edited and published by Bābā Tulasīdāsa in Vrindaban.

Goswami, Saranbihari. 1966. *Kṛṣṇa Bhakti Kāvya men Sakhī Bhāva*. 1st. Vārāṇasī: Chowkhambā Vidyābhavan. In Hindi.

Goswami, Vasudeva. 2009 Vikrama (1953). *Bhakta-kavi Vyāsa jī*. 1st. Mathurā: Prabhudayal Mital. In Hindi.

Gupt, Bharat. April-Sept 1982. "Origin of Dhruvapada and Krishna Bhakti in Brijabhasha." *Sangeet Natak* 64-65:55--63.

Gupta, Motilal. 1982. *Braj: The Centrum of Indian Culture*. 1st. Delhi: Agam Kala Prakashan.

Gupta, Usha. 1959. *Hindī ke Kṛṣṇa Bhakti Kālīn Sāhitya men Saṅgīt*. 1st. Lucknow: Lucknow University. In Hindi.

Hawley, John Stratton. 2009. *The Memory of Love: Sūrdās Sings to Krishna*. 1st. New York and Oxford: Oxford University Press.

Hitaharivaṃśa, Śrī. 1977. *Śrī Rādhā-rasa-sudhā-nidhi*. 1st. Edited by Śrī Kiśorī Śaraṇ Ālī. Vṛndāvana, India: Mohana Granthamālā.

Ho, Meilu. 2006. "The Liturgical Music of Pusti Marg of India: An Embryonic Form of the Classical Tradition." Ph.D. diss., U.C.L.A., Dissertation.

Karṇapūra, Kavi. 1999. *Ānanda-vṛndāvana-campū*. 1st. Vṛndāvana, India: Mahanidhi Swami. An English translation of Sanskrit work by Bhanu Swami and Subhag Swami. English edited by Mahanidhi Swami.

Khanna, Jatindra Simha. 1992. *Madhya-kālīn Dharmon men*

Sāstrīya Saṅgīta kā Tulanātmaka Adhyāyana. 1st. Candigarh: Abhishek Publications. In Hindi.

Lath, Mukund. 1978. *A Study of Dattilam: A Treatise on the Sacred Music of Ancient India*. 1st. New Delhi: Impex India.

McGregor, Ronald Stuart (R.S). 1973. *The Round Dance of Krishna and Uddhava's Message*. 1st. London: Luzac and Company. Nandadas' Hindi Ras-pancadhyayi in translation.

McIntosh, Solveig. 2005. *Hidden faces of Ancient Indian Song*. 1st. Burlington, VT: Ashgate Publishing.

Mital, Prabhudayal. 1968. *Braj ke Dharm Sampradayon ka Itihas*. 1st. Delhi: National Publishing House.

———. 1975. *Braj ki Kalao ka Itihas*. 1st. Mathura: Sahitya Samsthan.

———. 1981. "Bhakti Sangit ke Pracar men Radhavallabhiya Rasikon ka Yogdan." In *Rajata Jayanti Smarika*, edited by Vijayendra Snatak, 1st, 79--84. Vrindaban: Sri Hitasram Satsanga Bhumi.

Mutatkar, Sumati, ed. 1987a. *Aspects of Indian Music: A Collection of Essays*. 1st. Delhi: Sangeet Natak Academy.

———. 1987b. "Dhrupada: Its Legacy and Dynamics." In *Aspects of Indian Music: A Collection of Essays*, 1st, 76--83. Delhi: Sangeet Natak Academy.

Pauwels, Heidi R. M. 1996. *Round Dance Reconsidered: Hariram Vyas's Hindi Ras-pancadhyayi*. 1st. Surrey, UK: Curzon Press. Complete Braja Bhasha text with English translation, and notes, of Sri Hariram Vyas's "Ras-Pancadhyayi," 78-161.

———. 2002. *In Praise of Holy Men: Hagiographic Poems by and about Hariram Vyas*. 1st. Groningen: Egbert Forsten.

Prajnanananda, Swami. 1973. *The Historical Development of Indian Music: A Critical Study*. 1st. Calcutta: Firma KLM.

Preciado-Solis, Benjamin. 1984. *The Krsna Cycle in the Pu-*

ranas: Themes and Motifs in a Heroic Saga. 1st. Delhi: Motilal Banarsidass.

Raghavan, V. 1966. *The Great Integrators: The Saint-Singers of India.* 1st. Delhi: Ministry of Information.

Ray, Sukumar. 1985. *Music of Eastern India.* 1st. Calcutta: Firma KLM.

Rosenstein, Lucy. 1997. *The Devotional Poetry of Svami Haridas: A Study of Early Braj Bhasa Verse.* 1st. Groningen: Egbert Forsten.

———. 1998. "The Radhavallabha and the Haridasi Sampradayas: A Comparison." *Journal of Vaisnava Studies* 7 (1): 5--18 (Fall).

Rowell, Lewis. 1992. *Music and Musical Thought in Early India.* 1st. Chicago and London: University of Chicago Press.

Saksena, Rakesh Bala. 1981a. "Braj men Devalaya Sangit." In *Dhrupad-Samrāt Śrī Candanjī Caturvedī Smṛti Granth*, edited by Ramnarayan Agraval, 1st, 161--177. Mathurā: Kṛṣṇarī Candanjī Caturvedī Śatābdi Samāroha Samīti.

———. 1981b. "Sangit Jagat ko Hita Sampradaya ki Dena: Samaj Sangit." In *Rajata Jayanti Smarika*, edited by Vijayendra Snatak, 1st, 97--104. Vrindaban: Sri Hitasram Satsanga Bhumi.

———. 1990. *Madhya-Yugīn Vaiṣṇava Sampradāyon men Saṅgīt.* 1st. New Delhi: Rādhā Publications.

———. 1992. "Braj ke Vaisnava Devalaya men Kirtan tatha Samaj-Gayan Parampara." In *Braj Lok [Sri Ram Narayan Agraval Abhinandan Granth]*, edited by Sri Baijnath Dani, 1st, 115--123. Mathura: Braj Kala Kendra.

Sanyal, Ritwik, and Richard Widdess. 2004. *Dhrupad: Tradition and Performance in India Music.* 1st. Burlington, VT: Ashgate Publishing. (SOAS Musicology).

Schweig, Graham. 2005. *Dance of Divine Love: The Rasa Lila of Krishna from the Bhagavata Purana, India's Classic Sacred Love Story.* 1st. Princeton, NJ: Princeton University Press.

Sinha, Savitri. 1961. *Braj Bhasa ke Krsnabhakti Kavya men Abhivyanjana Silpa.* 1st. Delhi: National Publishing House.

Snatak, Vijayendra. 1957, 1968. *Radhavallabha Sampradaya Siddhanta aur Sahitya.* 1st. Delhi: National Publishing House.

———. 1981. *Rajata Jayanti Smarika.* 1st. Vrindaban: Sri Hitasram Satsanga Bhumi.

Snell, Rupert. 1983. "Metrical Forms in Braj Bhasa Verse: The Caurasi Pada in Performance." In *Bhakti in Current Research 1979-1982,* edited by Monika Theil-Horstmann, 1st, 353--383. Berlin: Dietrich Reimar Verlag.

———. 1991. *The Eighty-Four Hymns of Hita Harivamsa: An Edition of the Caurasi Pada.* 1st. Delhi and London: Motilal Banarsidass and School of Oriental and African Studies.

———. 1998. "The Nikunj as Sacred Space in the Poetry of the Radhavallabhi Tradition." *Journal of Vaisnava Studies* 7 (1): 63--84 (Fall).

Srivastava, Induram. 1980. *Dhrupada: A Study of its Origin, Historical Development, Structure, and Present State.* 1st. New Delhi: Motilal Banarsidass.

Theil-Horstmann, Monika, ed. 1983. *Bhakti in Current Research 1979-1982.* 1st. Berlin: Dietrich Reimar Verlag.

Thielemann, Selina. 1996. "Samaja, Haveli Samgita and Dhrupada: The Musical Manifestation of Bhakti." *Journal of Vaisnava Studies* 4 (2): 157--177 (Spring).

———. 1998. *Sounds of the Sacred: Religious Music in India.* 1st. New Delhi: APH Publishing Group.

———. 1999. *The Music of South Asia.* 1st. New Delhi: APH Publishing Group.

———. 2000. *Singing the Praises Divine: Music in the Hindu Tradition.* 1st. New Delhi: APH Publishing Group.

———. 2001. *Musical traditions of Vaisnava Temples in Vraja: A Comparative Study of Samaja and the Dhrupad Tradition of North Indian Classical Music*. 1st. New Delhi: Sagar Publishers.

———. 2002. *Divine Service and the Performing Arts in India*. 1st. New Delhi: APH Publishing Group.

Thite, G. U. 1997. *Music in the Vedas: Its Magico-Religious Significance*. 1st. Delhi: Sharada Publishing House.

Valpey, Kenneth Russell. 2006. *Attending Krishna's Image: Chaitanya Vaishnava Murti-Seva as Devotional Truth*. 1st. London: Routledge.

Vyasa, Gopal Prasad, ed. 1987. *Braj Vibhava*. 1st. New Delhi: Hindi Sahitya Sammelan.

Vyāsa, Harirāma. 1973. *Vyāsavāṇī*. 1st. Edited by Śrī Rādhākiśor Goswami. Mathura: Agarval Press.

Wade, Bonnie C. 1979. *Music in India: The Classical Traditions*. 1st. Englewood Cliffs, NJ: Prentice-Hall.

White, Charles S. J. 1977. *The Caurasi Pad of Sri Hit Harivams*. 1st. Honolulu: University of Hawaii Press. Reprinted as "'The Love of Radha,' A Translation of the Caurasi Pad of Sri Hit Harivams with Commentary." *Journal of Vaisnava Studies*, Vol. 7, No. 1 (Fall 1998): 101-180.

———. 1996. "The Remaining Hindi Works of Sri Hit Harivams." *Journal of Vaisnava Studies* 4 (4): 87--104 (Fall).

———. 2001. "Sri Radha and the Radhavallabha Sampraday." *Journal of Vaisnava Studies* 10 (1): 91--113 (Fall).